SPORT IN CONTEMPORARY SOCIETY

An Anthology

Eighth Edition

Edited by
D. Stanley Eitzen

Paradigm Publishers
Boulder • London

Paradigm Publishers is committed to preserving ancient forests and natural resources. We elected to print this title on 30% post consumer recycled paper, processed chlorine free. As a result, for this printing, we have saved:

18 Trees (40' tall and 6-8" diameter)
6,511 Gallons of Wastewater
12 million BTU's of Total Energy
836 Pounds of Solid Waste
1,569 Pounds of Greenhouse Gases

Paradigm Publishers made this paper choice because our printer, Thomson-Shore, Inc., is a member of Green Press Initiative, a nonprofit program dedicated to supporting authors, publishers, and suppliers in their efforts to reduce their use of fiber obtained from endangered forests.

For more information, visit www.greenpressinitiative.org

Environmental impact estimates were made using the Environmental Defense Paper Calculator. For more information visit: www.papercalculator.org.

Copyright © 2009 Paradigm Publishers

Published in the United States by Paradigm Publishers, 3360 Mitchell Lane, Suite E, Boulder, CO 80301 USA.

Paradigm Publishers is the trade name of Birkenkamp & Company, LLC,
Dean Birkenkamp, President and Publisher.

Library of Congress Cataloging-in-Publication Data

Sport in contemporary society : an anthology / edited by D. Stanley Eitzen. — 8th ed.
    p. cm.
    Includes bibliographical references.
    ISBN 978-1-59451-720-4 (pbk. : alk. paper)   1. Sports — Social aspects.   2.
Sports — Social aspects — United States.   I. Eitzen, D. Stanley
    GV706.5.S733 2009
    796.01—dc22

2008055767

Printed and bound in the United States of America on acid-free paper that meets the standards of the American National Standard for Permanence of Paper for Printed Library Materials.

Designed and Typeset by Straight Creek Bookmakers.

13 12 11 10 09   1 2 3 4 5

Contents

Part Thirteen
EXPANDING THE HORIZONS:
SPORT AND GLOBALIZATION   **373**

List of Tables and Figures

Preface

Most North Americans are at least somewhat interested in sport, and many are downright fanatical about it. They attend games, read the sports pages and sport magazines, participate in fantasy leagues, and talk endlessly about the subject. But even those fans who astound us with their knowledge of the most obscure facts about sport do not necessarily *understand* sport.

Do sport buffs know how sport is linked to other institutions of society? Do they understand the role of sport in socializing youngsters in both positive and negative ways? Do they know that the assumption that sport builds character is open to serious debate? Do they know that racism continues in sport? What about the ways in which sport perpetuates gender-role stereotypes in society? How do owners, coaches, and other sport authorities exercise power to maintain control over athletes? These are some of the issues this book examines.

There are two fundamental reasons for the ignorance of most North Americans about the role of sport in society. First, they have had to rely mainly on sportswriters and sportscasters for their information, and these journalists have typically been little more than describers and cheerleaders. Until recent years journalists have rarely examined sport critically. Instead they have perpetuated myths: "Football helped a whole generation of sons of coal miners escape the mines" or "Sport is an island free of prejudice and racism."

The second reason for our sports illiteracy is that sport has been ignored, for the most part, by North American academics. Only in the past generation or so have North American social scientists and physical educators begun to investigate seriously the social aspects of sport. Previously, as with sports journalism, academic research on sport has tended to be biased in support of existing myths. In particular, the early research by physical educators was aimed at proving that sports participation builds character. In this limited perspective, phenomena common to sport such as cheating, excessive violence, coaching tyranny, and the consequences of failure were, for the most part, simply ignored.

Today, however, not only academics but also a new breed of sports journalists are making insightful analyses of the role of sport in society. They examine the positive *and* negative consequences of sport for people, communities, schools, and nations. They demystify and demythologize sport. Most significantly, they document the reciprocal impact of sport on the various institutions of society: religion, education, politics, and economics. There is no danger that sport will suffer from such examination. Critical reflection leads, sometimes, to positive changes. Moreover, the scholarly scrutiny of sport reveals a subject far more complex and far more interesting than what we see on the fields and arenas and what we read in the sports pages.

This book is a collection of the writings representing this new era of critical appraisal. It includes contributions from both journalists and academics. The overriding criterion for inclusion of a particular article was whether it critically examined the role of sport in society. The praise of sport is not omitted, but such praise, as with condemnation, must be backed by fact, not mythology or dogma. (Occasionally a dogmatic piece has been included to challenge the critical faculties of the reader.) The selection of each article was also guided by such questions as: Is it interesting? Is it informative? Is it thought provoking? Does it communicate without the use of unnecessary jargon and sophisticated methodologies?

In short, the selections presented here not only afford the reader an understanding of sport that transcends the still prevalent stereotypes and myths; they also yield fascinating and important insights into the nature of society. Thus, this book has several groups of potential readers. First, it is intended to be the primary or supplementary text for courses in the sociology of sport, sport and society, and foundations of physical education. Second, the book can be used as a supplemental text for sociology courses such as the introduction to sociology, American society, and social institutions. A third audience for this book is general readers who wish to deepen their understanding and appreciation of sport.

The eighth edition of *Sport in Contemporary Society* has undergone extensive revision. Twenty of the forty selections are new to this edition. In keeping with my plan from previous editions, gender- and race-related articles are found throughout the collection, not just "ghettoized" into their appropriate sections. The result is an anthology of lively and timely chapters that will sharpen the reader's analysis and understanding both of sport *and* society.

I am indebted to the authors of the chapters in this volume. My thanks to them for their scholarship and, most significant, for their insights that help us unravel the mysteries of this intriguing and important part of social life.

D. Stanley Eitzen

SPORT IN CONTEMPORARY SOCIETY

PART ONE

Sport as a Microcosm of Society

The early part of the twenty-first century was a disheartening time in sports. Greed seemed to go unchecked. New stadiums were built at taxpayer expense *and the price of tickets went up.* Elite athletes were given astronomical salaries. Professional team owners threatened to move to different cities if they did not receive more subsidies. Parents were spending up to $100,000 annually to have their children groomed for the world of big-time sport. Scandals were commonplace in big-time college sport. Player and fan violence seemed rampant inside and outside the arenas. "Against this tawdry backdrop we've again been forced to face up to the sad truth that sport isn't a sanctuary. It reflects, often all too clearly, society. And, yes, today greed and violence are a big part of society."[1]

My thesis is that sport is a microcosm of society. If we know how sport is organized, the type of games played, the way winners and losers are treated, the type and amount of compensation given the participants, and the way rules are enforced, then we surely also know a great deal about the larger society in which it exists. Conversely, if we know the values of a society, the type of economy, the way minority groups are treated, and the political structure, then we would also have important clues about how sport in that society is likely organized.

The United States, for example, is a capitalistic society. It is not surprising, then, that in the corporate sport that dominates, American athletes are treated as property. In the professional ranks they are bought and sold. At the college level players once enrolled are unable to switch teams without waiting for a year. Even in youth sports, players are drafted and become the "property" of a given team.

Capitalism is also evident as team owners "carpetbag," i.e., move teams to more lucrative markets. At the same time these owners insist that the cities subsidize the construction of new stadiums, thereby making their franchises more profitable. The players, too, appear to have more loyalty to money than to their teams or fans.

1

Americans are highly competitive. This is easily seen at work, at school, in dating, and in sport. Persons are evaluated not on their intrinsic worth but on the criterion of achievement. As George H. Sage has written, "Sports have consented to measure the results of sports efforts in terms of performance and product—the terms which prevail in the factory and department store."[2]

Athletes are expected to deny self and sacrifice for the needs of the sponsoring organization. This requires, foremost, an acquiescence to authority. The coach is the ultimate authority and the players must obey. This is the way bureaucracies operate, and American society is highly bureaucratic whether it be in government, school, church, or business. As Paul Hoch has stated, "In football, like business ... every pattern of movement on the field is increasingly being brought under control of a group of nonplaying managerial technocrats who sit up in the stands ... with their headphones and dictate offenses, defense, special plays, substitutions, and so forth to the players below."[3]

Thus, American sport, like American society, is authoritarian, bureaucratic, and product-oriented. Winning is everything. Athletes use drugs to enhance their performances artificially in order to succeed. Coaches teach their athletes to bend the rules (to feign a foul, to hold without getting caught) in order to win. Even at America's most prestigious universities, coaches offer illegal inducements to athletes to attend their schools. And, as long as they win, the administrators at these offending schools usually look the other way. After all, the object is to win, and this mentality permeates sport as it does politics and the business world.

These are but some of the ways in which sport mirrors society. In this section we shall examine this relationship further through three selections. The first is from the introduction to sportswriter Dave Zirin's book *What's My Name, Fool? Sports and Resistance in the United States.* Zirin is a critical journalist with a keen eye for the inconsistencies, myths, and inequities in sport.

The second chapter is by D. Stanley Eitzen. This piece examines several para-doxes of U.S. sport at the beginning of the millennium: (1) Although seemingly a trivial pursuit, sport is important; (2) sport has the capacity to build character as well as encourage bad character; (3) while the nature of sport is competition where ability tells, the reality is that race restricts; and (4) schools emphasize sports because of the personal and social benefits for participants, yet these same schools have generally resisted efforts by girls and women for participation and resources equal to those of boys and men.

The final chapter, by sociologist Jay J. Coakley, enhances our understanding of sport and society by elaborating on the two contrasting theoretical approaches—functionalist and conflict—that guide much of the work of sport sociologists. The understanding of both of these perspectives is vitally important to the analyst of society. Each approach offers significant insights about society. However, the theo-retical approach guiding the structure of this book and the selection of readings is the conflict perspective. As I stated in the preface to Eitzen and Sage's *Sociology of North American Sport,*

[the] goal is to make the reader aware of the positive and negative consequences of the way sport is organized in society. We are concerned about some of the trends in sports, especially the move away from athlete-oriented activities toward the impersonality of what we term "corporate sport." We are committed to moving sport and society in a more humane direction, and this requires, as a first step, a thorough understanding of the principles that underlie the social structures and processes that create, sustain, and transform the social organizations within the institution of sport.[4]

NOTES

1. E. M. Switch, "Giving His All," *Sports Illustrated* (December 19, 1994): 88.

2. George H. Sage, "Sports, Culture, and Society," paper presented at the Basic Science of Sport Medicine Conference, Philadelphia (July 14–16, 1974), pp. 10–11.

3. Paul Hoch, *Rip Off the Big Game* (Garden City, NY: Doubleday Anchor, 1972), p. 9.

4. D. Stanley Eitzen and George H. Sage, *Sociology of North American Sport,* 8th ed. (Boulder, CO: Paradigm Publishers, 2009), p. xi.

1

Sports: An Offer We Can't Refuse

Dave Zirin

In *The Godfather, Part II,* dying mob boss Hymen Roth wheezes the obscene truth to young Don Michael Corleone. "Michael," he whispers, "we're bigger than U.S. Steel." This scene updated for today would have Yankees kingpin George Steinbrenner booming at pubescent Dallas Mavericks owner Mark Cuban, "Screw U.S. Steel. We're bigger than the damn mafia."

Just like Hymen Roth, "Big Stein" would be telling no lies. Professional sports are now the tenth largest industry in the United States, generating $220 billion in revenue every year. And just like Mr. Roth's rackets, it's a business that can stink to high heaven.

ROTTEN ROOTS

If, in 1900, a forward thinking person had predicted that sports would some day stand as one of the great pillars of American industry, that person would have been proclaimed mad and then subjected to some combination of leeching and lobotomy. Before the 1880s, everything from the World Series to a daily sports page was just a gleam in Uncle Sam's eye. The Victorian idea that sports undermined character and promoted a slothful work ethic dominated most people's perceptions of organized

Source: Dave Zirin, *What's My Name, Fool? Sports and Resistance in the United States* (Chicago: Haymarket Books, 2005): 17–22.

play. (The Victorians clearly considered child labor and building a better chastity belt more noble pursuits.) Their attitude, however, is easy to understand when you consider class. Competitive sports were a working-class pastime that reflected the brutality of early industrial life. Popular sports of the day included bare-knuckled boxing, "stick-battling," cock fighting, and animal baiting, which involved setting starved dogs against a bull or bear.

But at the end of the nineteenth century, an upstart generation of wealthy industrialists forged a new idea about these innocuous games. Industrialist J. P. Morgan and former President Teddy Roosevelt argued that organized athletics could be the means for instilling the character and values deemed necessary to make America a global power in the century to come. Sports could breed a sense of hard work, self-discipline, and the win-at-all-cost ethic of competition. Roosevelt once said, presumably while swinging a big stick,

> Virile, masterful qualities alone can maintain and defend this very civilization. There is no better way [to develop this] than by encouraging the sports which develop such qualities as courage, resolution, and endurance. No people has ever yet done great and lasting work if its physical type was infirm and weak.

Teddy and his ilk backed their words with bucks. Business scions funded organizations like the YMCA to teach sports and specifically to exclude "undesirable" ethnic groups, women, and Blacks.

As the popularity of sports rose among working people, factory owners began to see the benefit of starting plant teams as a form of labor management. This synthesis bore team factory names that remain today like the Green Bay Packers and the Milwaukee Brewers. The Chicago Bears, who used to be rooted in Decatur, Illinois, were known as the Decatur Staleys, named after the A. E. Staley Company. Their first coach, George "Papa Bear" Halas, was a Staley manager. Organized athletics became less a place to toughen up Teddy Roosevelt's gentlemen of leisure than a narrow window of opportunity for immigrants, white urban youth, and people right off the farm to claw their way out of poverty. Players who captured the country's imagination included a Baltimore orphan named "Babe" Ruth, Native American Olympic star Jim Thorpe, and the first renowned female athlete, a daughter of immigrants named Mildred "Babe" Didrikson. As another first-generation American, Joe DiMaggio, once said, "A ball player's got to be kept hungry to become a big-leaguer. That's why no boy from a rich family ever made the big leagues."

As the United States urbanized, it was evident that people would pay to see sports played at their highest level. The 1920s and 1950s, two decades with very similar economic landscapes, saw this take root. Both were periods of expansion and urbanization. Both eras saw revolutions in technology—radio in the 1920s and then TV in the 1950s—that could deliver sports into people's homes. But, most critically, both were times after brutal world wars that saw a population in the United States looking for relief, escape, and leisure.

SPORTS AND LEE GREENWOOD

In addition to becoming a profitable form of mass entertainment, pro sports were used by the political and financial elite as a way to package their values and ideas. This is why sports in this country reflect a distinctly U.S. project, rooted in aspirations for greatness as well as conquest and oppression. That's why the United States is so singular in its sports presentation. We are unique in playing the national anthem before every game (and, since 9/11, playing "God Bless America" during baseball's seventh inning stretch—even for all-American teams like the Toronto Blue Jays). We are unique in employing scantily clad women to tell us when to "cheer." We are unique in calling the winners of our domestic leagues "world champions." We are unique in the very sports we imbibe most heartily—especially football. (And don't tout NFL Europe as counter-evidence. There are more U.S. study-abroad students at those games than at your typical Amsterdam hash bar.) In many cities, the average Sunday NFL game contains more patriotic overkill than a USO show in Kuwait. First there's a military drum line to midfield. Then a standing sing-along to "I'm Proud to Be an American (Where at Least I Know I'm Free)" by Lee Greenwood. And then comes the "Star-Spangled Banner." You are certainly "free" to not stand, as long as you know that the person behind you will feel "free" to pour beer on your head. Save me, Lee Greenwood!

WHY SPORTS MATTERS

Many throughout the U.S. are repelled by pro sports today for a laundry list of reasons. People who otherwise enjoy competitive play performed at its highest levels don't want to be party to the cutthroat competition at its core. Many are also put off by the insane salaries of the games' top players, others by the backroom dealings that produce publicly funded stadiums at taxpayer expense. Then there is the abuse of steroids and other performance enhancing drugs, which some feel have taken long-hallowed baseball records and reduced them to rubbish. When you pile on the way racism and sexism can be used to sell sports, it can all seem about as appealing as a Sunday in the park with George Steinbrenner.

The way that the games have been shaped by profit and patriotism has quite understandably led many people to conclude that sports are little more than a brutal reflection of the savage inequalities that stream through our world. As esteemed left-wing critic Noam Chomsky noted in *Manufacturing Consent,*

> Sports keeps people from worrying about things that matter to their lives that they might have some idea of doing something about. And in fact it's striking to see the intelligence that's used by ordinary people in sports [as opposed to political and social issues]. I mean, you listen to radio stations where people call in—they have the most exotic information and understanding about all kinds of arcane issues. And the press undoubtedly does a lot with this.... Sports is a major factor

in controlling people. Workers have minds; they have to be involved in something and it's important to make sure they're involved in things that have absolutely no significance. So professional sports is perfect. It instills total passivity.

Chomsky quite correctly highlights how people use sports as a balm to protect themselves from the harsh realities of the world. He is also right that the intelligence and analysis many of us invest in sports far outstrips our dissecting of the broader world. It is truly amazing how we can be moved to fits of fury by a missed call or a blown play, but remain too under-confident to raise our voices in anger when we are laid off, lose our healthcare, or suffer the slings and arrows of everyday life in the United States. The weakness in Chomsky's argument, however, is that it disregards how the very passion we invest in sports can transform it from a kind of mindless escape into a site of resistance. It can become an arena where the ideas of our society are not only presented but also challenged. Just as sports can reflect the dominant ideas of our society, they can also reflect struggle. The story of the women's movement is incomplete without mention of Billie Jean King's match against Bobby Riggs. The struggle for gay rights has to include a chapter on Martina Navratilova. When we think about the Black freedom struggle, we picture Jackie Robinson and Muhammad Ali in addition to Martin Luther King Jr. and Malcolm X. And, of course, when remembering the movement for Black Power, we can't help but visualize one of the most stirring sights of our sports century: Tommie Smith and John Carlos's black-gloved medal-stand salute at the 1968 Olympics.

Chomsky's view also reflects a lack of understanding of why sports are, at their core, so appealing. Amid the politics and pain that engulf and sometimes threaten to smother big-time sports, there is also artistry that can take your breath away. To see Michael Vick zigzag his way through an entire defense, or Mia Hamm crush a soccer ball past a goalie's outstretched hands, or LeBron James use the eyes in the back of his head to spot a teammate cutting to the basket can be a glorious sight at the end of a tough day. It is a bolt of beauty in an otherwise very gray world. As a good friend said to me long ago, "Magic Johnson will always be my Miles Davis."

Lester "Red" Rodney, the editor of the *Daily Worker* sports section from 1934 to 1958 and a groundbreaking fighter in the battle to smash baseball's color line, puts it perfectly:

> Of course there is exploitation but there is fun and beauty too. I mean, what's more beautiful than a 6-4-3 double play perfectly executed where the shortstop fields a ground ball and flips it toward second base in one motion, the second baseman takes the throw in stride, pivots, avoids the base runner, and fires it to first on time. That's not a put-on. That's not fake. That's beyond all the social analysis of the game. The idea of people coming together and amazing the rest of us.

Sports as a whole do not represent black and white, good or bad, red state or blue state issues. Sports are neither to be defended nor vilified. Instead we need to look at sports for what they are, so we can take apart the disgusting, the beautiful, the ridiculous, and even the radical.

This book aims to recall moments of resistance past and rescue the underreported shows of struggle and humanity by athletes of the present, so we can appreciate the beauty of sports independent of the muck and fight for a future where skill, art, glory, and the joy of play belong to all of us.

2

American Sport in the New Millennium

D. Stanley Eitzen

I want to examine sport by focusing on several paradoxes that are central to sport as it has come to be.

Paradox: While seemingly a trivial pursuit, sport is important. On the one hand, sport is entertainment, a fantasy, a diversion from the realities of work, relationships, and survival. But if sport is just a game, why do we take it so seriously? Among the many reasons, let's consider four: First, sport mirrors the human experience. The introductory essay in *The Nation*, which was devoted to sport, said this:

> Sport elaborates in its rituals what it means to be human: the play, the risk, the trials, the collective impulse to games, the thrill of physicality, the necessity of strategy; defeat, victory, defeat again, pain, transcendence and, most of all, the certainty that nothing is certain—that everything can change and be changed.

Second, sport mirrors society in other profound ways as well. Sociologists, in particular, find the study of sport fascinating because we find there the basic elements and expressions of bureaucratization, commercialization, racism, sexism, homophobia, greed, exploitation of the powerless, alienation, and the ethnocentrism found in the larger society. Of special interest, too, is how sport has been transformed from an activity for individuals involved in sport for its own sake, to a money-driven, corporate entity where sport is work rather than play, and where loyalty to players,

Source: D. Stanley Eitzen, "American Sport at Century's End," *Vital Speeches of the Day* 65 (January 1, 1999): 189–191. Revised in 2008.

coaches, and owners is a quaint notion that is now rarely held. Also, now athletes are cogs in a machine where decisions by coaches and bureaucracies are less and less player-centered. I am especially concerned with the decisions made by big business bureaucracies (universities, leagues, cartels such as the NCAA, corporations, and sports conglomerates such as Rupert Murdoch's empire, which just in the U.S. includes ownership of the Fox network, FX, 22 local cable channels, the *New York Post,* 20 percent of L.A.'s Staples center, and the partial rights to broadcast NFL games for eight years and major league baseball for five years). Another powerful sports conglomerate is the Walt Disney Corporation, which owns ABC-TV, ESPN, and like Murdoch, partial rights for NFL games and major league baseball games. Time Warner is another sports empire, including ownership of *Sports Illustrated, Time Magazine,* CNN, HBO, TNT, TBS, and Warner Brothers. Obviously, sport is not a trivial pursuit by these media giants.

A third reason why sports are so compelling is that they combine spectacle with drama. Sports, especially football, involve pageantry, bands forming a liberty bell or unfurling a flag as big as the football field, and militaristic displays with the drama of a situation where the outcome is not perfectly predictable. Moreover, we see excellence, human beings transcending the commonplace to perform heroic deeds. There is also clarity—we know, unlike in many other human endeavors, exactly who won, by how much, and how they did it.

Finally, there is the human desire to identify with something larger than oneself. For athletes, it is to be part of a team, working and sacrificing together to achieve a common goal. For fans, by identifying with a team or a sports hero, they bond with others who share their allegiance; they belong and they have an identity. This bond of allegiance is becoming more and more difficult as players through free agency move from team to team, as coaches are hired and fired, and because many times when coaches are successful they break their contracts to go to a more lucrative situation, leaving their players, assistants, and fans in their wake. The owners of many professional teams blackmail their cities for more lucrative subsidies by threatening to move, which they sometimes do, leaving diehard fans without teams.

Paradox: Sport has the capacity to build character as well as encourage bad character. On the one hand, sports participation encourages hard work, perseverance, self-discipline, sacrifice, following the rules, obeying authority, and working with teammates to achieve a common goal. Sport promotes fair play. There are countless examples where competitors show respect for one another, where sportsmanship rules.

But for all of the honor and integrity found in sport there is also much about sport that disregards the ideals of fair play. Good sportsmanship may be a product of sport, but so is bad sportsmanship. Let me cite a few examples: (1) trash-talking and taunting opponents; (2) dirty play (an article in *Sports Illustrated* documented dirty play in the NFL, citing the ten worst offenders, saying that "there's a nasty breed of players who follow one cardinal rule: Anything goes, and that means biting, kicking, spearing, spitting, and leg-whipping"); (3) coaches who teach their players how to hold and not get caught; (4) faking being fouled so that a referee who is out of position will call an undeserved foul on the opponent; (5) trying to hurt an opponent; (6) coaches rewarding players for hurting an opponent; (7) throwing a spitter or corking a bat; (8) using illegal drugs to enhance performance; (9) crushing an opponent (a Laramie, Wyoming, girls junior high basketball team won a game a few years ago by a score of 81–1, using a full-court press the entire game); (10) fans yelling racial slurs; (11) coaches who, like Pat Riley of the Miami Heat, demand that their players not show respect for their opponents (Riley fines his players $1,500 if they help an opposing player get off the floor); (12) coaches who are sexist and homophobic, calling their male players "pussies" or "fags" if they are not aggressive enough; (13) a male locker room culture that tends to promote homophobia, sexism, and aggressive behaviors; and (14) coaches who recruit illegally, who alter transcripts and bribe teachers to keep players eligible, and who exploit players with no regard for their health or their education.

What lesson is being taught and caught when a coach openly asks a player to cheat? Consider this example. A few years ago, the Pretty Prairie Kansas High School had twin boys on its team. One of the twins was injured but suited up for a game where his brother was in foul trouble at half time. The coach had the twins change jerseys so that the foul-plagued twin would be in the second half with no fouls charged to the player's number he was now wearing. . . .

My point is that we live in a morally distorted sports world—a world where winning often supersedes all other considerations, where moral values have become confused with the bottom line. In this in-your-face, whip-your-butt climate, winning at any price often becomes the prevailing code of conduct. And when it does, I assert, sport does build character, but it is bad character. When we make the value of winning so important that it trumps morality, then we and sport are diminished.

Paradox: While the nature of sport is competition where ability tells, the reality is that race restricts. Just as in other social realms, we find in sport that the ascribed status of race gives advantage to some and disadvantage to others. Let's look at racism in sport, focusing on African Americans since they are the dominant racial minority in American sport.

At first glance, its seems impossible that Blacks are victims of discrimination in sport since some of them make huge fortunes from their athletic prowess, such as LaBron James who signed a seven-year deal with Nike for $90 million before he graduated from high school, and Tiger Woods who makes about $120 million annually. Moreover, it is argued that Blacks in sport are not victims of discrimination because, while only constituting 12 percent of the general population, they comprise 67 percent of the players in professional football, 77 percent of professional basketball players, and 8 percent of the players in major league baseball (and where Latinos constitute another 24 percent). Also about 60 percent of the football and basketball players in big-time college programs are African Americans.

Despite these empirical facts that seem to contradict racism in sport, it is prevalent in several forms. Let me cite some examples. First, Blacks are rarely found in those sports that require the facilities, coaching, and competition usually provided only in private—and typically racially segregated—clubs; sports such as swimming, golf, skiing, and tennis. Black athletes also are rarely found where it takes extraordinary up-front money, usually from corporate sponsors, to participate such as in automobile racing.

But even in the team sports where African Americans dominate numerically, there is evidence of discrimination. Sociologists have long noted that Blacks tend to be relegated to those team positions where the physical attributes of strength, size, speed, aggressiveness, and "instinct" are important but that they are underrepresented at those playing positions that require thinking and leadership and are the most crucial for outcome control. This phenomenon, known as stacking, continues today, at both the college and professional levels in football and baseball. Using professional football as the example, African Americans are underrepresented on offense and if on offense they tend to be at wide receiver and running back—the whitest positions are center, offensive guard, quarterback, punter, placekicker, and placekick holder. Blacks are overrepresented at all positions on defense, except middle linebacker. The existence of stacking reinforces negative stereotypes about racial minorities, as Whites appear, by the positions they play, to be superior to Blacks in cognitive ability and leadership qualities but behind them in physical prowess.

African Americans are also underrepresented in nonplaying leadership positions. At the professional level team ownership is an exclusively all-White club. In the league offices of the NCAA, major league baseball, the NBA, and the NFL, the employees are disproportionately White. The same is true, of course, for head coaches in big-time college and professional sports.

African Americans are also underrepresented in ancillary sports positions such as sports information director, ticket manager, trainer, equipment manager, scout, accountant, sportswriting, and sports broadcasting, especially play-by-play announcing.

Another consistent finding by sociologists is a form of discrimination known as "unequal opportunity for equal ability." This means that the entrance requirements for Blacks to obtain college scholarships or to play in the professional leagues are more rigorous than they are for Whites. In essence, Black players must be better than White players to succeed in the sports world. In baseball, for example, Blacks consistently have higher statistics (batting average, home runs, stolen bases, earned run average) than Whites. What's happening here is that superb Black athletes are not discriminated against but the substars do experience discrimination. The findings clearly indicate that the undistinguished Black player is less likely to play regularly than the equally undistinguished White player. As sociologist Jonathan Bower has said, "In sport mediocrity is a white luxury."

Paradox: Schools emphasize sports because of the personal and social benefits for participants, yet these same schools have generally resisted efforts by girls and women for participation and resources equal to that of boys and men. Research shows many benefits from sports for girls and women. When female athletes are compared to their nonathlete peers, they are found to have higher self-esteem and better body image. For high school girls, athletes are less likely than nonathletes to use illicit drugs; they are more likely to be virgins; if sexually active they are more likely to begin intercourse at a later age; and they are much less likely to get pregnant. These advantages are in addition to the standard benefits of learning to work with team-mates for a common goal, striving for excellence, and the lessons of what it takes to win and how to cope with defeat. Yet, historically, women have been denied these benefits. And, even today, the powerful male establishment in sport continues to drag its collective feet on gender equity.

Title IX, passed in 1972, mandated gender equity in school sports programs. While this affected schools at all levels, I'll focus on the college level because this is where women have met the most resistance. Since 1972 women's intercollegiate programs have made tremendous strides, with participation quadrupling from 30,000 women in 1971 to 160,000 in 2004. Athletic scholarships for women were virtually unknown in 1972; now women athletes receive 45 percent of college athletic schol-arship dollars. These increases in a generation represent the good news concerning gender equity in collegiate sport. The bad news, however, is quite significant. The Women's Sports Foundation has noted the following disparities by gender in big-time (Division I-A) programs:

1. Even though female students comprise 57 percent of college student popula-tions, female athletes receive only 43 percent of participation opportunities compared to their male counterparts.
2. Women's teams receive only 38 percent of college sport operating dollars and 33 percent of college athletic team recruitment spending.
3. Women coach 43 percent of women's teams and only 2 percent of men's teams, and hold only 8 percent of athletic director positions.
4. Head coaches of women's teams receive on average $932,700 less than head coaches of men's teams.

Clearly, as these data show, gender equity is not part of big-time college sports programs. In my view, universities must address the question: Is it appropriate for a college or university to deny women the same opportunities that it provides men? Shouldn't our daughters have the same possibilities as our sons in all aspects of higher education? Women are slightly more than half of the undergraduates in U.S. higher education. They receive half of all the master's degrees. Should they be second-class in any aspect of the university's activities? The present unequal state of affairs in sport is not inevitable. Choices have been made in the past that have given men advantage in university sports. They continue to do so, to the detriment of not only women's sports but so to the so-called minor sports for men.

These are a few paradoxes concerning contemporary sport in the United States. There are more but I'll let my colleagues and the other contributors speak directly or indirectly to them. Let me conclude my remarks with this statement and a plea. We celebrate sport for many good reasons. It excites and it inspires. We savor the great moments of sport when an athlete does the seemingly impossible or when the truly gifted athlete makes the impossible routine. We exult when a team or an athlete overcomes great odds to succeed. We are touched by genuine camaraderie among teammates and between competitors. We are uplifted by the biographies of athletes who have used sport to get an education that they would have been denied because of economic circumstance or who have used sport to overcome delinquency and drugs. But for all of our love and fascination with sport and our extensive knowledge of it, do we truly understand it? Can we separate the hype from the reality and the myths from the facts? Do we accept the way sport is organized without questioning? Unfortunately for many fans and participants alike there is a superficial, uncritical, and taken-for-granted attitude concerning sport. Sportswriter Rick Reilly of *Sports Illustrated* has written that "sport deserves a more critical examination. We need to ask more probing questions about sport." That has always been my goal; it continues to be my goal; and I hope that it is yours as well.

3

Sport in Society

An Inspiration or an Opiate?

Jay J. Coakley

People in American society generally see sport in a very positive way. Not only is sport assumed to provide a training ground for the development of desirable character traits and good citizens, but it is also believed to reaffirm a commitment to societal values emphasizing competition, success, and playing by the rules.

Does sport really do all these things? Is it as beneficial and healthy as people believe? These questions have generated considerable disagreement among sport sociologists. It seems that most of us in the sociology of sport are quick to agree that sport is a microcosm of society—that it mirrors the values, structure, and dynamics of the society in which it exists (Eitzen and Sage, 1978). However, we often disagree when it comes to explaining the consequences or the functions of sport in society. This disagreement grows out of the fact that sport sociologists have different theoretical conceptions of how society works. Therefore, they differ on their ideas about how sport functions within society. A description of the two major theoretical approaches used in sociology of sport will illustrate what I mean.

THE FUNCTIONALIST APPROACH

Sport Is an Inspiration

The majority of sport sociologists assume that society is most accurately conceptualized in terms of a *systems model*. They see society as an organized system of interrelated

Source: "Sport in Society: An Inspiration or an Opiate?" by Jay J. Coakley. From *Sport in Society: Issues and Controversies,* 2nd ed., by Jay J. Coakley. Copyright © 1982 by C. V. Mosby. Reprinted by permission.

parts. The system is held together and operates because (1) its individual members generally endorse the same basic values and (2) the major parts in the system (such as the family, education, the economy, government, religion, and sport) all fit together in mutually supportive and constructive ways. In sociology, this theoretical approach is called *functionalism.*

When the functionalists describe and analyze how a society, community, school, or any other system works, they are primarily concerned with how the parts of that system are related to the operation of the system as a whole. For example, if American society is the system being studied, a person using a functionalist approach would be concerned with how the American family, the economy, government, education, religion, and sport are all related to the smooth operation of the society as a whole. The analysis would focus on the ways in which each of these subparts of society helps to keep the larger system going.

The functionalists also assume that a social system will continue to operate smoothly only if the four following things happen:

1. The members of the system must learn the values and the norms (i.e., the general rules or guidelines for behavior) that will lead them to want to do what has to be done to keep the system in operation. This process of shaping the feelings, thoughts, and actions of individuals usually creates some frustration and tension. Therefore, there must also be some channels through which people can let off steam in harmless ways.
2. The system must contain a variety of social mechanisms that bring people together and serve as catalysts for building the social relationships needed for coordinated action. Without a certain degree of cohesion, solidarity, and social integration, coordinated action would be impossible and the social system would stop functioning smoothly.
3. The members of the system must have the opportunity to learn what their goals should be within the system and the socially approved ways of achieving those goals.
4. The social system must be able to adjust to the demands and challenges of the external environment. It must have ways of handling and coping with changes in the social and physical environments so that it can continue to operate with a minimal amount of interference and disruption.

According to those using a functionalist approach, these four "system needs" are the basic minimum requirements for the smooth operation of any social system whether it be a society, community, club, large corporation, or neighborhood convenience store (Parsons and Smelser, 1965). These four basic system requirements are referred to as:

1. The need for pattern maintenance and tension management
2. The need for integration
3. The need for goal attainment
4. The need for adaptation

When you start with a functionalist conception of how society works, the answer to the question of what sport does for a society or community is likely to emphasize the ways in which sport satisfies the four basic needs of the social system. A brief review of how sport is related to each of these needs is a good way to summarize this approach.

Pattern Maintenance and Tension Management

The functionalists generally conclude that sport provides learning experiences that reinforce and extend the learning occurring in other settings. In other words, sport serves as a backup or a secondary institution for primary social institutions such as the family, school, and church. Through sport people learn the general ways of thinking, feeling, and acting that make them contributing members of society. They become socialized so that they fit into the mainstream of American life and therefore reaffirm the stability and continued operation of our society (Schafer, 1976).[1]

The pattern maintenance function of sport applies to spectators as well as those who are active participants. Sport is structured so that those who watch or play learn the importance of rules, hard work, efficient organization, and a well-defined authority structure. For example, sociologist Gunther Luschen (1967) shows how sport helps to generate the high levels of achievement motivation necessary to sustain the commitment to work required in industrialized countries. Along similar lines, Kleiber and Kelly (1980) have reviewed a number of studies concluding that participation in competitive games helps children learn how to handle adult roles in general and competitive relationships in particular. In fact, some recent discussions of sex roles have suggested that women may be at a disadvantage in business settings partly because they have not been involved in competitive sports to the same degree as their male counterparts (Hennig and Jardim, 1977; Lever, 1978).

Sport has also been thought to serve tension management functions in society by providing both spectators and participants with an outlet for aggressive energy (Vanderzwaag, 1972; Proctor and Eckard, 1976; Marsh, 1978). This idea prompted two widely respected sociologists, Hans Gerth and C. Wright Mills (1953), to suggest the following: "Many mass audience situations, with their 'vicarious' enjoyments, serve psychologically the unintended function of channeling and releasing otherwise unplacable emotions. Thus, great volumes of aggression are 'cathartically' released by crowds of spectators cheering their favorite stars of sport—and jeering the umpire." The idea that sport may serve tension management functions is complex and controversial.

Integration

A functionalist approach also emphasizes how sport serves to bring people together and provide them with feelings of group unity, a sense of social identification, and a source of personal identity. In short, a functionalist explains how sport creates and reaffirms the linkages between people so that cooperative action is possible. Luschen

(1967) outlines how this occurs in the following: "Since sport is also structured along such societal subsystems as different classes, males, urban areas, schools, and communities, it functions for integration. This is obvious also in spectator sport, where the whole country or community identifies with its representatives in a contest. Thus, sport functions as a means of integration, not only for the actual participants, but also for the represented members of such a system."

Sport has been seen to serve integration functions in countries other than the United States also. For example, others have discussed how sport contributes to unity and solidarity in Switzerland (Albonico, 1967); France (Bouet, 1969); Germany (Brockmann, 1969); China (Chu and Segrave, 1979); the Soviet Union (Riordan, 1977); and Brazil (Lever, 1980).

Andrzej Wohl (1970), a sport sociologist from Poland, has argued that competitive sport could not exist if it recognized "local, nation or racial barriers or differences of world outlook." He points out that sport is so widely used to serve integration functions that it "is no secret for anybody any more."

Goal Attainment

Someone using a functionalist approach is likely to see sport as legitimizing and reinforcing the primary goals of the system as well as the means to be used to achieve those goals. In the United States, for example, sport is organized so that successful outcomes are heavily emphasized, and success is generally defined in terms of scores and win-loss records. Just as in the rest of society, the proper way to achieve success in sport is through a combination of competition, hard work, planning, and good organization. Therefore, the sport experience not only serves to legitimize the way things are done in other sectors of society but also it prepares people for participation in those sectors.

In other countries, different aspects of the sport experience are emphasized so that it serves as a supportive model for their goal priorities and the proper means to achieve goals. Capitalist countries are more likely to emphasize output and competition in sport while socialist countries will be more likely to emphasize cooperation and the development of a spirit of collectivism (Morton, 1963). Sport seems to be amazingly flexible in this respect; it has been shaped and defined in a variety of ways to serve goal attainment functions in many different social systems. This point has been developed and explained by Edwards (1973): "Most sports have few, if any, intrinsic and invariably social or political qualities ... and those qualities which such activities do possess are sufficiently 'liquid' to fit comfortably within many diverse and even conflicting value and cultural traditions."

Adaptation

In preindustrial societies it is easy to see how sport serves a system's need for adaptation. Since survival in such societies depends on the development and use of physical skills, participation in games and sport activities is directly related to coping with the surrounding environment (Luschen, 1967). Dunlap (1951) makes this case in her study of the Samoans. Additionally, she found that the "factors of physical strength and endurance which were essential for success in their games were also essential for success in their wars."

In industrial societies, it is more difficult to see how sport satisfies the adaptation needs of the social system. However, in two articles on the functions of sport, Wohl (1970, 1979) has suggested that it is in this area that sport makes its most important contributions. He points out that in any society with technologically advanced transportation and communications systems, sport becomes the only sphere of activities in which physical skills are developed and perfected. Through sport it is possible to measure and extend the range of human motor skills and to adapt them to the environments we have created. Without sport it would be difficult to maintain a population's physical well-being at the levels necessary to keep an industrial society operating efficiently. Sport is so crucial in this regard that Wohl (1979) calls for the use of all the sport sciences to plan and control its development. In this way the contributions of sport to satisfying adaptation needs could be maximized.

In concluding our review of the functionalist approach to sport it should be pointed out that social scientists are not the only ones who use such an approach in explaining the relationship between sport and society. Most people view society and the role of sport in terms very similar to those used by the functionalists. They look for the ways in which sport contributes to the communities in which they live. They see sport providing valuable lessons for their children and opportunities for themselves to release the tensions generated by a job or other life events. Sport gives them something to talk about with strangers as well as friends and it provides occasions for outings and get-togethers. Many people believe that sport can serve as a model of the goals we should strive for and the means we should use in trying to achieve those goals. Finally, sport is viewed as a healthy activity for individuals as well as the entire country; it can extend life and keep us physically prepared to defend our country in case of war.

These beliefs about sport have lead to policy decisions on Little League programs, the funding of high school and college athletics, the support of professional teams and the Olympic movement, the development of physical education programs in schools, and the use of sport activities in military academies to prepare young men and women to be "combat ready." The widespread acceptance and the pervasive influence of the functionalist approach make it necessary for us to be aware of its weaknesses.

Limitations of the Functionalist Approach

Using a functionalist approach to answer the question of how sport is related to society can provide us with valuable insights, but it is not without its problems. Such an approach tends to emphasize the positive aspects of sport. This is because those using it often assume that if some part or component of a social system has existed for a long time, it is likely to be contributing to the system in a favorable way; if it were not, it would have been eliminated or gradually faded out of existence on its own. Since sport has been around for some time and is an increasingly significant component of our social system, most functionalists conclude that it *does* make positive contributions to society. This conclusion leads them to ignore or underemphasize the negative aspects of sport. After all, it is also possible that sport could distort values and behavioral guidelines (norms). Sport could destroy motivation, create frustration and tensions, and disrupt social integration. It could impede goal attainment and interfere with methods of coming to terms with the external social and physical environment by diverting a group's attention away from crucial personal and social issues.

Another problem with the functionalist approach is that it is based on the assumption that the needs of the individual parts of a social system overlap with the needs of the system as a whole. The possibility of internal differences or basic conflicts of interests within a social system is inconsistent with the assumption that any system is held together by a combination of common values and an interrelated, mutually supportive set of parts. If the needs of the total system were in serious conflict with the needs of the individual parts, the validity of the functionalist approach would be called into question.

This is one of the major weaknesses of functionalism. Although we may agree that many people in our society hold similar values, can we also argue that the structure of American society serves the needs of everyone equally? It would be naive to assume that is does. In fact, it may even frustrate the needs of certain groups and individuals and generate conflict. To conclude that sport exists because it satisfies the needs of the total system overlooks the possibility that sport may benefit some segments of the population more than others. Furthermore, if the interests of some groups within the system are met at the expense of others, the consequences of sport could be described as positive only if you were viewing them from the perspective of those privileged groups. Unfortunately, a functionalist approach often leads to underemphasizing differences of interests as well as the possibility of exploitation and coercion within the social system. It also leads to ignoring the role of sport in generating conflict and maintaining a structure in which at least some relationships are based on exploitation and coercion.

In sociology the theoretical approach that calls attention to these unpleasant characteristics of social systems and how sport is related to them is called conflict theory.

CONFLICT THEORY

Sport Is an Opiate

Conflict theory is not as popular as functionalism. It does fit with what most people think about how society is organized and how it operates. Instead of viewing society as a relatively stable system of interrelated parts held together by common values and consensus, conflict theorists view it as an ever-changing set of relationships characterized by inherent differences of interests and held together by force, coercion, and subtle manipulation. They are concerned with the distribution and use of power rather than with common values and integration. Their analysis of society focuses on processes of change rather than on what is required for a social system to continue operating smoothly.

Most beginning students in the sociology of sport are not very receptive to the use of conflict theory in explaining the relationship between sport and society. They say that it is too negativistic and critical of our way of life and the institution of sport. They prefer the functionalist approach because it fits closely with what they have always believed and because it has implications that do not threaten the structure of either society or sport. My response is that although functionalism is useful, it can often lead us to look at the world unrealistically and ignore a dimension of the relationship between sport and society that should be considered. Neither American society nor sport is without problems. Awareness and understanding of these problems require critical thought, and conflict theory is a valuable stimulus for such thought.

Conflict theory is based primarily on an updated revision of the ideas of Karl Marx. Those who use it generally focus their attention on capitalist countries such as the United States, but it has also been used to describe and understand any social system in which individuals arc perceived as not having significant control over their own lives. According to many conflict theorists this includes capitalist systems along with fascist or military/police regimes and socialist systems controlled by centralized, bureaucratic governments (Brohm, 1978).

In order to understand how conflict theorists view the role of sport in society, we will start with a simplified description of capitalism and how contemporary organized sport fits into its structure. Any capitalist system requires the development of a highly efficient work process through which an increasing number of consumer goods can be mass produced. Industrial bureaucracies have been created to meet this need. This means that in the interest of efficiency and financial profit, workers end up performing highly specialized and alienating jobs. These jobs are generally in the production, marketing and sales, or service departments of large organizations where the workers themselves have little control over what they do and experience little or no excitement or satisfaction in their day-to-day work lives. This situation creates a need for escape and for tension-excitement in their nonwork lives. Within capitalist systems, people are subtly manipulated to seek the satisfaction they need through consumerism and mass entertainment spectacles. Sport in such societies has emerged as a major form of entertainment spectacle as well as a primary context for the consumption of material goods. Additionally, the structure of sport is so much like the structure of work organizations and capitalist society as a whole that it serves to stabilize the system and promote the interests of people who are in positions of power.

Conflict theorists see sport as a distorted form of physical exercise that has been shaped by the needs of a capitalist system of production. A specific example of how sport has developed in this manner has been outlined by Goodman (1979) in an analysis of the history of playground and street life in one of New York City's working-class neighborhoods. Goodman shows how the spontaneous, free-flowing play activities of children in New York were literally banned from the streets in order to force participation in organized playground programs. The original goals of the playgrounds are best described through the words of one of the influential playground supervisors early in this century (Chase, 1909); "We want a play factory; we want it to run at top speed on schedule time, with the best machinery and skilled operatives. We want to turn out the maximum product of happiness." Thus the organized activities and sport programs became a means for training the children of immigrants to fit into a world of work founded on time schedules, the stopwatch, and production-conscious supervisors.

For the parents of these children the playground and recreation center programs had a different goal. It was clearly explained in the following section of a 1910 New York City Department of Education report (cited in Goodman, 1979): "The great problem confronting the recreation center principal and teachers is the filling of the leisure time of the working men and women with a combination of recreation and athletic activities which will help make their lives more tolerable." As Goodman points out, the purpose of the centers was to provide controlled leisure activities to take the people's minds off the exploitation and poor working conditions experienced in their jobs. The supervised activities were meant to pacify the workers so that they could tolerate those conditions and continue contributing to the growth of the economy. When they needed to be replaced, the organized playground activities would have prepared their children to take their roles.

Other conflict theorists have not limited their focus to a local community setting. They have talked in more general terms about the relationship between sport and society. Their discussions emphasize four major aspects of the role of sport. These include:

1. How sport generates and intensifies alienation
2. How sport is used by the state and the economically powerful as a tool for coercion and social control
3. How sport promotes commercialism and materialism
4. How sport encourages nationalism, militarism, and sexism

The following sections summarize the discussions of the conflict theorists on each of these four topics.

Alienation

According to the conflict theorists, sport serves to alienate people from their own bodies. Sport focuses attention on time and output rather than on the individual. Standardized rules and rigid structure destroy the spontaneity, freedom, and inventiveness characteristic in play. Jean-Marie Brohm (1978), a French sport sociologist, explains how sport affects the connection between athletes and their bodies: "[In sport the body is] experienced as an object, an instrument, a technical means to an end, a reified factor of output and productivity, in short, as a machine with the job of producing maximum work and energy." In other words, sport creates a setting in which the body is no longer experienced as a source of self-fulfillment and pleasure in itself. Pleasure and fulfillment depend on *what is done* with the body. Satisfaction is experienced only if the contest is won, if a record is set or a personal goal achieved, and if the body performs the way it has been trained to perform. When this happens sport becomes a "prison of measured time" and alienates athletes from their own bodies (Brohm, 1978).

Mumford (1934) extends the idea of alienation even further. In a classic analysis of contemporary civilization he describes the sport stadium as an "industrial establishment producing running, jumping or football playing machines." Building on this notion conflict theorists argue that commercialized sport (any sport in which profits are sought) reduces athletes to material commodities (Hoch, 1972). Thus the body becomes a tool not only for the setting of records but also for generating financial profits for nonparticipants—from team owners and tournament sponsors to concession operators and parking lot owners. The athletes may also benefit, but their rewards require them to forfeit the control of their bodies and become "gladiators" performing for the benefit of others.

Conflict theorists have pointed to the use of drugs and computer technology in sport as support for their analysis of how sport affects the definition of an athlete's body (Brohm, 1978). When the body is seen as an instrument for setting records and the improvement of times is defined as the measure of human progress, then the use of drugs, even harmful drugs, will be seen as a valuable aid in the quest for achievement. Computer technology used to analyze and improve the body's productive capacity further separates the physical act of sport participation from the subjective experience of the athlete. Just as on the assembly line, efficiency comes to be the major concern in sport and the worker (athlete) loses control over the means of production (the body).

Coercion and Social Control

Goodman's (1979) study of the working-class neighborhood in New York City led him to conclude that sport in that city was used as a means of making the lives of shop workers more tolerable. Other conflict theorists expand this notion and describe sport as an opiate interfering with an awareness of social problems and subverting collective attempts to solve those problems. According to Hoch (1972), sport perpetuates problems by providing people with either "(1) a temporary high ... which takes their minds off problem[s] for a while but does nothing to deal with [them]; or (2) a distorted frame of reference or identification which encourages them to look for salvation through patently false channels."

Hoch's description of the personal and social impact of sport is similar to Marx's description of religion in society. To Marx, religion focuses attention on the supernatural, provides people with a psychological lift, and emphasizes improvement through changing the self rather than changing the social order. Religion destroys awareness of material reality and promotes the maintenance of the status quo by giving priority to the goal of spiritual salvation. Marx further concluded that organized religion can be exploited by people in positions of power in society. If the majority of individuals in a society believe that enduring pain, denying pleasure, and accepting their status in this life gains them spiritual salvation, those in power can be reasonably sure that those under their control will be hardworking and docile. If those in power go so far as to manifest their own commitment to religion, their hold over the people can be strengthened even further. Such a manifestation would, after all, show that they had something in common with the masses.

Conflict theorists make the case that in an advanced capitalist society where people are not likely to look to the supernatural for answers and explanations, religion may be supplemented by other activities with similar narcotic effects. Hoch points out that these contemporary "opiates" include "sport spectacles, whiskey, and repressively sublimated sex." These combined with other opiates such as nationalism, racism, and sexism distort people's perspectives and encourage self-defeating behavior. Among these, sport stands out as an especially powerful opiate. Unlike the others, sport spectatorship is often accompanied by an extremely intense identification with players, teams, and the values perceived to be the basis for success in athletics. According to Hoch, this identification brings sport further into the lives of the spectators and captures their attention on a long-term basis. When the game ends, fan involvement does not cease, but carries on between games and into the off-season. This means that workers think about and discuss the fate of their teams rather than the futility of their own lives. Thus they are less likely to become actively involved in political or revolutionary organizations. Petryszak (1978), in a historical analysis of sport, makes the case that the "ultimate consequence of . . . spectator sports in society is the reduction of the population to a position of complete passivity."

Beyond occupying people's time and distracting their attention and energy, sport helps maintain the position of those in power in other ways. Conflict theorists note that the major contact sports, such as football, hockey, and boxing, promote a justification for the use of "official" violence by those in authority positions. In other words, sport shapes our values in ways that lock us into a social system based on coercion and the exploitive use of power. The more we witness violent sports, the more we are apt to condone the use of official violence in other settings—even when it is directed against us.

Sport also serves the interests of those in power by generating the belief that success can be achieved only through hard work and that hard work always leads to success. Such a belief encourages people to look up to those who are successful as being paragons of virtue and to look down on the failures as being lazy and no good. For example, when teams win consistently, their success is attributed to hard work and discipline; when they lose consistently, losing often is blamed on a lack of hustle and poor attitude. Losses lead the fans to call for new players and coaches— not a restructuring of the game or its rules. Hoch (1972) points out that this way of looking at things blinds people to a consideration of the problems inherent in the social and economic structure and engenders the notion that success depends only on attitude and personal effort. It also leads to the belief that failure is to be blamed on the individual alone and is to be accepted as an indication of personal inadequacies and of a need to work harder in the future.

Conflict theories see sport as a tool for controlling people and maintaining the status quo. It is structured to promote specific political ideas and to regiment and organize the lives of young people so that they will become productive workers. For adults, the role of spectator reinforces a passive orientation toward life so that they will remain observers rather than the shapers of their own experience (Aronowitz, 1973).

Commercialism and Materialism

The conflict theorists emphasize that sport is promoted as a product to be consumed and that it creates a basis for capitalist expansion. For example, increasing numbers of individuals and families are joining athletic clubs where they pay to participate and pay for the lessons teaching them how to participate correctly and efficiently. Creating and satisfying these expanding interests have given rise to an entire new industry. Summer sport resorts, winter sport resorts, and local athletic clubs are all part of this profit-generating industry.

Furthermore, sporting goods manufacturers have found that effective advertising can lead more and more equipment to be defined as absolutely necessary for successful and healthy involvement. Potential consumers have been convinced that if they want to impress other people with their knowledge about the sport experience, they have to buy and show off only top-of-the-line equipment. It has come to the point where participants can prove themselves in sport through their ability to consume as well as their ability to master physical skills. Thus sport has been used to lead people to deal with one another in terms of material images rather than in terms of the human quality of experience.

Sport not only creates direct profits but also is used as an advertising medium (Brohm, 1978). Sport spectacles serve as important settings for selling cars, tires, beer, soft drinks, and insurance. The tendency for people to personally identify with athletes is also used to sell other products. The role of athlete, unlike most adult occupational roles, is highly visible, prestigious, and relatively easy to emulate. Therefore, the attachment to sport heroes serves as the basis for the creation of an interest in sport along with a general "need" for consumer goods.

This process affects young people as well as adults. Children are lured into the spectator role and the role of consumer by trading cards, Dallas Cowboy pajamas, Yankee baseball caps, NBA basketball shoes, and a multitude of other products that ultimately create adulthood desires to become season ticket purchasers. Participation in highly specialized sport programs leads children to conclude that the proper equipment is always necessary for a good time and that being a good runner, tennis player, and soccer player depends on owning three different pairs of the best shoes on the market.

Nationalism, Militarism, and Sexism

Conflict theorists point out that sport is used by most countries as the showplace for displaying their national symbols and military strength. In many developing countries, national sport programs are administered by the defense department; in industrialized countries sport is symbolically linked with warfare and strong militaristic orientations. The conflict theorists claim that the collective excitement generated by sport participation and mass spectator events can be converted into unquestioning allegiance to political beliefs and an irrational willingness to defend those beliefs. Nationalistic feelings are fed by an emphasis on demonstrating superiority over other countries and other political systems. Furthermore, sport provides a model of confrontation, which polarizes groups of people and stresses the necessity of being militarily prepared.

Finally, the conflict theorists argue that sport divides the sexes and perpetuates distorted definitions of masculinity and femininity. The organization of contemporary sport not only relegates women to a secondary, supportive role, but also leads people to define masculinity in terms of physical strength and emotional insensitivity. In fact, the model of the successful male is epitomized by the brute strength and the controlled emotions of the athlete. Sport further reinforces sexism by focusing attention on performance differences in selected physical activities. People then use those differences to argue that male superiority is grounded in nature and that the sexes should continue to be separated. This separation obscures the characteristics men and women have in common and locks members of both sexes into restrictive roles.

Conflict theorists see much of contemporary sport as a source of alienation and a tool of exploitation and control serving the needs of economic and political systems rather than the needs of human beings. They generally argue that it is impossible for sport to provide humanizing experiences when the society in which it exists is not humane and creative (Hoch, 1972).

Limitations of the Conflict Theory Approach

Like the functionalist approach, conflict theory has some weaknesses. The conflict theorists make good use of history, but they tend to overemphasize the role of capitalism in shaping all aspects, of social reality since the Industrial Revolution. Capitalism has been a significant force, but other factors must be taken into account in explaining what has happened during the last two centuries.

The emergence and growth of modern sport is a good case in point. Sport has been strongly influenced by capitalism, but the emergence of contemporary sport can be explained in terms of factors that existed prior to the Industrial Revolution. Guttmann (1978) has argued that modern sport is a product of a scientific approach to the world rather than of the needs of capitalist economic systems. This scientific approach to the world grew out of seventeenth-century discoveries in mathematics and is characterized by a commitment to quantification, measurement, and experimentation. According to Guttmann this scientific worldview has given rise to contemporary sport. This is the reason why sport is also popular in noncapitalist countries including China, Cuba, The Czech Republic, and the Soviet Union.

In their analysis of sport, many conflict theorists are too quick to conclude that sport inevitably creates alienation and serves as an "opiate of the masses." They tend to ignore the testimonials of athletes who claim that sport participation, even in a capitalist society, can be a personally creative, expressive, and liberating experience (Slusher, 1967; Spino, 1971; Bannister, 1980; Csikszentmihalyi, 1975; Sadler, 1977). This possibility, of course, is inconsistent with the idea that the athlete's body automatically becomes a tool of production controlled and used for the sake of political and economic goals.

The argument that sport is an opiate also has some weaknesses. It is probably true that athletes and fans are more likely than other people to have attitudes supportive of the status quo. However, it is not known if their involvement in sport caused these attitudes or if the attitudes existed prior to their involvement and caused them to be attracted to sport. It may be that sport attracts people who are already committed to the status quo. If this is the case, it is difficult to argue that sport provides an escape from reality for those who might otherwise be critical of the social order. Research suggests that the most alienated and the most dissatisfied people in society are the least likely to show an interest in sport. In fact, interest and involvement are greatest among those who are the most economically successful (Sillitoe, 1969; Edwards, 1973; Anderson and Stone, 1979).

Another weakness of conflict theory is that it often overemphasizes the extent to which sport is controlled by those in positions of power in society. The people who control the media, sport facilities, and sport teams do have much to say about the conditions under which top-level sport events are experienced and viewed by players and spectators alike. However, it is difficult to argue that all sport involvement is a result of the promotional efforts of capitalists or government bureaucrats. This is especially true when attention is shifted from professional level sport to sport at the local recreational level. Active sport participation generally occurs at levels where the interests of the participants themselves can be used as the basis for creating and developing programs.

Furthermore, certain sports have characteristics making them difficult to control by those who are not participants. Surfing is a good case in point; it does not lend itself to scheduling or television coverage, equipment needs are not extensive, and it does not generate much long-term spectator interest among those who have never been surfers. Therefore, the development of surfing and other similar sports has not been subject to heavy influence from outsiders whose main concerns are generating profits and creating sport spectacles.

SUMMARY AND CONCLUSION: WHO IS RIGHT?

Now that we have looked at the relationship between sport and society (see Table 3-1 for a review) from two different perspectives, which explanation is most correct? Is sport an inspiration or an opiate? I have found that the way people answer this question depends on what they think about the society in which sport exists. For example, those who are generally uncritical of American society will tend to agree with the functionalist approach when they look at sport in the United States. Those

Table 3-1 Functionalism and Conflict Theory: A Summary of Their Assumptions about the Social Order and Their Explanations of the Relationship between Sport and Society

Functionalist Approach	*Conflict Theory*
Assumptions about the Social Order	
Social order based on consensus, common values, and interrelated subsystems	Social order based on coercion, exploitation, and subtle manipulation of individuals
Major Concerns in the Study of Society	
What are the essential parts in structure of social system?	How is power distributed and used in society?
How do social systems continue to operate smoothly?	How do societies change and what can be done to promote change?
Major Concerns in the Study of Sport	
How does sport contribute to basic social system needs such as pattern maintenance and tension management, integration, goal attainment, and adaptation?	How does sport create personal alienation? How is sport used to control thoughts and behavior of people, and maintain economic and political systems serving interests of those in power?
Major Conclusions about the Sport-Society Relationship	
Sport is valuable secondary social institution benefitting society as well as individual members of society	Sport is distorted form of physical exercise shaped by needs of autocratic or production-conscious societies
Sport is basically a *source of inspiration* on personal and social level	Sport lacks creative and expressive elements of play; *it is an opiate*
Goals of Sport Sociology	
To discover ways in which sport's contribution to stability and maintenance of social order can be maximized at all levels	To promote development of humane and creative social order so that sport can be source of expression, creative experiences, and physical well-being
Major Weaknesses	
Assumes that existence and popularity of sport prove that it is serving positive functions	Assumes that structures and consequences of sport are totally determined by needs of political and economic order
Ignores possibility of internal differences and basic conflicts of interest within social systems and therefore assumes that sport serves needs, of all system parts and individuals equally	Ignores factors other than capitalism in analyzing emergence and development of contemporary sport Focuses too much attention on top-level spectator sport and overemphasizes extent to which all sport involvement is controlled and structured by power elite

who are critical of American society will side with the conflict theorists. However, when the country in question is East Germany or China rather than the United States, some people may shift perspective. Those who do not agree with the way of life in East Germany or China will quickly become conflict theorists in their discussions of sport in these countries; those supportive of socialist systems will tend to become functionalists. It can be confusing to say that sport is an inspiration in one country and an opiate in another.

In order to eliminate some of the confusion on this issue, we need detailed research on how the structure of physical activities is related to the subjective experiences of participants (players and spectators). We also need to know how those experiences are related to attitudes and behavior patterns. We can assume that under certain circumstances, the consequences of sport will be constructive, and under other circumstances they will be destructive. Our task is to be able to clearly describe the circumstances under which these different consequences occur and to explain why they occur the way they do. This means that studies cannot be limited to specific countries or to specific groups of people. We need cross-cultural and comparative research focusing on all dimensions of the phenomenon of sport.

In developing research and exploring these issues we need to be aware of the ideas of both the functionalists and the conflict theorists. Each of their explanations of the relationship between sport and society alerts us to questions that must be asked and hypotheses that must be tested. Unless these and other theoretical perspectives are used, our understanding of sport will be needlessly restricted.

Unfortunately, research will never be able to show us what the relationship between sport and society *should* be. It only alerts us to the possibilities and provides us with a starting point for shaping what it will be in the future.

NOTE

1. Although the focus in this [selection] is the United States, the pattern maintenance function of sport has been described in other countries, including the Soviet Union (Morton, 1963; Riordan, 1977); East Germany (Santomier and Ewees, 1979); China (Johnson, 1973; Chu and Segrave, 1979); Finland (Olin, 1979); Australia (Murray, 1979); and Samoa (Dunlap, 1951).

REFERENCES

Albonico, R. 1967. "Modern University Sport as a Contribution to Social Integration." *International Review of Sport Sociology* 2: 155–162.

Anderson, D., and G. P. Stone. 1979. "A Fifteen-Year Analysis of Socio-Economic Strata Differences in the Meaning Given to Sport by Metropolitans." In M. L. Krotee, ed., *The Dimensions of Sport Sociology.* West Point, NY: Leisure Press.

Aronowitz, S. 1973. *False Promises.* New York: McGraw-Hill.

Bannister, F. T. 1980. "Search for 'White Hopes' Threatens Black Athletes." *Ebony* 34, no. 4: 130–134.

Bouet, M. 1969. "Integrational Functions of Sport in the Light of Research Based on Questionnaires." *International Review of Sport Sociology* 4:129–134.

Brockmann, D. 1969. "Sport as an Integrating Factor in the Countryside." *International Review of Sport Sociology* 4: 151–170.

Brohm, J.-M. 1978. *Sport: A Prison of Measured Time.* London: Ink Links.

Chase, J. H. 1909. "How a Director Feels." *Playground* 3, no. 4: 13.

Chu, D. B., and J. O. Segrave. 1979. "Physical Culture in the People's Republic of China." *Journal of Sport Behavior* 2, no. 3: 119–135.

Csikszentmihalyi, M. 1975. *Beyond Boredom and Anxiety.* San Francisco: Jossey-Bass.

Dunlap, H. L. 1951. "Games, Sports, Dancing, and Other Vigorous Recreational Activities and Their Function in Samoan Culture." *Research Quarterly* 22, no. 3: 298–311.

Edwards, H. 1973. *Sociology of Sport.* Homewood, IL: Dorsey.

Eitzen, D. S., and G. H. Sage. 1978. *Sociology of American Sport.* Dubuque, IA: William C. Brown.

Gerth, H., and C. W. Mills. 1953. *Character and Social Structure.* New York: Harcourt Brace Jovanovich.

Goodman, C. 1979. *Choosing Sides.* New York: Schocken.

Guttmann, A. 1978. *From Ritual to Record: The Nature of Modern Sports.* New York: Columbia University Press.

Hennig, M., and A. Jardim. 1977. *The Managerial Woman.* New York: Anchor.

Hoch, P. 1972. *Rip Off the Big Game.* New York: Doubleday.

Johnson, W. O. 1973. "Faces on a New China Scroll." *Sports Illustrated* 39, no. 14: 42–67.

Kleiber, D. A., and J. R. Kelly. 1980. "Leisure, Socialization, and the Life Cycle." In S. Iso-Aloha, ed., *Social Psychological Perspectives on Leisure and Recreation.* Springfield, IL: Charles C. Thomas.

Lever, J. 1978. "Sex Differences in the Complexity of Children's Play." *American Sociological Review* 43, no. 4: 471–483.

Lever, J. 1980. "Multiple Methods of Data Collection: A Note on Divergence." Unpublished manuscript.

Luschen, G. 1967. "The Interdependence of Sport and Culture." *International Review of Sport Sociology* 2: 127–139.

Marsh, P. 1978. Aggro: *The Illusion of Violence.* London: J. M. Dent.

Morton, H. W. 1963. *Soviet Sport.* New York: Collier.

Mumford, L. 1934. *Technics and Civilization.* New York: Harcourt Brace Jovanovich.

Murray, L. 1979. "Some Ideological Qualities of Australian Sport." *Australian Journal of Health, Physical Education, and Recreation* 73: 7–10.

Olin, K. 1979. "Sport, Social Development, and Community Decision-Making." *International Review of Sport Sociology* 14, no. 3–4: 117–132.

Parsons, T., and N. J. Smelser. 1965. *Economy and Society.* New York: Free Press.

Petryszak, N. 1978. "Spectator Sports as an Aspect of Popular Culture—An Historical View." *Journal of Sport Behavior* 1, no. 1: 14–27.

Proctor, R. C., and W. M. Echard. 1976. "'Toot-Toot' or Spectator Sports: Psychological and Therapeutic Implications." *American Journal of Sports Medicine* 4, no. 2: 78–83.

Riordan, J. 1977. *Sport in Soviet Society.* New York: Cambridge University Press.

Sadler, W. A. 1977. "Alienated Youth and Creative Sports Experience." *Journal of the Philosophy of Sport* 4 (Fall): 83–95.

Santomier, J., and K. Ewees. 1979. "Sport, Political Socialization, and the German Democratic Republic." In M. L. Krotee, ed., *The Dimensions of Sport Sociology.* West Point, NY: Leisure Press.

Schafer, W. E. 1976. "Sport and Youth Counterculture: Contrasting Socialization Themes." In D. M. Landers, ed., *Social Problems in Athletics*. Urbana: University of Illinois Press.

Sillitoe, K. 1969. *Planning for Leisure*. London: University of Keele.

Slusher, H. S. 1967. *Man, Sport and Existence*. Philadelphia: Lea and Febiger.

Spino, M. 1971. *Running as a Spiritual Experience*. In J. Scott, ed., *The Athletic Revolution*. New York: Free Press.

Vanderzwaag, H. J. 1972. *Toward a Philosophy of Sport*. Reading, MA: Addison-Wesley.

Wohl, A. 1970. "Competitive Sport and Its Social Functions." *International Review of Sport Sociology* 5: 117–124.

Wohl, A. 1979. "Sport and Social Development." *International Review of Sport Sociology* 14, no. 3–4: 5–18.

✳ FOR FURTHER STUDY ✳

Coakley, Jay. 2007. *Sport in Society: Issues and Controversies*. 9th ed. New York: McGraw-Hill.

Coakley, Jay, and Eric Dunning, eds. 2000. *Handbook of Sport Studies*. London: Sage.

Crapeau, Dick. 1991–2001. Special Issue of *Aethlon: The Journal of Sport Literature* 20 (Fall).

Eitzen, D. Stanley. 2009. *Fair and Foul: Beyond the Myths and Paradoxes of Sport*. 4th ed. Lanham, MD: Rowman and Littlefield.

Eitzen, D. Stanley, and George H. Sage. 2009. *Sociology of North American Sport*. 8th ed. Boulder, CO: Paradigm.

Foer, Franklin. 2005. *How Soccer Explains the World*. New York: Harper Perennial.

Gerdy, John R. 2002. *Sports: The All-American Addiction*. Jackson: University of Mississippi Press.

Giulianotti, Richard. 2002. "Supporters, Followers, Fans, and *Flaneurs*." *Journal of Sport and Social Issues* 26 (February): 25–46.

Lever, Janet. 1983. *Soccer Madness*. Chicago: University of Chicago Press.

Loy, John W., and Jay Coakley. 2007. "Sport." Pp. 4643–4653 in *Blackwell Encyclopedia of Sport*. Vol. 9.

Nixon, Howard L. II. 2008. *Sport in a Changing World*. Boulder, CO: Paradigm.

Paolantonio, Sal. 2008. *How Football Explains America*. Chicago: Triumph.

Sage, George H. 1998. *Power and Ideology in American Sport: A Critical Perspective*. 2nd ed. Champaign, IL: Human Kinetics.

Zirin, Dave. 2008. *A People's History of Sports in the United States: 250 Years of Politics, Protest, People, and Play*. New York: New Press.

PART TWO

Sport and Socialization: Organized Sports and Youth

The involvement of young people in adult-supervised sport is characteristic of contemporary American society. Today, millions of boys and girls are involved in organized baseball, football, hockey, basketball, and soccer leagues. Others are involved in swimming, skating, golf, tennis, and gymnastics at a highly competitive level. School-sponsored sports begin about the seventh grade and are highly organized, win-oriented activities.

Why do so many parents in so many communities strongly support organized sports programs for youth? Primarily because most people believe that sports participation has positive benefits for those involved. The following quotation from *Time* summarizes this assumption.

> Sport has always been one of the primary means of civilizing the human animal, of inculcating the character traits a society desires. Wellington in his famous aphorism insisted that the Battle of Waterloo had been won on the playing fields of Eton. The lessons learned on the playing field are among the most basic: the setting of goals and joining with others to achieve them; an understanding of and respect for rules; the persistence to hone ability into skill, prowess into perfection. In games, children learn that success is possible and that failure can be overcome. Championships may be won; when lost, wait until next year. In practicing such skills as fielding a grounder and hitting a tennis ball, young athletes develop work patterns and attitudes that carry over into college, the marketplace and all of life.[1]

However, parents often ignore the negative side of sports participation, a position that is summarized by Charles Banham:

It [the conventional argument that sport builds character] is not sound because it assumes that everyone will benefit from sport in the complacently prescribed manner. A minority do so benefit. A few have the temperament that responds healthily to all the demands. These are the only ones able to develop an attractively active character. Sport can put fresh air in the mind, if it's the right mind; it can give muscle to the personality, if it's the right personality. But for the rest, it encourages selfishness, envy, conceit, hostility, and bad temper. Far from ventilating the mind, it stifles it. Good sportsmanship may be a product of sport, but so is bad sportsmanship.[2]

The problem is that sports produce positive and negative outcomes. This dualistic quality of sport is summarized by Terry Orlick: "For every positive psychological or social outcome in sports, there are possible negative outcomes. For example, sports can offer a child group membership or group exclusion, acceptance or rejection, positive feedback or negative feedback, a sense of accomplishment or a sense of failure, evidence of self-worth or a lack of evidence of self-worth. Likewise, sports can develop cooperation and a concern for others, but they can also develop intense rivalry and a complete lack of concern for others."[3]

The first chapter in this part, by sociologist Jay J. Coakley, describes the organized youth sports of today and compares them with the spontaneous games more characteristic of youth in previous generations.

The second chapter expresses a concern over the change in children's play as they are now more engaged in solitary computer games. This change stifles creativity, physical activity, and social engagement.

The final chapter, by sociologist Michael Messner, reports his research on the meanings that males attribute to their boyhood participation in organized sport. Messner concludes: "Organized sports is a 'gendered institution'—an institution constructed by gender relations. As such, its structure and values . . . reflect dominant conceptions of masculinity and femininity."

NOTES

1. "Comes the Revolution: Joining the Game at Last, Women Are Transforming American Athletics," *Time* (June 26, 1978): 55.
2. Charles Banham, "Man at Play," *Contemporary Review* 207 (August 1965): 62.
3. T. D. Orlick, "The Sports Environment: A Capacity to Enhance—A Capacity to Destroy," paper presented at the Canadian Symposium of Psycho-Motor Learning and Sports Psychology (1974), 2.

4

Play Group versus Organized Competitive Team

A Comparison

Jay J. Coakley

One way to begin to grasp the nature and extent of the impact of participation in sport is to try to understand the sport group as a context for the behavior and the relationships of youngsters. In a 1968 symposium on the sociology of sport, Gunther Luschen from the University of Illinois delivered a paper entitled "Small Group Research and the Group in Sport." While discussing the variety of different group contexts in which sport activities occur, he contrasted the spontaneously formed casual play group with the organized competitive team. He was primarily interested in the social organization and the amount of structural differentiation existing in sport groups in general, but some of his ideas give us a basis for comparing the characteristics of the spontaneous play group and the organized competitive Little League team in terms of their implications for youngsters. In general, any group engaging in competitive physical activity can be described in terms of the extent and complexity of its formal organization. Simply put, we can employ a continuum along which such groups could be located depending on how formally organized they are. Figure 4-1 illustrates this idea.

The spontaneous play group is an example of a context for competitive physical activities in which formal organization is absent. Its polar opposite is the sponsored

Source: "Play Group versus Organized Competitive Team: A Comparison" by Jay J. Coakley. From *Sport in Society: Issues and Controversies* by Jay J. Coakley. Copyright © 1978 by C. V. Mosby. Reprinted by permission.

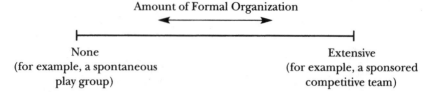

Amount of Formal Organization

None
(for example, a spontaneous
play group)

Extensive
(for example, a sponsored
competitive team)

Figure 4-1 A Formal Organization Continuum for Groups in Competitive Physical Activities

Table 4-1 Comparison of Two Groups

The Spontaneous Play Group: *No Formal Organization*	*The Sponsored Competitive Team:* *High Formal Organization*
Action is an outgrowth of the interpersonal relationships and of the decision-making processes of participating members.	Action is an outgrowth of a predesignated system of role relationships and of the role-learning abilities of group members.
Rewards are primarily intrinsic and are a function of the experience and the extent of the interpersonal skills of the group members.	Rewards are primarily extrinsic and are a function of the combined technical skills of group members.
Meanings attached to actions and situations are emergent and are subject to changes over time.	Meanings are predominantly predefined and are relatively static from one situation to the next.
Group integration is based on the process of exchange between group members.	Group integration is based on an awareness of and conformity to a formalized set of norms.
Norms governing action are emergent, and interpretation is variable.	Norms are highly formalized and specific, with variability resulting from official judgments.
Social control is internally generated among members and is dependent on commitment.	Social control is administered by an external agent and is dependent on obedience.
Sanctions are informal and are directly related to the maintenance of action in the situation	Sanctions are formal and are related to the preservation of values as well as order.
Individual freedom is high, with variability a function of the group's status structure.	Individual freedom is limited to the flexibility tolerated within role expectations.
Group is generally characterized by structural instability.	Group is generally characterized by structural stability.

competitive team in an organized league. It follows that the amount of formal organization has implications for the actions of group members, for their relationships with one another, and for the nature of their experiences. Table 4-1 outlines the characteristics of the two groups that would most closely approximate the polar extremes on the continuum.

Before going any further, I should point out that the two descriptions in Table 4-1 represent "ideal type" groups. In other words, the respective sets of characteristics represent hypothetical concepts that emphasize each group's most identifiable and important elements. Ideal types are necessarily extreme or exaggerated examples of the phenomenon under investigation and as such are to be used for purposes of comparison rather than as depictions of reality. Our concern here is to look at an actual group in which youngsters participate and to compare the actual group with the ideal types in order to make an assessment of what the real group might be like as a context for experience. Of course, the real group will not be an exact replica of either of the ideal types, but will more or less resemble one or the other.

GETTING THE GAME STARTED

The characteristics of each group suggest that the differences between the spontaneous play group and the organized competitive team would be quite apparent as soon as initial contact between the participants occurs. In the spontaneous play group, we might expect that the majority of time would be spent on dealing with organizational problems, such as establishing goals, defining means to those goals, and developing expectations of both a general and a specific nature for each of the participants. Being a member of a *completely* spontaneous play group would probably be similar to being involved in the initial organizational meeting of a group of unacquainted college freshmen who are supposed to come up with a class project. Both would involve a combination of some fun, a good deal of confusion, much talking, and little action. For the context of the organized competitive team, we might imagine a supervisor (coach) blowing a whistle that brings a group of preselected youngsters of similar ages and abilities running to fall into a routine formation to await an already known command. This would resemble a "brave new world" of sport where there would be some action, a good deal of listening to instructions, much routinization, and little fun. Fortunately, most group contexts for youngsters' sport participation fall somewhere between these two extremes. The trick is, of course, to find which points on the continuum would have a maximization of both fun and action along with the other characteristics seen as most beneficial to the young participants' development.

From my observations of youngsters in backyards, gyms, parks, and playgrounds, I have concluded that, for the most part, they are quite efficient in organizing their sport activities. The primary organizational details are often partially worked out by physical setting, available equipment, and time of the year, all of which influence the choice of activity and the form the activity will take. To the extent that the participants know one another and have played with each other before, there will be a minimum amount of time devoted to formation of norms—rules from previous games can be used. But despite the ability of most youngsters to get a competitive physical activity going, there seems to be a tendency for adults to become impatient with some of the "childish" disagreements of the young participants. Adults often become impatient because they do not understand the youngsters' "distortions" of the games—games the adults know are supposed to be played another way. Adults who want to teach youngsters to play the game the *right way* and to help young players avoid disagreements and discussions in order to build up more action time seem to be everywhere. These adults see a very clear need for organization, that is, establishing regular practice times, scheduling contests, and giving positive rewards and encouragement to those whose performances are seen as deserving. Although their motives may be commendable, these adults usually fail to consider all of the differences between the informally organized group and the formally organized team.

Most importantly, the game in the park is in the control of the youngsters themselves, whereas the organized competitive team is supervised and controlled by adults. In the play group, getting the game under way depends on the group members being able to communicate well enough to make organizational decisions and to evoke enough cooperation so that a sufficient amount of the group's behavior is conducive to the achievement of the goals of the game, however they have been defined. In this situation, interpersonal skills are crucial, and youngsters will probably be quick to realize that playing the game depends on being able to develop and maintain positive relationships or, at least, learning to cope with interpersonal problems in a way that will permit cooperative action. This constitutes a valuable set of experiences that become less available to participants as the amount of the group's formal organization increases. It is a rare adult coach who allows youngsters to make many decisions on how the game should be organized and played. In fact, most decisions have been made for the coach; the availability of the practice field has been decided, the roles defined, the rules made, the sanctions outlined, the team colors picked, the games scheduled, etc. Occasionally the players are allowed to vote on their team name, but that happens only if the team is new and does not already have one. In all, *the emphasis in the organized setting is on the development of sport skills, not on the development of interpersonal skills.*

PLAY OF THE GAME

Differences between the two groups do not disappear once the game begins. For the spontaneous play group, the game experience is likely to be defined as an end in itself, whereas for the organized team, the game is a means to an end. In the play group, the game is unlikely to have implications beyond the setting in which it occurs, and the participants are primarily concerned with managing the situation so that action can be preserved for as long as possible. To this end, it is quite common for the participating youngsters to develop sets of norms accompanied by rather complex sets of qualifications and to establish handicaps for certain participants. These tactics serve to compensate for skill differences and to ensure that the game proceeds with scores close enough so that excitement and satisfaction can be maximized for as many of the players as possible. For example, if one of the pitchers in an informal baseball game were bigger or stronger than the rest of the youngsters, he/she would be required to pitch the ball with "an arch on it" to minimize the ball's speed and to allow all the batters a chance to hit it. Exceptionally good batters might be required to bat left-handed (if they were right-handed) to minimize the chances of hitting a home run every time they came to bat. A youngster having a hard time hitting the ball might be given more than three strikes, and the pitcher might make a special effort to "put the ball over the plate" so that the batter would have a good chance of hitting the ball rather than striking out. Since a strikeout is a relatively unexciting event in a game where the primary goal is the involvement of all players, one of the most frequently made comments directed to the pitcher by his/her teammates in the field is "C'mon, let 'em hit it!"

Similar examples of norm qualifications and handicap systems can be found in other sport groups characterized by a low degree of formal organization. Sometimes these little adaptations can be very clever, and, of course, some participants have to be warned if they seem to be taking unfair advantage of them. This may occur in cases where a young player tends to call time-outs whenever the opposition has his team at a disadvantage or when someone begins to overuse an interference or a "do-over" call to nullify a mistake or a failure to make a play. Although the system of qualifications and handicaps may serve to allow the participants to have another chance when they make mistakes and to avoid the embarrassment associated with a relative lack of skills, the major function of such systems seems to be to equalize not only the players, but also the teams competing against one another. Through such techniques, scores will remain close enough that neither team will give up and destroy the game by quitting. In a sense, the players make an attempt to control the competition so that the fun of all will be safeguarded. Adults do the same thing when given the chance. None of us enjoys being overwhelmed by an opponent or overcoming an opponent so weak that we never had to make an effort.

For the formally organized competitive team, however, the play of the game may be considerably different. The goal of victory or the promotion of the team's place in the league standings replaces the goal of maximizing individual participant satisfaction. The meanings and rewards attached to the game are largely a function of how the experience is related to a desired outcome—either victory or "a good show." Players may even be told that a good personal performance is almost always nullified by a team defeat and that to feel satisfied with yourself without a team victory is selfish (as they say in the locker room, "There is no 'u' in team" or "Defeat is worse than death because you have to live with defeat").

Since victories are a consequence of the combined skills of the team members, such skills are to be practiced and improved and then utilized in ways that maximize the chances for team success. Granting the other team a handicap is quite rare unless any chance for victory is out of their grasp. If this is the case, the weaker players may be substituted in the lineup of the stronger team *unless*, of course, a one-sided score will serve the purpose of increasing the team's prestige or intimidating future opponents.

Also, if one player's skill level far exceeds that of the other participants, that player will often be used where he can be most effective. In the Little League game, it is frequently the bigger youngster with the strongest arm who is made the pitcher. This may help to ensure a team's chances for victory, but it also serves to nearly eliminate the rest of the team's chances for making fielding plays and for being involved in the defensive play of the game. In a 6-inning game, the fact that a large number of the 18 total outs for the opponents come as strikeouts means that a number of fielders may never have a chance to even touch the ball while they are out in the field. A similar thing happens in football. The youth-league team often puts its biggest and strongest players in the backfield rather than in the line. The game then consists of giving those youngsters the ball on nearly every play. For the smaller players on the defensive team, the primary task may be getting out of the way of the runner to avoid being stepped on. Thus on the organized team, intimidation may become a part of playing strategy. Unfortunately, intimidation increases apprehension and inhibits some of the action in the game as well as the involvement of some of the players. Generally, it seems that on the organized team the tendency to employ the skills of the players to win games takes precedence over devising handicaps to ensure fun and widespread participation.

One way to become aware of some of the differences between the informal play group and the formally organized competitive team is to ask the participants in each group the scores of their games. In the formally organized setting, the scores are often one-sided with members of the winning team even boasting about how they won their last football game 77 to 6, their last baseball games 23 to 1, or their last soccer game 14 to 0. Such scores lead me to question the amount of fun had by the players. In the case of the losers it would be rare to find players who would be able to maintain an interest in a game when they are so completely beaten. If the winners say they enjoyed themselves, the lesson they may be learning through such an experience should be seriously questioned. It may be that the major lesson is if your opponents happen to be weak, take advantage of that weakness so totally that they will never be able to make a comeback. Such experiences, instead of instilling positive relationships and a sincere interest in sport activities, are apt to encourage distorted assessments of self-worth and to turn youngsters off to activities that, in modified forms, could provide them with years of enjoyment.

In addition to the differences in how the game is organized and how the action is initiated, there are also differences in how action for the two groups is maintained. In the informally organized group, the members are held together through the operation of some elementary processes of exchange that, in a sense, serve as the basis for the participants obtaining what they think they deserve out of the experience (Polgar, 1976). When the range of abilities is great, the older, bigger, more talented participants have to compromise some of their abilities so that the younger, smaller, and less talented will have a chance to gain the rewards necessary to continue playing. The play of the game depends on maintaining a necessary level of commitment among all participants. This commitment then serves as a basis for social control during the action. Although there are some exceptions, those in the groups with the highest combined skill and social prestige levels act as leaders and serve as models of normal behavior. For these individuals to deviate from the norms in any consistent manner would most likely earn them the reputation of being cheaters or bad sports.

In fact, consistent deviation from the group norms by any of the participants is likely to be defined by the others as disruptive, and the violator will be reminded of his/her infraction through some type of warning or through a threat of future exclusion from group activities. When sanctions are employed in the informal play group, they usually serve an instrumental function—they bring behavior in line so that the game can continue. Sanctions are usually not intended to reinforce status distinctions, to preserve an established social structure, or to safeguard values and principles. Interestingly, self-enforcement of norms in the play group is usually quite effective. Deviation is not totally eliminated, but it is kept within the limits necessary to preserve action in the game. The emphasis is not so much on keeping norms sacred, but on making sure that the norms serve to maintain the goal of action. In fact, norms may change or be reinterpreted for specific individuals or in specific situations so that the level of action in the play activities can be maximized. The importance of maintaining a certain level of action is demonstrated by the informal sanctions directed at a participant who might always be insisting on too rigid an enforcement of norms. This is the person who continually cries "foul" or who always spots a penalty. To be persistent in such a hard-nosed approach to norm enforcement will probably earn the player the nonendearing reputation of being a baby, a crier, or a complainer.

In the informally organized play group, the most disruptive kind of deviant is the one who does not care about the game. It is interesting that the group will usually tolerate any number of different performance styles, forms, and individual innovations as long as they do not destroy action. Batting left-handed when one is right-handed is okay if the batter is at least likely to hit the ball, thus keeping the action going. Throwing behind-the-back passes and trying a crazy shot in basketball or running an unplanned pass pattern in football are all considered part of the game in the play group *if action is not destroyed.* Joking around will frequently be tolerated and sometimes even encouraged *if action can continue.* But if such behavior moves beyond the level of seriousness required to maintain satisfying action for all the participants, commitment decreases, and the group is likely to dissolve. In line with this, usually those participants with the highest amount of skill are allowed the greatest amount of freedom to play "as the spirit moves them." Although such behavior may seem to indicate a lack of seriousness to the outsider, the skill of the player is developed enough to avoid a "disruptive" amount of mistakes. At the same time, such freedom gives high-ability participants a means through which their interest level can be maintained. Similar free-wheeling behavior by a low-ability participant would be viewed with disfavor, since the behavior would frequently bring the action level below what would be defined as acceptable by the rest of the group.

In contrast to the play group, the maintenance of action on the formally organized team depends on an initial commitment to playing as a part of the team. This commitment then serves as a basis for learning and conforming to a preestablished set of norms.[1] The norms apply equally to everyone, and control is administered through the coach-supervisor. Regardless of how priorities are set with respect to goals, goal achievement rests primarily on obedience to the coach's directives rather than on the generation of personal interests based on mutually satisfying social exchange processes. Within the structure of the organized competitive team, deviation from the norms is defined as serious not only when it disrupts action, but also when it could have been disruptive or when it somehow challenges the organized structure through which action occurs. Thus sanctions take on a value-supportive function as well as an instrumental function. This is demonstrated by the coaches who constantly worry about their own authority, that is, whether they command the respect of their players.

In the interest of developing technical skills, the norms for the formally organized competitive team restrict not only the range of a player's action, but also the form of such actions. Unique batting, throwing, running, shooting, or kicking styles must be abandoned in the face of what the coach considers to be correct form. Joking around on the part of any team member is usually not tolerated regardless of the player's abilities, and the demonstration of skills is usually limited to the fundamentals of the game.

If commitment cannot be maintained under these circumstances, players are often not allowed to quit. They may be told by the coach that "We all have to take our bumps to be part of the team" or "Quitters never win and winners never quit." Parents may also point out that "Once you join a team, it is your duty to stick it out for the whole season" or "We paid our money for you to play the whole season; don't waste what we've given you." With this kind of feedback, even a total absence of personal commitment to the sport activity may not lead to withdrawal from participation. What keeps youngsters going is a commitment to personal honor and integrity or obedience to a few significant people in their lives.

WHEN THE GAME IS OVER: MEANING AND CONSEQUENCES

The implications of the game after completion are different for the members of the informal play group than they are for the members of the formally organized competitive team. For the latter, the game goes on record as a win or a loss. If the score was close, both winners and losers may initially qualify the outcome in terms of that closeness.[2] But, as other games are played, all losses and wins are grouped respectively regardless of the closeness of scores. In the informal play group, the score of a game may be discussed while walking home; however, it is usually forgotten quickly and considered insignificant in light of the actions of individual players. Any feelings of elation that accompany victory or of let-down that accompany defeat are short-lived in the play group—you always begin again on the next day, in the next game, or with the next activity. For the organized competitive team, such feelings are less transitory and are often renewed at some future date when there is a chance to avenge a previous loss or to show that a past victory was not just a fluke. Related to this is the fact that the organized team is usually geared to winning, with the coaches and players always reminding themselves, in the Norman Vincent Peale tradition, that "we can win ... if we only play like we can." This may lead to defining victories as the expected outcomes of games and losses as those outcomes that occur when you do not perform as you are able. When this happens, the elation and satisfaction associated with winning can be buried by the determination to win the next one, the next one, and so on. Losses, however, are not so quickly put away. They tend to follow you as a reminder of past failures to accomplish what you could have if you had executed your collective skills properly. The element of fun in such a setting is of only minor importance and may be eliminated by the seriousness and determination associated with the activity.

The final difference between the two groups is related to the stability of each. The informal play group is characteristically unstable, whereas the opposite is true of the organized team. If minimal levels of commitment cannot be maintained among some members of the play group, the group may simply dissolve. Dissolution may also result from outside forces. For example, since parents are not involved in the organization of the play group, they may not go out of their way to plan for their youngster's participation by delaying or arranging family activities around the time of the group's existence. When a parent calls a youngster home, the entire group may be in serious jeopardy. Other problems that contribute to instability are being told that you cannot play in the street, that someone's yard is off limits, that park space is inaccessible, or that necessary equipment is broken or unavailable. These problems usually do not exist for the organized team. Consent by parents almost guarantees the presence of a player at a scheduled practice or game, space and equipment are reserved in advance, and substitute players are available when something happens to a regular team member. Because the team is built around a structure of roles rather than a series of interacting persons, players can be replaced without serious disruption, and the action can continue.

NOTES

1. In some cases, "commitment" may not be totally voluntary on the part of the player. Parents may sign up a son or daughter without the youngster's full consent or may, along with peers, subtly coerce the youngster to play.

2. Such qualifications are, of course, used for different effects. Winners use them to show that their challengers were able or that victory came under pressure. Losers use them to show how close they came to victory.

5

Anyone Up for Stickball?
In a PlayStation World, Maybe Not

Timothy Williams and Cassi Feldman

On a few dirty squares of sidewalk in Crown Heights, Brooklyn, is a chalk drawing as mysterious to the uninitiated as hieroglyphics. Someone had, with great care, marked off a series of squares and given each a numerical value, although there did not seem to be any obvious pattern.

The drawing is a skelly board, for a game once so popular on the streets of New York that on some blocks adults had to walk in the street to avoid interrupting any of several games under way.

In a time before video games, trans fat or car alarms, in a city that seemed like a smaller version of present-day New York, screaming children ruled the streets. There was the whack of stickball on the asphalt, the singsong rhymes of double-dutch jump-rope on the sidewalk, the smack of curb ball in the gutter, the pained yelps arising out of a game called "booty's up," and the frantic counting of hide-and-seek in unexpected corners.

With joyous abandon, kids roller-skated, played ring-a-levio and steal the bacon, used sticks to roll discarded tires down the street, built go-carts and forts out of debris and wrenched open fire hydrants, drenching whoever dared go past.

Today, such loosely organized street play, outside of skateboarding and basketball, is on its last gasp in the city, a vestige of a simpler age for which a fast-paced world has little time.

"Parents drive children at a very young age to get them on the right track for success, so every waking moment is programmed, which doesn't leave lots of time for play," said Steven Zeitlin, executive director of City Lore, a nonprofit group on the Lower East Side of Manhattan that studies the nation's cultural heritage. "A lot is being lost as these old forms of play die out."

From the 1920s (and perhaps earlier) to the 1980s, the block in front of an apartment building in many neighborhoods was not just a child's backyard, but an extension of the living room and the classroom—a place where children learned to play by the rules, the simpler the better.

If, like Stephen Swid, a kid was lucky enough to live a few blocks from Yankee Stadium in the 1950s, players like Mickey Mantle or Tony Kubek might stop by to take a turn at stickball. Sometimes, it got even better.

Mr. Swid, 66, former chief executive officer of Knoll International Holdings and Spin magazine, said he remembered a day when Mantle hit a ball over a six-story building on Sheridan Avenue. Another day, a rival stickball team showed up wearing uniforms—an unusual touch for a working-class neighborhood. Later, Mr. Swid learned the black and gold uniforms had been designed by one of the team's adolescent players, Ralph Lifshitz, now known as Ralph Lauren.

The fun stopped, or moved inside, depending upon whom you ask, thanks to (pick two or three): television; two-income families; air-conditioning; digital technology; organized sports, crime; smaller families and roomier apartments; too much homework and other responsibilities; diverse, less cohesive neighborhoods; and perhaps most significantly, steady traffic, even on side streets.

Additionally, parents have not passed the games on to children, and newer immigrants have chosen to play soccer, cricket and badminton—sports not necessarily conducive to being played on the street.

While the games have largely faded away from city streets—and any sort of play beyond basketball, bicycle riding, handball or skateboarding has become unusual—some of the old games have held on, albeit with updated rules.

Brandon Santos, an 11-year-old with a crew cut who lives in the East Village, said his favorite is "off-the-ledge baseball," which years ago would have been called curb ball. A player throws a rubber ball against the curb, sending it airborne over the street. If a member of the opposing team falls to catch it, the thrower gets to run the bases, although in Brandon's version there is no running. Instead, the bases are accumulated in one's head.

"It's imaginary," he explained. "We don't run. We're kind of lazy." He and his friend Taylon Wilson, also 11, are part of a group of neighborhood kids that ebbs and swells as friends pass by on their way home, or appear from around a corner. The two, who had been playing handball, rattled off their favorite street games: fishies, fishies, cross my ocean; off-the-ledge baseball; booty's up; manhunt; taps.

Just off Avenue C, Brandon showed where he and friends had spray-painted a skelly board on the concrete—a task that in years past had been done with chalk.

They play their share of video games as well, said Taylon, who speaks in excited bursts, but the boys sometimes prefer to play on the street.

"It's kind of more fun," he said. "You get to make it like your own. You get to design your game and make the rules."

And besides, Taylon said about video games: "After a while, they kind of make your eyes water up. You start to drool." He pretended to drool. "You get bored of them."

As the boys came and went, Raynard Rembert, a 46-year-old security guard who grew up in the nearby Jacob Riis Houses, walked over after overhearing snippets of the conversation. His nickname, he said, is Radar.

One of Mr. Rembert's favorite childhood games was "Johnny-on-the-pony." The game, which had been among the most popular street games, involves two teams. One crouches into a single-file line, each person holding the waist of the person ahead of them. There are variations, but generally, members of they second team try one by one to hop atop the "pony" and to stay on for a certain amount of time before they are shaken off. Other versions involve jumping onto the pony, trying to make everyone fall to the ground.

Mr. Rembert said he had also played booty's up, though he and his friends called it "bunky's up" because they were not allowed to use the word "booty." That game involved throwing a hard rubber Spaldeen ball at someone's backside from close range. Few people seem to remember the precise rules, and doubt there were many anyhow.

The old games, Mr. Rembert said fondly, are "physical and they're challenging. They take coordination and balance and focus."

Perhaps allowing the sepia-tinged haze of his memories to forget the many welts raised by a round of booty's up and the noses bloodied during Johnny-on-the-pony, Mr. Rembert added, "It's good to pass down sports where the kids are competing but aren't trying to hurt each other."

For several years, a diverse collection of people have sought to revive street play in the city, not only with an eye on their own nostalgic views of childhood, but also with the belief that such games contribute to social cohesion and to healthier children.

"It was expected that you would go out after school, roam the neighborhood and play these games, and then come home for dinner," said Nick Green, a 53-year-old social worker who lives in South Jamaica, Queens, and operates a Web site, Streetplay.com, that celebrates the old games. "We didn't realize it at the time, but that was probably the golden age for children."

Last summer, Anthony Gigante, 48, of Brooklyn, organized a league to play what may be the most resilient of the traditional games—stickball—although its slow demise has been lamented for years.

The game is still played by a few adult leagues in the city, including the Major Stick-Ball League, which plays on schoolyard playgrounds, but Mr. Gigante wanted to teach the game to children after he learned that many could not afford the cost of participating in youth baseball leagues.

He got permission from the city to close Bay 22nd Street near Bath Avenue in Bensonhurst on Sunday mornings from 9 to noon. Every week, about 40 children, ages 5 to 11, showed up.

"We played ball every Sunday," he said. "We played stickball, box ball, Johnny-on-the-pony. You don't see kids playing on the street anymore because there's so many cars. It's a different culture."

The old games were rarely complicated, although their rules and names would often vary from block to block.

Skelly, for instance, is also known as skully, skilsies, skelsies, bottle caps and dead box. The game calls for players to use pieces, typically bottle caps, to navigate a board drawn on the pavement. The object is for a player to navigate through the board's 13 squares and back again. That player then has the right to roam the board, harassing other players, including "blasting" a rival's piece off the board.

Last year in Boerum Hill, Brooklyn, 58-year-old Delores Hadden Smith organized a street festival at the Gowanus Houses and had adults teach children games with candy-coated names that sounded like the made-up concoctions they were.

There was red devil; box ball; bluebird, bluebird through my window; hot peas and butter; a variation of ring-a-levio called cocolevio; steal the bacon; look who's here punch-a-nella; knockout; and duck duck goose.

"The older people said, 'No, that's not going to work, these children are too bad,'" Ms. Hadden Smith, a public school teacher, said triumphantly. "In the end, we had more than 300 people register, and we went all day without a single curse word."

Actually, Ms. Hadden Smith didn't last until the end of the day. She went to bed about 11 p.m. The games continued past midnight.

"We laughed and we hollered and we cried," she said. "We had the time of our lives."

It didn't matter that none of the children had known how to play the games, including performing simple tasks like turning a jump-rope, she said.

"Who's going to teach them?" she asked. "You don't see a lot of people jumping rope, do you?"

This summer, Ms. Hadden Smith expects an even larger turnout.

"The children were children like when we were children," she said. "They weren't little fidgety adults or little thugs or thugettes. Every single weekend since then, I can't go out to the corner store without them coming up to me saying, 'I'm ready! I'm ready! When are we going to do that again?'"

6

Boyhood, Organized Sports, and the Construction of Masculinities

Michael A. Messner

The rapid expansion of feminist scholarship in the past two decades has led to fundamental reconceptualizations of the historical and contemporary meanings of organized sport. In the nineteenth and twentieth centuries, modernization and women's continued movement into public life created widespread "fears of social feminization," especially among middle-class men (Hantover 1978; Kimmel 1987). One result of these fears was the creation of organized sport as a homosocial sphere in which competition and (often violent) physicality was valued, while "the feminine" was devalued. As a result, organized sport has served to bolster a sagging ideology of male superiority, and has helped to reconstitute masculine hegemony (Bryson 1987; Hall 1988; Messner 1988; Theberge 1981).

The feminist critique has spawned a number of studies of the ways that women's sport has been marginalized and trivialized in the past (Greendorfer 1977; Oglesby 1978; Twin 1978), in addition to illuminating the continued existence of structural and ideological barriers to gender equality within sport (Birrell 1987). Only recently, however, have scholars begun to use feminist insights to examine men's experiences in sport (Kidd 1987; Messner 1987; Sabo 1985). This article explores the relationship between the construction of masculine identity and boyhood participation in organized sports.

Source: Michael A. Messner, *Journal of Contemporary Ethnography,* 18, no. 4 (January 1990): 416–444, copyright © 1990 by Sage Publications, Inc. Reprinted by permission of Sage Publications, Inc.

I view gender identity not as a "thing" that people "have," but rather as a *process of construction* that develops, comes into crisis, and changes as a person interacts with the social world. Through this perspective, it becomes possible to speak of "gendering" identities rather than "masculinity" or "femininity" as relatively fixed identities or statuses.

There is an agency in this construction; people are not passively shaped by their social environment. As recent feminist analyses of the construction of feminine gender identity have pointed out, girls and women are implicated in the construction of their own identities and personalities, both in terms of the ways that they participate in their own subordination and the ways that they resist subordination (Benjamin 1988; Haug 1987). Yet this self-construction is not a fully conscious process. There are also deeply woven, unconscious motivations, fears, and anxieties at work here. So, too, in the construction of masculinity. Levinson (1978) has argued that masculine identity is neither fully "formed" by the social context, nor is it "caused" by some internal dynamic put into place during infancy. Instead, it is shaped and constructed through the interaction between the internal and the social. The internal gendering identity may set developmental "tasks," may create thresholds of anxiety and ambivalence, yet it is only through a concrete examination of people's interactions with others within social institutions that we can begin to understand both the similarities and differences in the construction of gender identities.

In this study I explore and interpret the meanings that males themselves attribute to their boyhood participation in organized sport. In what ways do males construct masculine identities within the institution of organized sports? In what ways do class and racial differences mediate this relationship and perhaps lead to the construction of different meanings, and perhaps different masculinities? And what are some of the problems and contradictions within these constructions of masculinity?

DESCRIPTION OF RESEARCH

Between 1983 and 1985, I conducted interviews with 30 male former athletes. Most of the men I interviewed had played the (U.S.) "major sports"—football, basketball, baseball, track. At the time of the interview, each had been retired from playing organized sports for at least five years. Their ages ranged from 21 to 48, with the median, 33; 14 were black, 14 were white, and two were Hispanic; 15 of the 16 black and Hispanic men had come from poor or working-class families, while the majority (9 of 14) of the white men had come from middle-class or professional families. All had at some time in their lives based their identities largely on their roles as athletes and could therefore be said to have had "athletic careers." Twelve had played organized sports through high school, 11 through college, and seven had been professional athletes. Though the sample was not randomly selected, an effort was made to see that the sample had a range of difference in terms of race and social class backgrounds, and that there was some variety in terms of age, types of sports played, and levels of success in athletic careers. Without exception, each man contacted agreed to be interviewed.

The tape-recorded interviews were semistructured and took from one and one-half to six hours, with most taking about three hours. I asked each man to talk about four broad eras in his life: (1) his earliest experiences with sports in boyhood, (2) his athletic career, (3) retirement or disengagement from the athletic career, and (4) life after the athletic career. In each era, I focused the interview on the meanings of "success and failure," and on the boy's/man's relationships with family, with other males, with women, and with his own body.

In collecting what amounted to life histories of these men, my overarching purpose was to use feminist theories of masculine gender identity to explore how masculinity develops and changes as boys and men interact within the socially constructed world of organized sports. In addition to using the data to move toward some generalizations about the relationship between "masculinity and sport," I was also concerned with sorting out some of the variations among boys, based on class and racial inequalities, that led them to relate differently to athletic careers. I divided my sample into two comparison groups. The first group was made up of 10 men from higher-status backgrounds, primarily white, middle-class, and professional families. The second group was made up of 20 men from lower-status backgrounds, primarily minority, poor, and working-class families.

BOYHOOD AND THE PROMISE OF SPORTS

Zane Grey once said, "All boys love baseball. If they don't they're not real boys" (as cited in Kimmel 1990). This is, of course, an ideological statement; in fact, some boys do *not* love baseball, or any other sports, for that matter. There are millions of males who at an early age are rejected by, become alienated from, or lose interest in organized sports. Yet all boys are, to a greater or lesser extent, judged according to their ability, or lack of ability, in competitive sports (Eitzen, 1975; Sabo, 1985). In this study I focus on those males who did become athletes—males who eventually poured thousands of hours into the development of specific physical skills. It is in boyhood that we can discover the roots of their commitment to athletic careers.

How did organized sports come to play such a central role in these boy's lives? When asked to recall how and why they initially got into playing sports, many of the men interviewed for this study seemed a bit puzzled: after all, playing sports was "just the thing to do." A 42-year-old black man who had played college basketball put it this way:

> It was just what you did. It's kind of like, you went to school, you played athletics, and if you didn't, there was something wrong with you. It was just like brushing your teeth: it's just what you did. It's part of your existence.

Spending one's time playing sports with other boys seemed as natural as the cycle of the seasons: baseball in the spring and summer, football in the fall, basketball in the winter—and then it was time to get out the old baseball glove and begin again. As a black 35-year-old former professional football star said:

> I'd say when I wasn't in school, 95 percent of the time was spent in the park playing. It was the only thing to do. It just came as natural.

And a black, 34-year-old professional basketball player explained his early experiences in sports:

> My principal and teacher said, "Now if you work at this you might be pretty damned good." So it was more or less a community thing—everybody in the community said, "Boy, if you work hard and keep your nose clean, you gonna be good." 'Cause it was natural instinct.

"It was natural instinct." "I was a natural." Several athletes used words such as these to explain their early attraction to sports. But certainly there is nothing "natural" about throwing a ball through a hoop, hitting a ball with a bat, or jumping over hurdles. A boy, for instance, may have amazingly dexterous inborn hand–eye coordination, but this does not predispose him to a career of hitting baseballs any more than it predisposes him to a life as a brain surgeon. When one listens closely to what these men said about their early experiences in sports, it becomes clear that their adoption of the self-definition of "natural athlete" was the result of what Connell (1990) has called "a collective practice" that constructs masculinities. The boyhood development of masculine identity and status—truly problematic in a society that offers no official rite of passage into adulthood—results from a process of interaction with people and social institutions. Thus, in discussing early motivations in sports, men commonly talk of the importance of relationships with family members, peers, and the broader community.

FAMILY INFLUENCES

Though most of the men in this study spoke of their mothers with love, respect, even reverence, their descriptions of their earliest experiences in sports are stories of an exclusively male world. The existence of older brothers or uncles who served as teachers and athletic role models—as well as sources of competition for attention and status within the family—was very common. An older brother, uncle, or even close friend of the family who was a successful athlete appears to have acted as a sort of standard of achievement against whom to measure oneself. A 34-year-old black man who had been a three-sport star in high school said:

> My uncles—my Uncle Harold went to the Detroit Tigers, played pro ball—all of 'em, everybody played sports, so I wanted to be better than anybody else. I knew

that everybody in this town knew them—their names were something. I wanted my name to be just like theirs.

Similarly, a black 41-year-old former professional football player recalled:

I was the younger of three brothers and everybody played sports, so consequently I was more or less forced into it. 'Cause one brother was always better than the next brother and then I came along and had to show them that I was just as good as them. My oldest brother was an all-city ballplayer, then my other brother comes along he's all-city and all-state, and then I have to come along.

For some, attempting to emulate or surpass the athletic accomplishments of older male family members created pressures that were difficult to deal with. A 33-year-old white man explained that he was a good athlete during boyhood, but the constant awareness that his two older brothers had been better made it difficult for him to feel good about himself, or to have fun in sports:

I had this sort of reputation that I followed from the playgrounds through grade school, and through high school. I followed these guys who were all-conference and all-state.

Most of these men, however, saw their relationships with their athletic older brothers and uncles in a positive light; it was within these relationships that they gained experience and developed motivations that gave them a competitive "edge" within their same-aged peer group. As a 33-year-old black man describes his earliest athletic experiences:

My brothers were role models. I wanted to prove—especially to my brothers—that I had heart, you know, that I was a man.

When asked, "What did it mean to you to be 'a man' at that age?" he replied:

Well, it meant that I didn't want to be a so-called scaredy-cat. You want to hit a guy even though he's bigger than you to show that, you know, you've got this macho image. I remember that at that young an age, that feeling was exciting to me. And that carried over, and as I got older, I got better and I began to look around me and see, well hey! I'm competitive with these guys, even though I'm younger, you know? And then of course all the compliments come—and I began to notice a change, even in my parents—especially in my father—he was proud of that, and that was very important to me. He was extremely important ... he showed me more affection, now that I think of it.

As this man's words suggest, if men talk of their older brothers and uncles mostly as role models, teachers, and "names" to emulate, their talk of their relationships with their fathers is more deeply layered and complex. Athletic skills and competition for status may often be learned from older brothers, but it is in boys' relationships with fathers that we find many of the keys to the emotional salience of sports in the development of masculine identity.

RELATIONSHIPS WITH FATHERS

The fact that boys' introductions to organized sports are often made by fathers who might otherwise be absent or emotionally distant adds a powerful emotional charge to these early experiences (Osherson 1986). Although playing organized sports eventually came to feel "natural" for all of the men interviewed in this study, many needed to be "exposed" to sports, or even gently "pushed" by their fathers to become involved in activities like Little League baseball. A white, 33-year-old man explained:

> I still remember it like it was yesterday—Dad and I driving up in his truck, and I had my glove and my hat and all that—and I said, "Dad, I don't want to do it." He says, "What?" I says, "I don't want to do it." I was nervous. That I might fail. And he says, "Don't be silly. Lookit: There's Joey and Petey and all your friends out there." And so Dad says, "You're gonna do it, come on." And in my memory he's never said that about anything else; he just knew I needed a little kick in the pants and I'd do it. And once you're out there and you see all the other kids making errors and stuff, and you know you're better than those guys, you know: Maybe I *do* belong here. As it turned out, Little League was a good experience.

Some who were similarly "pushed" by their fathers were not so successful as the aforementioned man had been in Little League baseball, and thus the experience was not altogether a joyous affair. One 34-year-old white man, for instance, said he "inherited" his interest in sports from his father, who started playing catch with him at the age of four. Once he got into Little League, he felt pressured by his father, one of the coaches, who expected him to be the star of the team:

> I'd go 0-for-four sometimes, strike out three times in a Little League game, and I'd dread the ride home. I'd come home and he'd say, "Go in the bathroom and swing the bat in the mirror for an hour," to get my swing level ... It didn't help much, though, I'd go out and strike out three or four times again the next game too [laughs ironically].

When asked if he had been concerned with having his father's approval, he responded:

> Failure in his eyes? Yeah, I always thought that he wanted me to get some kind of [athletic] scholarship. I guess I was afraid of him when I was a kid. He didn't

hit that much, but he had a rage about him—he'd rage, and that voice would just rattle you.

Similarly, a 24-year-old black man described his awe of his father's physical power and presence, and his sense of inadequacy in attempting to emulate him:

> My father had a voice that sounded like rolling thunder. Whether it was intentional on his part or not, I don't know, but my father gave me a sense, an image of him being the most powerful being on earth, and that no matter what I ever did I would never come close to him.... There were definite feelings of physical inadequacy that I couldn't work around.

It is interesting to note how these feelings of physical inadequacy relative to the father lived on as part of this young man's permanent internalized image. He eventually became a "feared" high school football player and broke school records in weight-lifting, yet,

> As I grew older, my mother and friends told me that I had actually grown to be a larger man than my father. Even though in time I required larger clothes than he, which should have been a very concrete indication, neither my brother nor I could ever bring ourselves to say that I was bigger. We simply couldn't conceive of it.

Using sports activities as a means of identifying with and "living up to" the power and status of one's father was not always such a painful and difficult task for the men I interviewed. Most did not describe fathers who "pushed" them to become sports stars. The relationship between their athletic strivings and their identification with their fathers was more subtle. A 48-year-old black man, for instance, explained that he was not pushed into sports by his father, but was aware from an early age of the community status his father had gained through sports. He saw his own athletic accomplishments as a way to connect with and emulate his father:

> I wanted to play baseball because my father had been quite a good baseball player in the Negro leagues before baseball was integrated, and so he was kind of a model for me. I remember, quite young, going to a baseball game he was in—this was before the war and all—I remember being in the stands with my mother and seeing him on first base, and being aware of the crowd ... I was aware of people's confidence in him as a serious baseball player. I don't think my father ever said anything to me like "play sports" ... [But] I knew he would like it if I did well. His admiration was important ... he mattered.

Similarly, a 24-year-old white man described his father as a somewhat distant "role model" whose approval mattered:

My father was more of an example ... he definitely was very much in touch with and still had very fond memories of being an athlete and talked about it, bragged about it.... But he really didn't do that much to teach me skills, and he didn't always go to every game I played like some parents. But he approved and that was important, you know. That was important to get his approval. I always knew that playing sports was important to him, so I knew implicitly that it was good and there was definitely a value on it.

First experiences in sports might often come through relationships with brothers or older male relatives, and the early emotional salience of sports was often directly related to a boy's relationship with his father. The sense of commitment that these young boys eventually made to the development of athletic careers is best explained as a process of development of masculine gender identity and status in relation to same-sex peers.

MASCULINE IDENTITY AND EARLY COMMITMENT TO SPORTS

When many of the men in this study said that during childhood they played sports because "it's just what everybody did," they of course meant that it was just what *boys* did. They were introduced to organized sports by older brothers and fathers, and once involved, found themselves playing within an exclusively male world. Though the separate (and unequal) gendered worlds of boys and girls came to appear as "natural," they were in fact socially constructed. Thorne's observations of children's activities in schools indicated that rather than "naturally" constituting "separate gendered cultures," there is considerable interaction between boys and girls in classrooms and on playgrounds. When adults set up legitimate contact between boys and girls, Thorne observed, this usually results in "relaxed interactions." But when activities in the classroom or on the playground are presented to children as sex-segregated activities and gender is marked by teachers and other adults ("boys line up here, girls over there"), "gender boundaries are heightened, and mixed-sex interaction becomes an explicit arena of risk" (Thorne 1986; 70). Thus sex-segregated activities such as organized sports as structured by adults, provide the context in which gendered identities and separate "gendered cultures" develop and come to appear natural. For the boys in this study, it became "natural" to equate masculinity with competition, physical strength, and skills. Girls simply did not (could not, it was believed) participate in these activities.

Yet it is not simply the separation of children, by adults, into separate activities that explains why many boys came to feel such a strong connection with sports activities, while so few girls did. As I listened to men recall their earliest experiences in organized sports, I heard them talk of insecurity, loneliness, and especially a need to connect with other people as a primary motivation in their early sports strivings. As a 42-year-old white man stated, "The most important thing was just being out there with the rest of the guys—being friends." Another 32-year-old interviewee was born in Mexico and moved to the United States at a fairly young age. He never knew his father, and his mother died when he was only nine years old. Suddenly he felt rootless, and threw himself into sports. His initial motivations, however, do not appear to be based on a need to compete and win:

> Actually, what I think sports did for me is it brought me into kind of an instant family. By being on a Little League team, or even just playing with all kinds of different kids in the neighborhood, it brought what I really wanted, which was some kind of closeness. It was just being there, and being friends.

Clearly, what these boys needed and craved was that which was most problematic for them: connection and unity with other people. But why do these young males find *organized sports* such an attractive context in which to establish "a kind of closeness" with others? Comparative observations of young boys' and girls' game-playing behaviors yield important insights into this question. Piaget (1965) and Lever (1976) both observed that girls tend to have more "pragmatic" and "flexible" orientations to the rules of games; they are more prone to make exceptions and innovations in the middle of a game in order to make the game more "fair." Boys, on the other hand, tend to have a more firm, even inflexible orientation to the rules of a game; to them, the rules are what protects any fairness. This difference, according to Gilligan (1982), is based on the fact that early developmental experiences have yielded deeply rooted differences between males' and females' developmental tasks, needs, and moral reasoning. Girls, who tend to define themselves primarily through connection with others, experience highly competitive situations (whether in organized sports or in other hierarchical institutions) as threats to relationships, and thus to their identities. For boys, the development of gender identity involves the construction of positional identities, where a sense of self is solidified through separation from others (Chodorow 1978). Yet feminist psychoanalytic theory has tended to oversimplify the internal lives of men (Lichterman 1986). Males do appear to develop positional identities, yet despite their fears of intimacy, they also retain a human need for closeness and unity with others. This ambivalence toward intimate relationships is a major thread running through masculine development throughout the life course. Here we can conceptualize what Craib (1987) calls the "elective affinity" between personality and social structure: For the boy who both seeks and fears attachment with others, the rule-bound structure of organized sports can promise to be a safe place in which to seek nonintimate attachment with others within a context that maintains clear boundaries, distance, and separation.

COMPETITIVE STRUCTURES AND CONDITIONAL SELF-WORTH

Young boys may initially find that sports gives them the opportunity to experience "some kind of closeness" with others, but the structure of sports and athletic careers often undermines the possibility of boys learning to transcend their fears of intimacy, thus becoming able to develop truly close and intimate relationships with others (Kidd 1990; Messner 1987). The sports world is extremely hierarchical, and an incredible amount of importance is placed on winning, on "being number one." For instance, a few years ago I observed a basketball camp put on for boys by a professional basketball coach and his staff. The youngest boys, about eight years old (who could barely reach the basket with their shots) played a brief scrimmage. Afterwards, the coaches lined them up in a row in front of the older boys who were sitting in the grandstands. One by one, the coach would stand behind each boy, put his hand on the boy's head (much in the manner of a priestly benediction), and the older boys in the stands would applaud and cheer, louder or softer, depending on how well or poorly the young boy was judged to have performed. The two or three boys who were clearly the exceptional players looked confident that they would receive the praise they were due. Most of the boys, though, had expressions ranging from puzzlement to thinly disguised terror on their faces as they awaited the judgments of the older boys.

This kind of experience teaches boys that it is not "just being out there with the guys—being friends," that ensures the kind of attention and connection that they crave; it is being *better* than the other guys—*beating* them—that is the key to acceptance. Most of the boys in this study did have some early successes in sports, and thus their ambivalent need for connection with others was met, at least for a time. But the institution of sport tends to encourage the development of what Schafer (1975) has called "conditional self-worth" in boys. As boys become aware that acceptance by others is contingent upon being good—a "winner"—narrow definitions of success, based upon performance and winning become increasingly important to them. A 33-year-old black man said that by the time he was in his early teens:

> It was expected of me to do well in all my contests—I mean by my coaches, my peers, and my family. So I in turn expected to do well, and if I didn't do well, then I'd be very disappointed.

The man from Mexico, discussed above, who said that he had sought "some kind of closeness" in his early sports experiences began to notice in his early teens that if he played well, was a *winner,* he would get attention from others:

> It got to the point where I started realizing, noticing that people were always there for me, backing me all the time—sports got to be really fun because I always had some people there backing me. Finally my oldest brother started going to all my games, even though I had never really seen who he was [laughs]—after the game, you know, we never really saw each other, but he was at all my baseball games, and it seemed like we shared a kind of closeness there, but only in those situations. Off the field, when I wasn't in uniform, he was never around.

By high school, he said, he felt "up against the wall." Sports hadn't delivered what he had hoped it would, but he thought if he just tried harder, won one more championship trophy, he would get the attention he truly craved. Despite his efforts, this attention was not forthcoming. And, sadly, the pressures he had put on himself to excel in sports had taken most of the fun out of playing.

For many of the men in this study, throughout boyhood and into adolescence, this conscious striving for successful achievement became the primary means through which they sought connection with other people (Messner 1987). But it is important to recognize that young males' internalized ambivalences about intimacy do not fully determine the contours and directions of their lives. Masculinity continues to develop through interaction with the social world—and because boys from different backgrounds are interacting with substantially different familial, educational, and other institutions, these differences will lead them to make different choices and define situations in different ways. Next, I examine the differences in the ways that boys from higher- and lower-status families and communities related to organized sports.

STATUS DIFFERENCES AND COMMITMENTS TO SPORTS

In discussing early attractions to sports, the experiences of boys from higher- and lower-status backgrounds are quite similar. Both groups indicate the importance of fathers and older brothers in introducing them to sports. Both groups speak of the joys of receiving attention and acceptance among family and peers for early successes in sports. Note the similarities, for instance, in the following descriptions of boyhood athletic experiences of two men. First, a man born in a white, middle-class family:

> I loved playing sports so much from a very early age because of early exposure. A lot of the sports came easy at an early age, and because they did, and because you were successful at something, I think that you're inclined to strive for that gratification. It's like, if you're good, you like it, because it's instant gratification. I'm doing something that I'm good at and I'm gonna keep doing it.

Second, a black man from a poor family:

> Fortunately I had some athletic ability, and, quite naturally, once you start doing good in whatever it is—I don't care if it's jacks—you show off what you do. That's your ability, that's your blessing, so you show it off as much as you can.

For boys from both groups, early exposure to sports, the discovery that they had some "ability," shortly followed by some sort of family, peer, and community recognition, all eventually led to the commitment of hundreds and thousands of hours of playing, practicing, and dreaming of future stardom. Despite these similarities, there are also some identifiable differences that begin to explain the tendency of males from lower-status backgrounds to develop higher levels of commitment to sports careers. The most clear-cut difference was that while men from higher-status backgrounds are likely to describe their earliest athletic experiences and motivations almost exclusively in terms of immediate family, men from lower-status backgrounds more commonly describe the importance of a broader community context. For instance, a 46-year-old man who grew up in a "poor working class" black family in a small town in Arkansas explained:

> In that community, at the age of third or fourth grade, if you're a male, they expect you to show some kind of inclination, some kind of skill in football or basketball. It was an expected thing, you know? My mom and my dad, they didn't push at all. It was the general environment.

A 48-year-old man describes sports activities as a survival strategy in his poor black community:

> Sports protected me from having to compete in gang stuff, or having to be good with my fists. If you were an athlete and got into the fist world, that was your business, and that was okay—but you didn't have to if you didn't want to. People would generally defer to you, give you your space away from trouble.

A 35-year-old man who grew up in "a poor black ghetto" described his boyhood relationship to sports similarly:

> Where I came from, either you were one of two things: you were in sports or you were out on the streets being a drug addict, or breaking into places. The guys who were in sports, we had it a little easier, because we were accepted by both groups.... So it worked out to my advantage, cause I didn't get into a lot of trouble—some trouble, but not a lot.

The fact that boys in lower-status communities faced these kinds of realities gave salience to their developing athletic identities. In contrast, sports were important to boys from higher-status backgrounds, yet the middle-class environment seemed more secure, less threatening, and offered far more options. By the time most of these boys got into junior high or high school, many had made conscious decisions to shift their attentions away from athletic careers to educational and (nonathletic) career goals. A 32-year-old white college athletic director told me that he had seen his chance to pursue a pro baseball career as "pissing in the wind," and instead, focused on education. Similarly, a 33-year-old white dentist who was a three-sport star in high school, decided not to play sports in college, so he could focus on getting into dental school. As he put it,

> I think I kind of downgraded the stardom thing. I thought it was small potatoes. And sure, that's nice in high school and all that, but on a broad scale, I didn't think it amounted to all that much.

This statement offers an important key to understanding the construction of masculine identity within a middle-class context. The status that this boy got through sports had been *very* important to him, yet he could see that "on a broad scale," this sort of status was "small potatoes." This sort of early recognition is more than a result of the oft-noted middle-class tendency to raise "future-oriented" children (Rubin 1976; Sennett and Cobb 1973). Perhaps more important, it is that the *kinds* of future orientations developed by boys from higher-status backgrounds are consistent with the middle-class context. These men's descriptions of their boyhoods reveal that they grew up immersed in a wide range of institutional frameworks, of which organized sports was just one. And—importantly—they could see that the status of adult males around them was clearly linked to their positions within various professions, public institutions, and bureaucratic organizations. It was clear that access to this sort of institutional status came through educational achievement, not athletic prowess. A 32-year-old black man who grew up in a professional-class family recalled that he had idolized Wilt Chamberlain and dreamed of being a pro basketball player, yet his father discouraged his athletic strivings:

> He knew I liked the game. I *loved* the game. But basketball was not recommended; my dad would say, "That's a stereotyped image for black youth.... When your basketball is gone and finished, what are you gonna do? One day, you might get injured. What are you gonna look forward to?" He stressed education.

Similarly, a 32-year-old man who was raised in a white, middle-class family, had found in sports a key means of gaining acceptance and connection in his peer group. Yet he was simultaneously developing an image of himself as a "smart student," and becoming aware of a wide range of nonsports life options:

> My mother was constantly telling me how smart I was, how good I was, what a nice person I was, and giving me all sorts of positive strokes, and those positive strokes became a self-motivating kind of thing. I had this image of myself as smart, and I lived up to that image.

It is not that parents of boys in lower-status families did not also encourage their boys to work hard in school. Several reported that their parents "stressed books first, sports second." It's just that the broader social context—education, economy, and community—was more likely to *narrow* lower-status boys' perceptions of real-life options, while boys from higher-status backgrounds faced an expanding world of options. For instance, with a different socioeconomic background, one 35-year-old black man might have become a great musician instead of a star professional football running back. But he did not. When he was a child, he said, he was most interested in music:

> I wanted to be a drummer. But we couldn't afford drums. My dad couldn't go out and buy me a drum set or a guitar even—it was just one of those things; he was just trying to make ends meet.

But he *could* afford, as could so many in his socioeconomic condition, to spend countless hours at the local park, where he was told by the park supervisor

> that I was a natural—not only in gymnastics or baseball—whatever I did, I was a natural. He told me I shouldn't waste this talent, and so I immediately started watching the big guys then.

In retrospect, this man had potential to be a musician or any number of things, but his environment limited his options to sports, and he made the best of it. Even within sports, he, like most boys in the ghetto, was limited:

> We didn't have any tennis courts in the ghetto—we used to have a lot of tennis balls, but no racquets. I wonder today how good I might be in tennis if I had gotten a racquet in my hands at an early age.

It is within this limited structure of opportunity that many lower-status young boys found sports to be *the* place, rather than *a* place, within which to construct masculine identity, status, the relationships. A 36-year-old white man explained that his father left the family when he was very young and his mother faced a very difficult struggle to make ends meet. As his words suggest, the more limited a boy's options, and the more insecure his family situation, the more likely he is to make an early commitment to an athletic career:

> I used to ride my bicycle to Little League practice—if I'd waited for someone to pick me up and take me to the ball park I'd have never played. I'd get to the ball park and all the other kids would have their dad bring them to practice or games. But I'd park my bike to the side and when it was over I'd get on it and go home. Sports was the way for me to move everything to the side—family problems, just all the embarrassments—and think about one thing, and that was sports … In the third grade, when the teacher went around the classroom and asked everybody, "What do you want to be when you grow up?," I said, "I want to be a major league baseball player," and everybody laughed their heads off.

This man eventually did enjoy a major league baseball career. Most boys from lower-status backgrounds who make similar early commitments to athletic careers are not so successful. As stated earlier, the career structure of organized sports is highly competitive and hierarchical. In fact, the chances of attaining professional status in sports are approximately 4:100,000 for a white man, 2:100,000 for a black man, and 3:1 million for a Hispanic man in the United States (Leonard and Reyman 1988). Nevertheless, the immediate rewards (fun, status, attention), along with the constricted (nonsports) structure of opportunity, attract disproportionately large numbers of boys from lower-status backgrounds to athletic careers as their major means of constructing a masculine identity. These are the boys who later, as young men, had to struggle with "conditional self-worth," and, more often than not, occupational dead ends.

Boys from higher-status backgrounds, on the other hand, bolstered their boyhood, adolescent, and early adult status through their athletic accomplishments. Their wider range of experiences and life chances led to an early shift away from sports careers as the major basis of identity (Messner 1989).

CONCLUSION

The conception of the masculinity–sports relationship developed here begins to illustrate the idea of an "elective affinity" between social structure and personality. Organized sports is a "gendered institution"—an institution constructed by gender relations. As such, its structure and values (rules, formal organization, sex composition, etc.), reflect dominant conceptions of masculinity and femininity. Organized sports is also a "gendering institution"—an institution that helps to construct the current gender order. Part of this construction of gender is accomplished through the "masculinizing" of male bodies and minds.

Yet boys do not come to their first experiences in organized sports as "blank slates," but arrive with already "gendering" identities due to early developmental experiences and previous socialization. I have suggested here that an important thread running through the development of masculine identity is males' ambivalence toward intimate unity with others. Those boys who experience early athletic successes find in the structure of organized sport an affinity with this masculine ambivalence toward intimacy: The rule-bound, competitive, hierarchical world of sport offers boys an attractive means of establishing an emotionally distant (and thus "safe") connection with others. Yet as boys begin to define themselves as "athletes," they learn that in order to be accepted (to have connection) through sports, they must be winners. And in order to be winners, they must construct relationships with others (and with themselves) that are consistent with the competitive and hierarchical values and structure of the sports world. As a result, they often develop a "conditional self-worth" that leads them to construct more instrumental relationships with themselves and others. This ultimately exacerbates their difficulties in constructing intimate relationships with others. In effect, the interaction between the young male's preexisting internalized ambivalence toward intimacy with the competitive hierarchical institution of sport has resulted in the construction of a masculine personality that is characterized by instrumental rationality, goal orientation, and difficulties with intimate connection and expression (Messner 1987).

This theoretical line of inquiry invites us not simply to examine how social institutions "socialize" boys, but also to explore the ways that boys' already-gendering identities interact with social institutions (which, like organized sport, are themselves the product of gender relations). This study has also suggested that it is not some singular "masculinity" that is being constructed through athletic careers. It may be correct, from a psychoanalytic perspective, to suggest that all males bring ambivalences toward intimacy to their interactions with the world, but "the world" is a very different place for males from different racial and socioeconomic backgrounds. Because males have substantially different interactions with the world, based on class, race, and other differences and inequalities, we might expect the construction of masculinity to take on different meanings for boys and men from differing backgrounds (Messner 1989). Indeed, this study has suggested that boys from higher-status backgrounds face a much broader range of options than do their lower-status counterparts. As a result, athletic careers take on different meanings for these boys. Lower-status boys are likely to see athletic careers as *the* institutional context for the construction of their masculine status and identities, while higher-status males make an early shift away from athletic careers toward other institutions (usually education and nonsports careers). A key line of inquiry for future studies might begin by exploring this irony of sports careers: Despite the fact that "the athlete" is currently an example of an exemplary form of masculinity in public ideology, the vast majority of boys who become most committed to athletic careers are never well-rewarded for their efforts. The fact that class and racial dynamics lead boys from higher-status backgrounds, unlike their lower-status counterparts, to move into nonsports careers illustrates how the construction of different kinds of masculinities is a key component of the overall construction of the gender order.

REFERENCES

Birrell, S. 1987. "The Woman Athlete's College Experience: Knowns and Unknowns." *Journal of Sport and Social Issues* 11: 82–96.

Benjamin, J. 1988. *The Bonds of Love: Psychoanalysis, Feminism, and the Problem of Domination.* New York: Pantheon.

Bryson, L. 1987. "Sport and the Maintenance of Masculine Hegemony." *Women's Studies International Forum* 10: 349–360.

Chodorow, N. 1978. *The Reproduction of Mothering.* Berkeley: University of California Press.

Connell, R. W. 1987. *Gender and Power.* Stanford, CA: Stanford University Press.

Connell, R. W. (1990) "An Iron Man: The Body and Some Contradictions of Hegemonic Masculinity." In M. A. Messner and D. F. Sabo, eds., *Sport, Men and the Gender Order: Critical Feminist Perspectives.* Champaign, IL: Human Kinetics.

Craib, I. 1987. "Masculinity and Male Dominance." *Sociological Review* 38: 721–743.

Eitzen, D. S. 1975. "Athletics in the Status System of Male Adolescents: A Replication of Coleman's *The Adolescent Society.*" *Adolescence* 10: 268–276.

Gilligan, C. 1982. *In a Different Voice: Psychological Theory and Women's Development.* Cambridge, MA: Harvard University Press.

Greendorfer, S. L. 1977. "The Role of Socializing Agents in Female Sport Involvement." *Research Quarterly* 48: 304–310.

Hall, M. A. 1988. "The Discourse on Gender and Sport: From Femininity to Feminism." *Sociology of Sport Journal* 5: 330–340.

Hantover, J. 1978. "The Boy Scouts and the Validation of Masculinity." *Journal of Social Issues* 34: 184–195.

Haug, F. 1987. *Female Sexualization.* London: Verso.

Kidd, B. 1987. "Sports and Masculinity." Pp. 250–265 in M. Kaufman, ed., *Beyond Patriarchy: Essays by Men on Pleasure, Power, and Change.* Toronto: Oxford University Press.

———. 1990. "The Men's Cultural Centre: Sports and the Dynamic of Women's Oppression/ Men's Repression." In M. A. Messner and D. F. Sabo, eds., *Sport, Men and the Gender Order: Critical Feminist Perspectives*. Champaign, IL: Human Kinetics.

Kimmel, M. S. 1987. "Men's Responses to Feminism at the Turn of the Century." *Gender and Society* 1: 261–283.

———. 1990. "Baseball and the Reconstitution of American Masculinity: 1880–1920." In M. A. Messner and D. F. Sabo, eds., *Sport, Men and the Gender Order: Critical Feminist Perspectives*. Champaign, IL: Human Kinetics.

Leonard, W. M. II, and J. M. Reyman. 1988. "The Odds of Attaining Professional Athlete Status: Refining the Computations." *Sociology of Sport Journal* 5: 162–169.

Lever, J. 1976. "Sex Differences in the Games Children Play." *Social Problems* 23: 478–487.

Levinson, D. J. et al. 1978. *The Seasons of a Man's Life*. New York: Ballantine.

Lichterman, P. 1986. "Chodorow's Psychoanalytic Sociology: A Project Half-Completed." *California Sociologist* 9: 147–166.

Messner, M. 1987. "The Meaning of Success: The Athletic Experience and the Development of Male Identity." Pp. 193–210 in H. Brod, ed., *The Making of Masculinities: The New Men's Studies*. Boston: Allen and Unwin.

———. 1988. "Sports and Male Domination: The Female Athlete as Contested Ideological Terrain." *Sociology of Sport Journal* 5: 197–211.

———. 1989. "Masculinities and Athletic Careers." *Gender and Society* 3: 71–88.

Oglesby, C. A., ed. 1978. *Women and Sport: From Myth to Reality*. Philadelphia: Lea and Febiger.

Osherson, S. 1986. *Finding Our Fathers: How a Man's Life Is Shaped by His Relationship with His Father*. New York: Fawcett Columbine.

Piaget, J. H. 1965. *The Moral Judgment of the Child*. New York: Free Press.

Rubin, L. B. 1976. *Worlds of Pain: Life in the Working Class Family*. New York: Basic Books.

Sabo, D. 1985. "Sport, Patriarchy, and Male Identity: New Questions about Men and Sport." *Arena Review* 9: 2.

Schafer, W. E. 1975. "Sport and Male Sex Role Socialization." *Sport Sociology Bulletin* 4: 47–54.

Sennett, R., and J. Cobb. 1973. *The Hidden Injuries of Class*. New York: Random House.

Theberge, N. 1981. "A Critique of Critiques: Radical and Feminist Writings on Sport." *Social Forces* 60: 2.

Thorne, B. 1986. "Girls and Boys Together … but Mostly Apart: Gender Arrangements in Elementary Schools." Pp. 167–184 in W. W. Hartup and Z. Rubin, eds., *Relationships and Development*. Hillsdale, NJ: Lawrence Erlbaum.

Twin, S. L., ed. 1978. *Out of the Bleachers: Writings on Women and Sport*. Old Westbury, NY: Feminist Press.

✻ FOR FURTHER STUDY ✻

Bissenger, H. G. 1990. *Friday Night Lights: A Town, A Team, and a Dream.* New York: Perseus.

Cavanaugh, Ed. 2003. "Basketball Lifts Cairo's Gloom." *Chicago Tribune,* March 14, 1, 28.

Coakley, Jay. 2007. *Sports in Society: Issues and Controversies,* 9th ed. New York: McGraw-Hill.

Curry, Timothy Jon. 2001. Reply to "A Conversation (Re)Analysis of Fraternal Bonding in the Locker Room." *Sociology of Sport Journal* 18 (3): 339–344.

Curtis, James, William McTeer, and Philip White. 2003. "Do High School Athletes Earn More Pay? Youth Sports Participation and Earnings as an Adult." *Sociology of Sport Journal* 20 (1): 60–76.

Eitle, Tamela McNulty, and David J. Eitle. 2002. "Just Don't Do It: High School Sports Participation and Young Female Adult Sexual Behavior." *Sociology of Sport Journal* 19 (4): 403–418.

Eitzen, D. Stanley. 2009. *Fair and Foul: Beyond the Myths and Paradoxes of Sport.* 4th ed. Lanham, MD: Rowman and Littlefield.

Eitzen, D. Stanley, and George H. Sage, 2009. *Sociology of North American Sport.* 8th ed. Boulder, CO: Paradigm.

Ferguson, Andrew. 1999. "Inside the Crazy Culture of Kids Sports." *Time* (July 12): 52–60.

Foley, Douglas E. 1990. *Learning Capitalist Culture: Deep in the Heart of Tejas.* Philadelphia: University of Pennsylvania Press.

Frey, Darcy. 1991. *The Last Shot: City Streets, Basketball Dreams.* Boston: Houghton Mifflin.

Gatz, Margaret, Michael A. Messner, and Sandra J. Ball-Rokeach, eds. 2002. *Paradoxes of Youth and Sport.* Albany: State University of New York Press.

Goldsmith, Pat Antonio. 2003. "Race Relations and Racial Patterns in School Sports Participation." *Sociology of Sport Journal* 20 (2): 147–171.

Hyman, Mark. 2001. "Reading, Writing—and Winning." *Business Week* (April 2): 58–60.

Jimerson, Jason B. 2001. "A Conversation (Re)Analysis of Fraternal Bonding in the Locker Room." *Sociology of Sport Journal* 18 (3): 317–338.

Latimer, Clay. 2003. "Pulling Strings: For Better or Worse, Parents' Role in Prep Sports Evolving into More Agent than Cheerleader." *Rocky Mountain News,* March 8, 1B, 11B-13B.

May, Reuben A. Buford. 2001. "The Sticky Situation of Sportsmanship: Contexts and Contradictions in Sportsmanship among High School Boys Basketball Players." *Journal of Sport and Social Issues* 25 (November): 372–389.

Nixon, Howard L. II. 2008. *Sport in a Changing World.* Boulder, CO: Paradigm.

Rees, C. Roger, and Andrew W. Miracle. 2001. "Education and Sport." Pp. 277–290 in Jay Coakley and Eric Dunning eds., *Handbook of Sports Studies.* London: Sage.

Ryan, Joan. 1995. *Little Girls in Pretty Boxes: The Making and Breaking of Elite Gymnasts and Figure Skaters.* New York: Warner.

Telander, Rick. 1976. *Heaven Is a Playground.* New York: Simon and Schuster.

Watts, Jay. 2002. "Perspectives on Sport Specialization." *JOPERD* 73 (October): 33–37, 50.

Wolff, Alexander. 2002. "The High School Athlete." *Sports Illustrated,* three-part series (November 18, 25, and December 2).

PART THREE

Sport and Socialization: The Mass Media

The mass media have a tremendous impact on sports. First, the popularity of sport is due in large measure to the enormous attention it receives from the mass media. Second, television has infused huge sums of money into sport, affecting franchise moves and salaries. Third, television (and the money it offers) has changed the way sports are played (for example, the scheduling of games, the interruption of the flow of games for commercial breaks, the shift from match play to medal play in tournament golf, and rule changes such as liberalizing offensive holding in football to increase scoring and, therefore, viewer interest). Fourth, television has affected college sports by making recruiting more national than regional and by focusing the nation's attention (and heaping television's money) on the games by a relatively few schools. Thus, television has exacerbated the gap between the "haves" and the "have nots." Moreover, since television money goes to the successful, it has heightened the pressure to win, and for some, the necessity to cheat in order to win.

Another consequence of the media—the effect on perceptions—is the focus of this section. The media direct attention toward certain acts and away from others. While the media appear to simply report what is happening, or what has just happened, during a sporting event, they actually provide a constructed view by what they choose to cover, their focus, and the narrative themes they pursue.[1] As Alan and John Clarke have said:

> It selects *between* sports for those which make "good television," and it selects *within* a particular event, it highlights particular aspects for the viewers. This selective highlighting is not "natural" or inevitable—it is based on certain criteria, certain media assumptions about what is "good television." But the media do not only select, they also provide us with definitions of what has been selected. They interpret events for us, provide us with frameworks of meaning in which to make sense of

69

the event. To put it simply, television does not merely consist of pictures, but also involves a commentary on the pictures—a commentary which explains to us what we are seeing. . . . These selections are socially constructed—they involve decisions about what to reveal to the viewers. The presentation of sport through the media involves an active process of re-presentation: what we see is not the event, but the event transformed into something else—a media event.[2]

The first chapter in this section, by Michael A. Messner, Michele Dunbar, and Darnell Hunt, explores themes in televised sports that combine to construct a masculinity formula consistent with the entrenched interests of the sports/media/commercial complex.

The second chapter, by sociologists Michael A. Messner and Jeffrey Montez de Oca, examines the gendered themes in advertising, focusing on beer and liquor advertising. They found "a pattern of men being depicted as 'losers,' as chumps, whose shortcomings and insecurities could be best overcome, the ads suggested, through nonemotional bonding with other guys, preferably over a few beers. Women are absent from many of these ads. But when they do appear, they are depicted either as wives or girlfriends who threaten men's freedom to have fun with the guys, or as fantasy sex objects.[3]

NOTES

1. D. Stanley Eitzen and George H. Sage, *Sociology of North American Sport,* 8th ed. (Boulder, CO: Paradigm Publishers, 2008), chap. 9.

2. Alan Clarke and John Clarke, "Highlights and Action Replays—Ideology, Sport, and the Media," in *Sport, Culture, and Ideology,* Jennifer Hargreaves, ed. (Boston: Routledge and Kegan Paul, 1982), pp. 69, 71.

3. Michael A. Messner, *Out of Play: Critical Essays on Gender and Sport* (Albany: State University of New York Press, 2007), pp. 167–168.

7

The Televised Sports Manhood Formula

Michael A. Messner, Michele Dunbar, and Darnell Hunt

A recent national survey found 8- to 17-year-old children to be avid consumers of sports media, with television most often named as the preferred medium (Amateur Athletic Foundation of Los Angeles, 1999). Although girls watch sports in great numbers, boys are markedly more likely to report that they are regular consumers of televised sports. The most popular televised sports with boys, in order, are pro football, men's pro basketball, pro baseball, pro wrestling, men's college basketball, college football, and Extreme sports.[1] Although counted separately in the Amateur Athletic Foundation (AAF) study, televised sports highlights shows also were revealed to be tremendously popular with boys.

What are boys seeing and hearing when they watch these programs? What kinds of values concerning gender, race, aggression, violence, and consumerism are boys exposed to when they watch their favorite televised sports programs, with their accompanying commercials? This chapter, based on a textual analysis, presents the argument that televised sports, and their accompanying commercials, consistently present boys with a narrow portrait of masculinity, which we call the Televised Sports Manhood Formula.

SAMPLE AND METHOD

We analyzed a range of televised sports that were identified by the AAF study as those programs most often watched by boys. Most of the programs in our sample aired

Source: Michael A. Messner, Michele Dunbar, and Darnell Hunt, "The Televised Sports Manhood Formula," *Journal of Sport and Social Issues* 24 (November 2000): 380–394.

during a single week, May 23–29, 1999, with one exception. Because pro football is not in season in May, we acquired tapes of two randomly chosen National Football League (NFL) *Monday Night Football* games from the previous season to include in our sample. We analyzed televised coverage, including commercials and pregame, halftime, and postgame shows (when appropriate), for the following programs:

1. two broadcasts of *SportsCenter* on ESPN (2 hours of programming);
2. two broadcasts of Extreme sports, one on ESPN and one on Fox Sports West (approximately 90 minutes of programming);
3. two broadcasts of professional wrestling, including *Monday Night Nitro* on TNT and *WWF Superstars* on USA (approximately 2 hours of programming);
4. two broadcasts of National Basketball Association (NBA) play-off games, one on TNT and the other on NBC (approximately 7 hours of programming);
5. two broadcasts of NFL *Monday Night Football* on ABC (approximately 7 hours of programming); and
6. one broadcast of Major League Baseball (MLB) on TBS (approximately 3 hours of programming).

We conducted a textual analysis of the sports programming and the commercials. In all, we examined about 23 hours of sports programming, nearly one quarter of which was time taken up by commercials. We examined a total of 722 commercials, which spanned a large range of products and services. We collected both quantitative and qualitative data. Although we began with some sensitizing concepts that we knew we wanted to explore (e.g., themes of violence, images of gender and race, etc.), rather than starting with preset categories we used an inductive method that allowed the dominant themes to emerge from our reading of the tapes.

Each taped show was given a first reading by one of the investigators, who then constructed a preliminary analysis of the data. The tape was then given a second reading by another of the investigators. This second independent reading was then used to modify and sharpen the first reading. Data analysis proceeded along the lines of the categories that emerged in the data collection. The analyses of each separate sport were then put into play with each other and common themes and patterns were identified. In one case, the dramatic pseudosport of professional wrestling, we determined that much of the programming was different enough that it made little sense to directly compare it with the other sports shows; therefore, we only included data on wrestling in our comparisons when it seemed to make sense to do so.

DOMINANT THEMES IN TELEVISED SPORTS

Our analysis revealed that sports programming presents boys with narrow and stereotypical messages about race, gender, and violence. We identified 10 distinct themes that, together, make up the Televised Sports Manhood Formula.

Table 7-1 **Race and Sex of Announcers**

White Men	White Women	Black Men	Black Women
24	3	3	1

White Males Are the Voices of Authority

Although one of the two *SportsCenter* segments in the sample did feature a White woman coanchor, the play-by-play and ongoing color commentary in NFL, wrestling, NBA, Extreme sports, and MLB broadcasts were conducted exclusively by White, male play-by play commentators (see Table 7-1).

With the exception of *SportsCenter,* women and Blacks never appeared as the main voices of authority in the booth conducting play-by-play or ongoing color commentary. The NFL broadcasts occasionally cut to field-level color commentary by a White woman, but her commentary was very brief (about 3½ minutes of the nearly 3 hours of actual game and pregame commentary). Similarly, one of the NBA broadcasts used a Black man for occasional on-court analysis and a Black man for pregame and halftime analysis, whereas the other NBA game used a White woman as host in the pregame show and a Black woman for occasional on-court analysis. Although viewers commonly see Black male athletes—especially on televised NBA games—they rarely hear or see Black men or women as voices of authority in the broadcast booth (Sabo and Jansen, 1994). In fact, the only Black commentators that appeared on the NBA shows that we examined were former star basketball players (Cheryl Miller, Doc Rivers, and Isaiah Thomas). A Black male briefly appeared to welcome the audience to open one of the Extreme sports shows but he did not do any play-by-play; in fact, he was used only to open the show with a stylish, street, hip-hop style for what turned out to be an almost totally White show.

Sports Is a Man's World

Images or discussion of women athletes is almost entirely absent in the sports programs that boys watch most. *SportsCenter's* mere 2.9 percent of news time devoted to women's sports is slightly lower than the 5 percent to 6 percent of women's sports coverage commonly found in other sports news studies (Duncan and Messner, 1998). In addition, *SportsCenter's* rare discussion of a women's sport seemed to follow men's in newsworthiness (e.g., a report on a Professional Golfers' Association [PGA] tournament was followed by a more brief report on a Ladies Professional Golf Association [LPGA] tournament). The baseball, basketball, wrestling, and football programs we watched were men's contests so they could not perhaps have been expected to cover or mention women athletes. However, Extreme sports are commonly viewed as "alternative" or "emerging" sports in which women are challenging masculine hegemony (Wheaton and Tomlinson, 1998). Despite this, the Extreme sports shows we watched devoted only a single 50-second interview segment to a woman athlete.

Table 7-2 Sex Composition of 722 Commercials

Men Only	Women Only	Women and Men	No People
279 (38.6%)	28 (3.9%)	324 (44.9%)	91 (12.6%)

This segment constituted about 1 percent of the total Extreme sports programming and, significantly, did not show this woman athlete in action. Perhaps this limited coverage of women athletes on the Extreme sports shows we examined is evidence of what Rinehart (1998) calls a "pecking order" in alternative sports, which develops when new sports are appropriated and commodified by the media.

Men Are Foregrounded in Commercials

The idea that sports is a man's world is reinforced by the gender composition and imagery in commercials. Women almost never appear in commercials unless they are in the company of men, as Table 7-2 shows.

That 38.6 percent of all commercials portray only men actually understates the extent to which men dominate these commercials for two reasons. First, nearly every one of the 91 commercials that portrayed no visual portrayals of people included a male voice-over. When we include this number, we see that more than 50 percent of commercials provide men-only images and/or voiceovers, whereas only 3.9 percent portray only women. Moreover, when we combine men-only and women and men categories, we see that men are visible in 83.5 percent of all commercials and men are present (when we add in the commercials with male voice-overs) in 96.1 percent of all commercials. Second, in the commercials that portray both women and men, women are often (although not exclusively) portrayed in stereotypical, and often very minor, background roles.

Women Are Sexy Props or Prizes for Men's Successful Sport Performances or Consumption Choices

Although women were mostly absent from sports commentary, when they did appear it was most often in stereotypical roles as sexy, masculinity-validating props, often cheering the men on. For instance, "X-sports" on Fox Sports West used a bikini-clad blonde woman as a hostess to welcome viewers back after each commercial break as the camera moved provocatively over her body Although she mentioned the show's sponsors, she did not narrate the actual sporting event. The wrestling shows generously used scantily clad women (e.g., in pink miniskirts or tight Spandex and high heels) who overtly displayed the dominant cultural signs of heterosexy attractiveness[2] to escort the male wrestlers to the ring, often with announcers discussing the women's provocative physical appearance. Women also appeared in the wrestling shows as sexually provocative dancers (e.g., the "Gorgeous Nitro Girls" on TNT).

In commercials, women are numerically more evident, and generally depicted in more varied roles, than in the sports programming. Still, women are underrepresented

Table 7-3 Instances of Women Being Depicted as Sexy Props or Prizes for Men

	SportsCenter	Extreme	Wrestling	NBA	MLB	NFL
Commercials	5	5	3	10	4	6
Sport programs	0	5	13	3	0	4
Total	5	10	16	13	4	10

Note: NBA = National Basketball Association, MLB = Major League Baseball, and NFL = National Football League.

and rarely appear in commercials unless they are in the company of men. Moreover, as Table 7-3 illustrates, the commercials' common depiction of women as sexual objects and as "prizes" for men's successful consumption choices articulates with the sports programs' presentation of women primarily as sexualized, supportive props for men's athletic performances. For instance, a commercial for Keystone Light Beer that ran on *SportsCenter* depicted two White men at a baseball game. When one of the men appeared on the stadium big screen and made an ugly face after drinking an apparently bitter beer, women appeared to be grossed out by him. But then he drank a Keystone Light and reappeared on the big screen looking good with two young, conventionally beautiful (fashion-model-like) women adoring him. He says, "I hope my wife's not watching!" as the two women flirt with the camera.

As Table 7-3 shows, in 23 hours of sports programming, viewers were exposed to 58 incidents of women being portrayed as sexy props and/or sexual prizes for men's successful athletic performances or correct consumption choices. Put another way, a televised sports viewer is exposed to this message, either in commercials or in the sports program itself, on an average of twice an hour. The significance of this narrow image of women as heterosexualized commodities should be considered especially in light of the overall absence of a wider range of images of women, especially as athletes (Duncan and Messner, 1998; Kane and Lenskyj, 1998).

Whites Are Foregounded in Commercials

The racial composition of the commercials is, if anything, more narrow and limited than the gender composition. As Table 7-4 shows, Black, Latino, or Asian American people almost never appear in commercials unless the commercial also has White people in it (the multiracial category in the table).

To say that 52.2 percent of the commercials portrayed only Whites actually understates the extent to which images of White people dominated the commercials for two reasons. First, if we subtract the 91 commercials that showed no actual people, then we see that the proportion of commercials that actually showed people was 59.7 percent White only. Second, when we examine the quality of the portrayals of Blacks, Latinos, and Asian Americans in the multiracial commercials, we see that people of color are far more often than not relegated to minor roles, literally in the background of scenes that feature Whites, and/or they are relegated to stereotypical or negative roles.

Table 7-4 Racial Composition of 722 Commercials

White Only	Black Only	Latino/a Only	Asian Only	Multiracial	Undeter-mined	No People
377 (52.2%)	28 (3.9%)	3 (0.4%)	2 (0.3%)	203 (28.1%)	18 (2.5%)	91 (12.6%)

For instance, a Wendy's commercial that appeared on several of the sports programs in our sample showed White customers enjoying a sandwich with the White owner while a barely perceptible Black male walked by in the background.

Aggressive Players Get the Prize; Nice Guys Finish Last

As Table 7-5 illustrates, viewers are continually immersed in images and commentary about the positive rewards that come to the most aggressive competitors and of the negative consequences of playing "soft" and lacking aggression.

Commentators consistently lauded athletes who most successfully employed physical and aggressive play and toughness. For instance, after having his toughness called into question, NBA player Brian Grant was awarded redemption by *SportsCenter* because he showed that he is "not afraid to take it to Karl Malone." *SportsCenter* also informed viewers that "the aggressor usually gets the calls [from the officials] and the Spurs were the ones getting them." In pro wrestling commentary, this is a constant theme (and was therefore not included in our tallies for Table 7-5 because the theme permeated the commentary, overtly and covertly). The World Wrestling Federation (WWF) announcers praised the "raw power" of wrestler "Shamrock" and approvingly dubbed "Hardcore Holly" as "the world's most dangerous man." NBA commentators suggested that it is okay to be a good guy off the court but one must be tough and aggressive on the court: Brian Grant and Jeff Hornacek are "true gentlemen of the NBA ... as long as you don't have to play against them. You know they're great off the court; on the court, every single guy out there *should* be a killer."

When players were not doing well, they were often described as "hesitant" and lacking aggression, emotion, and desire (e.g., for a loose ball or rebound). For instance, commentators lamented that "the Jazz aren't going to the hoop, they're being pushed and shoved around," that Utah was responding to the Blazers' aggression "passively, in a reactive mode," and that "Utah's got to get Karl Malone toughened up." *SportsCenter* echoed this theme, opening one show with a depiction of Horace

Table 7-5 Statements Lauding Aggression or Criticizing Lack of Aggression

SportsCenter	Extreme	NBA	MLB	NFL
3	4	40	4	15

Note: NBA = National Basketball Association, MLB = Major League Baseball, and NFL = National Football League.

Grant elbowing Karl Malone and asking of Malone, "Is he feeble?" Similarly, NFL broadcasters waxed on about the virtues of aggression and domination. Big "hits"; ball carriers who got "buried," "stuffed," or "walloped" by the defense; and players who get "cleaned out" or "wiped out" by a blocker were often shown on replays, with announcers enthusiastically describing the plays. By contrast, they clearly declared that it is a very bad thing to be passive and to let yourself get pushed around and dominated at the line of scrimmage. Announcers also approvingly noted that going after an opposing player's injured body part is just smart strategy: In one NFL game, the Miami strategy to blitz the opposing quarterback was lauded as "brilliant"— "When you know your opposing quarterback is a bit nicked and something is wrong, Boomer, you got to come after him."

Previous research has pointed to this heroic framing of the male body-as-weapon as a key element in sports' role in the social construction of narrow conceptions of masculinity (Messner, 1992; Trujillo, 1995).

This injunction for boys and men to be aggressive, not passive, is reinforced in commercials, where a common formula is to play on the insecurities of young males (e.g., that they are not strong enough, tough enough, smart enough, rich enough, attractive enough, decisive enough, etc.) and then attempt to convince them to avoid, overcome, or mask their fears, embarrassments, and apparent shortcomings by buying a particular product. These commercials often portray men as potential or actual geeks, nerds, or passive schmucks who can overcome their geekiness (or avoid being a geek like the guy in the commercial) by becoming decisive and purchasing a particular product.

Boys Will Be (Violent) Boys

Announcers often took a humorous "boys will be boys" attitude in discussing fights or near-fights during contests, and they also commonly used a recent fight, altercation, or disagreement between two players as a "teaser" to build audience excitement (see Table 7-6).

Fights, near-fights, threats of fights, or other violent actions were overemphasized in sports coverage and often verbally framed in sarcastic language that suggested that this kind of action, although reprehensible, is to be expected. For instance, as *Sports-Center* showed NBA centers Robinson and O'Neill exchanging forearm shoves, the commentators said, simply, "much love." Similarly, in an NFL game, a brief scuffle between players is met with a sarcastic comment by the broadcaster that the players

Table 7-6 **Humorous or Sarcastic Discussion of Fights or Near-Fights**

SportsCenter	Extreme	NBA	MLB	NFL
10	1	2	2	7

Note: NBA = National Basketball Association, MLB = Major League Baseball, and NFL = National Football League.

are simply "making their acquaintance." This is, of course, a constant theme in pro wrestling (which, again, we found impossible and less than meaningful to count because this theme permeates the show). We found it noteworthy that the supposedly spontaneous fights outside the wrestling ring (what we call unofficial fights) were given more coverage time and focus than the supposedly official fights inside the ring. We speculate that wrestling producers know that viewers already watch fights inside the ring with some skepticism as to their authenticity so they stage the unofficial fights outside the ring to bring a feeling of spontaneity and authenticity to the show and to build excitement and a sense of anticipation for the fight that will later occur inside the ring.

Give Up Your Body for the Team

Athletes who are "playing with pain," "giving up their body for the team," or engaging in obviously highly dangerous plays or maneuvers were consistently framed as heroes; conversely, those who removed themselves from games due to injuries had questions raised about their character, their manhood (see Table 7-7).

This theme cut across all sports programming. For instance, *SportsCenter* asked, "Could the dominator be soft?" when a National Hockey League (NHL) star goalie decided to sit out a game due to a groin injury. Heroically taking risks while already hurt was a constant theme in Extreme sports commentary. For instance, one bike competitor was lauded for "overcoming his fear" and competing "with a busted up ankle" and another was applauded when he "popped his collarbone out in the street finals in Louisville but he's back on his bike here in Richmond, just 2 weeks later!" Athletes appear especially heroic when they go against doctors' wishes not to compete. For instance, an X Games interviewer adoringly told a competitor, "Doctors said don't ride but you went ahead and did it anyway and escaped serious injury." Similarly, NBA player Isaiah Rider was lauded for having "heart" for "playing with that knee injury." Injury discussions in NFL games often include speculation about whether the player will be able to return to this or future games. A focus on a star player in a pregame or halftime show, such as the feature on 49ers' Garrison Hearst, often contain commentary about heroic overcoming of serious injuries (in this case, a knee blowout, reconstructive surgery, and rehabilitation). As one game began, commentators noted that 37-year-old "Steve Young has remained a rock ... not bad for a guy who a lotta people figured was, what, one big hit from ending his career." It's especially impressive when an injured player is able and willing to continue to play with aggressiveness and reckless abandon: "Kurt Scrafford at right guard-bad neck

Table 7-7 Comments on the Heroic Nature of Playing Hurt

SportsCenter	Extreme	NBA	MLB	NFL
9	12	6	4	15

Note: NBA = National Basketball Association, MLB = Major League Baseball, and NFL = National Football League.

and all—is just out there wiping out guys." And announcers love the team leader who plays hurt:

> Drew Bledsoe gamely tried to play in loss to Rams yesterday; really admirable to try to play with that pin that was surgically implanted in his finger during the week; I don't know how a Q.B. could do that. You know, he broke his finger the time we had him on Monday night and he led his team to two come-from-behind victories, really gutted it out and I think he took that team on his shoulders and showed he could play and really elevated himself in my eyes, he really did.

Sports Is War

Commentators consistently (an average of nearly five times during each hour of sports commentary) used martial metaphors and language Of war and weaponry to describe sports action (e.g., battle, kill, ammunition, weapons, professional sniper, depth charges, taking aim, fighting, shot in his arsenal, reloading, detonate, squeezes the trigger, attack mode, firing blanks, blast, explosion, blitz, point of attack, a lance through the heart, etc.) (see Table 7-8).

Some shows went beyond commentators' use of war terminology and actually framed the contests as wars. For instance, one of the wrestling shows offered a continual flow of images and commentary that reminded the viewers that "RAW is WAR!" Similarly, both NFL *Monday Night Football* broadcasts were introduced with explosive graphics and an opening song that included lyrics "Like a rocket burning through time and space, the NFL's best will rock this place . . . the battle lines are drawn." This sort of use of sport/war metaphors has been a common practice in televised sports commentary for many years, serving to fuse (and confuse) the distinctions between values of nationalism with team identity and athletic aggression with military destruction (Jansen and Sabo, 1994). In the shows examined for this study, war themes also were reinforced in many commercials, including commercials for movies, other sports programs, and in the occasional commercial for the U.S. military.

Show Some Guts!

Commentators continually depicted and replayed exciting incidents of athletes engaging in reckless acts of speed, showing guts in the face of danger, big hits, and violent crashes (see Table 7-9).

Table 7-8 Martial Metaphors and Language of War and Weaponry

SportsCenter	Extreme	Wrestling	NBA	MLB	NFL
9	3	15	27	6	23

Note: NBA = National Basketball Association, MLB = Major League Baseball, and NFL = National Football League.

Table 7-9 Depictions of Guts in Face of Danger, Speed, Hits, Crashes

SportsCenter	Extreme	NBA	MLB	NFL
4	21	5	2	8

Note: NBA = National Basketball Association, MLB = Major League Baseball, and NFL = National Football League.

This theme was evident across all of the sports programs but was especially predominant in Extreme sports that continually depicted crashing vehicles or bikers in an exciting manner. For instance, when one race ended with a crash, it was showed again in slow-motion replay, with commentators approvingly dubbing it "unbelievable" and "original." Extreme sports commentators; commonly raised excitement levels by saying "he's on fire" or "he's going huge!" when a competitor was obviously taking greater risks. An athlete's ability to deal with the fear of a possible crash, in fact, is the mark of an "outstanding run": "Watch out, Richmond," an X-games announcer shouted to the crowd, "He's gonna wreck this place!" A winning competitor laughingly said, "I do what I can to smash into [my opponents] as much as I can." Another competitor said, "If I crash, no big deal; I'm just gonna go for it." NFL commentators introduced the games with images of reckless collisions and during the game a "fearless" player was likely to be applauded: "There's no chance that Barry Sanders won't take when he's running the football." In another game, the announcer noted that receiver "Tony Simmons plays big. And for those of you not in the NFL, playing big means you're not afraid to go across the middle and catch the ball and make a play out of it after you catch the ball." Men showing guts in the face of speed and danger was also a major theme in 40 of the commercials that we analyzed.

THE TELEVISED SPORTS MANHOOD FORMULA

Tens of millions of U.S. boys watch televised sports programs with their accompanying commercial advertisements. This study sheds light on what these boys are seeing when they watch their favorite sports programs. What values and ideas about gender, race, aggression, and violence are being promoted? Although there are certainly differences across different kinds of sports, as well as across different commercials, when we looked at all of the programming together, we identified 10 recurrent themes, which we have outlined above. Taken together, these themes codify a consistent and (mostly) coherent message about what it means to be a man. We call this message the Televised Sports Manhood Formula:

> What is a Real Man? A Real Man is strong, tough, aggressive, and above all, a winner in what is still a Man's World. To be a winner he has to do what needs to be done. He must be willing to compromise his own long-term health by showing guts in the face of danger, by fighting other men when necessary, and by "play-

ing hurt" when he's injured. He must avoid being soft; he must be the aggressor, both on the "battle fields" of sports and in his consumption choices. Whether he is playing sports or making choices about which snack food or auto products to purchase, his aggressiveness will net him the ultimate prize: the adoring attention of conventionally beautiful women. He will know if and when he has arrived as a Real Man when the Voices of Authority—White Males—*say* he is a Real Man. But even when he has finally managed to win the big one, has the good car and the right beer, and is surrounded by beautiful women, he will be reminded by these very same Voices of Authority just how fragile this Real Manhood really is: After all, he has to come out and prove himself all over again tomorrow. You're only as good as your last game (or your last purchase).

The major elements of the Televised Sports Manhood Formula are evident, in varying degrees, in the football, basketball, baseball, Extreme sports, and *SportsCenter* programs and in their accompanying commercials. But it is in the dramatic spectacle of professional wrestling that the Televised Sports Manhood Formula is most clearly codified and presented to audiences as an almost seamless package. Boys and young men are drawn to televised professional wrestling in great numbers. Consistently each week, from four to six pro wrestling shows rank among the top 10 rated shows on cable television. Professional wrestling is not a real sport in the way that baseball, basketball, football, or even Extreme sports are. In fact, it is a highly stylized and choreographed "sport as theatre" form of entertainment. Its producers have condensed—and then amplified—all of the themes that make up the Televised Sports Manhood Formula. For instance, where violence represents a thread in the football or basketball commentary, violence makes up the entire fabric of the theatrical narrative of televised pro wrestling. In short, professional wrestling presents viewers with a steady stream of images and commentary that represents a constant fusion of all of the themes that make up the Televised Sports Manhood Formula: This is a choreographed sport where all men (except losers) are Real Men, where women are present as sexy support objects for the men's violent, monumental "wars" against each other. Winners bravely display muscular strength, speed, power, and guts. Bodily harm is (supposedly) intentionally inflicted on opponents. The most ruthlessly aggressive men win, whereas the passive or weaker men lose, often shamefully. Heroically wrestling while injured, rehabilitating oneself from former injuries, and inflicting pain and injury on one's opponent are constant and central themes in the narrative.

GENDER AND THE SPORTS/MEDIA/ COMMERCIAL COMPLEX

In 1984, media scholar Sut Jhally pointed to the commercial and ideological symbiosis between the institutions of sport and the mass media and called it the sports/media complex. Our examination of the ways that the Televised Sports Manhood Formula reflects and promotes hegemonic ideologies concerning race, gender, sexuality, aggression, violence, and consumerism suggests adding a third dimension to Jhally's analysis: the huge network of multi-billion-dollar automobile, snack food, alcohol, entertainment, and other corporate entities that sponsor sports events and broadcasts. In fact, examining the ways that the Televised Sports Manhood Formula cuts across sports programming and its accompanying commercials may provide important clues as to the ways that ideologies of hegemonic masculinity are both promoted by—and in turn serve to support and stabilize—this collection of interrelated institutions that make up the sports/media/commercial complex. The Televised Sports Manhood Formula is a master discourse that is produced at the nexus of the institutions of sport, mass media, and corporations who produce and hope to sell products and services to boys and men. As such, the Televised Sports Manhood Formula appears well suited to discipline boys' bodies, minds, and consumption choices within an ideological field that is conducive to the reproduction of the entrenched interests that profit from the sports/media/commercial complex. The perpetuation of the entrenched commercial interests of the sports/media/commercial complex appears to be predicated on boys accepting—indeed glorifying and celebrating—a set of bodily and relational practices that resist and oppose a view of women as fully human and place boys' and men's long-term health prospects in jeopardy.

At a historical moment when hegemonic masculinity has been destabilized by socioeconomic change, and by women's and gay liberation movements, the Televised Sports Manhood Formula provides a remarkably stable and concrete view of masculinity as grounded in bravery, risk taking, violence, bodily strength, and heterosexuality. And this view of masculinity is given coherence against views of women as sexual support objects or as invisible and thus irrelevant to men's public struggles for glory. Yet, perhaps to be successful in selling products, the commercials sometimes provide a less than seamless view of masculinity. The insecurities of masculinity in crisis are often tweaked in the commercials, as we see weak men, dumb men, and indecisive men being eclipsed by strong, smart, and decisive men and sometimes being humiliated by smarter and more decisive women. In short, this commercialized version of hegemonic masculinity is constructed partly in relation to images of men who don't measure up.

This analysis gives us hints at an answer to the commonly asked question of why so many boys and men continue to take seemingly irrational risks, submit to pain and injury, and risk long-term debility or even death by playing hurt. A critical examination of the Televised Sports Manhood Formula tells us why: The costs of masculinity (especially pain and injury), according to this formula, appear to be well worth the price; the boys and men who are willing to pay the price always seem to get the glory, the championships, the best consumer products, and the beautiful women. Those who don't—or can't—pay the price are humiliated or ignored by women and left in the dust by other men. In short, the Televised Sports Manhood Formula is a pedagogy through which boys are taught that paying the price, be it one's bodily health or one's money, gives one access to the privileges that have been historically linked to hegemonic masculinity—money, power, glory, and women. And the barrage of images of femininity as model-like beauty displayed for and in the service of successful men suggests that heterosexuality is a major lynchpin of the Televised Sports

Manhood Formula, and on a larger scale serves as one of the major linking factors in the conservative gender regime of the sports/media/commercial complex.

On the other hand, we must be cautious in coming to definitive conclusions as to how the promotion of the values embedded in the Televised Sports Manhood Formula might fit into the worlds of young men. It is not possible, based merely on our textual analysis of sports programs, to explicate precisely what kind of impact these shows, and the Televised Sports Manhood Formula, have on their young male audiences. That sort of question is best approached through direct research with audiences. Most such research finds that audiences interpret, use, and draw meanings from media variously, based on factors such as social class, race/ethnicity, and gender (Hunt, 1999; Whannel, 1998). Research with various subgroups of boys that explores their interpretations of the sports programs that they watch would enhance and broaden this study.

Moreover, it is important to go beyond the preferred reading presented here that emphasizes the persistent themes in televised sports that appear to reinforce the hegemony of current race, gender, and commercial relations (Sabo and Jansen, 1992). In addition to these continuities, there are some identifiable discontinuities within and between the various sports programs and within and among the accompanying commercials. For instance, commercials are far more varied in the ways they present gender imagery than are sports programs themselves. Although the dominant tendency in commercials is either to erase women or to present them as stereotypical support or sex objects, a significant minority of commercials present themes that set up boys and men as insecure and/or obnoxious schmucks and women as secure, knowledgeable, and authoritative. Audience research with boys who watch sports would shed fascinating light on how they decode and interpret these more complex, mixed, and paradoxical gender images against the dominant, hegemonic image of the Televised Sports Manhood Formula.

NOTES

1. There are some differences, and some similarities, in what boys and girls prefer to watch. The top seven televised sports reported by girls are, in order, gymnastics, men's pro basketball, pro football, pro baseball, swimming/diving, men's college basketball, and women's pro or college basketball.

2. Although images of feminine beauty shift, change, and are contested throughout history, female beauty is presented in sports programming and commercials in narrow ways. Attractive women look like fashion models (Banet-Weiser, 1999): They are tall, thin, young, usually (although not always) White, with signs of heterosexual femininity encoded and overtly displayed through hair, makeup, sexually provocative facial and bodily gestures, large (often partially exposed) breasts, long (often exposed) legs, and so forth.

REFERENCES

Amateur Athletic Foundation of Los Angeles. 1999. *Children and Sports Media.* Los Angeles: Author.

Banet-Weiser, S. 1999. *The Most Beautiful Girl in the World: Beauty Pageants and National Identity.* Berkeley: University of California Press.

Duncan, M. C., and Messner, M. A. 1998. "The Media Image of Sport and Gender." Pp. 170–195 in L. A. Wenner, ed., *MediaSport.* New York: Routledge.

Hunt, D. 1999. *O.J. Simpson: Facts and Fictions,* New York: Cambridge University Press.

Jansen, S. C., and Sabo, D. 1994. The "Sport/War Metaphor: Hegemonic Masculinity, the Persian Gulf War, and the New World Order." *Sociology of Sport Journal* 11: 1–17.

Jhally, S. 1984. "The Spectacle of Accumulation: Material and Cultural Factors in the Evolution of the Sports/Media Complex." *Insurgent Sociologist* 12, no. 3: 41–52.

Kane, M. J., and Lenskyj, H. J. 1998. "Media Treatment of Female Athletes: Issues of Gender and Sexualities." Pp. 186–201 in L. A. Wenner, ed., *MediaSport.* New York: Routledge.

Messner, M. A. 1992. *Power at Play: Sports and the Problem of Masculinity.* Boston: Beacon.

Rinehart, R. 1998. "Inside of the Outside: Pecking Orders within Alternative Sport at ESPN's 1995 'The eXtreme Games.'" *Journal of Sport and Social Issues* 22: 398–415.

Sabo, D., and Jansen, S. C. 1992. "Images of Men in Sport Media: The Social Reproduction of Masculinity." Pp. 169–184 in S. Craig, ed., *Men, Masculinity, and the Media.* Newbury Park, CA: Sage.

———. 1994. "Seen but Not Heard: Images of Black Men in Sports Media." Pp. 150–160 in M. A. Messner and D. F. Sabo, eds., *Sex, Violence, and Power in Sports: Rethinking Masculinity.* Freedom, CA: Crossing Press.

Trujillo, N. 1995. "Machines, Missiles, and Men: Images of the Male Body on ABC's *Monday Night Football.*" *Sociology of Sport Journal* 12: 403–423.

Whannel, G. 1998. "Reading the Sports Media Audience." Pp. 221–232 in L. A. Wenner, ed., *MediaSport.* New York: Routledge.

Wheaton, B., and Tomlinson, A. 1998. "The Changing Gender Order in Sport? The Case of Windsurfing Subcultures." *Journal of Sport and Social Issues* 22: 252–274.

8

The Male Consumer as Loser: Beer and Liquor Ads in Mega Sports Media Events

Michael A. Messner and Jeffrey Montez de Oca

The historical development of modern men's sport has been closely intertwined with the consumption of alcohol and with the financial promotion and sponsorship provided by beer and liquor producers and distributors, as well as pubs and bars (Collins and Vamplew 2002). The beer and liquor industry plays a key economic role in commercialized college and professional sports (Zimbalist 1999; Sperber 2000). Liquor industry advertisements heavily influence the images of masculinity promoted in sports broadcasts and magazines (Wenner 1991). Alcohol consumption is also often a key aspect of the more dangerous and violent dynamics at the heart of male sport cultures (Curry 2000; Sabo, Gray, and Moore 2000). By itself, alcohol does not "cause" men's violence against women or against other men; however, it is commonly one of a cluster of factors that facilitate violence (Koss and Gaines 1993; Leichliter et al. 1998). In short, beer and liquor are central players in "a high holy trinity of alcohol, sports, and hegemonic masculinity" (Wenner 1998).

This article examines beer and liquor advertisements in two "mega sports media events" consumed by large numbers of boys and men—the 2002 and 2003 Super Bowls and the 2002 and 2003 *Sports Illustrated* swimsuit issues. Our goal is to illuminate tropes of masculinity that prevail in those ads. We see these ads as establishing a pedagogy of youthful masculinity that does not passively teach male consumers about the qualities of their products so much as it encourages consumers to think of their products as essential to creating a stylish and desirable lifestyle. These ads do more than just dupe consumers into product loyalty; they also work with consumers to construct a consumption-based masculine identity relevant to contemporary social conditions. Drawing on insights from feminist cultural studies (Walters 1999), we argue that these gendered tropes watched by tens of millions of boys and men offer a window through which we can broaden our understanding of contemporary continuities, shifts, and strains in the social construction of masculinities.

GENDER, MEN'S SPORTS, AND ALCOHOL ADS

Although marketing beer and liquor to men is not new, the imagery that advertisers employ to pitch their product is not static either. Our analysis of past Super Bowls and *Sports Illustrated* beer and liquor ads suggests shifting patterns in the gender themes encoded in the ads. Consistently, over time, the ads attempt not to simply "plug" a particular product but to situate products within a larger historically specific way of life. Beer and liquor advertisers normally do not create product differentiation through typical narratives of crisis and resolution in which the product is the rescuing hero. Instead, they paint a series of images that evoke feelings, moods, and ways of being. In short, beer and liquor advertising engages in "lifestyle branding." Rather than simply attaching a name to a product, the brand emanates from a series of images that construct a plausible and desirable world to consumers. Lifestyle branding—more literary and evocative than simple crisis/resolution narratives—theorizes the social location of target populations and constructs a desiring subject whose consumption patterns can be massaged in specific directions. As we shall see, the subject constructed by the beer and liquor ads that we examined is an overtly gendered subject.

Beer and alcohol advertising construct a "desirable lifestyle" in relation to contemporary social conditions, including shifts and tensions in the broader gender order. Ads from the late 1950s through the late 1960s commonly depicted young or middle-aged white heterosexual couples happily sharing a cold beer in their suburban backyards, in their homes, or in an outdoor space like a park.

In these ads, the beer is commonly displayed in a clear glass, its clean, fresh appearance perhaps intended to counter the reputation of beer as a working-class male drink. Beer in these ads symbolically unites the prosperous and happy postwar middle-class couple. By the mid-1970s, women as wives and partners largely disappeared from beer ads. Instead of showing heterosexual couples drinking in their homes or backyards, these ads began primarily to depict images of men drinking with other men in public spaces. Three studies of beer commercials of the 1970s and 1980s found that most ads pitched beer to men as a pleasurable reward for a hard day's work. These ads told men that "For all you do, this Bud's for you." Women were rarely depicted in these ads, except as occasional background props in male-dominated bars (Postman et al. 1987; Wenner 1991; Strate 1992).

The 1950s and 1960s beer ads that depicted happy married suburban couples were part of a moment in gender relations tied to postwar culture and Fordist relations of production. White, middle-class, heterosexual masculinity was defined as synonymous with the male breadwinner, in symmetrical relation to a conception of femininity grounded in the image of the suburban housewife. In the 1970s and early 1980s, the focus on men's laboring bodies, tethered to their public leisure with other men, expressed an almost atavistic view of hegemonic masculinity at a time when women were moving into public life in huge numbers and blue-collar men's jobs were being eliminated by the tens of thousands.

Both the postwar and the postindustrial ads provide a gendered pedagogy for living a masculine lifestyle in a shifting context characterized by uncertainty. In contrast to the depiction of happy white families comfortably living lives of suburban bliss, the postwar era was characterized by anxieties over the possibility of a postwar depression, nuclear annihilation, suburban social dislocation, and disorder from racial and class movements for social justice (Lipsitz 1981; May 1988; Spigel 1992). Similarly, the 1970s and 1980s beer ads came in the wake of the defeat of the United States in the Vietnam War, the 1972 gas crisis, the collapse of Fordism, and the turbulence in gender relations brought on by the women's and gay/lesbian liberation movements. All of these social ruptures contributed to produce an anxious white male subject (Connell 1995; Lipsitz 1998). Therefore, there is a sort of crisis/resolution narrative in these beer ads: the "crisis" lies broadly in the construction of white masculinities in the latter half of the twentieth century (Kimmel 1987), and the resolution lies in the construction of a lifestyle outside of immediate anxieties. The advertisements do not straightforwardly tell consumers to buy; rather, they teach consumers how to live a happy, stress-free life that includes regular (if not heavy) consumption of alcoholic beverages.

The 2002 and 2003 ads that we examine here primarily construct a white male "loser" whose life is apparently separate from paid labor. He hangs out with his male buddies, is self-mocking and ironic about his loser status, and is always at the ready to engage in voyeurism with sexy fantasy women but holds committed relationships and emotional honesty with real women in disdain. To the extent that these themes find resonance with young men of today, it is likely because they speak to basic insecurities that are grounded in a combination of historic shifts: deindustrialization, the declining real value of wages and the male breadwinner role, significant cultural shifts brought about by more than three decades of struggle by feminists and sexual minorities, and challenges to white male supremacy by people of color and by immigrants. This cluster of social changes has destabilized hegemonic masculinity and defines the context of gender relations in which today's young men have grown toward adulthood.

In theorizing how the loser motif in beer and liquor ads constructs a version of young white masculinity, we draw on Mikhail Bakhtin's (1981) concept of the chronotope. This is especially relevant in analyzing how lifestyle branding goes beyond the reiteration of a name to actually creating desirable and believable worlds in which consumers are beckoned to place themselves. The term *chronotope*—literally meaning "time-space"—describes how time and space fuse in literature to create meaningful structures separate from the text and its representations (Bakhtin 1981). The ads that we looked at consistently construct a leisure-time lifestyle of young men meeting in specific sites of sports and alcohol consumption: bars, television rooms, and stadiums. This meeting motif gives a temporal and spatial plane to male fantasy where desire can be explored and symbolic boundaries can simultaneously be transgressed and reinscribed into the social world.

TWO MEGA SPORTS MEDIA EVENTS

This article brings focus to the commercial center of sports media by examining the gender and sexual imagery encoded in two mega sports media events: the 2002 and 2003 Super Bowls and the 2002 and 2003 *Sports Illustrated* swimsuit issues. (See the appendix for a complete list of the ads and commercials.)[1]

Mega sports media events are mediated cultural rituals (Dayan and Katz 1988) that differ from everyday sports media events in several key ways: sports media actively build audience anticipation and excitement throughout the year for these single events; the Super Bowl and the swimsuit issue are each preceded by major pre-event promotion and hype—from the television network that will broadcast the Super Bowl to *Sports Illustrated* and myriad other print and electronic media; the Super Bowl and the swimsuit issue are used as marketing tools for selling the more general products of National Football League (NFL) games and *Sports Illustrated* magazine subscriptions; the Super Bowl and the swimsuit issue each generate significant spin-off products (e.g., videos, books, "making of" TV shows, calendars, frequently visited Web pages); the Super Bowl and the swimsuit issue generate significantly larger audiences than does a weekly NFL game or a weekly edition of *Sports Illustrated;* and advertisements are usually created specifically for these mega sports media events and cost more to run than do ads in a weekly NFL game or a weekly edition of *Sports Illustrated.*

To be sure, the Super Bowl and the *Sports Illustrated* swimsuit issue are different in some fundamental ways. First, the Super Bowl is a televised event, while the swimsuit issue is a print event. Second, the Super Bowl is an actual sporting contest, while the swimsuit issue is a departure from *Sports Illustrated*'s normal coverage of sports. However, for our purposes, we see these two events as comparable, partly because they are mega sports media events but also because their ads target young males who consume sports media.

Super Bowl Ads

Since its relatively modest start in 1967, the NFL Super Bowl has mushroomed into one of the most expensive and most watched annual media events in the United States, with a growing world audience (Martin and Reeves 2001), the vast majority of whom are boys and men. Increasingly over the past decade, Super Bowl commercials have been specially created for the event. Newspapers, magazines, television news shows, and Web sites now routinely run pre–Super Bowl stories that focus specifically on the ads, and several media outlets run post–Super Bowl polls to determine which ads were the most and least favorite. Postgame lists of "winners" and "losers" focus as much on the corporate sponsors and their ads as on the two teams that—incidentally?—played a football game between the commercials.

Fifty-five commercials ran during the 2003 Super Bowl (not counting pregame and postgame shows), at an average cost of $2.1 million for each thirty-second ad. Fifteen of these commercials were beer or malt liquor ads. Twelve of these ads were run by Anheuser-Busch, whose ownership of this Super Bowl was underlined at least twenty times throughout the broadcast, when, after commercial breaks, the camera lingered on the stadium scoreboard, atop which was a huge Budweiser sign. On five other occasions, "Bud" graphics appeared on the screen after commercial breaks, as voice-overs reminded viewers that the Super Bowl was "brought to" them by Budweiser. This represented a slight increase in beer advertising since the 2002 Super Bowl, which featured thirteen beer or malt liquor commercials (eleven of them by Anheuser-Busch), at an average cost of $1.9 million per thirty-second ad. In addition to the approximately $31.5 million that the beer companies paid for the 2003 Super Bowl ad slots, they paid millions more creating and testing those commercials with focus groups. There were 137.7 million viewers watching all or part of the 2003 Super Bowl on ABC, and by far the largest demographic group watching was men, aged twenty-five to fifty-five.

Sports Illustrated Swimsuit Issue Ads

Sports Illustrated began in 1964 to publish an annual February issue that featured five or six pages of women modeling swimsuits, embedded in an otherwise normal sixty-four-page magazine (Davis 1997). This modest format continued until the late 1970s, when the portion of the magazine featuring swimsuit models began gradually to grow. In the 1980s, the swimsuit issue morphed into a special issue in which normal sports coverage gradually disappeared. During this decade, the issue's average length had grown to 173 pages, 20 percent of which were focused on swimsuit models. By the 1990s the swimsuit issue averaged 207 pages in length, 31 percent of which featured swimsuit models. The magazine has continued to grow in recent years. The 2003 issue was 218 pages in length, 59 percent of which featured swimsuit models. The dramatic growth in the size of the swimsuit issue in the 1990s, as well as the dropping of pretense that the swimsuit issue had anything to do with normal "sports journalism," were facilitated by advertising that began cleverly to echo and spoof the often highly sexualized swimsuit imagery in the magazine. By 2000, it was more the rule than the exception when an ad in some way utilized the swimsuit theme. The gender and sexual themes of the swimsuit issue became increasingly seamless, as ads and *Sports Illustrated* text symbiotically echoed and played off of each other. The 2002 swimsuit issue included seven pages of beer ads and seven pages of liquor ads, which cost approximately $230,000 per full page to run. The 2003 swimsuit issue ran the equivalent of sixteen pages of beer ads and thirteen pages of liquor ads. The ad space for the 2003 swimsuit issue sold for $266,000 per full-page color ad.

The millions of dollars that beer and liquor companies spent to develop and buy space for these ads were aimed at the central group that reads the magazine: young and middle-aged males. *Sports Illustrated* estimates the audience size of its weekly magazine at 21.3 million readers, roughly 76 percent of whom are males.[2] Nearly half of the male audience is in the coveted eighteen- to thirty-four-year-old demographic group, and three quarters of the male *Sports Illustrated* audience is between the ages of eighteen and forty-nine. A much larger number of single-copy sales gives the swimsuit issue a much larger audience, conservatively estimated at more than 30 million readers.[3]

The Super Bowl and the *Sports Illustrated* swimsuit issue are arguably the biggest single electronic and print sports media events annually in the United States. Due to their centrality, size, and target audiences, we suggest that mega sports media events such as the Super Bowl and the swimsuit issue offer a magnified view of the dominant gender and sexual imagery emanating from the center of the sports-media-commercial complex. Our concern is not simply to describe the stereotypes of masculinity and femininity in these ads; rather, we use these ads as windows into the ways that cultural capitalism constructs gender relationally, as part of a general lifestyle. In this article, we will employ thick description of ads to illuminate the four main gender relations themes that we saw in the 2002 and 2003 ads, and we will follow with a discussion of the process through which these themes are communicated: erotic and often humorous intertextual referencing. We will end by discussing some of the strains and tensions in the ads' major tropes of masculinity.

LOSERS AND BUDDIES, HOTTIES AND BITCHES

In the 2002 and 2003 beer and liquor ads that we examined, men's work worlds seem mostly to have disappeared. These ads are less about drinking and leisure as a reward for hard work and more about leisure as a lifestyle in and of itself. Men do not work in these ads; they recreate. And women are definitely back in the picture, but not as wives who are partners in building the good domestic life. It is these relations among men as well as relations between men and women that form the four dominant gender themes in the ads we examined. We will introduce these four themes by describing a 2003 Super Bowl commercial for Bud Lite beer.

Two young, somewhat nerdy-looking white guys are at a yoga class, sitting in the back of a room full of sexy young women. The two men have attached prosthetic legs to their bodies so that they can fake the yoga moves. With their bottles of Bud Lite close by, these voyeurs watch in delight as the female yoga teacher instructs the class to "relax and release that negative energy ... inhale, arch, *thrust* your pelvis to the sky and exhale, *release* into the stretch." As the instructor uses her hands to push down on a woman's upright spread-eagled legs and says "focus, focus, focus," the camera (serving as prosthesis for male spectators at home) cuts back and forth between close-ups of the women's breasts and bottoms, while the two guys gleefully enjoy their beer and their sexual voyeurism. In the final scene the two guys are standing outside the front door of the yoga class, beer bottles in hand, and someone throws their fake legs out the door at them. As they duck to avoid being hit by the legs, one of them comments, "*She's* not very relaxed."

We begin with this ad because it contains, in various degrees, the four dominant gender themes that we found in the mega sports media events ads:

1. Losers: Men are often portrayed as chumps, losers. Masculinity—especially for the lone man—is precarious. Individual men are always on the cusp of being publicly humiliated, either by their own stupidity, by other men, or worse, by a beautiful woman.
2. Buddies: The precariousness of individual men's masculine status is offset by the safety of the male group. The solidity and primacy—and emotional safety—of male friendships are the emotional center of many of these ads.
3. Hotties: When women appear in these ads, it is usually as highly sexualized fantasy objects. These beautiful women serve as potential prizes for men's victories and proper consumption choices. They sometimes serve to validate men's masculinity, but their validating power also holds the potential to humiliate male losers.
4. Bitches: Wives, girlfriends, or other women to whom men are emotionally committed are mostly absent from these ads. However, when they do appear, it is primarily as emotional or sexual blackmailers who threaten to undermine individual men's freedom to enjoy the erotic pleasure at the center of the male group.

To a great extent, these four gender themes are intertwined in the Super Bowl "Yoga Voyeurs" ad. First, the two guys are clearly not good-looking, high-status, muscular icons of masculinity. More likely they are intended to represent the "every-man" with whom many boys and men can identify. Their masquerade as sensitive men allows them to transgress the female space of the yoga class, but they cannot pull the masquerade off and are eventually "outed" as losers and rejected by the sexy women. But even if they realize that they are losers, they do not have to care because they are so happy and secure in their bond with each other. Their friendship bond is cemented in frat-boy-style hijinks that allow them to share close-up voyeurism of sexy women who, we can safely assume, are way out of these men's league. In the end, the women reject the guys as pathetic losers. But the guys do not seem too upset. They have each other and, of course, they have their beers.

Rarely did a single ad in our study contain all four of these themes. But taken together, the ads show enough consistency that we can think of these themes as in-tertwined threads that together make up the ideological fabric at the center of mega sports media events. Next, we will illustrate how these themes are played out in the 2002 and 2003 ads, before discussing some of the strains and tensions in the ads.

REAL FRIENDS, SCARY WOMEN

Five twenty-something white guys are sitting around a kitchen table playing poker. They are laughing, seemingly having the time of their lives, drinking Jim Beam whiskey. The caption for this ad reflects the lighthearted, youthful mood of the group: "Good Bourbon, ice cubes, and whichever glasses are clean." This ad, which appeared in the 2002 *Sports Illustrated* swimsuit issue, is one in a series of Jim Beam ads that have run for the past few years in *Sports Illustrated* and in other magazines aimed at young men.[4] Running under the umbrella slogan of "Real Friends, Real Bourbon," these Jim Beam ads hail a white, college-age (or young college-educated) crowd of men with the appeal of playful male bonding through alcohol consumption in bars or pool halls. The main theme is the safety and primacy of the male group, but the accompanying written text sometimes suggests the presence of women. In one ad, four young white guys partying up a storm together and posing with arms intertwined are accompanied by the caption, "Unlike your girlfriend, they never ask where this relationship is going." These ads imply that women demand levels of emotional commitment and expression undesirable to men, while life with the boys (and the booze) is exciting, emotionally comfortable, and safe. The comfort that these ads suggest is that bonding and intimacy have clear (though mostly unspoken) boundaries that limit emotional expression in the male group. When drinking with the guys, a man can feel close to his friends, perhaps even drape an arm over a friend's shoulder, embrace him, or tell him that he loves him. But the context of alcohol consumption provides an escape hatch that contains and rationalizes the eruption of physical intimacy.

Although emotional closeness with and commitment to real women apparently are to be avoided, these ads also do suggest a role for women. The one ad in the Jim Beam series that includes an image of a woman depicts only a body part (*Sports Illustrated* ran this one in its 2000 swimsuit issue in 3-D). Four guys drinking together in a bar are foregrounded by a set of high-heeled legs that appear to be an exotic dancer's. The guys drink, laugh, and seem thoroughly amused with each other. "Our lives would make a great sitcom," the caption reads, and continues, "of course, it would have to run on cable." That the guys largely ignore the dancer affirms the strength and primacy of their bond with one another—they do not need her or any other women, the ad seems to say. On the other hand—and just as in the "Yoga Voyeurs" commercial—the female dancer's sexualizing of the chronotopic space affirms that the bond between the men is safely within the bounds of heterosexuality.

Although these ads advocate keeping one's emotional distance from women, a commitment to heterosexuality always carries the potential for developing actual relationships with women. The few ads that depict real women portray them consistently as signs of danger to individual men and to the male group. The ads imply that what men really want is sex (or at least titillation), a cold beer, and some laughs with the guys. Girlfriends and wives are undesirable because they push men to talk about feelings and demonstrate commitment to a relationship. In "Good Listener," a 2003 Super Bowl ad for Budweiser, a young white guy is sitting in a sports bar with his girlfriend while she complains about her best friend's "totally self-centered and insensitive boyfriend." As he appears to listen to this obviously boring "girl talk," the camera pulls to a tight close-up on her face. She is reasonably attractive, but the viewer is not supposed to mistake her for one of the model-perfect fantasy women in other beer ads. The close-up reveals that her teeth are a bit crooked, her hair a bit stringy, and her face contorts as she says of her girlfriend that "she has these *emotional* needs he can't meet." Repelled, the guy spaces out and begins to peer over her shoulder at the television. The camera takes the guy's point of view and focuses on the football game while the speaking woman is in the fuzzy margins of his view. The girlfriend's monologue gets transposed by a football announcer describing an exciting run. She stops talking, and just in time his gaze shifts back to her eyes. She lovingly says, "You're such a great listener." With an "aw-shucks" smile, he says "thanks," and the "Budweiser TRUE" logo appears on the screen. These ads suggest that a sincere face and a bottle of beer allow a guy to escape the emotional needs of his partner while retaining regular access to sex. But the apparent dangers of love, long-term commitment, and marriage remain. The most overtly misogynist ad in the 2003 Super Bowl broadcast was "Sarah's Mom." While talking on the phone to a friend, a young, somewhat nerdy-looking white guy prepares to meet his girlfriend's mother for the first time. His friend offers him this stern advice: "Well, get a good look at her. 'Cause in twenty years, that's what Sarah's gonna look like." The nerd expresses surprised concern, just as there is a knock on the door. Viewed through the door's peephole, the face of Sarah's mother appears as young and beautiful as Sarah's, but it turns out that Sarah's mother has grotesquely large hips, thighs, and buttocks. The commercial ends with the screen filled mostly with the hugeness of the mother's bottom, her leather pants audibly stretching as she bends to pet the dog, and Sarah shoveling chips and dip into her mouth, as she says of her mother, "Isn't she incredible?" The guy replies, with obvious skepticism, "yeah."

The message to boys and men is disturbing. If you are nerdy enough to be thinking about getting married, then you should listen to your male friends' warnings about what to watch out for and what is important. If you have got to have a wife, make sure that she is, and always will be, conventionally thin and beautiful.

In beer ads, the male group defines men's need for women as sexual, not emotional, and in so doing it constructs women as either whores or bitches and then suggests ways for men to negotiate the tension between these two narrow and stereotypical categories of women. This, we think, is a key point of tension that beer and liquor companies are attempting to exploit to their advantage. They do so by creating a curious shift away from the familiar "madonna-whore" dichotomy of which Western feminists have been so critical, where wives/mothers/girlfriends are put on a pedestal and the women one has sex with are put in the gutter. The alcohol industry would apparently prefer that young men not think of women as madonnas. After all, wives and girlfriends to whom men are committed, whom they respect and love, often do place limits on men's time spent out with the boys, as well as limits on men's consumption of alcohol. The industry seems to know this: as long as men remain distrustful of women, seeing them either as bitches who are trying to ensnare them and take away their freedom or as whores with whom they can party and have sex with no emotional commitment attached, then men remain more open to the marketing strategies of the industry.

WINNERS AND LOSERS

In the 2002 and 2003 Super Bowls, Budweiser's "How Ya Doin'?" ads featured the trope of a country bumpkin, or hick, in the big city to highlight the rejection of men who transgress the symbolic boundaries of the male peer group. These ads also illustrate the communication and emotional processes that police these boundaries. Men may ask each other "how's it goin'," but they do not want to hear how it's *really* goin'. It is these unspoken limits that make the group bond feel like an emotionally safe place: male buddies at the bar will not ask each other how the relationship is going or push each other to get in touch with their feminine sides. But men who transgress these boundaries, who do not understand the unwritten emotional rules of the male group, are suspect, are branded as losers, and are banished from the inner circle of the group.

REVENGE OF THE REGULAR GUYS

If losers are used in some of these ads to clarify the bounds of masculine normality, this is not to say that hypermasculine men are set up as the norm. To the contrary, overly masculine men, muscle men, and men with big cars who flash their money around are often portrayed as the real losers, against whom regular guys can sometimes turn the tables and win the beautiful women. In the ads we examined, however, this "regular guy wins beautiful fantasy woman" outcome was very rare. Instead, when the regular guy does manage to get the beautiful fantasy woman's attention, it is usually not in the way that he imagined or dreamed. A loser may want to win the attention of—and have sex with—beautiful women. But ultimately, these women are unavailable to a loser; worse, they will publicly humiliate him if he tries to win their attention. But losers can always manage to have another beer.

If white-guy losers risk punishment or humiliation from beautiful women in these ads, the level of punishment faced by black men can be even more severe. Although nearly all of the television commercials and print ads that we examined depict white people, a very small number do focus centrally on African Americans.[5] In "Pick-Up Lines," a Bud Lite ad that ran during the 2002 Super Bowl, two black males are sitting at a bar next to an attractive black female. Paul, the man in the middle, is obviously a loser; he's wearing a garish shirt, and his hair looks like an Afro gone terribly wrong. He sounds a bit whiny as he confides in his male friend, "I'm just not good with the ladies like you, Cedric." Cedric, playing Cyrano de Bergerac, whispers opening pickup lines to him. The loser turns to the woman and passes on the lines. But just then, the bartender brings another bottle of beer to Cedric, who asks the bartender, "So, how much?" Paul, thinking that this is his next pickup line, says to the woman, "So, how much?" Her smile turns to an angry frown, and she delivers a vicious kick to Paul's face, knocking him to the floor. After we see the Budweiser logo and hear the voice-over telling us that Bud Lite's great taste "will never let you down," we see a stunned Paul rising to his knees and trying to pull himself up to his bar stool, but the woman knocks him down again with a powerful backhand fist to the face.

This Bud Lite "Pick-Up Lines" ad—one of the very few ads that depict relations between black men and black women—was the only ad in which we saw a man being physically beaten by a woman. Here, the African American woman as object turns to subject, inflicting direct physical punishment on the African American man. The existence of these very few "black ads" brings into relief something that might otherwise remain hidden: most of these ads construct a youthful white masculinity that is playfully self-mocking, always a bit tenuous, but ultimately lovable. The screwups that white-guy losers make are forgivable, and we nearly always see these men, in the end, with at least a cold beer in hand. By contrast, the intersection of race, gender, and class creates cultural and institutional contexts of suspicion and punishment for African American boys and men (Ferguson 2000). In the beer ads this translates into the message that a black man's transgressions are apparently deserving of a kick to the face.

EROTIC INTERTEXTUALITY

One of the dominant strategies in beer and liquor ads is to create an (often humorous) erotic tension among members of a "threesome": the male reader/viewer, a woman depicted as a sexy fantasy object, and a bottle of cold beer. This tension is accomplished through intertextual referencing between the advertising text and the sport text. For instance, on returning to live coverage of the Super Bowl from a commercial break, the camera regularly lingered on the stadium scoreboard, above which was a huge Budweiser sign. One such occasion during the 2003 Super Bowl was particularly striking. Coors had just run its only commercial (an episode from its successful "Twins" series) during this mega sports media event that seemed otherwise practically owned by Anheuser-Busch. Immediately on return from the commercial break to live action, the handheld field-level camera focused one by one on dancing cheerleaders (once coming so close that it appears that the camera bumped into one of the women's breasts), all the while keeping the Budweiser sign in focus in the background. It was almost as though the producers of the Super Bowl were intent on not allowing the Coors "twins" to upstage Anheuser-Busch's ownership of the event.

Omnipresent advertising images in recent years have continued to obliterate the already blurry distinction between advertising texts and other media texts (Goldman and Papson 1996). This is surely true in the world of sport: players' uniforms, stadium walls, the corner of one's television screen, and even moments within telecasts are regularly branded with the Nike swoosh or some other corporate sign. Stephanie O'Donohoe argues that "popular texts have 'leaky boundaries,' flowing into each other and everyday life.... This seems especially true of advertising" (1997, 257–58). The "leakiness" of cultural signs in advertising is facilitated, O'Donohoe argues, "by increasing institutional ties between advertising, commercial media, and mass entertainment.... Conglomeration breeds intertextuality" (257–58). When ads appropriate or make explicit reference to other media (e.g., other ads, celebrities, movies, television shows, or popular music), they engage in what Robert Goldman and Stephen Papson call "cultural cannibalism" (1998, 10). Audiences are then invited to make the connections between the advertised product and the cultural meanings implied by the cannibalized sign; in so doing, the audience becomes "the final author, whose participation is essential" (O'Donohoe 1997, 259). As with all textual analyses that do not include an audience study, we must be cautious in inferring how differently situated audiences might variously take up, and draw meanings from, these ads. However, we suspect that experiences of "authorship" in the process of decoding and drawing intertextual connections are a major part of the pleasure of viewing mass media texts.

The 2002 and 2003 *Sports Illustrated* swimsuit issues offer vivid examples of texts that invite the reader to draw intertextual connections between erotically charged ads and other non-ad texts. Whereas in the past the *Sports Illustrated* swimsuit issue ran ads that were clearly distinct from the swimsuit text, it has recently become more common for the visual themes in the ads and the swimsuit text to be playfully intertwined, symbiotically referencing each other. A 2003 Heineken ad shows a close-up of two twenty-four-ounce "keg cans" of Heineken beer, side by side. The text above the two cans reads, "They're big. And yeah, they're real." As if the reference to swimsuit models' breast size (and questions about whether some of the models have breast implants) were perhaps too subtle, *Sports Illustrated* juxtaposed the ad with a photo of a swimsuit model, wearing a suit that liberally exposed her breasts.

For the advertisers and for *Sports Illustrated,* the payoff for this kind of intertextual coordination is probably large: for the reader, the text of the swimsuit issue becomes increasingly seamless, as ads and swimsuit text melt into each other, playfully, humorously, and erotically referencing each other. As with the Super Bowl ads, the *Sports Illustrated* swimsuit issue ads become something that viewers learn not to ignore or skip over; instead, the ads become another part of the pleasure of consuming and imagining.

In 2003, Miller Brewing Company and *Sports Illustrated* further developed the symbiotic marketing strategy that they had introduced in 2002. The 2003 swimsuit issue featured a huge Miller Lite ad that included the equivalent of fourteen full pages of ad text. Twelve of these pages were a large, pull-out poster, one side of which was a single photo of "Sophia," a young model wearing a bikini with the Miller Lite logo on the right breast cup. On the opposite side of the poster were four one-page photos and one two-page photo of Sophia posing in various bikinis, with Miller Lite bottles and/or logos visible in each picture. As it did in the 2002 ad, Miller invites viewers to enter a contest to win a trip to the next *Sports Illustrated* swimsuit issue photo shoot. The site of the photo shoot fuses the text-based space of the magazine with the real space of the working models in exotic, erotic landscapes of desire that highlight the sexuality of late capitalist colonialism (Davis 1997). The accompanying text invites the reader to "visit http://www.cnnsi.com" to "check out a 360 degree view of the *Sports Illustrated* swimsuit photo shoot." And the text accompanying most of the photos of Sophia and bottles of Miller Lite teasingly encourages the reader to exercise his consumer power: "So if you had to make a choice, which one would it be?"

This expansive ad evidences a multilevel symbiosis between *Sports Illustrated* and Miller Brewing Company. The playful tease to "choose your favorite" (model, swimsuit, and/or beer) invites the reader to enter another medium—the *Sports Illustrated* swimsuit Web site, which includes access to a *Sports Illustrated* swimsuit photo shoot video sponsored by Miller. The result is a multifaceted media text that stands out as something other than mere advertisement and other than business-as-usual *Sports Illustrated* text. It has an erotic and commercial charge to it that simultaneously teases the reader as a sexual voyeur and hails him as an empowered consumer who can freely choose his own beer and whichever sexy woman he decides is his "favorite."

"LIFE IS HARSH": MALE LOSERS AND ALCOHOLIC ACCOMMODATION

In recent years, the tendency in the *Sports Illustrated* swimsuit issue to position male readers as empowered individuals who can "win" or freely choose the sexy fantasy object of their dreams has begun to shift in other directions. To put it simply, many male readers of the swimsuit issue may find the text erotically charged, but most know that these are two-dimensional images of sexy women who in real life are unavailable to them. In recent years, some swimsuit issue ads have delivered this message directly. In 1997, a two-page ad for Tequila Sauza depicted six women in short red skirts, posing flirtatiously, some of them lifting their blouses provocatively to reveal bare midriffs, or opening their blouses to reveal parts of their breasts. In small letters, across the six women's waists, stretching all the way across the two pages, the text reads, "We can say with 99.9 percent accuracy that there is no possible way whatsoever in this lifetime that you will ever get a date with one of these women." Then, to the side of the ad is written "LIFE IS HARSH. Your tequila shouldn't be." A similar message appears in other ads. For instance, in the 1999 swimsuit issue, a full-page photo of a Heineken bottle included the written text "The only heiny in this magazine you could actually get your hands on."

These ads play directly to the male reader as loser and invite him to accommodate to his loser status, to recognize that these sexy fantasy women, though "real," are unavailable to him, and to settle for what he can have: a good bottle of Tequila Sauza or a cold (rather than a hot) "Heiny." The Bud Lite Super Bowl commercials strike a similar chord. Many Bud Lite ads either titillate the viewer with sexy fantasy women, point to the ways that relationships with real women are to be avoided, or do both simultaneously. The break that appears near the end of each Bud Lite ad contrasts sharply with the often negative depiction of men's relations with real women in the ad's story line. The viewer sees a close-up of a bottle of Bud Lite. The bottle's cap explodes off, and beer ejaculates out, as a male voice-over proclaims what a man truly can rely on in life: "For the great taste that won't fill you up, and never lets you down ... make it a Bud Lite."

REVENGE OF THE LOSERS

The accommodation theme in these ads may succeed, momentarily, in encouraging a man to shift his feelings of being a sexual loser toward manly feelings of empowerment through the consumption of brand-name beers and liquor. If the women in the ads are responsible for heightening tensions that result in some men's sense of themselves as losers, one possible outcome beyond simply drinking a large amount of alcohol (or one that accompanies the consumption of alcohol) is to express anger toward women and even to take revenge against them. This is precisely a direction that some of the recent ads have taken.

A full-page ad in the 2002 swimsuit issue showed a large photo of a bottle of Maker's Mark Whiskey. The bottle's reflection on the shiny table on which it sits is distorted in a way that suggests an hourglass-shaped female torso. The text next to the bottle reads, " 'Your bourbon has a great body and fine character. I WISH the same could be said for my girlfriend.' D. T., Birmingham, AL." This one-page ad is juxtaposed with a full-page photo of a *Sports Illustrated* model, provocatively using her thumb to begin to pull down the right side of her bikini bottom.

Together, the ad text and *Sports Illustrated* text angrily express the bitch-whore dichotomy that we discussed above. D. T.'s girlfriend is not pictured, but the description of her clearly indicates that not only does she lack a beautiful body; worse, she's a bitch. While D. T.'s girlfriend symbolizes the real woman whom each guy tolerates, and to whom he avoids committing, the juxtaposed *Sports Illustrated* model is the beautiful and sexy fantasy woman. She is unavailable to the male reader in real life; her presence as fantasy image highlights that the reader, like D. T., is stuck, apparently, with his bitchy girlfriend. But at least he can enjoy a moment of pseudo-empowerment by consuming a Maker's Mark whiskey and by insulting his girlfriend's body and character. Together, the Maker's Mark ad and the juxtaposed *Sports Illustrated* model provide a context for the reader to feel hostility toward the real women in his life.

This kind of symbolic male revenge toward women is expressed in a different way in a four-page Captain Morgan rum ad that appeared in the 2003 *Sports Illustrated* swimsuit issue. On the first page, we see only the hands of the cartoon character "Captain Morgan" holding a fire hose spraying water into the air over what appears to be a tropical beach. When one turns the page, a three-page foldout ad reveals that "the Captain" is spraying what appears to be a *Sports Illustrated* swimsuit issue photo shoot. Six young women in tiny bikinis are laughing, perhaps screaming, and running for cover (five of them are huddled under an umbrella with a grinning male character who looks suspiciously like Captain Morgan). The spray from the fire hose causes the women's bathing suits to melt right off their bodies. The readers do not know if the swimsuits are painted on or are made of meltable candy or if perhaps Captain Morgan's ejaculate is just that powerfully corrosive. One way or the other, the image suggests that Captain Morgan is doing a service to the millions of boys and men who read this magazine. Written across a fleeing woman's thigh, below her melting bikini bottom, the text reads "Can you say birthday suit issue?"

Two men—apparently photographers—stand to the right of the photo, arms raised to the heavens (with their clothing fully intact). The men in the picture seem ecstatic with religious fervor. The male reader is perhaps invited to identify with these regular guys: like them, he is always good enough to look at these beautiful women in their swimsuits but never good enough to get them to take it off for him. But here, "the Captain" was clever enough to strip the women naked so that he and all of his male buddies could enjoy a vengeful moment of voyeurism. The relational gender and sexual dynamics of this ad—presented here without overt anger and with cartoonish humor—allegorize the common dynamics of group sexual assaults (Beneke 1982). These sexy women have teased men enough, the ad suggests. First they arouse men, and then they inevitably make them feel like losers. They deserve to be stripped naked against their will. As in many male rape fantasies, the ad suggests that women ultimately find that they like it. And all of this action is facilitated by a bottle of rum, the Captain's magical essence.

TENSION, STABILIZATION, AND MASCULINE CONSUMPTION

We argued in our introduction that contemporary social changes have destabilized hegemonic masculinity. Examining beer and liquor ads in mega sports media events gives us a window into the ways that commercial forces have seized on these destabilizing tendencies, constructing pedagogical fantasy narratives that aim to appeal to a very large group—eighteen- to thirty-four-year-old men. They do so by appealing to a broad zeitgeist among young (especially white, heterosexual) men that is grounded in widespread tensions in the contemporary gender order.[6] The sexual and gender themes of the beer and liquor ads that we examine in this article do not stand alone; rather they reflect, and in turn contribute to, broader trends in popular culture and marketing to young white males. Television shows like *The Man Show,* new soft-core porn magazines like *Maxim* and *FHM,* and radio talk shows like the syndicated *Tom Leykus Show* share similar themes and are targeted to similar audiences of young males. Indeed, radio talk show hosts like Leykus didactically instruct young men to avoid "girlie" things, to eschew emotional commitment, and to think of women primarily as sexual partners (Messner 2002, 107–8). The chronotope of these magazines and television and radio shows constructs young male lifestyles saturated with sexy images of nearly naked, surgically enhanced women; unabashed and unapologetic sexual voyeurism shared by groups of laughing men; and explicit talk of sexual exploits with "hotties" or "juggies." A range of consumer products that includes—often centrally, as in *The Man Show*—consumption of beer as part of the young male lifestyle stitches together this erotic bonding among men. Meanwhile, real women are either absent from these media or they are disparaged as gold diggers (yes, this term has been resuscitated) who use sex to get men to spend money on them and trick them into marriage. The domesticated man is viewed as a wimpy victim who has subordinated his own pleasures (and surrendered his paychecks) to a woman. Within this framework, a young man should have sex with as many women as he can while avoiding (or at least delaying) emotional commitments to any one woman. Freedom from emotional commitment grants 100 percent control over disposable income for monadic consumption and care of self. And that is ultimately what these shows are about: constructing a young male consumer characterized by personal and emotional freedom who can attain a hip lifestyle by purchasing an ever-expanding range of automobile-related products, snack foods, clothes, toiletries, and, of course, beer and liquor.

At first glance, these new media aimed at young men seem to resuscitate a 1950s "*Playboy* philosophy" of men's consumption, sexuality, and gender relations (Ehrenreich 1983). Indeed, these new media strongly reiterate the dichotomous bitch-whore view of women that was such a lynchpin of Hugh Hefner's "philosophy." But today's tropes of masculinity do not simply reiterate the past; rather, they give a postfeminist twist to the *Playboy* philosophy. A half-century ago, Hefner's pitch to men to recapture the indoors by creating (purchasing) one's own erotic "bachelor pad" in which to have sex with women (and then send them home) read as a straightforwardly masculine project. By contrast, today's sexual and gender pitch to young men is delivered with an ironic, self-mocking wink that operates, we think, on two levels. First, it appears to acknowledge that most young men are neither the heroes of the indoors (as Hefner would have it) nor of the outdoors (as the 1970s and 1980s beer ads suggested). Instead, the ads seem to recognize that young white men's unstable status leaves them always on the verge of being revealed as losers. The ads plant seeds of insecurity on this fertile landscape, with the goal of creating a white guy who is a consistent and enthusiastic consumer of alcoholic beverages. The irony works on a second level as well: the throwback sexual and gender imagery—especially the bitch-whore dichotomization of women—is clearly a defensively misogynistic backlash against feminism and women's increasing autonomy and social power. The wink and self-mocking irony allow men to have it both ways: they can engage in humorous misogynist banter and claim simultaneously that it is all in play. They do not take themselves seriously, so anyone who takes their misogyny as anything but boys having good fun just has no sense of humor. The humorous irony works, then, to deflect charges of sexism away from white males, allowing them to define themselves as victims, as members of an endangered species. We suspect, too, that this is a key part of the process that constructs the whiteness in current reconstructions of hegemonic masculinity. As we have suggested, humorous "boys-will-be-boys" misogyny is unlikely to be taken ironically and lightly when delivered by men of color.

The white-guy-as-loser trope, though fairly new to beer and liquor ads, is certainly not new to U.S. media. Part of the irony of this character is not that he is a loser in every sense; rather he signifies the typical everyman who is only a loser in comparison to versions of masculinity more typical to beer and liquor ads past—that is, the rugged guys who regularly get the model-beautiful women. Caught between the excesses of a hypermasculinity that is often discredited and caricatured in popular culture and the increasing empowerment of women, people of color, and homosexuals, while simultaneously being undercut by the postindustrial economy, the "Average Joe" is positioned as the ironic, vulnerable but lovable hero of beer and liquor ads. It is striking that the loser is not, or is rarely, your "José Mediano," especially if we understand the construction as a way to unite diverse eighteen- to thirty-four-year-old men. This is to say that the loser motif constructs the universal subject as implicitly white, and as a reaction against challenges to hegemonic masculinity it represents an ongoing possessive investment in whiteness (Lipsitz 1998).

Our analysis suggests that the fact that male viewers today are being hailed as losers and are being asked to identify with—even revel in—their loser status has its limits. The beer and liquor industry dangles images of sexy women in front of men's noses. Indeed, the ads imply that men will go out of their way to put themselves in position to be voyeurs, be it with a TV remote control, at a yoga class, in a bar, or on the *Sports Illustrated*/ Miller Beer swimsuit photo shoot Web site. But ultimately, men know (and are increasingly being told in the advertisements themselves) that these sexy women are not available to them. Worse, if men get too close to these women, these women will most likely humiliate them. By contrast, real women—women who are not model-beautiful fantasy objects—are likely to attempt to ensnare men into a commitment, push them to have or express feelings that make them uncomfortable, and limit their freedom to have fun watching sports or playing cards or pool with their friends. So, in the end, men have only the safe haven of their male friends and the bottle.

This individual sense of victimization may feed young men's insecurities while giving them convenient scapegoats on which to project anger at their victim status. The cultural construction of white males as losers, then, is tethered to men's anger at and desire for revenge against women. Indeed, we have observed that revenge-against-women themes are evident in some of the most recent beer and liquor ads. And it is here that our analysis comes full circle. For, as we suggested in the introduction, the cultural imagery in ads aimed at young men does not simply come from images "out there." Instead, this imagery is linked to the ways that real people live their lives. It is the task of future research—including audience research—to investigate and flesh out the specific links between young men's consumption of commercial images, their consumption of beer and liquor, their attitudes toward and relationships with women, and their tendencies to drink and engage in violence against women.

APPENDIX

Table 8-1 Commercials and Advertisements in the Sample

2002 Super Bowl:
  Michelob Lite, "Free to Be"
  Budweiser, "Robobash"
  Budweiser, "Pick-Up Lines"
  Bud Lite, "Hawk"
  Budweiser, "Clydesdales"
  Bud Lite, "Greeting Cards"
  Budweiser, "How Ya Doin'?"
  Bud Lite, "Black Teddy"
  Budweiser, "Meet the Parents"
  Budweiser, "History of Budweiser"
  Budweiser, "Designated Driver"
  Smirnoff Ice

2003 Super Bowl:
  Budweiser, "Zebras"
  Bud Lite, "Refrigerator"
  Bud Lite, "Clown"
  Bud Lite, "Rasta Dog"
  Bud Lite, "Conch"
  Bud Lite, "Date Us Both"
  Smirnoff Lite, "Blind Date"
  Bud Lite, "Sarah's Mom"
  Bud Lite, "Three Arms"
  Coors, "Twins"
  Budweiser, "Good Listener"
  Budweiser, " 'How Ya Doin'?' Redux"
  Michelob Ultra, "Low-Carb Bodies"
  Bud Lite, "Yoga Voyeurs"

2002 *Sports Illustrated* swimsuit issue
    (no. of pages):
  Miller Lite (2)
  Jim Beam (1)
  Miller Genuine Draft (2, plus card insert)
  Heineken (1)
  Budweiser (1)
  Captain Morgan Rum (1)
  Martell (1)
  Sam Adams Utopia (1)
  Maker's Mark Whiskey (1)
  Bacardi Rum (1.25)
  José Cuervo Tequila (1)
  Crown Royal (1)
  Chivas (1)

2003 *Sports Illustrated* swimsuit issue
    (no. of pages):
  Budweiser (1)
  José Cuervo Tequila (1)
  Smirnoff Vodka (1)
  Captain Morgan Rum (4)
  Seagrams (1)
  Miller Lite (11, including poster pullout)
  Crown Royal (1)
  Heineken (1)
  Skyy Vodka (1)
  Knob Whiskey (1)
  Chivas (1)

NOTES

We thank Cheryl Cooky and Sarah Banet-Weiser for their helpful suggestions on an earlier draft of this article and Wayne Wilson for his research assistance. We also give thanks to the editors and anonymous readers at *Signs,* whose criticisms and suggestions helped tighten and improve this article.

1. We first conducted a content analysis of the Super Bowl tapes and the *Sports Illustrated* swimsuit issues to determine how many beer and liquor ads there were and where they were placed in the texts. Next, we employed textual analysis to identify common thematic patterns in the ads. We also sought to identify tensions, discontinuities, and contradictory gender themes in the ads. Finally, we examined the ways that the advertisements meshed with, respectively, the actual Super Bowl football game broadcast and the *Sports Illustrated* swimsuit issue text. We sought to understand how the intertextual cross-referencing of beer and liquor ads' gender themes with the game or the swimsuit models might variously create tensions in the dominant gender codings of the texts, reinforce these tensions, or both.

In the absence of a systematic study of the various ways that audiences interpret and use these texts, our textual analysis is obviously limited.

2. *Sports Illustrated*'s rate card claims 3,137,523 average weekly subscribers and additional single-copy sales of 115,337. The company then uses a multiplier of 6.55 readers per issue to estimate the total size of its audience at 21,306,468.

3. In addition to *Sports Illustrated*'s 3,137,523 average weekly subscribers, the company's rate card claims 1,467,228 single-copy sales of the swimsuit issue. According to the same multiplier of 6.55 readers per magazine that *Sports Illustrated* uses for estimating the total size of its weekly audience, the swimsuit issue audience is over 30 million. More than likely, the multiplier for the swimsuit issue is higher than that of the weekly magazine, so the swimsuit issue audience is probably much larger than 30 million.

4. Most of the Jim Beam "Real Friends" ads discussed here did not appear in the two *Sports Illustrated* swimsuit issues on which we focus. However, it enhances our understanding of the gender themes in the Jim Beam ads to examine the thematic consistencies in the broader series of Jim Beam "Real Friends" ads.

5. Of the twenty-six beer and malt liquor ads in the two Super Bowls, twenty-four depicted people. Among the twenty-four ads that depicted people, eighteen depicted white people only, three depicted groups that appear to be of mixed race, and three focused on African American main characters. Thirteen of the twenty-four beer and liquor ads in the two *Sports Illustrated* swimsuit issues depicted people: twelve depicted white people only, and one depicted what appears to be the silhouette of an African American couple. No apparent Latino/as or Asian Americans appeared in any of the magazine or television ads.

6. These same beer companies target different ads to other groups of men. Suzanna Danuta Walters (2001) analyzes Budweiser ads, e.g., that are aimed overtly at gay men.

REFERENCES

Bakhtin, Mikhail. 1981. "Forms of Time and the Chronotope in the Novel." Pp. 84–258 in Caryl Emerson and Michael Holmquist, trans., *The Dialogic Imagination: Four Essays.* Austin: University of Texas Press.

Beneke, Timothy. 1982. *Men on Rape.* New York: St. Martin's.

Collins, Tony, and Wray Vamplew. 2002. *Mud, Sweat, and Beers: A Cultural History of Sport and Alcohol.* New York: Berg.

Connell, R. W. 1995. *Masculinities.* Berkeley: University of California Press.

Curry, Timothy. 2000. "Booze and Bar Fights: A Journey to the Dark Side of College Athletics." Pp. 162–175 in Jim McKay, Donald F. Sabo, and Michael A. Messner, eds., *Masculinities, Gender Relations, and Sport.* Thousand Oaks, CA: Sage.

Davis, Laurel L. 1997. *The Swimsuit Issue and Sport: Hegemonic Masculinity in* Sports Illustrated. Albany: State University of New York Press.

Dayan, Daniel, and Elihu Katz. 1988. "Articulating Consensus: The Ritual and Rhetoric of Media Events." Pp. 161–186 in Jeffrey C. Alexander, ed., *Durkheimian Sociology: Cultural Studies.* Cambridge, UK: Cambridge University Press.

Ehrenreich, Barbara. 1983. *The Hearts of Men: American Dreams and the Flight from Commitment.* New York: Anchor Doubleday.

Ferguson, Ann Arnett. 2000. *Bad Boys: Public Schools in the Making of Black Masculinity.* Ann Arbor: University of Michigan Press.

Goldman, Robert, and Stephen Papson. 1996. *Sign Wars: The Cluttered Landscape of Advertising.* New York: Guilford.

———. 1998. *Nike Culture: The Sign of the Swoosh.* Thousand Oaks, CA: Sage.

Kimmel, Michael S. 1987. "Men's Responses to Feminism at the Turn of the Century." *Gender and Society* 1, no. 3: 261–283.

Koss, Mary, and John A. Gaines. 1993. "The Prediction of Sexual Aggression by Alcohol Use, Athletic Participation, and Fraternity Affiliation." *Journal of Interpersonal Violence* 8, no. 1: 94–108.

Leichliter, Jami S., Philip W. Meilman, Cheryl A. Presley, and Jeffrey R. Cashin. 1998. "Alcohol Use and Related Consequences among Students with Varying Levels of Involvement in College Athletics." *Journal of American College Health* 46, no. 6: 257–262.

Lipsitz, George. 1981. *Class and Culture in Cold War America: "A Rainbow at Midnight."* New York: Praeger.

———. 1998. *The Possessive Investment in Whiteness: How White People Profit from Identity Politics.* Philadelphia, PA: Temple University Press.

Martin, Christopher R., and Jimmie L. Reeves. 2001. "The Whole World Isn't Watching (but We Thought They Were): The Super Bowl and U.S. Solipsism." *Culture, Sport, and Society* 4, no. 2: 213–254.

May, Elaine Tyler. 1988. *Homeward Bound: American Families in the Cold War Era.* New York: Basic Books.

Messner, Michael A. 2002. *Taking the Field: Women, Men, and Sports.* Minneapolis: University of Minnesota Press.

O'Donohoe, Stephanie. 1997. "Leaky Boundaries: Intertextuality and Young Adult Experiences of Advertising." Pp. 257–275 in Mica Nava, Andrew Blake, Ian McRury, and Barry Richards, eds., *Buy This Book: Studies in Advertising and Consumption.* London: Routledge.

Postman, Neil, Christine Nystrom, Lance Strate, and Charlie Weingartner. 1987. *Myths, Men, and Beer: An Analysis of Beer Commercials on Broadcast Television, 1987.* Washington, DC: AAA Foundation for Traffic Safety.

Sabo, Don, Phil Gray, and Linda Moore. 2000. "Domestic Violence and Televised Athletic Events: 'It's a Man Thing.'" Pp. 127–146 in Jim McKay, Don Sabo, and Michael A. Messner, eds., *Masculinities, Gender Relations, and Sport.* Thousand Oaks, CA: Sage.

Sperber, Murray. 2000. *Beer and Circus: How Big-Time College Sports Is Crippling Undergraduate Education.* New York: Henry Holt.

Spigel, Lynn. 1992. *Make Room for TV: Television and the Family Ideal in Postwar America.* Chicago: University of Chicago Press.

Strate, Lance. 1992. "Beer Commercials: A Manual on Masculinity." Pp. 78–92 in Steve Craig, ed., *Men, Masculinity, and the Media.* Thousand Oaks, CA: Sage.

Walters, Suzanna Danuta. 1999. "Sex, Text, and Context: (In) Between Feminism and Cultural Studies." Pp. 222–257 in Myra Marx Ferree, Judith Lorber, and Beth B. Hess, eds., *Revisioning Gender.* Thousand Oaks, CA: Sage.

———. 2001. *All the Rage: The Story of Gay Visibility in America.* Chicago: University of Chicago Press.

Wenner, Lawrence A. 1991. "One Part Alcohol, One Part Sport, One Part Dirt, Stir Gently: Beer Commercials and Television Sports." Pp. 388–407 in Leah R. Vende Berg and Lawrence A. Wenner, eds., *Television Criticism: Approaches and Applications.* New York: Longman.

———. 1998. "In Search of the Sports Bar: Masculinity, Alcohol, Sports, and the Mediation of Public Space." Pp. 303–332 in Genevieve Rail, ed., *Sport and Postmodern Times.* Albany: State University of New York Press.

Zimbalist, Andrew. 1999. *Unpaid Professionals: Commercialism and Conflict in Big-Time College Sports.* Princeton, NJ: Princeton University Press.

✳ FOR FURTHER STUDY ✳

Bishop, Ronald. 2003. "Missing in Action: Feature Coverage of Women's Sports in *Sports Illustrated*." *Journal of Sport and Social Issues* 27 (May): 184–194.

Brookes, R. 2002. *Representing Sport*. London: Arnold.

Coakley, Jay. 2007. *Sports in Society: Issues and Controversies*. New York: McGraw-Hill.

Crawford, Garry. 2004. *Consuming Sport: Fans, Sport, and Culture*. New York: Routledge.

Denham, Bryan E., Andrew C. Billings, and Kelby K. Halone. 2002. "Differential Accounts of Race in Broadcast Commentary of the 2000 NCAA Men's and Women's Final Four Basketball Tournaments." *Sociology of Sport Journal* 19 (3): 315–332.

Duncan, Margaret Carlisle, and Michael A. Messner. 2005. *Gender in Televised Sports: News and Highlights Shows, 1989–2004*. Los Angeles: Amateur Athletic Foundation.

Eitzen, D. Stanley, and George H. Sage. 2009. *Sociology of North American Sport*. 8th ed. Boulder, CO: Paradigm.

Juffer, Jane. 2002. "Who's the Man? Sammy Sosa, Latinos, and Televisual Redefinitions of the 'American' Pastime." *Journal of Sport and Social Issues* 26 (November): 381–402.

Malcolm, Dominic. 2007. "Sports Industry." Pp. 4713–4717 in *Blackwell Encyclopedia of Sport*. Vol. 9.

Messner, Michael A., Margaret Carlisle Duncan, and Cheryl Cooky. 2003. "Silence, Sports Bras, and Wrestling Porn." *Journal of Sport and Social Issues* 27 (February): 38–51.

Messner, Michael A., Margaret Carlisle Duncan, and Kerry Jensen. "Separating the Men from the Girls: The Gendered Language of Televised Sports." *Gender and Society* 7 (1992): 121–137.

Nixon, Howard L. II. 2008. *Sport in a Changing World*. Boulder, CO: Paradigm.

Owusu, Jeanette, and Aretha Faye Marbley. 2008. "Institutional Racism within the Print Media," *Journal for the Study of Sports and Athletes in Education* 2 (Spring): 29–49.

Raney, Arthur A., and Jennings Bryant, eds. 2006. *Handbook of Sports and Media*. Mahwah, NJ: Lawrence Erlbaum.

Stempel, Carl. 2006. "Televised Sports, Masculinist Moral Capital, and Support for the U.S. Invasion of Iraq." *Journal of Sport and Social Issues* 30 (February): 79–106.

Wannel, G. 2000. "Sports and the Media." Pp. 291–308 in Jay Coakley and Eric Dunning, eds., *Handbook of Sport Studies*. London: Sage.

PART FOUR

Sport and Socialization: Symbols

A symbol is anything that carries a particular meaning recognized by members of a culture. A wink, a raised finger (which one is important), a green light, a double stripe on the highway, and a handshake are all symbols with meaning for people in the United States. Part of the socialization process for children or other newcomers to a culture is the learning of symbols. While some symbols are relatively unimportant, others—such as the Constitution, the U.S. flag, or a cross—have great importance to certain segments of the population. Some of the symbols found in sport are very important.

The four chapters in this section consider four symbols. The first, by journalist John Branch, examines the trend toward the use of huge U.S. flags at athletic events. The second, by journalist Douglas Lederman, describes the use of the Confederate flag and the singing of the Southern anthem, "Dixie," in conjunction with sports at the University of Mississippi. These symbols represent pride by whites in their heritage. For others, especially African Americans, these are symbols of centuries of racial oppression. Should these symbols be used by a school that is supposed to represent all of the citizens of Mississippi?

The third chapter, by Laurel R. Davis-Delano, highlights another battle over symbols. Here the issue is the use of Native American names, mascots, and ceremonial acts by athletic teams. There are teams such as the Scalpers and the Savages, as well as the Indians with mascots dressed in war paint and fans doing the "tomahawk chop." Many Native Americans object to these common practices because they demean Native American heritage and encourage negative stereotypes.

The fourth chapter, by D. Stanley Eitzen and Maxine Baca Zinn, looks at sexist naming of women's athletic teams. They found in a study of all four-year colleges and universities in the United States that over half had sexist names, logos, or mascots. This use of demeaning symbols for women's teams has several negative functions for women: through their use women are trivialized, made invisible, and de-athleticized.

107

9

American Flags as Big as Fields

John Branch

On the field before the All-Star Game, Major League Baseball plans to assemble the largest gathering of Hall of Fame players in baseball history. And as fans salute their heroes, the former players will join the crowd in saluting the American flag—one that is roughly 75 feet by 150 feet, as long as a 15-story building is tall, spread horizontally over the Yankee Stadium turf.

That is a relatively small flag by big-event standards in American sports these days. But it will signal the latest can't-miss blend of sports and patriotism, a combination increasingly presenting itself through gigantic American flags, unfurled by dozens or hundreds of people in an attempt to elicit a sense of awe and nationalism in the surrounding crowd.

Once the gaudy lure of attention-seeking car dealerships or other roadside attractions, big flags have found a comfortable home inside the ballparks, arenas and raceways of American sporting events.

"It is an American phenomenon, no doubt about it," said Frank Supovitz, the N.F.L.'s senior vice president for events, who oversees such spectacles as the Super Bowl and has helped stage events around the world.

A small industry has formed to supply the flags, usually at a cost of a few thousand dollars an appearance. Some colleges and bowl games, tired of renting them frequently, have bought their own field-sized flags.

"People are getting more on the bandwagon," said Doug Green, who has long rented giant flags to teams and leagues, and recently supplied one for the Indianapolis 500. "Nascar's doing it more and more, the N.F.L. is doing it more and more."

The trend began nearly 25 years ago, spiked after 9/11 and now seems simply part of the cultural backdrop in American sports. Where there is a big game, there is a big flag, often the size of the playing field itself.

Far too big for a pole, the flags raise something else—the question of whether a bigger flag is a more patriotic one, or just a bigger one.

"For big, spectacular events, big just happens because it paints a more vibrant picture," said Tim Brosnan, the executive vice president for business at Major League Baseball. "I don't think bigger is necessarily better, but it is a celebration."

These can be touchy times for interpreting the use of the flag as a symbol of patriotism. A tiny flag on a lapel, or the absence of one, fueled debate in the presidential campaign. And the Olympics will provide plenty of chances for medal-winning Americans, handed flags as celebratory props, to create a stir with their reaction. Some past Olympians were accused of disrespecting the flag by wrapping themselves in it or wearing it like a cape.

But there is little debate over the use of field-size or court-size flags during the national anthem or other sporting rituals. They have received the tacit approval of the military, which often supplies the people to present the flags, and are routinely greeted with wide-eyed cheers.

"People go ape when they see it," said Jim Alexander, a retired Coast Guard commander who runs Superflag, the company that basically invented the industry and once held the world record for the largest flag, which temporarily hung on the Hoover Dam. It was 255 by 505 feet and has been surpassed by a flag in Israel that measures 2,165 by 330 feet. "It's a feeling. It's a feeling that takes over a whole stadium. If anyone in the stands opened their mouth and objected, there would be hell to pay."

The eccentric founder of Superflag, Thomas Demski, known as Ski, commissioned a 95-by-160-foot American flag—about half the size of a football field—that made its debut in 1984 at Super Bowl XVIII.

Mr. Green soon designed a big flag of his own, made to come apart in 14 pieces for easy transport. Now, as the vice president of Sky's the Limit Productions, he has two football-field-sized flags. The other unfastens into four pieces, packed into separate trunks that, when filled, weigh 400 pounds each. Each of the 50 stars on those flags is about 5 feet across, according to Pete Van de Putte, the president of the Dixie Flag Manufacturing in San Antonio, which has made four football-field-sized flags.

At games, flags are typically unfurled quickly by volunteers, sometimes hundreds of them, creating an effect like a slow-motion firework or a fast-motion blooming of a flower. Once the flag is fully displayed, often at a particular point in the national anthem, the holders sometimes shake their arms, creating ripples to conjure a flag in a breeze.

Mr. Green says that the only complaint he hears is that the flags sometimes touch the ground. Sheer size makes it nearly impossible to avoid. Plastic is often placed on the ground when the flags are packed and unpacked. Superflag recommends having 265 volunteers to hold the football-field-sized flag—most to hold the edges, but about 100 of them to be stationed beneath the flag to help keep it aloft.

Mike Buss, an assistant director at the American Legion's national headquarters in Indianapolis, and the organization's flag guru, said that the belief that a flag that touched the ground was somehow soiled and must be destroyed "is an old wives' tale."

"All we ask is, no matter the size, that the flag is treated with dignity and respect," Mr. Buss said.

Event planners say they sense that there are limits, but do not think they have yet been exceeded. Still, every team is different. Mr. Green has supplied flags to the Yankees for opening days, playoff games and other occasions for about 10 years.

"The Yankees like one of the smallest flags I own—about the size of a basketball court, 45 by 90," Mr. Green said.

That means, for the All-Star Game on July 15, a decision was made by baseball: We need a bigger flag than usual at Yankee Stadium. But not the biggest.

"The smell test is, is it exploitative?" said Mr. Brosnan, the Major League Baseball vice president.

Mr. Buss, from the American Legion, says he has yet to see flags go too far—or too big. "Huge flags?" he said. "That's great."

10

Old Times Not Forgotten

A Battle over Symbols

Douglas Lederman

As the ball carrier sprints across the goal line for a touchdown, thousands of University of Mississippi students erupt in cheers.

They thrust their arms to the sky, many holding flags aloft, as the band breaks into a stirring song. Backs are slapped, high fives exchanged. It is one of those magical moments that bring classmates together and unify a community.

But not one of the university's 700 black undergraduates is seated among the thousands in the students' section. Most blacks say they don't feel at home there, in part because the flags the students are waving are those of the Confederacy, and the song is the Southern anthem, "Dixie."

Much has changed here since 1962, when the university and the state gained national notoriety for resisting James Meredith's attempts to enroll as the institution's first black student. Blacks are now integrated into most aspects of daily life on the campus.

But the progress is obscured, and even undermined, by an enduring battle over the university's continued use of its Old South symbols, official and informal. The debate ignited again last spring when three black members of the band refused to

Source: "Old Times Not Forgotten: A Battle over Symbols Obscures U. of Mississippi's Racial Changes" by Douglas Lederman. From *The Chronicle of Higher Education.* Copyright 1993. Reprinted with permission.

play "Dixie," saying the song should not be performed at university-sponsored events because it offends black students.

Most white students and alumni insist—no, more than that, they practically swear—that there is nothing racist in their use of the symbols. Whatever link the flag and song might once have had with slavery and the South's segregationist past, they argue, has been supplanted in their hearts and minds by an association with the university they love. Waving the flag and cheering the playing of "Dixie" evince Southern heritage, they say, not bigotry.

"THEY'RE OUR FRIENDS"

They just represent Ole Miss to us," says Lettye Williams, a retired schoolteacher who picnicked with her husband and fellow alumni before a football game last month. "We do not see these as racist symbols. Just because you're proud to be a Southerner doesn't mean you don't like blacks. They're our friends. We work with them. We live with them."

Black students don't believe that everyone who waves the Confederate battle flag or claps along to "Dixie" is racist. But history, most of them agree, has forever tainted the flag and the song, making them inappropriate symbols for an institution that is supposed to represent all of Mississippi's citizens. The flag and "Dixie" were adopted by the university only in the late 1940s, embraced defiantly by students opposed to integration. Mississippians who violently protested Mr. Meredith's admission also rallied around the flag and "Dixie," a fact not easily forgotten by many blacks here.

They, along with many faculty members, believe Mississippi must cast off the vestiges of its Old South past if it is to thrive in the New South. Symbols, they argue, should unite, not divide, especially at a public institution in a state with a black population of 35 percent.

"No matter how much things have changed, African Americans will always remember why all of this was brought here—to keep us out," says Jesse Holland, a black senior who edits the *Daily Mississippian,* the student newspaper.

Many critics of "Dixie" want the university's chancellor, R. Gerald Turner, to stop or at least discourage the band from playing the song, just as the university officially dissociated itself from the Confederate flag a decade ago.

Many white alumni and students vow to fight such a move, and some alums say they will halt their financial support if Mississippi abandons "Dixie." Some professors also complain that banning the song by fiat would be a form of censorship.

Mr. Turner has been grappling with this issue on and off since he got here in 1983, and he has won praise from many quarters for his efforts to improve race relations. The chancellor is under pressure from all sides, but he is asking for patience. Mississippi, he believes, must at some point formally review the appropriateness of all its symbols, but he says the time is not yet right for such a study.

When that discussion does take place, Mr. Turner and others say, it will focus on a broader question raised by the dispute over "Dixie": Is it possible for an institution to shed its Confederate roots, yet remain fervently, profoundly Southern?

The university is not alone in facing that dilemma. Georgia, for instance, is bitterly divided over whether to strip the Confederate battle flag from its state banner. And just this month, the University of Alabama stirred protests when it adopted an Old South theme for its football homecoming. But few institutions have been identified so closely with the Old South legacy, good and bad, as this one.

"If this university isn't Southern," Mr. Turner says, "it's not anything."

CULTIVATING AN IMAGE

That's true partly because of its location and history. The main administration building was a hospital for Civil War soldiers, over 700 of whom are buried in a graveyard here. And the university and Oxford have been home to Southern writers who have shaped the country's perceptions of the region, from William Faulkner to Eudora Welty.

The university has also cultivated that image, carving out a niche among other public universities in the region as a bastion of the Old South. It has done that largely through its use of symbols, which extend well beyond the flag and "Dixie," which is neither fight song nor alma mater, but a popular, unofficial theme song.

The sports teams are called the Rebels, and the mascot is Colonel Reb, a caricature of an Old South plantation owner. Even the university's nickname, Ole Miss, has antebellum origins. It isn't short for Old Mississippi, as most people think, but rather is what some slaves called the wives of their owners.

The institution's image attracts students who yearn as much for its conservative, traditional nature as for the beauty of its campus and the quality of its education. But Mississippi has had trouble distancing itself from the negative aspects of what the Old South stood for, despite its advances.

"THERE IS A NEW ORDER HERE"

Signs of those advances are plentiful. This summer Mr. Turner hired the university's first black vice-chancellor; its basketball coach is also black. This year's group of 701 black undergraduates (8 percent of the 10,369 total) is its largest in history, and two white fraternities became integrated last year for the first time.

"You see white and black students together here today in ways that never before were possible," says William Ferris, director of the university's Center for the Study of Southern Culture. "That gives you hope. There is a new order here."

That's not so obvious on Saturdays during football season.

Ten hours before an evening home game, alumni and students begin filling the tree-lined expanse known as "the Grove" with picnic tables and tents. For the rest of the day, they eat, reminisce, and get fired up for the game. The people are friendly, the atmosphere inviting.

THE OLD OLE MISS

But Confederate flags hang from trees and serve as centerpieces amid the fried chicken and iced tea on many a picnic table. And just as at the game, blacks are virtually invisible in the Grove—except when the football squad, half of whose players are black, parades through the crowd en route to the stadium.

This is the *old* Ole Miss, the one that was in its prime when the university first embraced its Confederate trappings.

The university's teams became known as "the Rebels" in 1936, but Confederate flags and "Dixie" did not become an exalted part of the football ritual until 1948, when dozens of Mississippi students took part in the "Dixiecrat" political convention, which was dedicated to the fight against desegregation.

"The song and the Confederate battle flag were adopted by the all-white university specifically as a gesture of white supremacy," says Warren Steel, a music professor whose arguments helped persuade the Faculty Senate last spring to discourage the playing of "Dixie" at campus events. "People can honestly say, 'I don't think about bigotry,' but the history is there."

Tim Jones didn't know that history when he joined Mississippi's band. But after learning the origins of the university's affiliation with "Dixie" and its other symbols, he decided he could no longer play the song in good conscience.

TIME FOR PROTEST

So at a basketball game last spring, as the band took up "Dixie," Mr. Jones put down his drum, got to his feet, and crossed his arms in front of his chest.

"There's a line in the song that says, 'Old times there are not forgotten,'" says Mr. Jones, a senior. "When you talk about old times in the South, the only thing my people think about is slavery."

Mr. Jones's protest, which was backed by the Black Student Union, came 10 years after the last major flare-up over the symbols. In 1983, a black cheerleader refused to carry the Rebel flag and the alumni association discouraged its use. Saying the flag's meaning had changed because it had been appropriated by groups like the Ku Klux Klan, the university abandoned it as an official symbol.

Mississippi stopped distributing flags before games and selling them in the bookstore, and dropped the symbol from all its T-shirts and other items. The university also introduced the "Battle M" flag, a blue M with white stars on a red background, hoping it would replace the Confederate flag in its fans' hearts.

That hasn't happened. Although use of the Confederate banner waned in the mid-1980s, Rebel flags now vastly outnumber the "Battle M" at football games. If anything, the dispute over the university's symbols seems to make many whites more, not less, inclined to cling to the past.

"If it wasn't so controversial, we probably wouldn't want to wave them," says John Kennedy, a junior. "I can understand how they feel, but we feel kind of abused. If they take 'Dixie' away, I think race relations will get worse."

"AN ESCAPE" FROM DISCUSSION

The widening gap between the two sides is evidenced by T-shirts. On the front of one is the "X" popularized by the movie *Malcolm X,* under the words "you wear yours . . ." On the back is the Confederate flag, framed by the words "We'll wear ours."

"The controversy tends to polarize people and worsen race relations, and it is an escape from discussing real issues in race relations," says Mr. Steel, the music professor. "That's why I wish we would just resolve this now."

Mr. Turner says the issue will be decided not by the advocates on either side but by the "middle ground," which he says has not yet formed a consensus. The chancellor admits that people may be uneasy about the continuing debate, but he says it is necessary. Meanwhile, Mr. Turner is formulating what he calls a "framework" for the coming debate about how the university should present itself in the future.

"It is difficult to communicate how much things have changed here when you have symbols that are Confederate, not Southern," says Mr. Turner. "Somehow we need to ferret out things that are Southern from those that are Confederate."

UPDATING TRADITION

Charles Reagan Wilson, a professor of history and Southern studies, argues that for Southern tradition to survive, it must be "extended," or updated, to take recent history into account. The trick for the university, he argues, is to remain relevant to all Mississippians, black and white, without losing its distinctive character.

One alternative, he says, is to mix symbols of the confederacy with those of the civil-rights movement, reflecting Mississippi's "complex, tortured history by focusing on the two events that most shaped the South."

Another option, he says, is to give new meaning to traditional symbols. Keep using the Confederate flag, Mr. Wilson says, but redefine it: "Make a new flag that shows a white and a black hand grasping the Confederate flag," for instance. As for "Dixie," he and others say, the band's repertoire already includes a compromise: "From Dixie with Love," which meshes "Dixie" with "The Battle Hymn of the Republic," and "All My Trials," an old spiritual, reflecting all of the factors at work in the Civil War.

A third possibility, Mr. Wilson says, is to focus on Southern cultural symbols that are "anchored in the past but are not Confederate." A flag featuring a magnolia tree, for example, could be a "good common symbol of the South and of Mississippi."

Whether any of those solutions would appease either side of the debate is another question.

The problem, says Charles W. Eagles, a history professor who specializes in race relations and the civil-rights movement, is that the campus houses two very different institutions: the University of Mississippi and Ole Miss.

Every time Mr. Eagles walks through the student union, he is irked by a quotation from an alumnus that adorns a wall. It says: "The University is respected, but Ole Miss is loved. The University gives a diploma and regretfully terminates tenure, but one never graduates from Ole Miss."

CAPTURING THE PLACE

"That captures this place. For some of us—those who believe in the University of Mississippi—the symbols prevent the university from being everything it can be. Others—those that are faithful to Ole Miss—think that if you took the symbols away, there wouldn't be anything there.

"The symbols are seen as a real burden for the University of Mississippi. But they're the backbone of Ole Miss."

11

The Problems with Native American Mascots

Laurel R. Davis-Delano

Sport has not been widely discussed in the field of multicultural education. Yet, sport is central to the lives of many students. It is critical that multicultural educators attend to the field of sport, because it plays a significant role in the socialization of youth. There are many sport-related topics that multicultural educators could address. This chapter focuses on the existence of Native American mascots in school-sponsored sport.

Because of the prevalence of stereotypes of Native Americans in United States popular culture, many have difficulty understanding the problems with Native American mascots. Even those who oppose these mascots often have trouble clearly articulating the reasons for their opposition. The purpose of this chapter is to lay out the main arguments against the use of Native American mascots. All of the arguments mentioned in this chapter are used by activists who are working to eliminate these mascots.

THE MASCOTS ARE RACIST STEREOTYPES

The most common argument against Native American mascots is that they represent racist stereotypes of Native Americans. Stereotypes of Native Americans appear

Source: Laurel R. Davis-Delano, "The Problems with Native American Mascots," *Multicultural Education* 9 (Summer 2002): 11–15.

throughout United States popular culture, such as in movies; government seals; advertisements and symbols for products like butter, beer, and paper; and statues and paintings that non-Natives have in their homes. Scholars have observed two main stereotypes: the "bloodthirsty savage," which conveys the notions that Native Americans are wild, aggressive, violent, and brave; and the "noble savage," which conveys the notions that Native Americans are primitive, childlike, silent, and part of the natural world (Bataille and Silet, 1980; Hilger, 1986; Lyman, 1982; Williams, 1980).

It is the stereotype of Native Americans as bloodthirsty savage that led non-Natives to choose Native American mascots for sport. Traits associated with this stereotype, such as having a fighting spirit, and being aggressive, brave, stoic, dedicated, and proud, are associated with sport, and thus selecting a Native American mascot links sport teams with such traits. The appeal of this stereotype to many in sport is illustrated by the following quotations from supporters of Native American mascots: "I can think of no greater tribute to the American Indian than to name a team's warriors after courageous, cunning and feared warriors of the Indian nations, the braves" (Shepard, 1991, p. 14A); and "I look at that mascot, that Indian head, and it stirs me up. I think of getting real aggressive, and it brings out the aggressiveness in me. And it makes me go out there and really wrestle hard and fight hard, you know, because that's what those Indians were" (cited in Davis, 1993, p. 15).

When all the mascots representing Native Americans are considered (e.g., Indians, Redskins, Braves, Chiefs), it turns out that Native Americans are the most common mascot in United States sport. The other mascots that are most common are animals, most of which are also associated with aggression and fighting (e.g., tigers). Of course it is offensive that Native Americans are perceived, and used as symbols, in the same way as animals.

Stereotypes are misleading generalizations about a category of people. When people believe stereotypes they tend to think that all, or almost all, people who belong to a particular category behave in the same way, and they tend to ignore the wide diversity of behavior exhibited by people within the category. So, regarding the stereotype associated with the mascots, not all Native Americans in the past were aggressive, brave, dedicated fighters. And today, most Native Americans do not occupy their time fighting. And many non-Natives are aggressive, brave, dedicated fighters. Of course, many Native Americans take pride in their ethnic/racial background and are dedicated people. But, do they have more pride and dedication than other groups? And, since Native Americans have extremely high rates of suicide, health problems, and poverty, asserting that this racial group has more pride than other groups is shallow.

The stereotype of Native Americans as aggressive is particularly offensive because it distorts the historical reality of European and European-American aggression (i.e., white invasion of Native American lands and conquering of people on these lands). Belief in this stereotype works to obscure the oppression, violence, and genocide initiated by European Americans against Native Americans, and serves as justification for these acts. This stereotype is part of a mythological history of the Western United States, according to which cowboys and so-called pioneers led a glorious and adventurous life fighting Native Americans. One reason the resistance to elimination of Native American mascots is so vigorous and emotionally charged is because when the activists critique the mascots they are also criticizing a form of American identity that is linked to myths about the Western United States (Davis, 1993).

Native American mascots, and most other images of Native Americans in popular culture, are stereotypes that focus on the past, and thus these stereotypes reinforce the problematic view that associates Native Americans only with the past. Thus, this stereotyping works to obscure the lives of contemporary Native Americans. As one interview subject said, "Respect the living Indian, you know. Don't memorialize us . . . [The mascots are] almost like a monument to the vanished American Indian" (Davis, 1993, p. 13). Of course, recognizing and understanding the lives of contemporary Native Americans challenges this stereotype.

Native American mascots misrepresent, distort, and trivialize many aspects of Native American cultures, such as drumming, dancing, singing, and some aspects of religion. As an interview subject stated, "I compose memorial songs, I compose burial songs for my grandmothers and my grandfathers, my family. And, when people [imitate that at an athletic event, like at a baseball game, it hurts me, to see that people are making a mockery of me. We don't do that, what they're doing, this chanting" (Davis, 1993, p. 13). Most of those who support the mascots do not understand the meanings or realities of Native American lives and cultures. Thus, it is particularly ironic that many who want to retain Native American mascots think they are honoring Native Americans. As an interview subject asserted, "How can you honor me, when you don't know the first damn thing about me?" (Davis, 1993, p. 14).

Another irony related to the belief that Native Americans are being honored by the mascots is that "positive" views of Native Americans, and the practice of using symbols of Native Americans to represent sport teams and the like, began soon after the last of the Native American nations were conquered or subdued (Davis, 1993). Thus, one has to ask, who is being "honored" by Native American mascots, Native Americans or those who subdued Native Americans?

The mascots, and most other images of Native Americans in popular culture, lump all nations (i.e., "tribes") of Native Americans together, incorrectly conveying that there is a single Native American culture and rendering the diversity of Native American cultures invisible. For example, only some Native American nations have political structures that are dominated by a male chief, and headdresses are worn by members of only some nations.

Ethnic/racial groups other than Native Americans have occasionally been used as mascots. There are several reasons why these mascots are not as problematic as Native American mascots. First, these other mascots tend to either represent a people that lived in the past and are not alive today (e.g., Spartans), or they were selected by people from this ethnic group (e.g., Scots). Second, most of the mascots that represent other ethnic groups do not have the same association with aggression (e.g., Irish). And, third, Native Americans should not have to condition their responses to be the same as other ethnic/racial groups.

One of the reasons many do not see Native American mascots, and other images of Native Americans in popular culture, as stereotypes and as racist is that the majority of these images seem to be positive. Most stereotypes of racial/ethnic groups are obviously negative, such as African Americans as criminals and Mexican Americans as lazy. It is easier to understand that overtly negative stereotypes are stereotypes and are racist. On the other hand, some stereotypes appear to be positive, such as Asians as intelligent, Jews as good at business, and Native Americans as brave. Yet, despite their positive tone, these are problematic stereotypes, in that many people from these groups do not fit the stereotype, and underneath the positive facade lie some problematic beliefs and consequences. For example, the stereotype that all Asians are intelligent contributes to the extra pressure and discrimination many Asian Americans face, and this stereotype is often used to disparage other Persons of Color. The stereotype that all Jews are good in business serves as a foundation for another stereotype—that Jews are taking over the world economy, a stereotype which has been used to legitimate anti-Semitic actions such as the Holocaust. There are problematic beliefs and consequences that stem from the so-called positive stereotypes of Native Americans as well.

Some people argue that they should be able to retain their Native American mascots if they portray the mascots in a culturally authentic and nonstereotypical manner. There are three problems with this idea. One is that a school/team cannot control how others, such as the media and other schools/teams, use their mascot. For example, the media might print a headline announcing an "attack" by the school/team with the Native American mascot. The second problem with this idea is that the schools/teams with the Native American mascots will not be able to avoid stereotypes. Native Americans are a category of people that live in many different societies, each with a different culture, and within each Native American society there is much diversity. Thus, how does one portray what Native Americans are "really like"? Imagine creating a mascot that represented African Americans, Jewish Americans, Puerto Ricans, or European Americans. Because of the wide diversity of people within these categories, any mascot one could imagine would be a stereotype. Third, it is inappropriate for non-Natives to imitate Native Americans, even if they do so in a culturally accurate way. We would find it offensive to see a Christian portray her/himself as Jewish or an European American portray her/himself as African American, even if the portrayal is culturally accurate (e.g., using an authentic dialect and clothing). Imitating another's culture, even if we do it accurately, seems like we are mimicking and mocking the other, especially if the imitation is done for entertainment, like it is at a sporting event.

The mascot stereotypes, and other images of Native Americans in popular culture, influence the way non-Natives both perceive and treat Native Americans.

The mascot stereotypes, and other similar images, limit the abilities of the public to understand Native American realities. As the late Michael Dorris (1992) put it, "War-bonnetted apparitions pasted to football helmets or baseball caps act as opaque, impermeable curtains, solid walls of white noise that for many citizens block or distort all vision of the nearly 2 million native Americans today" (p. 19A).

A second argument against the mascots, and many other images of Native Americans in popular culture, is that they have a negative impact on Native American lives. Many people argue that symbols, such as images and language, are trivial issues that do not matter. Yet, reams of scholarship demonstrate that symbols exert a significant influence on both our perceptions and behaviors.

Native American mascots create a hostile climate for many Native Americans, and sensitive non-Natives, in the schools and communities with these mascots. It is hard to feel comfortable in and committed to a school/community, and perform to the best of one's ability in school or work, when constantly surrounded by stereotypes that offend.

The mascots, and many other images of Native Americans in popular culture, negatively influence the self-image and self-esteem of Native Americans, especially children. One activist tells the story of how she instilled pride in her children regarding their Native American heritage and how she thought her children were secure. Yet, when she took them to a game with a Native American mascot she witnessed a major "blow to their self-esteem" as they "sank in their seats," not wanting to be identified as Native American (Davis, 1993). Another activist called the mascot issue a "mental health" issue (Ode, 1992, p. 2E).

Mascot stereotypes (and other images of Native Americans in popular culture) affect more than mental health and comfort within a school/community. Other problems Native Americans commonly face, such as poverty, cultural destruction, poor health, and inadequate education, are intertwined with public images of Native Americans. These images played a role in creating such problems, and now these images constrain Native American efforts to effectively address such problems.

Because of the current power structure in the United States, the quality of lives Native Americans will lead in the future depends on whether the general public has an accurate understanding of past and present Native American lives. If the public cannot understand the problem with Native American mascots, and other images of Native Americans in popular culture, they certainly will not understand sovereignty or other issues that affect the quality of Native American lives.

NATIVE AMERICANS SHOULD CONTROL IMAGES OF THEMSELVES

A third argument against the mascots is that Native Americans should have control over societal definitions of who they are. Currently, Native Americans have little power to shape public images of themselves, and the voices of Native Americans are rarely heard. Non-Natives continually assert that the mascots are honoring Native Americans, despite the fact that most pan-ethnic Native American organizations (i.e., organizations consisting of Native American nations from throughout the United States) have stated otherwise (Rosenstein, 1996). One Native American writer said: "I'll decide what honors me and what doesn't.... Minority groups have had enough of whites telling them what to think" (MacPhie, 1991, p. 19A). It is plain arrogance, and lack of respect, for non-Natives to think that they know more about Native Americans, and what honors them, than Native Americans themselves.

Of course, one can find some people from every racial/ethnic group to agree with any opinion, as people from one racial/ethnic group never all have the same opinion, so supporters of Native American mascots have been able to find Native Americans (and other People of Color) to defend their use of these mascots. Many Native Americans have learned stereotypes of Native Americans from the same sources that non-Natives have. Some Native Americans have even profited from selling images of these stereotypes to non-Natives. It is important not to blame these Native Americans, but to recognize the social forces that affect them, such as the media, extreme poverty, and inadequate education, In light of the fact that most pan-ethnic Native American organizations have issued statements against the mascots, it is offensive for non-Natives to use Native Americans, or other People of Color, to justify the position that the mascots should be retained.

OTHER ISSUES ASSOCIATED WITH THE MASCOTS

Finally, there are several other issues associated with the Native American mascot controversy that need to be addressed. The first issues are tradition and intent. Supporters of Native American mascots regularly point out that they do not intend to offend anyone, they intend to honor Native Americans, and they are just having fun and affirming tradition. It is worth pointing out that not all traditions are good ones. Some examples of bad traditions are racially segregated facilities and the exclusion of women from schools. Many people have benefitted from the elimination of such traditions.

It is also crucial to note that intent is not the most important issue here. If a belief or action has problematic consequences (i.e., if it has negative societal effects), then we should eliminate it, regardless of intent. For example, drunk drivers or men who continually comment on the sexual attractiveness of women they work with, usually do not intend to harm anyone, and yet the consequences of such actions are often problematic and thus we should work to eliminate these behaviors. Many times, despite our best intentions, when we lack the necessary knowledge, our behavior can be quite harmful to others. Although most people who support Native American mascots do not intend to harm Native Americans, the consequences of the mascots are problematic and therefore the mascots should be eliminated.

The final issue is the small percentage of people who object to Native American mascots. Many supporters of Native American mascots argue that the mascots must not be problematic because only a small number of people object to them. Polls do indicate that if this issue were put to voters, the majority of people in most parts of the United States would vote to retain the mascots (Sigelman, 1998). Yet, there are two reasons that the focus on numbers and majority rule is problematic.

First, it is important to note that the majority of people in the United States are uncritical of stereotypes of Native Americans, including the mascots, because of lack of education about Native American issues. Most Americans have had little to no substantial contact with Native Americans and thus have distorted perspectives that come from television, movies (especially "Westerns"), and "tourist traps" that feature stereotypes of Native Americans. We have been inundated with stereotypes of Native Americans in United States popular culture from birth, so we have come to believe these stereotypes (Green, 1988). So, it is not surprising that large numbers of people do not understand this issue.

It seems that in areas of the United States where the Native American population is larger and politically active, the non-Native population has a greater understanding of Native American issues because they have been educated by local Native Americans and media coverage of these Native Americans (Davis, 1993). The task of educating the United States public or regional populations about Native American stereotypes and lives is a difficult one.

Second, Native Americans represent only about one percent of the United States population, so issues they care about, and most others do not, will not likely win public approval. People who are Jewish, and people who travel in wheelchairs, also represent a small percentage of the United States population, yet this does not mean that others should ignore their feelings and concerns. Even if the percentage of people who are offended is small, others should still try to be sensitive. Part of being a good citizen is trying to empathize with other people, especially those who are different from ourselves. Of course, we should attempt to understand why other people are offended by something, but even if we cannot achieve this understanding, the considerate thing to do is to respond to others' concerns.

Those who support the use of Native American mascots often claim that they want to retain the mascots because they "respect" Native Americans. Respect is a meaningless word when the positions of most pan-ethnic Native American organizations are ignored. Real respect is carefully listening to, attempting to understand, and addressing Native American concerns about this issue. On a related note, it is not accurate to say that every possible symbol or mascot will be objectionable to someone. There are many symbols, including most other sport mascots, that are not offensive to any groups of people.

CONCLUSION

In conclusion, equality and justice in society depend on our abilities to empathize with those who are different from us. If we listen carefully to the Native American individuals and organizations that call for an elimination of Native American mascots, it will be clear that there are valid reasons why we should work to eliminate these mascots, and other problematic images of Native Americans, in society. The state of Minnesota has made a coordinated effort to eliminate Native American mascots in its public schools and has been quite successful. The rest of the country needs to follow its lead.

REFERENCES

Bataille, G., and Silet, C. L. P., eds. 1980. *The Pretend Indians: Images of Native Americans in the Movies.* Ames: Iowa State University.

Davis, L. R. 1993. "Protest against the Use of Native American Mascots: A Challenge to Traditional American Identity." *Journal of Sport and Social Issues* 17, no. 1: 9–22.

Dorris, M. 1992. "Crazy Horse Isn't a Good Name for a Malt Liquor." *Star Tribune,* April 24, 19A.

Green, R. 1988. "The Tribe Called Wannabee: Playing Indian in America and Europe." *Folklore* 99: 30–55.

Hilger, M. 1986. *The American Indian in Film.* Methuen, NJ: Scarecrow.

Lyman, C. M. 1982. *The Vanishing Race and Other Illusions.* Washington, DC: Smithsonian Institute.

MacPhie, R. P. 1991. "This 'Real Live Indian' Offended by Chop." *Star Tribune,* October 25, 19A.

Ode, K. 1992. "Bellecourt's New AIM." *Star Tribune,* January 23, 1E-2E.

Rosenstein, J. 1996. *In Whose Honor? American Indian Mascots in Sports.* Video produced and directed by Jay Rosenstein. Champaign, IL: Jay Rosenstein.

Shepard, B. 1991. [Letter to the Editor.] *Star Tribune,* October 26, 14A.

Sigelman, L. 1998. "Hail to the Redskins? Public Reactions to a Racially Insensitive Team Name." *Sociology of Sport Journal* 15, no. 4: 317–325.

Williams, L. E. 1980. "Foreword." Pp. ix–xvi in J. E. O'Conner, *The Hollywood Indian: Stereotypes of Native Americans in Films.* Trenton: New Jersey State Museum.

12

The De-Athleticization of Women

The Naming and Gender Marking of Collegiate Sport Teams

D. Stanley Eitzen and Maxine Baca Zinn

Sport is an institution with enormous symbolic significance that contributes to and perpetuates male dominance in society (Hall, 1984, 1985). This occurs through processes that exclude women completely, or if they do manage to participate, processes that effectively minimize their achievements. Bryson (1987) has argued that sport reproduces patriarchal relations through four minimalizing processes: definition, direct control, ignoring, and trivialization. This chapter examines several of these processes but focuses especially on how the trivialization of women occurs through the sexist naming practices of athletic teams.

THE PROBLEM

American colleges and universities typically have adopted nicknames, songs, colors, emblems, and mascots as identifying and unifying symbols. This practice of using symbols to achieve solidarity and community is a common group practice, as Durk-

Source: Reprinted by permission from D. S. Eitzen and M. B. Zinn, "The De-Athleticization of Women: The Naming and Gender Marking of Collegiate Sport Teams," *Sociology of Sport Journal* 65, no. 4, (1989): 362–370.

heim showed in his analysis of primitive religions (Durkheim, 1947). Durkheim noted that people in a locality believed they were related to some totem, which was usually an animal but was occasionally a natural object as well. All members of a common group were identified by their shared symbol, which they displayed by the emblem of their totem. This identification with an animal, bird, or other object is common in institutions of higher learning where students, former students, faculty members, and others who identify with the local academic community display similar colors, wave banners, wear special clothing and jewelry, and chant or sing together. These behaviors usually center around athletic contests. Janet Lever (1983, p. 12) connects these activities with totemism: "Team worship, like animal worship, makes all participants intensely aware of their own group membership. By accepting that a particular team represents them symbolically, people enjoy ritual kinship based on a common bond. Their emblem, be it an insignia or a lapel pin or a scarf with team colors, distinguishes fellow fans from both strangers and enemies."

A school nickname is much more than a tag or a label. It conveys, symbolically as Durkheim posits, the characteristics and attributes that define the institution. In an important way, the school's symbols represent the institution's self-concept. Schools may have names that signify the school's ethnic heritage (e.g., the Bethany College Swedes), state history (University of Oklahoma Sooners), mission (U.S. Military Academy at West Point Cadets), religion (Oklahoma Baptist College Prophets), or founder (Whittier College Poets). Most schools, though, use symbols of aggression and ferocity (e.g., birds such as hawks, animals such as bulldogs, human categories such as pirates, and even the otherworldly such as devils) (see Fuller and Manning, 1987).

While school names tend to evoke strong emotions of solidarity among followers, there is also a potential dark side. The names chosen by some schools are demeaning or derogatory to some groups. In the past two decades or so, Native American activists have raised serious objections to the use of Indians as school names or mascots because their use typically distorts Native American traditions and reinforces negative stereotypes about them by depicting them as savages, scalpers, and the like. A few colleges (e.g., Stanford and Dartmouth) have taken these objections seriously and deleted Indian names and mascots. Most schools using some form of reference to Indians, however, have chosen to continue that practice despite the objections of Native Americans. In fact, Indian or some derivative is a popular name for athletic teams. Of the 1,251 four-year schools reported by Franks (1982), some 21 used Indian, 13 were Warriors, 7 were Chiefs, 6 were Redmen, 5 were Braves, 2 were Redskins, and individual schools were Nanooks, Chippewas, Hurons, Seminoles, Choctaws, Mohawks, Sioux, Utes, Aztecs, Savages, Tribe, and Raiders. Ironically though, Native Americans is the only racial/ethnic category used by schools where they are not a significant part of the student body or heritage of the school. Yet the members of schools and their constituencies insist on retaining their Native American names because these are part of their collective identities. This allegiance to their school symbol is more important, apparently, than an insensitivity to the negative consequences evoked from the appropriation and depiction of Native Americans.

The purpose of this chapter is to explore another area of potential concern by an oppressed group—women—over the names given their teams. The naming of women's teams raises parallel questions to the issues raised by Native Americans. Are the names given to university and college women's sport teams fair to women in general and women athletes in particular, or do they belittle them, diminish them, and reinforce negative images of women and their secondary status?

THEORETICAL BACKGROUND: LANGUAGE AND GENDER

Gender differentiation in language has been extensively documented and analyzed. An expanding body of literature reveals that language reflects and helps maintain the secondary status of women by defining them and their place (Henley, 1987, p. 3). This is because "every language reflects the prejudices of the society in which it evolved" (Miller and Swift, 1980, p. 3). Language places women and men within a system of differentiation and stratification. Language suggests how women and men are to be evaluated. Language embodies negative and positive value stances and valuations related to how certain groups within society are apprised (Van Den Bergh, 1987, p. 132). Language in general is filled with biases about women and men. Specific linguistic conventions are sexist when they isolate or stereotype some aspect of an individual's nature or the nature of a group of individuals based on their sex.

Many studies have pointed to the varied ways in which language acts in the defining, deprecation, and exclusion of women in areas of the social structure (Thorne, Kramarae, and Henley, 1985, p, 3). Our intent is to add to the literature by showing how the linguistic marking systems adopted by many college and university teams promote male supremacy and female subordination.

Names are symbols of identity as well as being essential for the construction of reality. Objects, events, and feelings must be named in order to make sense of the world. But naming is not a neutral process. Naming is an application of principles already in use, an extension of existing rules (Spender, 1980, p. 163). Patriarchy has shaped words, names, and labels for women and men, their personality traits, expressions of emotion, behaviors, and occupations. Names are badges of femininity and masculinity, hence of inferiority and superiority. Richardson (1981, p. 46) has summarized the subconscious rules governing the name preference in middle-class America:

> Male names tend to be short, hard-hitting, and explosive (e.g., Bret, Lance, Mark, Craig, Bruce, etc.). Even when the given name is multisyllabic (e.g., Benjamin, Joshua, William, Thomas), the nickname tends to imply hardness and energy (e.g., Ben, Josh, Bill, Tom, etc.). Female names, on the other hand, are longer, more melodic, and softer (e.g., Deborah, Caroline, Jessica, Christina) and easily succumb to the diminutive "ie" ending form (e.g., Debbie, Carrie, Jessie, Christie). And although feminization of male names (e.g., Fredricka, Roberta, Alexandra) is not uncommon, the inverse rarely occurs.

While naming is an important manifestation of gender differentiation, little research exists on naming conventions other than those associated with gender and given names. Only one study (Fuller and Manning, 1987) examines the naming practices of college sport teams, but it focuses narrowly on the sexism emanating from the violence commonly attributed to these symbols. Because of their emphasis Fuller and Manning considered only three sexist naming practices. The study presented here builds on the insights of Fuller and Manning by looking at eight sexist naming categories. The goal is to show that the naming traditions of sports teams can unwittingly promote the ideology of male superiority and sexual difference.

Our argument is that the names of many women's and men's athletic teams reinforce a basic element of social structure—that of gender division. Team names reflect this division as well as the asymmetry that is associated with it. Even after women's advances in sport since the implementation of Title IX, widespread naming practices continue to mark female athletes as unusual, aberrant, or invisible.

DATA AND METHODS

The data source on the names and mascots of sports teams at 4-year colleges and universities was Franks (1982). This book provides the required information plus a history of how the names were selected for 1,251 schools. Since our research focused on comparing the names for men's and women's teams, those schools limited to one sex were not considered. Also, schools now defunct were omitted from the present analysis. This was determined by eliminating those schools not listed in the latest edition of *American Universities and Colleges* (American Council of Education, 1987). Thus the number of schools in the present study was 1,185.

The decision on whether a school had sexist names for its teams was based on whether the team names violated the rules of gender neutrality. A review of the literature on language and gender revealed a number of gender-linked practices that diminish and trivialize women (Henley, 1987; Lakoff, 1975; Miller and Swift, 1980; Schulz, 1975; Spender, 1980).

1. Physical markers: One common naming practice emphasizes the physical appearance of women ("belle"). As Miller and Swift (1980, p. 87) argue, this practice is sexist because the "emphasis on the physical characteristics of women is offensive in contexts where men are described in terms of achievement."

2. Girl or gal: The use of "girl" or "gal" stresses the presumed immaturity and irresponsibility of women. "Just as *boy* can be blatantly offensive to minority men, so *girl* can have comparable patronizing and demeaning implications for women" (Miller and Swift, 1980, p. 71).

3. Feminine suffixes: This is a popular form of gender differentiation found in the names of athletic, social, and women's groups. The practice not only marks women but it denotes a feminine derivative by establishing a "female

negative trivial category" (Miller and Swift, 1977, p. 58). The devaluation is accomplished by tagging words with feminine suffixes such as "ette" or "esse."

4. Lady: This label has several meanings that demean women athletes. Often "lady" is used to indicate women in roles thought to be unusual, if not unfortunate (Baron, 1986, p. 114). Lady is used to "evoke a standard of propriety, correct behavior, and elegance" (Miller and Swift, 1977, p. 72), characteristics decidedly unathletic. Similarly, lady carries overtones recalling the age of chivalry. "This makes the term seem polite at first, but we must also remember that these implications are perilous: they suggest that a 'lady' is helpless, and cannot do things for herself" (Lakoff, 1975, p. 25).

5. Male as a false generic: This practice assumes that the masculine in language, word, or name choice is the norm while the feminine is ignored altogether. Miller and Swift (1980, p. 9) define this procedure as, "Terms used of a class or group that are not applicable to all members." The use of "mankind" to encompass both sexes has its parallel among athletic teams where both men's and women's teams are the Rams, Stags, or Steers. Dale Spender (1980, p. 3) has called this treatment of the masculine as the norm as "one of the most pervasive and pernicious rules that has been encoded."

6. Male name with a female modifier: This practice applies the feminine to a name that usually denotes a male. This gives females lower status because it indicates inferior quality (Baron, 1986, p. 112). Examples among sports teams are the Lady Friars, Lady Rams, and Lady Gamecocks. Using such oxymorons "reflects role conflict and contributes to the lack of acceptance of women's sport" (Fuller and Manning, 1987, p. 64).

7. Double gender marking: This occurs when the name for the women's team is a diminutive of the men's team name and adding "belle" or "lady" or other feminine modifier. For example, the men's teams at Mississippi College are known as the Choctaws, while the women's teams are designated as the Lady Chocs. At the University of Kentucky the men's teams are the Wildcats and the women's teams are the Lady Kats. By compounding the feminine, the practice intensifies women's secondary status. Double gender marking occurs "perhaps to underline the inappropriateness or rarity of the feminine noun or to emphasize its negativity" (Baron, 1986, p. 115).

8. Male-female-paired polarity: Women's and men's teams can be assigned names that represent a female/male opposition. When this occurs, the names for the men's teams always are positive in that they embody competitive and other traits associated with sport while the names for women's teams are lighthearted or cute. The essence of sports is competition in which physical skills largely determine outcomes. Successful athletes are believed to embody such traits as courage, bravura, boldness, self-confidence, and aggression. When the names given men's teams imply these traits but the names for women's teams suggest that women are playful and cuddly, then women are trivialized and de-athleticized. Some egregious examples of this practice are:

Fighting Scots/Scotties, Blue Hawks/Blue Chicks, Bears/Teddy Bears, and Wildcats/Wildkittens.

Although these eight categories make meaningful distinctions, they are not mutually exclusive. The problem arises with teams using the term lady. They might be coded under "lady" (Lady Threshers), or "male name with a female modifier" (Lady Rams), or "double gender marking" (Lady Kats). Since team names of all three types could be subsumed under the "lady" category, we opted to separate those with lady that could be included in another category. In other words, the category "lady" includes only those teams that could not be placed in either of the other two categories.

FINDINGS

The extent and type of symbolic derogation of women's teams were examined in several ways. We found, first, that of the 1,185 four-year schools in the sample, 451 (38.1 percent) had sexist names for their athletic teams. Examining only team logos (903 schools, or 76 percent of the sample, provided these data), 45.1 percent were sexist. For those schools with complete information on both names and logos, 493 of the 903 (54.6 percent) were sexist on one or both. We found that many schools have contradictory symbols, perhaps having a gender-neutral name for both male and female teams (Bears, Tigers) but then having a logo for both teams that was clearly having stereotypical and therefore unathletic characteristics. The important finding here is that when team names and logos are considered, more than half of the colleges and universities trivialize women's teams and women athletes.

The data on names were analyzed by the mode of discrimination, using the naming practices elaborated in the previous section (see Table 12-1). This analysis reveals, first, that over half the cases (55.0 percent) fall into the category of using a male name as a false generic. This usage contributes to the invisibility of women's teams. The next popular type of sexism in naming is the use of "lady" (25.3 percent) in Table 12-1, but actually 30.8 percent since some of the teams using lady are classified in what we considered more meaningful categories (see second footnote under Table 12-1). This popular usage clearly de-athleticizes women by implying their fragility, elegance, and propriety. This is also the consequence of the use of the feminine suffix (6.4 percent). Another 5.8 percent of the schools with sexist naming patterns use the male/female paired polarity where male teams have names with clear referents to stereotypically masculine traits while the names for women's teams denote presumed feminine traits that are clearly unathletic. The other important category was the use of a male name with a female modifier (4.7 percent). This naming practice clearly implies that men are more important than women; men are represented by nouns whereas women are represented by adjectives. Few schools use the other linguistic categories (physical markers, girl or gal, and double gender marking).

The next question addressed was whether the institutions that diminished women through team naming were clustered among certain types of schools or in

Table 12-1 Naming Practices That De-Athleticize Women's Teams

Naming Practices	N	%	Examples
Physical markers	2	0.4	Belles, Rambelles
Girl or Gal[a]	1	0.2	Green Gals
Feminine suffix	29	6.4	Tigerettes, Duchesses
Lady[b]	114	25.3	Lady Jets, Lady Eagles
Male as false generic	248	55.0	Cowboys, Hokies, Tomcats
Male name with female modifier	21	4.7	Lady Rams, Lady Centaurs, Lady Dons
Double gender marking	10	2.2	Choctaws/Lady Chocs, Jaguars/Lady Jags
Male-/Female-paired polarity	26	5.8	Panthers/Pink Panthers, Bears/Teddy Bears
Totals	451	100.0	

[a]Several female teams were designated as Cowgirls but they were not included if the male teams were Cowboys. We assumed this difference to be nonsexist.

[b]Actually 139 of the 451 schools (30.8%) used Lady, but we placed 25 of them in other, more meaningful categories.

a particular geographical region. We thought perhaps that religious schools might be more likely to employ traditional notions about women than public schools or private secular schools (see Table 12-2). The data show that while religious colleges and universities are slightly more likely to have sexist naming practices than public or independent schools, the differences were not statistically significant.

We also controlled for region of the country, assuming that southern schools might be less likely than schools in other regions of the United States to be progressive about gender matters (see Table 12-3). The data show that the differences between schools in the South and the non-South are indeed statistically different, with Southern schools more likely to use sexist names for their athletic teams. Table 12-4 analyzes these data by type of discrimination. Three interesting and statistically significant

Table 12-2 Prevalence of Sexist Team Names by Type of School

Naming Practice	PUBLIC[a]		INDEPENDENT		RELIGIOUS	
	N	%	N	%	N	%
Nonsexist	289	64.7	135	63.4	310	59.0
Sexist	158	35.3	78	36.6	215	41.0
Totals	447	100.0	213	100.0	525	100.0

$\chi^2 = 3.45$, $df = 2$, not significant.

[a]The determination of public, independent, or religious was provided in the description of each school in American Council of Education (1987).

Table 12-3 Prevalence of Sexist Team Names by Region

Naming Practice	NON-SOUTH		SOUTH[a]	
	N	*%*	*N*	*%*
Nonsexist	500	65.4	264	34.6
Sexist	264	34.6	187	44.4
Totals	764	100.0	451	100.0

$\chi^2 = 10.79$, corrected for continuity *df = 1, p < .001.*

[a]Included in the South are schools from Missouri, Arkansas, Virginia, West Virginia, Mississippi, Maryland, Texas, Oklahoma, Louisiana, Alabama, Georgia, Kentucky, Tennessee, North Carolina, South Carolina, Florida, and the District of Columbia.

Table 12-4 Naming Practices That De-Athleticize Women's Teams by Region

Naming Practices	NON-SOUTH		SOUTH		*Level of Significance*
	N	*%*	*N*	*%*	
Physical markers	0	0.0	2	100.0	n.s.
Girl or Gal	0	0.0	1	100.0	n.s.
Feminine suffix	10	34.4	19	65.6	p < .025
Lady	47	41.2	67	58.8	p < .001
Male as false generic	173	70.0	75	30.0	p < .001
Male name with female modifier	14	66.7	7	33.3	n.s.
Double gender marking	5	50.0	5	50.0	n.s.
Male-/Female-paired polarity	15	58.0	11	42.0	n.s.
Totals	264	58.5	187	41.0	

differences are found. Southern schools are much more likely than non-Southern schools to incorporate feminine suffixes and use lady in their naming of female teams. Both of these naming practices emphasize traditional notions of femininity. The other difference in this table is in the opposite direction—non-Southern schools are more likely to use male names as a false generic than are Southern schools. This naming practice ignores women's teams. Southern schools on the other hand, with their disproportionate use of feminine suffixes and lady, call attention to their women's teams but emphasize their femininity rather than their athleticism.

DISCUSSION

This research has shown that approximately three-eighths of American colleges and universities employ sexist names and over half have sexist names and/or logos for their athletic teams. This means that the identity symbols for athletic teams contribute to the maintenance of male dominance within college athletics. As Polk (1974) has noted in an article on the sources of male power, since men have shaped society's institutions they tend to fit the value structure of such institutions. Nowhere is this more apparent than in sport. Since the traditional masculine gender role matches most athletic qualities better than the traditional feminine gender role, the images and symbols are male. Women do not fit in this scheme. They are "others" even when they do participate. Their team names and logos tend to perpetuate and strengthen the image of female inferiority by making them either invisible or trivial or consistently nonathletic.

Institutional sexism is deeply entrenched in college sports. The mere changing of sexist names and logos to nonsexist ones will not alter this structural inequality, but it is nevertheless important. As institutional barriers to women's participation in athletics are removed, negative linguistic and symbolic imagery must be replaced with names and images that reflect the new visions of women and men in their expanding and changing roles.

In the past decade the right of women to rename or relabel themselves and their experiences has become a tool of empowerment. For feminists, changing labels to reflect the collective redefinition of what it means to be female has been one way to gain power. As Van Den Bergh (1987) explains, renaming can create changes for the powerless group as well as promoting change in social organization. Renaming gives women a sense of control of their own identity and raises consciousness within their group and that of those in power. Because language is intimately intertwined with the distribution of power in society, the principle of renaming can be an important way of changing reality.

Since language has a large impact on people's values and their conceptions of women's and men's rightful place in the social order, the pervasive acceptance of gender marking in the names of collegiate athletic teams is not a trivial matter. Athletes, whether women or men, need names that convey their self-confidence, their strength, their worth, and their power.

REFERENCES

American Council of Education. 1987. *American Universities and Colleges,* 14th ed. New York: de Gruyter.

Baron, D. 1986. *Grammar and Gender.* New Haven, CT: Yale University Press.

Bryson, L. 1987. "Sport and the Maintenance of Masculine Hegemony." *Women's Studies International Forum* 10: 349–360.

Durkheim, E. 1947. *The Elementary Forms of Religious Life,* trans. J. W. Sivain. New York: Free Press.

Franks, R. 1982. *What's in a Nickname? Exploring the Jungle of College Athletic Mascots.* Amarillo, TX: Ray Franks.

Fuller, J. R., and E. A. Manning. 1987. "Violence and Sexism in College Mascots and Symbols: A Typology." *Free Inquiry in Creative Sociology* 15: 61–64.

Hall, M. A. 1984. "Feminist Prospects for the Sociology of Sport." *Arena Review* 8: 1–9.

————. 1985. "Knowledge and Gender: Epistemological Questions in the Social Analysis of Sport." *Sociology of Sport Journal,* 25–42.

Henley, N. M. 1987. "This New Species That Seeks a New Language: On Sexism in Language and Language Change." Pp. 3–27 in J. Penfield, ed., *Women and Language in Transition.* Albany: State University of New York Press.

Lakoff, R. 1975. *Language and Woman's Place.* New York: Harper and Row.

Lever, J. 1983. *Soccer Madness.* Chicago: University of Chicago Press.

Miller, C., and Swift, K. 1977. *Words and Women: New Language in New Times.* Garden City, NY: Doubleday/Anchor.

Miller, C., and Swift, K. 1980. *The Handbook of Nonsexist Writing.* New York: Lippincott and Crowell.

Polk, B. B. 1974. "Male Power and the Women's Movement." *Journal of Applied Behavioral Sciences* 10, no. 3: 415–431.

Richardson, L. W. 1981. *The Dynamics of Sex and Gender,* 2nd ed. Boston: Houghton Mifflin.

Schulz, M. 1975. "The Semantic Derogation of Women." Pp. 64–75 in B. Thorne and N. Henley, eds., *Language and Sex: Difference and Dominance.* Rowley, MA: Newbury House.

Spender, D. 1980. *Man-Made Language.* London: Routledge and Kegan Paul.

Thorne, B., C. Kramarae, and N. Henley. 1985. "Language, Gender, and Society: Opening a Second Decade of Research." Pp. 7–24 in B. Thorne and N. Henley, eds., *Language, Gender, and Society.* Rowley, MA: Newbury House.

Van Den Bergh, N. 1987. "Renaming: Vehicle for Empowerment." Pp. 130–136 in J. Penfield, ed., *Women and Language and Transition.* Albany: State University of New York Press.

✳ FOR FURTHER STUDY ✳

Charmaz, Kathy. 2006. "The Power of Names." *Journal of Contemporary Ethnography* 35: 396–399.

Churchill, Ward. 1993. "Crimes against Humanity." *Z Magazine* 6: 43–47.

Davis-Delano, Laurel. 2007. "Eliminating Native American Mascots: Ingredients for Success." *Journal of Sport and Social Issues* 31 (4): 340–373.

Eitzen, D. Stanley. 2009. *Fair and Foul: Beyond the Myths and Paradoxes of Sport.* 4th ed. Lanham, MD: Rowman and Littlefield.

King, C. Richard. 2004. "Reclaiming Indianness: Critical Perspectives on Native American Mascots." *Journal of Sport and Social Issues* 28 (February): entire issue.

King, C. Richard, and C. F. Springwood, eds. 2001. *Team Spirits: The Native American Mascots Controversy.* Lincoln: University of Nebraska Press/Bison Books.

King, C. Richard, Ellen J. Staurowsky, Lawrence Baca, Laurel R. Davis, and Cornel Pewewardy. 2002. "Of Polls and Race Prejudice: *Sports Illustrated*'s Errant 'Indian Wars.'" *Journal of Sport and Social Issues* 26 (November): 381–402.

Pelak, Cynthia Fabrizio. 2008. "The Relationship between Sexist Naming Practices and Athletic Opportunities at Colleges and Universities in the Southern United States." *Sociology of Education* 81 (April): 189–210.

Staurowsky, Ellen J. 2000. "The Cleveland 'Indians': A Case Study in American Indian Cultural Dispossession." *Sociology of Sport Journal* 17 (4): 307–330.

Van Den Bergh, Nan. 1987. "Renaming: Vehicle for Empowerment." Pp. 130–136 in Joyce Penfield, ed., *Women and Language in Transition.* Albany: State University of New York Press.

PART FIVE

Problems of Excess: Overzealous Athletes, Parents, and Coaches

This section examines some forms of deviance in sport. One manifestation of this—positive deviance—is by the athletes. We usually think of deviance as the rejection of commonly accepted norms and expectations for behavior. Positive deviance, however, results from the overacceptance of and overconformity to norms and expectations.[1] Athletes may pursue goals in sports with such zeal that it undermines family relationships and work responsibilities. Athletes may harm themselves as they use drugs to become bigger, faster, and stronger. They may starve themselves to meet weight requirements. They may injure themselves by overtraining.

The first chapter, by journalist Joan Ryan, shows how positive deviance by the athletes combined with incredibly demanding coaches and ambitious parents results, sometimes, in damaged bodies and psyches of young female elite gymnasts and ice skaters.

The second chapter, by *Los Angeles Times* writer Mike Bresnahan, describes the intrusion of the corporate world, in this case Nike, into high school sports.

The third chapter, by journalist John Feinstein, describes the coaching style of legendary basketball coach Bob Knight. This style is authoritarian. The athletes are under his total command. When they fall short of his expectations, they incur his wrath. His demanding ways have led to winning games. He is successful, but at what cost?

NOTE

1. Jay J. Coakley, *Sport in Society: Issues and Controversies,* 6th ed. (New York: McGraw-Hill. 1998), chap. 6.

13

Female Gymnasts and Ice Skaters
The Dark Side

Joan Ryan

Unlike women's tennis, a sport in which teenage girls rise to the highest echelon year after year in highly televised championships, gymnastics and figure skating flutter across our screens as ephemerally as butterflies. We know about tennis burnout, about Tracy Austin, Andrea Jaeger, Mary Pierce, and, more recently, about Jennifer Capriati, who turned pro with $5 million in endorsement contracts at age thirteen and ended up four years later in a Florida motel room, blank-eyed and disheveled, sharing drugs with runaways. But we hear precious little about the young female gymnasts and figure skaters who perform magnificent feats of physical strength and agility, and even less about their casualties. How do the extraordinary demands of their training shape these young girls? What price do their bodies and psyches pay?

I set out to answer some of these questions during three months of research for an article that ran in the *San Francisco Examiner,* but when I finished I couldn't close my notebook. I took a year's leave to continue my research, focusing this time on the girls who never made it, not just on the champions.

What I found was a story about legal, even celebrated, child abuse. In the dark troughs along the road to the Olympics lay the bodies of the girls who stumbled on the way, broken by the work, pressure, and humiliation. I found a girl whose father left the family when she quit gymnastics at age thirteen, who scraped her arms and

Source: Excerpted from *Little Girls in Pretty Boxes,* by Joan Ryan, pp. 3–15. Copyright © 1996 by Joan Ryan. Used by permission of Doubleday, a division of Random House, Inc.

legs with razors to dull her emotional pain, and who needed a two-hour pass from a psychiatric hospital to attend her high school graduation. Girls who broke their necks and backs. One who so desperately sought the perfect, weightless gymnastics body that she starved herself to death. Others-many-who became so obsessive about controlling their weight that they lost control of themselves instead, falling into the potentially fatal cycle of bingeing on food, then purging by vomiting or taking laxatives. One who was sexually abused by her coach and one who was sodomized for four years by the father of a teammate. I found a girl who felt such shame at not making the Olympic team that she slit her wrists. A skater who underwent plastic surgery when a judge said her nose was distracting. A father who handed custody of his daughter over to her coach so she could keep skating. A coach who fed his gymnasts so little that federation officials had to smuggle food into their hotel rooms. A mother who hid her child's chicken pox with makeup so she could compete. Coaches who motivated their athletes by calling them imbeciles, idiots, pigs, cows.

I am not suggesting that gymnastics and figure skating in and of themselves are destructive. On the contrary, both sports are potentially wonderful and enriching, providing an arena of competition in which the average child can develop a sense of mastery, self-esteem, and healthy athleticism. But this chapter isn't about recreational sports or the average child. It's about the elite child athlete and the American obsession with winning that has produced a training environment wherein results are bought at any cost, no matter how devastating. It's about how our cultural fixation on beauty and weight and youth has shaped both sports and driven the athletes into a sphere beyond the quest for physical performance.

The well-known story of Tonya Harding and Nancy Kerrigan did not happen in a vacuum; it symbolizes perfectly the stakes now involved in elite competition—itself a reflection of our national character. We created Tonya and Nancy not only by our hunger for winning but by our criterion for winning, an exaggeration of the code that applies to ambitious young women everywhere: Talent counts, but so do beauty, class, weight, clothes, and politics. The anachronistic lack of ambivalence about femininity in both sports is part of their attraction, hearkening back to a simpler time when girls were girls, when women were girls for that matter: coquettish, malleable, eager to please. In figure skating especially, we want our athletes thin, graceful, deferential, and cover-girl pretty. We want eyeliner, lipstick, and hair ribbons. Makeup artists are fixtures backstage at figure-skating competitions, primping and polishing. In figure skating, costumes can actually affect a score. They are so important that skaters spend $1500 and up on one dress—more than they spend on their skates. Nancy Kerrigan's dresses by designer Vera Wang cost upward of $5000 each.

Indeed, the costumes fueled the national fairy tale of Tonya and Nancy. Nancy wore virginal white. She was the perfect heroine, a good girl with perfect white teeth, a 24-inch waist, and a smile that suggested both pluck and vulnerability. She remained safely within skating's pristine circle of grace and femininity. Tonya, on the other hand, crossed all the lines. She wore bordello red-and-gold. She was the perfect villainess, a bad girl with truck stop manners, a racy past, and chunky thighs. When she became convinced Nancy's grace would always win out over her own explosive strength, Tonya crossed the final line, helping to eliminate Nancy from competition. The media frenzy tapped into our own inner wranglings about the good-girl/bad-girl paradox, about how women should behave, about how they should look and what they should say. The story touched a cultural nerve about women crossing societal boundaries—of power, achievement, violence, taste, appearance—and being ensnared by them. In the end, both skaters were trapped, Tonya by her ambition and Nancy by the good-girl image she created for the ice—an image she couldn't live up to. The public turned on Nancy when foolish comments and graceless interviews made it clear she wasn't Snow White after all.

Both sports embody the contradiction of modern womanhood. Society has allowed women to aspire higher, but to do so a woman must often reject that which makes her female, including motherhood. Similarly, gymnastics and figure skating remove the limits of a girl's body, teaching it to soar beyond what seems possible. Yet they also imprison it, binding it like the tiny Victorian waist or the Chinese woman's foot. The girls aren't allowed passage into adulthood. To survive in the sports, they beat back puberty, desperate to stay small and thin, refusing to let their bodies grow up. In this way the sports pervert the very femininity they hold so dear. The physical skills have become so demanding that only a body shaped like a missile—in other words, a body shaped like a boy's—can excel. Breasts and hips slow the spins, lower the leaps, and disrupt the clean, lean body lines that judges reward. "Women's gymnastics" and "ladies' figure skating" are misnomers today. Once the athletes become women, their elite careers wither.

In the meantime, their childhoods are gone. But they trade more than their childhoods for a shot at glory. They risk serious physical and psychological problems that can linger long after the public has turned its attention to the next phenom in pigtails. The intensive training and pressure heaped on by coaches, parents, and federation officials—the very people who should be protecting the children—often result in eating disorders, weakened bones, stunted growth, debilitating injuries, and damaged psyches. In the last six years two U.S. Olympic hopefuls have died as a result of their participation in elite gymnastics.

Because they excel at such a young age, girls in these sports are unlike other elite athletes. They are world champions before they can drive. They are the Michael Jordans and Joe Montanas of their sports before they learn algebra. Unlike male athletes their age, who are playing quarterback in high school or running track for the local club, these girls are competing on a worldwide stage. If an elite gymnast or figure skater fails, she fails globally. She sees her mistake replayed in slow motion on TV and captured in bold headlines in the newspaper. Adult reporters crowd around, asking what she has to say to a country that had hung its hopes on her thin shoulders. Tiffany Chin was seventeen when she entered the 1985 U.S. Figure Skating Championships as the favorite. She was asked at the time how she would feel if she didn't win. She paused, as if trying not to consider the possibility. "Devastated," she said quietly. "I don't know. I'd probably die."

Chin recalled recently that when she did win, "I didn't feel happiness. I felt relief. Which was disappointing." Three months before the 1988 Olympics, Chin retired when her legs began to break down. Some, however, say she left because she could no longer tolerate the pressure and unrelenting drive of her stern mother. "I feel I'm lucky to have gotten through it," she said of skating. "I don't think many people are that lucky. There's a tremendous strain on people who don't make it. The money, the sacrifices, the time. I know people emotionally damaged by it. I've seen nervous breakdowns, psychological imbalances."

An elite gymnast or figure skater knows she takes more than her own ambitions into a competition. Her parents have invested tens of thousands of dollars in her training, sometimes hundreds of thousands. Her coach's reputation rides on her performance. And she knows she might have only one shot. By the next Olympics she might be too old. By the next year she might be too old. Girls in these sports are under pressure not only to win but to win quickly. They're running against a clock that eventually marks the lives of all women, warning them they'd better hurry up and get married and have children before it's too late. These girls hear the clock early. They're racing against puberty.

Boys, on the other hand, welcome the changes that puberty brings. They reach their athletic peak after puberty when their bodies grow and their muscles strengthen. In recent years Michael Chang and Boris Becker won the French Open and Wimbledon tennis titles, respectively, before age eighteen, but in virtually every male sport the top athletes are men, not boys. Male gymnastics and figure-skating champions are usually in their early to mid-twenties; female champions are usually fourteen to seventeen years old in gymnastics and sixteen to early twenties in figure skating.

In staving off puberty to maintain the "ideal" body shape, girls risk their health in ways their male counterparts never do. They starve themselves, for one, often in response to their coaches' belittling insults about their bodies. Starving shuts down the menstrual cycle—the starving body knows it cannot support a fetus—and thus blocks the onset of puberty. It's a dangerous strategy to save a career. If a girl isn't menstruating, she isn't producing estrogen. Without estrogen, her bones weaken. She risks stunting her growth. She risks premature osteoporosis. She risks fractures in all bones, including her vertebrae, and she risks curvature of the spine. In several studies over the last decade, young female athletes who didn't menstruate were found to have the bone densities of postmenopausal women in their fifties, sixties, and seventies. Most elite gymnasts don't begin to menstruate until they retire. Kathy Johnson, a medalist in the 1984 Olympics, didn't begin until she quit the sport at age twenty-five.

Our national obsession with weight, our glorification of thinness, has gone completely unchecked in gymnastics and figure skating. The cultural forces that have produced extravagantly bony fashion models have taken their toll on gymnasts and skaters already insecure about their bodies. Not surprisingly, eating disorders are common in both sports, and in gymnastics they're rampant. Studies of female college gymnasts show that most practice some kind of disordered eating. In a 1994 University of Utah study of elite gymnasts—those training for the Olympics—59 percent admitted to some form of disordered eating. And in interviewing elites for this book, I found only a handful who had not tried starving, throwing up, or taking laxatives or diuretics to control their weight. Several left the sport because of eating disorders. One died. Eating disorders among male athletes, as in the general male population, are virtually unknown.

"Everyone goes through it, but nobody talks about it, because they're embarrassed," gymnast Kristie Phillips told me. "But I don't put the fault on us. It's the pressures that are put on us to be so skinny. It's mental cruelty. It's not fair that all these pressures are put on us at such a young age and we don't realize it until we get older and we suffer from it."

Phillips took laxatives, thyroid pills, and diuretics to lose weight. She had been the hottest gymnast in the mid-1980s, the heir apparent to 1984 Olympic superstar Mary Lou Retton. But she not only didn't win a medal at the 1988 Summer Games, she didn't even make the U.S. team. She left the sport feeling like a failure. She gained weight, then became bulimic, caught in a cycle of bingeing and vomiting. Distraught, she took scissors to her wrists in a botched attempt to kill herself. "I weighed ninety-eight pounds and I was being called [by her coach] an overstuffed Christmas turkey," Phillips said in our interview. "I was told I was never going to make it in life because I was going to be fat. I mean, in *life*. Things I'll never forget."

Much of the direct blame for the young athletes' problems falls on the coaches and parents. Obviously, no parent wakes up in the morning and plots how to ruin his or her child's life. But the money, the fame, and the promise of great achievement can turn a parent's head. Ambition gets perverted. The boundaries of parents and coaches bloat and mutate, with the parent becoming the ruthless coach and coach becoming the controlling parent. One father put gymnastics equipment in his living room and for every mistake his daughter made at the gym she had to repeat the skill hundreds of times at home. He moved the girl to three gyms around the country, pushing her in the sport she came to loathe. He said he did it because he wanted the best for her.

Coaches push because they are paid to produce great gymnasts. They are relentless about weight because physically round gymnasts and skaters don't win. Coaches are intolerant of injuries because in the race against puberty, time off is death. Their job is not to turn out happy, well-adjusted young women; it is to turn out champions. If they scream, belittle, or ignore, if they prod an injured girl to forget her pain, if they push her to drop out of school, they are only doing what the parents have paid them to do. So sorting out the blame when a girl falls apart is a messy proposition; everyone claims he was just doing his job.

The sports' national governing bodies, for their part, are mostly impotent. They try to do well by the athletes, but they, too, often lose their way in a tangle of ambition and politics. They're like small-town governments: personal, despotic, paternalistic, and absolutely without teeth. The federations do not have the power that the commissioners' offices in professional baseball, football, and basketball do. They cannot revoke a coach's or an athlete's membership for anything less than criminal activity. (Tonya Harding was charged and sentenced by the courts before the United States Figure Skating Association expelled her.) They cannot fine or suspend a coach whose athletes regularly leave the sport on stretchers.

There simply is no safety net protecting these children. Not the parents, the coaches, or the federations.

Child labor laws prohibit a thirteen-year-old from punching a cash register for forty hours a week, but that same child can labor for forty hours or more inside a gym or an ice skating rink without drawing the slightest glance from the government. The U.S. government requires the licensing of plumbers. It demands that even the tiniest coffee shop adhere to a fastidious health code. It scrutinizes the advertising claims on packages of low-fat snack food. But it never asks a coach, who holds the lives of his young pupils in his hands, to pass a minimum safety and skills test. Coaches in this country need no license to train children, even in a high-injury sport like elite gymnastics. The government that forbids a child from buying a pack of cigarettes because of health concerns never checks on the child athlete who trains until her hands bleed or her knees buckle, who stops eating to achieve the perfect body, who takes eight Advils a day and offers herself up for another shot of cortisone to dull the pain, who drinks a bottle of Ex-Lax because her coach is going to weigh her in the morning. The government never takes a look inside the gym or the rink to make sure these children are not being exploited or abused or worked too hard. Even college athletes—virtually all of whom are adults—are restricted by the NCAA to just twenty hours per week of formal training. But no laws, no agencies, put limits on the number of hours a child can train or the methods a coach can use.

Some argue that extraordinary children should be allowed to follow extraordinary paths to realize their potential. They argue that a child's wants are no less important than an adult's and thus she should not be denied her dreams just because she is still a child. If pursuing her dream means training eight hours a day in a gym, withstanding abusive language, and tolerating great pain, and if the child wants to do it and the parents believe it will build character, why not let her? Who are we to tell a child what she can and cannot do with her life?

In fact, we tell children all the time what they can and cannot do with their lives. Restricting children from certain activities is hardly a revolutionary concept. Laws prohibit children from driving before sixteen and drinking before twenty-one. They prohibit children from dropping out of school before fifteen and working full-time before sixteen. In our society we put great value on protecting our children from physical harm and exploitation, and sometimes that means protecting them from their own poor judgment and their parents' poor judgment. No one questions the wisdom of the government in forbidding a child to work full-time, so why is it all right for her to train full-time with no rules to ensure her well-being? Child labor laws should address all labor, even that which is technically nonpaid, though top gymnasts and figure skaters *do* labor for money.

In recent years the federations have begun to pay their top athletes a stipend based on their competition results. The girls can earn bonuses by representing the United States in certain designated events. Skaters who compete in the World Figure Skating Championships and the Olympic Games, for example, receive $15,000. They earn lesser amounts for international competitions such as Skate America. They also earn money from corporate sponsors and exhibitions. The money might not cover much more than their training expenses, which can run $75,000 for a top skater and $20,000 to $30,000 per year for a top gymnast, but it's money—money that is paid specifically for the work the athletes do in the gym and the skating rink.

The real payoff for their hard work, however, waits at the end of the road. That's what the parents and athletes hope anyway. When Mary Lou Retton made millions on Madison Avenue after winning the gold medal at the 1984 Olympics, she changed gymnastics forever. "Kids have agents now before they even make it into their teens," Retton says. Now the dream is no longer just about medals but about Wheaties boxes and appearance fees, about paying off mom and dad's home equity loans, and trading in the Toyota for a Mercedes. It doesn't seem to matter that only six girls every four years reach the Olympics and that winning the gold once they get there is the longest of long shots. Even world champion Shannon Miller didn't win the all-around Olympic gold in 1992.

Figure skating, even more than gymnastics, blinds parents and athletes with the glittering possibilities, and for good reason. Peggy Fleming and Dorothy Hamill are still living off gold medals won decades ago. Nancy Kerrigan landed endorsements with Reebok, Evian, Seiko, and Campbell's soup with only a bronze medal in 1992. With glamorous and feminine stars like Kerrigan and Kristi Yamaguchi to lead the way, the United States Figure Skating Association has seen the influx of corporate sponsorship climb 2000 percent in just five years. Money that used to go to tennis is now being shifted to figure skating and gymnastics as their popularity grows. The payoff in money and fame now looms large enough to be seen from a distance, sparkling like the Emerald City, driving parents and children to extremes to reach its doors.

I'm not suggesting that all elite gymnasts and figure skaters emerge from their sports unhealthy and poorly adjusted. Many prove that they can thrive under intense pressure and physical demands and thus are stronger for the experience. But too many can't. There are no studies that establish what percentage of elite gymnasts and figure skaters are damaged by their sports and in what ways. So the evidence I've gathered for this book is anecdotal, the result of nearly a hundred interviews and more than a decade of covering both sports as a journalist.

The bottom line is clear. There have been enough suicide attempts, enough eating disorders, enough broken bodies, enough regretful parents, and enough bitter young women to warrant a serious reevaluation of what we're doing in this country to produce Olympic champions. Those who work in these sports know this. They know the tragedies all too well. If the federations and coaches truly care about the athletes and not simply about the fame and prestige that come from trotting tough little champions up to the medal stand, they know it is past time to lay the problems on the table, examine them, and figure out a way to keep their sports from damaging so many young lives. But since those charged with protecting young athletes so often fail in their responsibility, it is time the government drops the fantasy that certain sports are merely games and takes a hard look at legislation aimed at protecting elite child athletes.

It is also my hope that by dramatizing the particularly intense subculture of female gymnastics and figure skating, we can better understand something of our own nature as a country bent on adulating, and in some cases sacrificing, girls and young women in a quest to fit them into our pretty little boxes.

14

Swoosh Comes to Shove

Mike Bresnahan

Even before the start of the season, when Westchester High boys' basketball team was ranked no. 1 in the nation, opposing coaches were saying it.

Westchester, with its top eight players all likely to earn college scholarships, was so much better than the rest that it belonged in a league of its own.

Now that the season has ended with a state championship and a 32–2 record, many in the City basketball coaching ranks are still talking about the Comets.

They say Westchester has an edge—corporate sponsorship—that is ruining the competitive balance of the playing court.

"What you have is professional players in high school," said Ronald Quiette, the boys' basketball coach at Los Angeles Jordan. "Let them all play each other. Set up two leagues: The semi-professional league, and the rest of us."

Westchester and Santa Ana Mater Dei were among a select 15 teams in the nation that sports apparel giant Nike outfitted for free this season. For Westchester players, that meant an investment of more than $15,000. From headbands to high-tops, each Comet player received more than $1,300 in gear—including five pairs of the newest top-of-the-line shoes. And there is more.

The team had its expenses to a prestigious holiday tournament in Houston paid for by a Nike affiliate. The estimated cost of that trip: $7,000. Westchester also played in three other out-of-state events last season, trips worth about $20,000 that

Source: Mike Bresnahan, "Swoosh Comes to Shove," *Los Angeles Times,* April 10, 2002. Copyright © 2002 *Los Angeles Times.* Used by permission.

were paid for almost entirely by organizers seeking a prominent headliner for their tournaments.

Special associations such as the one between Westchester and Nike concern high-ranking school sports administrators, who worry that the lines of fair play are being erased.

The California Interscholastic Federation, which governs athletic competition for the state's 1,292 high schools, doesn't have rules prohibiting such arrangements. But some might be coming in at least one of its 10 sections.

The director of the CIF's largest section said he is tired of endorsement deals such as the ones between Nike and Westchester that seem to allow continued success for "the privileged few."

James Staunton, commissioner of the 522-school Southern Section, said he thinks that restrictive legislation is a potential hot topic for an April 25 meeting of athletic representatives, where voting members from each of his section's 73 leagues will be in attendance.

"The only thing we can do would be to alter our bylaws to make it impossible to do this, even if a district would accept it through their policies," Staunton said. "If the time is right and the council can craft a rule that can at least put a damper on this, I think it would pass in a heartbeat."

Even though Westchester is a member of the Los Angeles City Section, any policy-making decision by the Southern Section is sure to be considered by the CIF's other regional governing bodies.

Staunton, a former high school principal, said Nike's "selectivity" is what disturbs him. "It's not the product; it's how they're doing it," he said. "It's run so contrary to what we're trying to do with the kids. Their business decision interferes with our attempts to try to provide a level playing field … and to get away from direct influence on kids."

While most high school teams do car washes and bake sales to raise funds for equipment, uniforms, and travel, Westchester, a public school, attracts all-star-caliber athletes from across the South Bay and parts of Los Angeles. The players admit they have been at least partially enticed by thousands of dollars in free apparel and paid trips to national tournaments that are attended by hundreds of college scouts.

"People who don't play [for Westchester], they're like, 'Damn you're lucky,'" said Scott Cutley, a starter for the Comets at forward. "They see our shoes. They see us traveling. They say things like, 'I'll sit on the end of the bench just to be a part of everything.'"

Some do. Jonathan Smith, a top player at Lawndale Leuzinger High, transferred to Westchester before this season only to become an end-of-the-bench reserve. But he doesn't regret his choice.

"There's a lot of exposure," he said. "At Leuzinger, we only traveled to tournaments in the South Bay. At Westchester, we travel everywhere. The shoes, they're nice too."

And, he added, "We win a lot."

WINNING TRADITION

In the five years they have been partners with Nike, the Comets have won four City Section championships and two state titles. Mater Dei, the other school with full sponsorship, has won Southern Section titles in 10 of the past 11 years.

Fairfax, Crenshaw, Compton Dominguez, Bellflower St. John Bosco, Santa Margarita, Santa Monica Crossroads, and Glendora, which received smaller Nike contributions—most often, shoes and equipment bags—also are perennial power-houses.

Westchester opponents think this is not a coincidence, although at all of these schools it is hard to determine what arrived first—success or Nike.

"That's Nike's money and they can do whatever they want with it, but it creates parity problems," Reseda Coach Mike Wagner said. "No kid in his right mind is not going to want to go to Westchester, where they get their shoes and sweats and bags."

The result, Wagner said, was a season played to a nearly predetermined climax. It is why a meeting of City Section coaches in October was noticeably void of the usual preseason optimism.

"Every coach in the room knew there was Westchester, Fairfax, and then 58 other schools," Wagner said. "We all knew they'd play for the City championship."

They were right. Westchester defeated Fairfax for the City title and then swept its way to the state Division I championship.

Wagner isn't the only local coach who wishes Nike would share the wealth.

"Let them help all the schools, not just individual schools," said Dave Uyeshima, coach at Hamilton High, which lost two games to Westchester by a combined 109 points.

Almost as aggravating to local coaches as the Comets' tie to Nike is that Westchester's banner season came courtesy of 12 players all hailing from places outside the school's primary attendance area.

Critics say that loose transfer rules, along with Nike's sponsorship money, encouraged a collection of star athletes to converge at Westchester, which is located within window-rattling distance of Los Angeles International Airport.

Hassan Adams, the 6-foot-4 guard who was the Comets' best player, is attending his third high school. He is from Inglewood, as are starting point guard Ashanti Cook, sixth man Brandon Heath, and reserve Bobby Brown. The others come from Santa Monica, Hawthorne, Torrance, Lawndale, Carson, Hancock Park, and the Crenshaw district.

Only one month into the season, four of the Comets' five seniors had already signed letters of intent with major-college basketball programs—Adams to Arizona, Cook to New Mexico, Heath to San Diego State and Brandon Bowman to Georgetown. At least two others—juniors Cutley and Trevor Ariza—are considered certain major-college recruits for next season.

"An all-star team," Wagner said. "There are college teams they could beat."

PAST PENALTIES

Three times in the past two years Westchester has been formally accused of breaking City Section rules, and twice it has been penalized. The Comets were slapped with a year's probation when Adams played for the team in a 2000 summer tournament before his transfer to the school was official, and 6' 7" center Ashton Thomas was declared ineligible for varsity competition this season because of an improper transfer from Leuzinger.

Westchester had two transfers in its title-winning starting lineup this season—Adams and Bowman, a senior forward who transferred in as a sophomore. Neither player says he was "recruited," although Adams acknowledges a long friendship with Westchester assistant Marlon Morton, whom he met 10 years ago while playing on the courts of St. Andrews Park in South Los Angeles.

Barbara Fiege, commissioner of athletics for the 62 high schools in the Los Angeles Unified School District, understands the frustration of coaches who struggle to compete with the Comets, but she stops well short of accusing Westchester of recruiting.

"When there are transfer students that go to a school, you can't jump to that first conclusion that they were recruited by people at the school," she said.

While critics say that a roster lacking a single player from the school's neighborhood is evidence enough of recruiting, other coaches defend Westchester's Ed Azzam and members of his staff by saying that top players are sophisticated enough to know which teams are equipped to offer them the most.

The winning equation isn't complicated: Free gear + free travel = talented players, and a team entices even more top players because of the exposure it gets and the college recruiters it attracts.

Azzam said coaches who complain about his team's partnership with Nike are expressing "sour grapes" and "maybe a little jealousy."

"I don't think the kids come to the school because we wear Nike or we get this or that," he said. "Some people think they're going to get exposure or free shoes. But I hope it's because we teach. I'd like to think they come here because they get better and because they want to go to a program where they have the opportunity to win."

Some of his coaching colleagues remain unconvinced.

"It's tough when people say we'll give you three pairs of Nikes and two sweat suits and we'll go to Vegas or Houston or other places," said Travis Showalter, the recently resigned Leuzinger coach who lost Smith and Thomas to the Comets before last season. "That's tough to compete against. There's no way I [could] match up financially."

SONNY DAYS

Shoe companies such as Nike and competitors Adidas, AND 1, and Reebok, which also sponsor high school basketball teams, know they are in a position to be criticized for their ties to teenage athletes. It's a calculated risk. Forming a bond with a top high school player is potentially lucrative if that player one day signs an NBA contract and becomes a star.

Nike won't soon forget the image of Sonny Vaccaro, a former consultant who left the company to become a prominent member of Adidas, sitting with Kobe Bryant's family at the 1996 NBA draft. When Bryant was selected with the 13th pick, he popped out of his chair and embraced his family, then his friends, and then Vaccaro, with whom he had formed a bond during his years at Philadelphia's Lower Merion High.

Two NBA championships with the Lakers later, Bryant still has a contract with Adidas. His "Kobe Two" shoes hit stores in February. Retail price: $130.

Adidas, Nike's closest competitor, has a budget of about $250,000 to support partnerships with about 40 high schools nationwide, a company source said.

Nike won't divulge what it spends on its "grass roots basketball operation"—its sponsorship of high school and age-group youth teams—but industry experts estimate that in recent years it has grown to $3 million to $4 million annually.

Tony Dorado, the director of Nike's high school basketball operation, believes it is money well spent, especially with so many teenagers jumping directly to the NBA or into the starting lineups of major colleges. That exposure may easily be worth $3–4 million.

Most of the 150 high schools connected with Nike get free shoes, T-shirts, and balls or athletic bags for each player, donations that are tied for the company's sales and marketing strategy rather than charity.

"We're a for-profit company," Dorado said. "I was hired to make sound business decisions, and that's what I do."

Critics might howl, but one prominent sports marketing analyst said Nike and other shoe companies "are just following the tenets of capitalism. The strong survive and the good get better."

Rick Burton, executive director of the Warsaw Sports Marketing Center at the University of Oregon, said, "When we look at the commercialism of youth athletics, we can't speak about total purity, Corporations have been asked to fund and sponsor Little League teams for 40 years. We're OK with it when it was the local Albertsons or the barber shop."

Dorado said Nike's deal with Westchester fits the company's business philosophy of partnering with winners, "We're always going to be associated with the best," Dorado said, "whether it be Westchester or a gold-medal speed skater."

NOT ONLY SPORTS

Local administrators have been grappling for a solution almost as long as coaches have been grumbling about inequity.

Commissioner Fiege said Nike sponsored the City Section basketball championships a few years ago, but was turned down by district officials when it expressed interest in expanding its contribution. The reason: The television program *60 Minutes* had just broadcast its October 1996 investigative piece on Nike and child labor.

"It just didn't seem like the right fit at the time," Fiege said.

Fiege said the CIF, and its individual sections, have occasionally considered strictly regulating sports sponsorships, but decided against it for a variety of reasons.

"If you single out donations to athletic teams, what do you do about the $25,000 worth of computers IBM gives to such and such a school for their business department?" Fiege said, "Once you open those doors to discussion, it's not as easy as one would think to keep it to athletics. You're singling out athletes if you take a hard line and single out Adidas or Nike, but then it's OK to accept IBM or Coca-Cola. How can I sit here and say Coca-Cola is OK and Nike isn't? It's murky."

Marlene Canter, the LAUSD's board member from Westchester's area, District 4, said that while she was proud of the Comets' achievements, the team's Nike contract was an example of "overabundance."

"On the one hand, I'm happy to have attracted Nike's attention," she said. "On the other hand, I'd feel much more comfortable if Nike would be looking at Westchester as a school, saying, 'What can we do to help school [academic] achievement?' Academics is really the ball we need to keep our eye on."

Uyeshima, who recently completed his 18th season as Hamilton's coach, said local administrators need to start looking at teams like Westchester with a more critical eye.

"Downtown, they don't care," he said, referring to Fiege and other City Section officials. "They get a team that goes to the state championship every year. It's frustrating. It seems like they have so many schools and so many things going on, they can't look into it."

In addition to calling for Nike to more equally distribute its sponsorship riches, Uyeshima and others would like to see rules instituted on transfers.

LACK OF CONTROL?

From the local real-estate agent who advertises in the football program to the car dealership that has a banner on the outfield fence of the softball diamond, many high school sports programs have sponsors.

But Marie Ishida, the CIF's executive director, said many schools don't seem aware that there are established guidelines for accepting corporate gifts.

"We've tried to address in our constitution and bylaws that the school's district determines how to divvy up that stuff so that no one group of kids gets all of it," she said. "I'm not sure how many districts are doing that, however, or if they're necessarily aware they should be doing that." One CIF rule stipulates that teams are supposed to report single-source donations of $500 or more to an administrative source—most often, the school principal.

Westchester's basketball team easily surpassed that standard—per player—but Principal Dana Perryman said the team had "established a practice" with a previous principal and that she "didn't know that much" about the Comets' association with Nike.

"Other than tennis shoes, I don't know what else they gave them," she said. "I trust Mr. Azzam and I trust Mr. [Brian] Henderson [athletic director]. They care about the kids. I don't think they would do anything to jeopardize them."

Dave Goosen, whose Venice High teams never beat the Comets during his five years as coach, said the Westchester administration's lack of institutional control makes it culpable for what he says is illegal recruiting by the basketball staff.

"They're just willing to look the other way because when Westchester wins a state title it's publicity for the school," said Goosen, who resigned before the past season, in part because he was tired of being overrun by his Nike-powered foes in the Western League.

"I felt like we were going to war with sticks and stones, and Westchester and Fairfax had machine guns," Goosen said.

15

One Coaching Style
The Total Control of Coach Bob Knight

John Feinstein

Knight was incapable of accepting failure. Every defeat was personal; *his* team lost, a team *he* had selected and coached. None of the victories or milestones of the past mattered. The fact that he could quit right then and know that his place in history was secure didn't matter. Failure on any level all but destroyed him, especially failure in coaching because it was coaching that gave him his identity, made him special, set him apart.

And so on this rainy, ugly Sunday, beginning the final week of preparation for another season, Knight was angry. He was angry because as his team scrimmaged he could see its flaws. Even playing perfectly, following every instruction he gave, this team would be beatable. How could that be? Knight believed—and his record seemed to back him up—that the system he had devised over the years was the best way there was to play basketball. He always told his players that. "Follow our rules, do exactly what we tell you and you will not lose," he would say. "But boys, you have to listen to me."

The boys listened. Always, they listened. But they didn't always assimilate, and sometimes, even when they did, they could not execute what they had been told. That was what frightened Knight—yes, frightened him—about this team. It might do everything it was told and still not be very good. He liked these players; there wasn't, in his view, a bad kid on the team. But he wondered about their potential as basketball players.

Source: John Feinstein, *A Season on the Brink* (New York: Macmillan, 1986). Excerpt from pp. 3–9.

Today the player bothering him most was Daryl Thomas. In Thomas, Knight saw a player of huge potential. Thomas has what coaches call a "million dollar body." He was strong and wide, yet quick. He could shoot the basketball with both hands, and when he went past bigger men to the basket, they had little choice but to foul him.

But Thomas was not one of those basketball players who like to get up on game day and eat nails for breakfast to get ready. He was a middle-class kid from Chicago, extremely bright and sensitive. Knight's angry words often hurt him. Other Indiana players, Alford for one, knew that Knight would say almost anything when he was angry and that the only way to deal with that was to ignore the words of anger and listen to the words of wisdom. Dan Dakich, who had graduated the previous spring to become a graduate assistant coach, had told the freshman Calloway, "When he's calling you an asshole, don't listen. But when he starts telling you *why* you're an asshole, listen. That way you'll get better."

Thomas couldn't shut off some words and hear others. He heard them all, and they hurt.

Knight didn't want to hurt Thomas. He wanted to make him a better player, but he honestly believed that some days Thomas had to be hurt if he was going to get better. He had used this tactic on Landon Turner, another sensitive black youngster with immense ability. Turner, 6-10 and 250 pounds, had emerged from a shell of mediocrity as a junior to play a key role in Indiana's 1981 run to the national championship. That summer he was crippled in an automobile accident. Knight, who had once put Tampax in Turner's locker, who had cursed him and called him names for three years, spent the next six months raising money to pay Landon Turner's medical bills.

Now, he was hoping that Thomas would bloom as a junior the way Turner had. Some days he cajoled. Other days he joked. Today, though, he raged. Practice had not gone well; after three straight good practices, the team had been sluggish. Intellectually, Knight knew this was inevitable. Emotionally, it drove him to the brink of complete hysteria.

First, he screamed at Thomas for playing carelessly. Then, he banished him from the scrimmage, sending him to a lone basket at the end of the court to practice with Magnus Pelkowski, a 6'10" sophomore who was not scrimmaging because of an injury.

"Daryl," he screamed as Thomas walked toward where Pelkowski was working, "get the f__ out of my sight. If that's the best you can give us after two days' rest, get away from me. There is absolutely no way you'll start on Saturday. No way. You cost yourself that chance today by f____ around. You are so terrible, it's just awful. I don't know what the f__ you are thinking about. You think I was mad last year? You saw me, I was the maddest sonofabitch you ever saw. You want another year like that? Just get the f__ out of my sight."

When Knight is angry, he spews profanities so fast they're hard to keep track of. In the right mood, he can talk for hours without ever using an obscenity. In this mood, every other word was one. Turning to his assistant coaches, Knight added, "F____

Daryl Thomas. Don't even mess with him anymore. We've worked three years with the sonofabitch. Use him to make Magnus a better player. At least *he* wants to play."

They played on without Thomas. Finally, after about twenty minutes, he was allowed to return. But he was tight. Some players react to Knight's anger with anger of their own and play better. Not Thomas; he tightens up. When Courtney Witte, a backup forward with far less natural ability than Thomas, scored over him from inside, Knight blew up again. "Daryl, get in the game or get out! Do you know you haven't scored a basket inside since Jesus Christ was lecturing in Omaha? Just get out, Daryl. Get him the f__ in the locker room. He hasn't done a f____ thing since we got out here."

Thomas departed. His teammates felt for him, because every one of them had been in his shoes at some point. Especially the better players; Knight rarely picks on the second teamers. The rest of the team lasted two plays before Knight blew up again and told them all to join Thomas in the locker room. Knight was genuinely angry, but he was also playing a game with his team. It was a dangerous game, but one he had played successfully for twenty years: put pressure on them now so they will react well to pressure from opponents later. But this was a delicate team and a delicate situation. Last year's team had folded under Knight's pressure. Knight knew that. Some days this fall he restrained himself because of that. But not today.

In the locker room, Knight ordered the assistant coaches to play back the tape of the day's practice. As often happens when Knight is angry, he began invoking the past. "I'd like to know when somebody in here is going to go up and grab somebody and punch them when they watch this bullshit. [Quinn] Buckner would have hit somebody by now. Do you know that? He just would have gone up and hit one of you f____. People I played with in college would have killed you people if you pulled that shit on them."

Quinn Buckner had been the captain of the 1976 national championship team. He was, without question, Knight's all-time favorite player. He had been a leader, a coach on the floor, but no one could remember him hitting a teammate. Part of that was because any time two players squared off in practice, Knight would say to them, "Anybody who wants to fight, you can fight me." No one wanted to fight Knight.

Knight stormed out, leaving the assistants to go through the tape with the players. The room was dark, almost quiet. The four assistant coaches, Kohn Smith, Joby Wright, Royce Waltman, and Ron Felling, gingerly began pointing out mistakes. With the exception of Felling, they had all lived through the nightmare of the previous year, and they didn't want a repeat, either. But no one was really listening as the coaches droned on about missed screens and lack of concentration. Everyone in the room knew Knight was going to be back. Most people get angry, scream and yell, and then calm down. Knight, more often than not, gets even angrier.

Sure enough, five minutes later, he returned. Thomas was on his mind. "Daryl, you know you are a f____ joke," he said. "I have no more confidence in your ability to go out and play hard than I did when you were a freshman. I don't know how you've f____ up your head in the last two weeks but you're as f____ up now as you've ever been. I wouldn't turn you loose in a game if you were the last guy I had because of your f____ head. This is just bullshit.

"Honest to Christ I want to just go home and cry when I watch this shit. Don't you boys understand? Don't you know how bad I want to see Indiana play basketball? I want to see Indiana play so bad I can f_____ taste it. I want a good team so bad it hurts. I want to go out there and kick somebody's ass."

He looked at Winston Morgan, a fifth-year senior playing without a scholarship. "Do you?" Morgan nodded assent. *"Bullshit. Lying sonofabitch. Show me out there and I'll believe it. I come out here to practice and see this and I just want to quit. Just go home and never come back."*

Knight was hoarse from yelling. His voice was almost choking with emotion. He stopped. The tape started. It ran for one play. "Stop, stop it," Knight said. "Daryl, look at that. You don't even run back down the floor hard. That's all I need to know about you, Daryl. All you want to be out there is comfortable. You don't work, you don't sprint back. Look at that! You never push yourself. You know what you are Daryl? You are the worst f_____ pussy I've ever seen play basketball at this school. The absolute worst pussy ever. You have more goddamn ability than 95 percent of the players we've had here but you are a pussy from the top of your head to the bottom of your feet. An absolute f_____ pussy. That's my assessment of you after three years."

Finally, with Thomas fighting back tears, Knight turned on the rest of his team. For ten more minutes he railed at them, called them names, told them they couldn't beat anybody. He told them not to bother coming to practice the next day, or the day after. He didn't care what they did. "Get them out of here," he finally told the assistants. "Get them the f__ out."

Knight walked out onto the floor. He was drained. He turned to Kohn Smith. "Go talk to Daryl," he said. Knight knew he had gone too far with Thomas, and undoubtedly he had regretted many of the words as soon as they were out of his mouth. But he couldn't take them back. Instead, he would send Smith, who was as quiet and gentle as Knight was loud and brutal, to talk to Thomas.

Thomas cried. Smith comforted him. Thomas was facing the same question everyone who comes in contact with Knight faces sooner or later: Is it worth it? Does the end justify the means? He knew Knight just wanted him to be a better player. He knew Knight liked him and cared about him. He knew that if anyone ever attacked him, Knight would come to his defense. But was all that worth it for this? This was Knight at his meanest. Every player who comes to Indiana faces the screaming, raving Knight at some point in his life. Some leave because it isn't worth it to them, but most stay. And most leave convinced Knight's way is the right way. But now Daryl Thomas wondered. He had to wonder; he wouldn't have been human if he hadn't wondered, if he hadn't cried.

They practiced early the next morning, but without Knight: he stayed home, not wanting to put himself or his team through another emotional trauma.

One morning later, Knight called Thomas into his locker room. He put his arm around Thomas and told him to sit down. He spoke softly, gently. There were no other coaches, no teammates in the room. "Daryl, I hate it when I get on you the way I did Sunday, I really do," he said. "But do you know why I do it?"

Thomas shook his head. "Because, Daryl, sometimes I think I want you to be a great player more than you want you to be a great player. And that just tears me up inside. Because there is no way you will ever be a great player unless *you* want it. You have the ability. But I can coach, teach, scream, and yell from now until Doomsday and you won't be any good unless you want it as bad as I do. Right now, I *know* you don't want it as bad as I do. Somehow, I have to convince you to feel that way. I don't know if this is the right way, but it's my way. You know it's worked for other people in the past. Try, Daryl, please try. That's all I ask. If you try just as hard as you can, I promise you it will be worth it. I know it will. Don't try for me, Daryl. Try for you."

Thomas listened to all this. Unlike some players who might not understand what Knight was saying, he understood. This was the way his coach coached; that would never change. Thomas was going through the same emotional swings that other gifted Knight players had gone through. One in particular, Isiah Thomas (no relation to Daryl) had come out of the Chicago ghetto and had lit up Indiana basketball for two years with his talent and his personality. He and Knight had fought for two years while Thomas starred for Indiana, and had continued to fight after Thomas left Indiana early to turn pro.

At a clinic once, someone asked Isiah Thomas what he really thought about Knight. "You know there were times," Isiah Thomas answered, "when if I had had a gun, I think I would have shot him. And there were other times when I wanted to put my arms around him, hug him, and tell him that I loved him."

Those words, perhaps better than any others, sum up the love-hate relationship between Knight and his players, even between Knight and his friends. To know Bob Knight is to love him. To know Bob Knight is to hate him. Because he views the world and everyone in it in strict black-and-white terms, he is inevitably viewed that way by others.

In less than forty-eight hours, Daryl Thomas had seen the black and the white. He had felt the full range of emotions. That Saturday, when Indiana played its first game of the season, Daryl Thomas was Indiana's best player. Not for Knight. For himself. But it was only one game. A long season lay ahead.

✳ FOR FURTHER STUDY ✳

Adler, Patricia, and Peter Adler. 1998. *Peer Power: Preadolescent Culture and Identity.*

Anderson, Sally. 2001. "Practicing Children: Consuming and Being Consumed by Sports." *Journal of Sport and Social Issues* 25 (August): 229–250.

Bissinger, Buzz. 2008. "Creep Show." *New York Times,* August 9. Available at http://www.nytimes.com/2008/08/09/opinion/09bissinger.html.

Coakley, Jay. 2006. "The Good Father: Parental Expectations and Youth Sports." *Leisure Studies* 25 (2).

———. 2007. *Sports in Society: Issues and Controversies.* 9th ed. New York: McGraw-Hill.

Eitzen, D. Stanley. 2009. *Fair and Foul: Beyond the Myths and Paradoxes of Sport.* Lanham, MD: Rowman and Littlefield.

Eitzen, D. Stanley, and George H. Sage. 2009. *Sociology of North American Sport.* 8th ed. Boulder, CO: Paradigm.

King, Kelley. 2002. "High School Sports: The Ultimate Jock School." *Sports Illustrated* (November 25): 49–54.

Fejgin, Naomi, and Ronit Hanegby. 2001. "Gender and Cultural Bias in Perceptions of Sexual Harassment in Sport." *International Review for the Sociology of Sport* 36 (December): 459–478.

Sokolove, Michael. 2004. "The Thoroughly Designed American Childhood: Constructing a Teen Phenom." *New York Times Magazine,* section 6 (November 28): 80.

Watts, Jay. 2002. "Perspectives on Sport Specialization." *JOPERD* 73 (October): 33–37, 50.

PART SIX

Problems of Excess: Sport and Deviance

Sport and *deviance* would appear on the surface to be antithetical terms. After all, sports contests are bound by rules, school athletes must meet rigid grade and behavior standards in order to compete, and there is a constant monitoring of athletes' behavior because they are public figures. Moreover, sport is assumed by many to promote those character traits deemed desirable by most in society: fair play, sportsmanship, obedience to authority, hard work, and commitment to excellence.

The selections in this part show, to the contrary, that deviance is not only prevalent in sport but that the structure of sport in American society actually promotes deviance. Players and coaches sometimes cheat to gain an advantage over an opponent. Some players engage in criminal violence on and off the playing field. Some players use performance-enhancing drugs. Some players are sexually promiscuous.

The first chapter, by D. Stanley Eitzen, provides an overview of deviance by looking at the dark side of competition in society as well as sport. This is an important consideration because the value Americans place on competition is at the heart of much deviance.

The second chapter, by Todd W. Crosset, Jeffrey R. Benedict, and Mark A. McDonald, reports the results of a survey about campus sexual assault and participation in NCAA athletics. Their tentative findings are that male college student-athletes, compared with the rest of the male student population, are responsible for a significantly higher percentage of the sexual assaults reported to judicial affairs offices on the campuses of big-time colleges and universities.

The final chapter, by Richard E. Lapchick, counters the implications of the preceding chapter that athletes are prone toward sexual violence. He argues that male athletes are unfairly stereotyped as being more likely than others their age to be violent and, especially, gender violent. He concludes that "the distortions about

159

our athletes and the crimes that a few of them commit need to be put in their real social context. The misleading perceptions need to be corrected so we can focus on the truth and what is really necessary."

16

Ethical Dilemmas in American Sport
The Dark Side of Competition

D. Stanley Eitzen

Although there are a number of prominent American values, I am going to focus on the consequences of the two that I consider the most central—achievement and competition. We Americans glorify individual achievement in competitive situations. A recent book, *The Winner-Take-All Society,* shows how we heap incredible rewards on winners and barely reward others in a number of markets including sport.

The values we promote throughout American society are believed to be good. They motivate. They promote excellence. They make individuals and society productive. They fit with capitalism. And, they make life interesting.

We believe that sports participation for children and youth prepares them for success in a competitive society. According to folk wisdom, these young people will take on a number of desirable character traits from sport. They will learn to persevere, to sacrifice, to work hard, to follow orders, to work together with others, and to be self-disciplined. Assuming that these traits are learned through sport, what else is learned through the sports experience? This is the central question I wish to discuss. I will focus on the dark side of competition, emphasizing ethical dilemmas.

Now I want you to know that while I am going to be critical of sport, much of the time I celebrate sport. I was an athlete in high school and college. I have coached youth sports and several high school sports. My children participated from youth

Source: D. Stanley Eitzen, "Ethical Dilemmas in American Sport: The Dark Side of Competition," *Vital Speeches of the Day* (January 1, 1996): 182–185.

161

sports through college sport. The last 25 years I have been an active researcher and teacher in the sociology of sport. I am energized by sport. Going to sports events and watching them on television adds zest to my existence. I savor the great moments of sport, when my favorite team and athletes overcome great odds to defeat superior opponents. I am transfixed by the excellence of athletes. I am moved by the genuine camaraderie among teammates. Of course, I suffer when these same athletes make mistakes and fall short of expectations. The key is that I genuinely love sport. I want you to place my critical analysis of sport within the context of my great affection for sport. I love sport, and in criticizing it, I hope to improve it.

Sport has a dark side. It is plagued with problems. Big-time sport has corrupted academe. Coaches sometimes engage in outrageous behaviors, but if they win, they are rewarded handsomely. Gratuitous violence is glorified in the media. Some athletes take drugs. Some athletes are found guilty of gang rape and spouse abuse. Many athletes cheat to achieve a competitive edge. Sports organizations take advantage of athletes. In the view of many, these problems result from bad people. I believe that stems from a morally distorted sports world—a world where winning supersedes all other consider-ations, where moral values have become confused with the bottom line. And winning-at-any-price has become the prevailing code of conduct in much of sport.

This chapter is divided into three parts: (1) a brief examination of the high value placed on success in sport; (2) the ethical dilemmas in sport that can be traced to this emphasis on success; and (3) the consequences of unethical practices in sport.

SUCCESS: WINNING IS EVERYTHING

My thesis is that American values are responsible for many of the ethical problems found in sport. We glorify winners and forget losers. As Charles Schulz, the creator of the Peanuts comic strip, puts it: "Nobody remembers who came in second." Let me quote a few famous coaches on the importance of winning:

- "Winning isn't everything, it is the only thing." (Vince Lombardi)
- "Defeat is worse than death because you have to live with defeat." (Bill Musselman)
- "In our society, in my profession, there is only one measure of success, and that is winning. Not just any game, not just the big game, but the last one." (John Madden)
- "There are only two things in this league, winning and misery." (Pat Riley)
- "Our expectations are to play for and win the national championship every year ... second, third, fourth, and fifth don't do you any good in this business." (Dennis Erickson, when he was head football coach at the University of Miami)

Americans want winners, whether winning is in school or in business or in politics or in sport. In sport, we demand winners. Coaches are fired if they are not successful; teams are booed if they play for ties. The team that does not win the

Super Bowl in a given year is a loser. My team, the Denver Broncos, has made it to the Super Bowl three times and lost that big game each time. In the minds of the Bronco coaches, players, fans, as well as others across the United States, the Broncos were losers in each of those years even though they were second out of twenty-eight teams, which, if you think about it, is not too shabby an accomplishment.

One other example shows how we exalt first place and debase second place. A football team composed of fifth graders was undefeated going into the Florida state championship game. They lost that game in a close contest. At a banquet for these boys following that season, each player was given a plaque on which was inscribed a quote from Vince Lombardi: "There is no room for second place. I have finished second twice at Green Bay and I never want to finish second again. There is a second place bowl game but it is a game for losers played by losers. It is and always has been an American zeal to be first in anything we do and to win and to win and to win."

In other words, the parents and coaches of these boys wanted them to not be satisfied with being second. Second is losing. The only acceptable placement is first.

If second is unacceptable and all the rewards go to the winners, then some will do whatever it takes to be first. It may require using steroids, or trying to injure a competitor, or altering the transcript of a recruit so that he or she can play illegally. These, of course, are unethical practices in sport, the topic of this chapter.

ETHICAL DILEMMAS

This section points to some questionable practices in sport that need to be examined more closely for their ethical meaning and consequences.

The Culture of Certain Sports

The essence of sport is competition. The goal is to win. But to be ethical this quest to win must be done in a spirit of fairness. Fairness tends to prevail in certain sports such as golf and tennis but in other sports the prevalent mood is to achieve an unfair advantage over an opponent. Getting such a competitive edge unfairly is viewed by many in these sports as "strategy" rather than cheating. In these sports some illegal acts are accepted as part of the game. Coaches encourage them or look the other way, as in the case of steroid use. Rule enforcers such as referees and league commissioners rarely discourage them, impose minimal penalties, or ignore them altogether.

The forms of normative cheating are interesting and important to consider because they are more widespread and they clearly violate ethical principles. Nevertheless, they are accepted by many. In basketball, for example, it is common for a player to pretend to be fouled in order to receive an undeserved free throw and give the opponent an undeserved foul. In football players are typically coached to use illegal techniques to hold or trip opponents without detection. The practice is common in baseball for the home team to "doctor" its field to suit its strengths and minimize the strengths of a particular opponent. A fast team can be neutralized, for example, by slowing down the base paths with water or sand.

Home teams have been known to gain an edge by increasing the heat by several degrees from normal in the visitors' dressing room to make the athletes sluggish. At my school the visiting football team's dressing room is painted pink. This upset the coach of Hawaii because the color pink, he argued, reduces strength and makes people less aggressive.

Let's look at sportspersonship in sport, using three examples. First, in a state championship basketball game in Colorado, Agate was playing Stratton. Agate because of a mix-up over keys could not dress in time. The referees called a technical foul, allowing Stratton to begin the game with two free throws. The Stratton coach, however, told his player to miss the shots.

A second example involves a football game between Dartmouth and Cornell a number of years ago, with Dartmouth winning. Later, after reviewing the films, it was established that Dartmouth had received a fifth down on its winning drive. The Dartmouth president forfeited the win.

As a third example, consider the case of a basketball team in Alabama a few years ago that won the state championship—the first ever for the school. A month or so later, the coach found that he had unknowingly used an ineligible player. No one else knew of the problem. Moreover, the player in question was in the game only a minute or two and had not scored. The coach notified the state high school activities association and, as a result, the only state championship in the school's history was forfeited.

Each of these examples has an unusual resolution. They represent acts of true sportspersonship. Usually, we hear of the opposite situations, a team scoring with a fifth down as the University of Colorado did to defeat Missouri in the year Colorado won the national championship but refused to forfeit (not only did this school accept the victory, so, too, did its coach, the very religious Bill McCartney). Last year, Stanford and Northwestern played to a 41–41 tie. After reviewing the films, the referees admitted that they gave Stanford an undeserved touchdown, yet Stanford did not forfeit. What did the fans of these offending schools say? What did the media outlets say? What did the school administrations say? At my school, Colorado State, the football team upset LSU in 1992. On CSU's winning drive there was a fumble. A LSU player fell on the ball, but in the ensuing pile up, a CSU player ended up with the ball illegally. The player, Geoff Grenier, was quoted in the newspaper that he elbowed and kicked a player in the pile to get the ball. The referees did not see this action and awarded the ball to CSU. CSU's coach, Earle Bruce, said: "One player who should get credit for the victory is Geoff Grenier. If we had lost the ball, the game was over. Geoff found a way to get the ball." The point: the coaches, players, and fans of the "winning" teams accepted these ill-gotten gains as victories. Isn't this strange behavior in an activity that pretends to be built on a foundation of rules and sportspersonship. To the contrary. Such activities involved "normative cheating"—acts to achieve an unfair advantage that are accepted as part of the game. The culture of most sports is to get a competitive advantage over the opponent even if it means taking an unfair advantage. When this occurs, I argue, sport is sending a message—winning is more important than being fair. In this way, sport is a microcosm of society where the bottom line is more important than how you got there. That, my friends, is a consequence of the huge importance we put on success in our society.

Violence

Another area of ethical concern has to do with normative violence in sport. Many popular sports encourage player aggression. These sports demand body checking, blocking, and tackling. But the culture of these sports sometimes goes beyond what is needed. Players are taught to deliver a blow to the opponent, not just to block or tackle him. They are taught to gang tackle, to make the ball carrier "pay the price." The assumption is that physically punishing the other player will increase the probability of the opponent fumbling, losing his concentration, and executing poorly the next time, or having to be replaced by a less talented substitute. Coaches often reward athletes for extra hard hits. In this regard, let me cite several examples from a few years ago:

- At the University of Florida a football player received a "dead roach" decal for his helmet when he hit an opponent so hard that he lay prone with his legs and arms up in the air.
- Similarly, University of Miami football players were awarded a "slobber knocker" decal for their helmets if they hit an opposing player so hard that it knocked the slobber out of his mouth.
- The Denver Broncos coaching staff, similar to other NFL teams yet contrary to league rules, gave monetary awards each week to the players who hit their opponents the hardest.

To show the assumption of unethical violence by opponents in football, in a 1993 playoff game, a player from the Buffalo Bills put a splint on the outside of his good leg so that opponents would concentrate on that leg rather than on his bad leg.

This emphasis on intimidating violence is almost universally held among football and hockey coaches, their players, and their fans. The object is not to just hit, but to hit to punish, and even to injure. The unfortunate result is a much higher injury rate than necessary. Clearly, these behaviors are unethical. John Underwood, a writer for *Sports Illustrated,* has said this about these practices: "Brutality is its own fertilizer. From 'get by with what you can' it is a short hop to the deviations that poison sport.... But it is not just the acts that border on criminal that are intolerable, it is the permissive atmosphere they spring from. The 'lesser' evils that are given tacit approval as 'techniques' of the game, even within the rules."

Player Behavior

Players engage in a number of acts that are unethical but are considered part of their sport. These include: (a) use of intimidation (physical aggression, verbal aggression such as taunting and "trash talking," physical threats, and racial insults); (b) use of drugs to enhance performance (steroids, amphetamines, blood doping); (c) use of illegal equipment (changing a baseball with a "foreign" substance, or roughing one side, a "corked" bat, and a hockey stick curved beyond the legal limits); and (d) use of unethical tactics (e.g., a punter acting as if he had been hit by a defender).

The Behavior of Coaches

Coaches are rewarded handsomely if they win. In addition to generous salary raises, successful college coaches receive lucrative contracts from shoe companies and for other endorsements, media deals, summer camps, speaking engagements, country club memberships, insurance annuities, and the like. With potential income of college coaches approaching $1 million at the highest levels, the temptations are great to offer illegal inducements to prospective athletes or to find illicit ways to keep them eligible (phantom courses, surrogate test takers, altered transcripts). Because winning is so important, some coaches drive their athletes too hard, take them out of the classroom too much, and encourage them to use performance-enhancing drugs. They may also abuse their athletes physically. Verbal assaults by coaches are routine.

Coaches may encourage violence in their players. Vince Lombardi, the famous football coach, once said that "to play this game, you have to have that fire within you, and nothing stokes that fire like hate." Let me cite two examples of how coaches have tried to whip their players into a frenzy that could lead to violence: (1) you'll likely remember that Jackie Sherrill, the coach at Mississippi State, at the end of the last practice before they were to play the Texas Longhorns, had a bull castrated in front of his players. (2) In a less celebrated case, a high school coach in Iowa playing a team called the "Golden Eagles" spray-painted a chicken gold and had his players stomp it to death in the locker room before the contest.

Are these actions by coaches in educational settings appropriate? What lesson is being taught to athletes when their coaches blatantly ask the players to cheat? Consider, for example, the situation when a high school football coach in Portland sent a player into the game on a very foggy night. The player asked: "Who am I going in for?" "No one," the coach replied, "the fog is so thick the ref will never notice you."

Is it all right for coaches to crush the opposition? This is the case in college football this season, as it is imperative to be ranked in the top two at season's end, so your team can play in the Fiesta Bowl for the national championship (and, by the way, each team receives $12 million). But this happens at other levels as well. A Laramie, Wyoming, girls' junior high school basketball team won a game by a score of 81–1, using a full-court press the entire game. Is that OK?

In general it appears coaches condone cheating, whether it be an offensive line-man holding his opponent or a pitcher loading a baseball so that it is more difficult to hit. For example, consider this statement by Sparky Anderson, the former manager of the Detroit Tigers: "I never teach cheating to any of my players but I admire the guys who get away with it. The object of the game is to win and if you can cheat and win, I give you all the credit in the world."

Spectator Behavior

Spectator behavior such as rioting and throwing objects at players and officials is excessive. The question is how are we to evaluate other common but unsportspersonlike practices? Spectators not only tolerate violence, they sometimes encourage it. They do so, when they cheer an opponent's injury, or with bloodlust cheers such as:

> Kill, Kill!
> Hate, Hate,
> Murder, Murder!
> Mutilate!

What about those unethical instances where fans try to distract opponents by yelling racial slurs, or as in the case of Arizona State fans several years ago chanting "P-L-O" to Arizona's Steve Kerr, whose father had been killed by terrorists in Beirut?

Athletic Directors and Other Administrators

The administrators of sport have the overall responsibility to see that the athletic programs abide by the spirit of the rules and that their coaches behave ethically. They must provide safe conditions for play, properly maintained equipment, and appropriate medical attention. Are they showing an adequate concern for their players, for example, when they choose artificial turf over grass, knowing that the rate and severity of injuries are higher with artificial turf?

There are several other areas where athletic directors and administrators may be involved in questionable ethics. They are not ethical when they "drag their feet" in providing equal facilities, equipment, and budgets for women's athletic programs. Clearly, athletic directors are not ethical when they schedule teams that are an obvious mismatch. The especially strong often schedule the especially weak to enhance their record and maintain a high ranking while the weak are enticed to schedule the strong for a good pay day, a practice, 1 suggest, that is akin to prostitution.

Finally, college administrators are not ethical when they make decisions regarding the hiring and firing of coaches strictly on the won-lost record. For the most part school administrators do not fire coaches guilty of shady transgressions if they win. As John Underwood has characterized it, "We've told them it doesn't matter how clean they keep their program. It doesn't matter what percentage of their athletes graduate or take a useful place in society. It doesn't even matter how well the coaches teach the sport. All that matters are the flashing scoreboard lights."

The Behavior of Parents

Parents may push their children too far, too fast. Is it appropriate to involve children as young as five in triathlons, marathons, and tackle football? Should one-year-olds be trying to set records as was the case in 1972 when the national record for the mile run for a one-year-old was set by Steve Parsons of Normal, Illinois, at 24:16.6 (one day short of his second birthday). Is such a practice appropriate or is it a form of child abuse? Is it all right to send ten-year-old children away from home to work out eight hours a day with a gymnastics coach in Houston, a swimming coach in Mission Viejo, California, or a tennis coach in Florida?

Parents may encourage their child to use drugs (diuretics for weight control, drugs to retard puberty, growth hormones, or steroids).

Parents sometimes are too critical of their children's play, other players, coaches, and referees. Some parents are never satisfied. They may have unrealistic expectations for their children and in doing so may rob them of their childhood and their self-esteem.

The Behaviors of Team Doctors and Trainers

There are essentially two ethical issues facing those involved in sports medicine, especially those employed by schools or professional teams. Most fundamentally these team doctors and trainers often face a dilemma resulting from their ultimate allegiance—is it to their employer or to the injured athlete? The employer wants athletes on the field not in the training room. Thus, the ethical question—should pain-killing drugs be administered to an injured player so that he or she can return to action sooner than is prudent for the long-term health of the athlete?

A second ethical issue for those in sports medicine is whether they should dispense performance-enhancing drugs and the related issue of whether or not they should help drug-using athletes pass a drug test.

Organizational Behavior

Immorality is not just a matter of rule breaking or bending the rules—the rules themselves may be immoral. Powerful organizations such as universities, leagues, Little League baseball, and the U.S. Olympic Committee have had sexist rules and they exploit athletes. The rules of the NCAA are consistently unfair to college athletes. For example, the NCAA rules require that athletes commit to a four-year agreement with a school, yet schools only have to abide by a year by year commitment to the athlete. Moreover, the compensation of athletes is severely limited while the schools and the NCAA make millions.

This listing of areas of ethical concern for various aspects of sport is not meant to be exhaustive but rather to highlight the many ethical dimensions present in the sports world. I now turn to the consequences of unethical practices.

THE ETHICAL CONSEQUENCES OF UNETHICAL PRACTICES IN SPORT

A widely held assumption of parents, educators, banquet speakers, and editorial writers is that sport is a primary vehicle by which youth are socialized to adopt the values and morals of society. The ultimate irony is, however, that sport as it is presently conducted in youth leagues, schools, and at the professional level does not enhance positive character traits. As philosopher Charles Banham has said, many do benefit from the sports experience but for many others sport "encourages selfishness, envy, conceit, hostility, and bad temper. Far from ventilating the mind, it stifles it. Good sportsmanship may be a product of sport, but so is bad sportsmanship."

The "winning-at-all-costs" philosophy pervades sport at every level and this leads to cheating by coaches and athletes. It leads to the dehumanization of athletes and to their alienation from themselves and from their competitors. Under these conditions, it is not surprising that research reveals consistently that sport stifles moral reasoning and moral development. For example, from 1987 to the present physical educators Sharon Stoll and Jennifer Beller have studied over 10,000 athletes from the ninth grade through college. Among their findings:

1. Athletes score lower than their non-athlete peers on moral development.
2. Male athletes score lower than female athletes in moral development.
3. Moral reasoning scores for athletic populations steadily decline from the ninth grade through university age, whereas scores for non-athletes tend to increase.

This last point is very significant: the longer an individual participates in sport, the less able they are to reason morally. Stoll and Beller say: "While sport does build character if defined as loyalty, dedication, sacrifice, and teamwork, it does not build moral character in the sense of honesty, responsibility, and justice." Thus, I believe the unethical practices so common in sport have negative consequences for the participants. Gresham's law would seem to apply to sport—bad morality tends to defeat good morality; unfairness tends to encourage unfairness. Sociologist Melvin Tumin's principle of "least significant morality" also makes this point: "In any social group, the moral behavior of the group as an average will tend to sink to that of the least moral participant, and the least moral participant will, in that sense, control the group unless he is otherwise restrained and/or expelled.... Bad money may not always drive out good money, though it almost always does. But 'bad' conduct surely drives out 'good' conduct with predictable vigor and speed."

The irony, as sport psychologists Brenda Jo Bredemeir and David Shields have pointed out, is that often "to be good in sports, you have to be bad." You must, as we have seen, take unfair advantage and be overly aggressive if you want to win. The implications of this are significant. Moral development theorists agree that the fundamental structure of moral reasoning remains relatively stable from situation to situation. Thus, when coaches and athletes in their zeal to succeed corrupt the ideals of sportspersonship and fair play, they are likely to employ or condone similar tactics outside sport. They might accept the necessity of dirty tricks in politics, the manipulation of foreign governments for our benefit, and business practices that include using misleading advertising and selling shoddy and/or harmful products. The ultimate goal in politics, business, and sport, after all, is to win. And winning may require moving outside the established rules. Unfortunately, this lesson is learned all too often in sport.

Sport has the potential to ennoble its participants and society. Athletes strain, strive, and sacrifice to excel. But if sport is to exalt the human spirit, it must be practiced within a context guided by fairness and humane considerations. Competition is great but it can go too far. Personally, I know that my competitive drive has gone too far when:

1. The activity is no longer enjoyable—i.e., there is too much emphasis on the outcome and not enough on the process.
2. I treat my opponents with disrespect.
3. I am tempted to gain an unfair advantage.
4. I cannot accept being less than the best even when I have done my best.

I believe that many times those intimately involved in sport have stepped over these lines. When they make those choices, when the goal of winning supersedes other goals, they and sport are diminished. Sport, then, rather than achieving its ennobling potential has the contrary effect. Rather than making the best of our American emphasis on success and competition, unethical sport perverts these values.

It is time we who care about sport recognize the dangers in what sport has become and strive to change it. Above all, we must realize, to win by going outside the rules and the spirit of the rules is not really to win at all.

17

Male Student-Athletes Reported for Sexual Assault

A Survey of Campus Police Departments and Judicial Affairs Offices

Todd W. Crosset, Jeffrey R. Benedict, and Mark A. McDonald

In recent years, an ongoing public debate has developed regarding the propensity of athletes to commit sexual assault. A succession of publicized rape cases during the 1980s involving high-profile athletes led to increased coverage of sexual assault by sports reporters. During the first half of the 1990s, the unabated number of allegations involving athletes in rape cases (for a summary, see Nelson 1994) has fed the debate. Some members of the media have suggested that athletes are more prone to commit acts of sexual aggression (Eskanazi 1990; Hofmann 1986; Kirshenbaum 1989; Larimer 1991; Toufexis 1990). This claim is disputed by those who believe that athletes are scrutinized more intensely because of their notoriety (Dershowitz 1994). They contend that thousands of rape cases go unmentioned in news reports each year, yet seldom does a case involving an athlete or any other celebrity go unpublicized. This practice, they argue, creates a distorted perception regarding the proportion of athletes who commit sexual assault and fails to account for the large number of athletes who do not commit sexually aggressive acts.

Source: Todd W. Crosset, Jeffrey R. Benedict, and Mark A. McDonald, *Journal of Sport and Social Issues,* 19 (1995): 126–140. Copyright © 1995 Sage Publications. Reprinted by permission of Sage Publications, Inc.

Social scientists have offered little to inform this debate. The purpose of this study is to research the association between reported incidents of sexual assault and athletic affiliation in a rigorous fashion.

INTRODUCTION

Social Milieu and Sexual Aggression

A number of researchers concerned with sexually aggressive behavior adopt what Malamuth, Sockloskie, Koss, and Tanaka (1991) call an "ecological approach." This approach starts with the recognition that sexually aggressive behavior is a form of violence and not a form of sexuality. It argues that aggression against women results from a complex combination of social and psychological factors, with primary emphasis on sociological factors. Employing multiple regression analysis, Malamuth et al. note that proximate social factors such as peer group environment and masculine hostility toward women have far more influence as predictors of sexual aggression than do distal factors such as violence experienced as a child. Malamuth et al. conclude that future research should focus on the following social factors: (a) factors that contribute to the practice and acceptance of coercion and hostility, (b) factors that promote aggression against targets perceived as weaker or as out groups (e.g., sex segregation), and (c) factors that promote sexism and violence against women (e.g., eroticism of domination).

This approach is supported by the work of anthropologist Peggy Sanday (1981), who found that the frequency of rape varied substantially from one tribal society to another. Cultures that displayed a high level of tolerance for violence, male dominance, and sex segregation had the highest frequency of rape (both individual and gang). These societal characteristics are the basis of what Sanday (1990) calls "rape cultures," which lack the social constraints that discourage sexual aggression or contain social arrangements that encourage sexual aggression. Sanday's findings support the contention that sexual assault is not simply the result of an individual's biological makeup or psychological disposition; rather, it is a behavior that is socially encouraged (Brownmiller 1975; Russell 1975; Sanday 1981, 1990).

Athletes and Sexual Assault

Beginning in the late 1970s, academics and social critics began discussing connections between the culture of sport and violence against women (Sabo and Runfola 1980). In many regards, men's sport resembles a "rape culture." Athletics is highly sex segregated. By design, dominant forms of sport promote hostile attitudes toward rivals and gaining at the expense of another team or person (Kidd 1990; Messner 1992; Messner and Sabo 1994). Male athletic teams often garner high status for physically dominating others (Sabo 1980). Further, organized competitive sports for men have been described as supporting male dominance and sexist practices (Bryson

1987; Kidd 1990; MacKinnon 1987; Messner 1992; Whitson 1990). Curry (1991), in his study of conversation fragments from a male locker room, found statements that were consistent with what might be found in a "rape culture."

Social scientists have been conducting empirical research on the relationship between athletic participation and sexual assault for a relatively short period of time (Koss and Gaines 1993). Prior to the early 1990s, there were few attempts to document the connection between athletes and sexual assault.

To date, most academic references to athletes as sexual aggressors involve gang rapes (Ehrhart and Sandler 1985, as cited by Koss and Gaines 1993; O'Sullivan 1991). This literature identifies members of fraternities, followed by members of athletic teams, as the "most likely to engage in group sexual assault" (O'Sullivan 1991, p. 144).[1] O'Sullivan argues that cohesiveness gained through team membership, sex-segregated housing, and prestige can be factors in facilitating illicit activities. The group dynamics outlined by O'Sullivan confirm those identified by Sanday (1990), who has conducted extensive research on gang rape in college fraternities. Sanday concludes that the group environment binds men emotionally to one another and contributes to their seeing sex relations from a position of power and status.

There is little doubt that men in sex-segregated groups (sports teams, fraternities, military, etc.) are more likely to commit acts of group sexual assault (Ehrhart and Sandler 1992; O'Sullivan 1991; Sanday 1981, 1990). However, there is a lack of scholarly research on athletes as individual perpetrators of simple rape or aggravated rape.

Using multiple regression analysis of data collected through self-reports, Koss and Gaines (1993) attempted to ascertain the influence of athletic affiliation on sexual aggression. They compared the influence of alcohol use, nicotine use, fraternity membership, and athletic affiliation on sexual aggressive behavior on a Division I college campus. Whereas alcohol and nicotine use were strongly associated with the incidence of sexual assault, varsity athletic participation in "revenue-producing sports" was weakly associated with sexually aggressive behavior by men against women at the university.

The study by Koss and Gaines (1993) has limitations. Because they examined only one campus, Koss and Gaines are reluctant to make generalizations applicable to other universities. Further, their comparison population was taken from introductory courses consisting predominantly of first- and second-year students whose average age was 18.9 years. The athletic population was oversampled and selected from all years. The result is a comparison of the group-affiliated student–athlete against "newer" students less likely to have developed strong campus affiliations. In addition, the study used only self-reported data, which carries inherent limitations on validity (Koss and Gaines 1993). Finally, Koss and Gaines do not distinguish between individual rape and gang rape. Despite these limitations, the research of Koss and Gaines is a groundbreaking step in understanding sexual aggression and college athletes. It is the first rigorous empirical research that identifies athletic affiliation as a predictor (albeit slight) of sexual aggression.

The nature of sexual assault makes it difficult to study. Clinical research in this area is both impractical and unethical. Correlational data can be collected from self-reports or official reports, but both types of data have limitations. Further, we cannot draw conclusions about causality from correlational research. Muehlenhard and Linton (1987) recommend that data from different types of studies converge to provide insight into the problem of sexual assault. Therefore, the design and methodology of this study is to address some of the limitations of the work of Koss and Gaines (1993) and Curry (1991) and determine whether the findings based on official reports of sexual assault are consistent with the findings of previous studies.

The objective of the present study is to examine the relationship between membership on men's varsity sports teams in NCAA Division I universities and officially reported sexual assaults. The study compares the rates of reported sexual assaults for varsity athletes with the rest of the male student population. The data were obtained from records at 30 Division I American universities; 107 cases of sexual assault were examined. The study uses statistical analyses to test the purported relationship between membership on a varsity sports team and officially reported sexual assaults.

METHOD

In general, there are three locations on a college campus where a victim can officially report sexual assault: campus police, judicial affairs,[2] or a rape crisis/counseling center. Of these, only the first two keep records on the perpetrator. However, at nearly all institutions, neither campus police nor judicial affairs offices indicate whether an alleged perpetrator is a student–athlete. Institutions participating in our study were asked to provide the total number of male students enrolled, student–athletes enrolled, sexual assaults reported, and sexual assaults reported that involved a student–athlete by cross-referencing the names of accused perpetrators with the names on official athletic rosters. The figures were calculated at each institution to protect privacy rights.

We purposely selected Division I institutions and, whenever possible, selected schools with highly ranked popular sports. We assumed that these institutions were most likely to support insulated athletic subworlds and systems of affiliation among athletes that, according to the literature (Curry 1991; Messner 1992; Messner and Sabo 1994; Sabo 1980), might lead to problematic behavior.

Two Data Sets

We speculated that the initial response to and subsequent adjudication of incidents of sexual assault differed considerably between campus police and judicial affairs officials. Further, we thought that these differences are understood on some level by victims. Campus police officers operate under the same guidelines as do civil police officers. In most cases, a victim would file an official report with campus police only if she desired to file criminal charges and pursue justice through the state court system. By contrast, administrators in judicial affairs are empowered to independently determine the facts in an alleged assault without being subjected to the strict laws of evidence required in a court of law. Although unable to mete out punishment in the same manner as the criminal justice system, institutions are able to provide more immediate recourse to a victim while maintaining her privacy. Through either a student court or a private hearing conducted by a judicial officer or dean, a school can stipulate disciplinary action that ranges from probation to expulsion. A victim who is seeking a timely response, an immediate separation from the perpetrator with respect to housing or class schedules, or adjudication without a criminal trial may be more inclined to report the incident to judicial affairs.

In other words, although both judicial affairs and campus police process official reports of sexual assault, their functions are not identical. Therefore, we have approached the data as two distinct sample sets. Data were collected from 20 campus police departments and 10 judicial affairs offices.

Campus Police Data Set. With regard to campus police departments, our survey group includes institutions from all geographic regions of the United States. We targeted schools with perennial Top 20 basketball or football teams. Schools that landed teams in the men's Top 20 poll for either basketball or football in at least 2 of the 3 years between 1991 and 1993 were mailed surveys. Of the 49 schools targeted, 20 responded—a response rate of 41 percent. All the reports were usable. The high rate of usability was enhanced by the Campus Security Act (1987), which requires campus police departments to allow public access to information regarding all crime on campus.

Judicial Affairs Data Set. Because judicial affairs offices are not required by the Campus Security Act to reveal information regarding violations of the student codes of conduct, data were much more difficult to obtain than they were from campus police departments. To facilitate a high response rate, we conducted telephone interviews with a judicial affairs representative from institutions in the original sample. Many institutions with Top 20 basketball and football teams were reluctant to participate in this study. Therefore, in addition to 8 Division I institutions with Top 20 athletic programs, we petitioned 8 Division I institutions that did not have perennial Top 20 basketball or football teams. Of these 16 schools that initially agreed to be part of the survey, 12 were able to complete the project (75 percent response rate) and 10 provided usable data. Judicial affairs offices were asked to provide 3 years of data, covering the academic years from 1991 through 1993. Among the respondents, 2 schools did not have records for 1991 and 1 school did not have data from 1993. Of the 10 schools supplying usable data, 5 were perennial Top 20 football or basketball schools according to our operational definition.

Problems and Solutions

Asking for information regarding sexual assaults on campuses poses a number of problems for the researcher. First, this information is extremely sensitive and potentially damaging to the reputation of an institution. Initially, we assured confidentiality to all potential participants. To overcome further hesitancy on the part of institutions, we garnered the support of two influential people—Jim Ferrier, a member of the

International Association of Campus Law Enforcement Administrators, and Carol Bohmer, a legal scholar who has trained judicial affairs officers at institutions around the country. We included their names in the cover letter of our survey. As a result, we were able to gain the cooperation of both police departments and judicial affairs offices at a significant number of schools.

Second, each institution has an obligation to protect the privacy of both the victim and the accused. In keeping with privacy protection laws, the names of individuals accused of sexual assault were neither requested nor revealed. Instead, each participating institution was asked to internally review the names of those students accused of sexual offenses and determine whether they appeared on a varsity team roster at the time of the assault. This required a considerable amount of effort on the part of participating institutions.

Finally, the institutions we surveyed do not adhere to universal definitions for student codes of conduct violations. Rather than asking participating schools to conform to a researcher-created definition of sexual assault, we allowed each institution to maintain its own definition of sexual assault. This procedure ensures that we are reporting data based on codes of conduct violations as described at each institution. The overlap between institutional definitions of sexual assault ensures that all perpetrators reported in this study are accused of either rape, attempted rape, unwanted touching of intimate parts of another person, or the use of threats or intimidation to gain an advantage in nonconsensual sexual contact.

FINDINGS

A summary of the data collected from the two sample sets is listed in Table 17-1.[3]

Male student–athletes comprised 3.8 percent of the total male student population yet represented 5.5 percent of the reported sexual assaults to campus police ($n = 38$). For the combined 3 years of the 10 judicial affairs offices, male student–athletes comprised 3.3 percent of the total male population, yet represented 19 percent of the perpetrators reported ($n = 69$). A two-tailed t test was conducted on these data

Table 17-1 **Summary of Data Collected from Two Sample Sources**

	Campus Police Questionnaire[a]	Judicial Affairs Questionnaire (1991–1993)[b]
Men not on intercollegiate sport teams		
Student population	182,091	252,630
Perpetrators	36	56
Men on intercollegiate sport teams		
Athlete population	6,975	8,739
Perpetrators	2	13

[a]Institutions reporting = 20.

[b]Institutions reporting = 10; annual reports = 27 (1991 = 8, 1992 = 10, 1993 = 9).

Table 17-2 Results of *t* Test for Campus Police Questionnaire (CPQ) and
Judicial Affairs Questionnaire (JAQ)

Survey	Number of Male Nonvarsity Athlete Perpetrators	Men/1,000 Incident Rate	Number of Male Student–Athlete Perpetrators	Men/1,000 Incident Rate	*t* Statistics
CPQ (1992)	36	0.19	2	0.33	–0.70
JAQ (1991)	16	0.20	5	2.21	–2.45*
JAQ (1992)	19	0.21	6	1.72	–1.29
JAQ (1993)	23	0.25	2	0.67	–0.57
JAQ (1991–1993)	56	0.22	13	1.49	–2.47*

*$p < .05$.

to compare the sexual assault perpetrator rate of male student–athletes with that of the rest of the male student population. This test was chosen because we did not hypothesize from the outset the direction of the difference between the student–athletes and the rest of the male student population. We tested for significance to the .05 level, or a confidence level of higher than 95 percent.

Because the judicial affairs data come from different years at the same campuses, we needed to test the appropriateness of combining the 3 years of judicial affairs data. First, the annual data were tested for significance. Then a regression analysis was conducted to determine the appropriateness of combining the 3 years of data for further analysis.[4] Because we found no significant difference between the years, we were able to combine the 3 years to create a larger sample for analysis.

Table 17-2 shows the results of the *t* test for the campus police questionnaire, each year of the judicial affairs questionnaire, and the combined data from judicial affairs.

Campus Police Questionnaire Results

The *t* test reveals that, in the reported sexual assaults to campus police, there is no significant difference between male student–athletes and other male students, $t = –0.70$, $p = .490$. That is, given the current data sample, we cannot state with confidence that collegiate athletes are reported to campus police at a higher rate than are other male students.

Judicial Affairs Questionnaire Results

For the annual data collected from the judicial affairs offices, only in the 1991 academic year are there statistically significant differences between male student–athletes and other male students, $t = –2.45$, $p < .05$, with regard to the rate of being reported for sexual assault. In this year, male student–athletes comprised 2.8 percent of the total male student population and represented 24 percent of the perpetrators reported to judicial affairs for sexual assault ($n = 21$).

By contrast, there were no significant differences in sexual assault incident rates between these two groups based on the 1992 data, $t = -1.29$, $p = .229$, or on the 1993 data, $t = -0.57$, $p = .582$. In 1992, student–athletes comprised 3.7 percent of the total male student population and represented 24 percent of the perpetrators reported to judicial affairs for sexual assault ($n = 25$). In 1993, student–athletes comprised 3.4 percent of the population and represented 8.7 percent of the perpetrators reported to judicial affairs for sexual assault ($n = 25$).

The t test performed on the combined judicial affairs data (1991–1993) reveals statistically significant differences between male student–athletes and other male students, $t = -2.47$, $p < .05$. For the combined 3 years, male student–athletes comprised 3.3 percent of the total male population yet represented 19 percent of the reported perpetrators ($n = 69$). This result indicates an association between collegiate athletic membership and reports of sexual assault to judicial affairs offices.

Finally, we conducted a comparison of student–athletes involved in the revenue-producing contact sports of football and basketball to all other student–athletes. This comparison was made with the combined judicial affairs data (1991–1993). A two-tailed t test indicated that the difference in incident rates between these groups approached significance but was not quite statistically significant, $t = 1.41$, $p = .17$. However, it should be noted that, in this sample, male football and basketball players comprised 30 percent of the student–athlete population, yet are responsible for 67 percent of the reported sexual assaults.

Limitations

Our data included only those sexual assaults officially reported to either campus police or judicial affairs. Some estimates suggest that 84 percent of all rapes go unreported (National Victim's Center, 1992). Although the conditions under which women will report sexual assault are not fully understood, we can assume that reports are not random. Any sample based on official reports, therefore, is not a representative sample of sexual assaults that take place on college campuses. The benefit of working with officially reported sexual assaults is the general high reliability of the claims.[5] Further, the small sample size prevents us from using highly sophisticated statistical tests in our data analysis. Therefore, our study does not include an analysis of all the factors associated with men's sexual aggression toward women; we have no information on the circumstances in which actual cases of sexual aggression occurred. We know only whether the reported perpetrator was a member of an intercollegiate sport team. Given the limitations of the data, we can report only on the statistical relationship between membership on men's intercollegiate sport teams in Division I universities and the incidence of reported sexual assaults at those universities.

CONCLUSION

Given the nature and scope of this research, conclusions based on the data are necessarily limited. For example, to draw conclusions as to the frequency of sexual assault committed by athletes would be a misapplication of these findings. Further, it needs to be reiterated that it is not clear whether the association between athletic affiliation and sexual assault is causal or the result of behavior only indirectly related to sport.

Nonetheless, this research indicates that male college student–athletes, compared with the rest of the male student population, are responsible for a significantly higher percentage of the sexual assaults reported to judicial affairs offices on the campuses of Division I institutions. Although reports of sexual assault by student–athletes to campus police are not statistically different from those by other male students, athletes are nonetheless slightly overrepresented. When the two data sets are viewed concurrently, athletes appear to be disproportionately involved in incidents of sexual assault on college campuses. Further, these findings lend support to other research that links athletic participation and sexual aggression (Curry 1991; Koss and Gaines 1993).

This research makes three significant contributions to this area of study. First, because it relies on official reports, it can be used to counter those who would dismiss the findings based on data from self-reports (Koss and Gaines 1993). The findings of this study do not contradict those of Koss and Gaines, enhancing the validity of their findings. We can state with increasing confidence that there is some connection between the dynamics of being involved on a men's intercollegiate sports team, particularly in the contact sports of football and basketball in Division I universities, and reported cases of sexual assault at those institutions.

Second, we investigated 30 Division I institutions across the United States, 25 of which support top-ranked teams in either football or basketball. Previous researchers have been reluctant to make broad conclusions on the basis of research drawn from single institutions (Curry 1991; Koss and Gaines 1993). Because we sampled a number of institutions, we can assume that our conclusions are generally representative of other large Division I campuses with strong athletic programs.

Finally, this study contributes to a small body of empirical research on an issue that is much discussed yet rarely studied. Popular sports journalism and scholarship alike have attributed one in three sexual assaults committed on college campuses to athletes (Bohmer and Parrot 1993; Deford 1993; Eskanazi 1990; Kane and Disch 1993; Kirshenbaum 1989; Melnick 1992; Nelson 1991, 1994; Toufexis 1990). However, after extensive review of the literature, there does not appear to be any empirical evidence to substantiate this claim, which appears consistently in both academic and sport journalism publications.

Claims that one in three campus sexual assaults is committed by a student–athlete have two primary sources: Richard Hofmann (1986) of the *Philadelphia Daily News* and Gerald Eskanazi (1990) of the *New York Times*. In 1986, Hofmann wrote a four-part series on athletes and sexual assault. Hofmann does not contend that his investigation is scientific. He acknowledges that the figures used in his articles were based on an informal poll of university officials. The findings from this poll were then compared to FBI Uniform Crime Reports. Despite the obvious flaws in this type of comparison, both scholars and journalists have relied on the Hofmann piece to assert that athletes are much more likely to commit sexual assaults.

Eskanazi (1990) misrepresented the work of a leading researcher in the area of sexual assault on campus, Mary Koss. He cites a 3-year National Institute of Mental Health study by Koss claiming that, of the cases studied, athletes were involved about a third of the time. Koss did not control for athletic affiliation in this study and disputes the findings Eskanazi attributes to her.[6]

Implications

Clearly, caution must be employed when discussing the implications of our findings. The popular press has overstated the problem in the past, in part by misrepresenting scientific research. At the same time, the findings of this research clearly indicate the existence of a problem. To suggest that all of these cases are simply a result of athletes being targeted because of their high profile status denies reality. The best interest of institutions cannot be served until those working within the institution admit that a problem exists. Athletic departments and coaches have an obvious interest in learning about and addressing the factors that are contributing to athletes being reported for individual acts of sexual assault (and gang rapes) at a higher rate than that of other male students. Reducing the number of sexual attacks committed by athletes on campus will require a significant effort from athletic departments, coaches, and other educational personnel.

Further Research

The lack of rigorous research in this area points to one obvious avenue of study: replication. In addition to replication, we see three broad research needs: exploration of variables associated with sexually aggressive behavior, factors influencing reporting rates, and efficacy of intervention programs.

From the current research, we are unable to explain the association between varsity athletic membership and sexual assault. It is possible that the association we found has little to do with athletic participation but rather is associated with some other behavior only indirectly related to athletics. Despite the association between intercollegiate athletic membership and reported sexual assaults, far stronger associations have been found between sexual assault and alcohol use, nicotine use, and hostile attitudes toward women (Koss and Gaines 1993). Those who attempt replication, then, will want to test more variables.

Further, there is a need for more studies so that we can learn more about patterns within and between universities and develop explanations for those patterns. For example, although the sample size was small, the data hinted that sexual assault was not endemic to all sports. Contact sports such as football and basketball were overrepresented, raising the possibility that athletes trained to use physical domination on the field are more likely to carry these lessons into their relationships. Even here, reports were not uniform from school to school, suggesting that the social environment of programs may vary significantly and have a substantial impact on the rate of sexual assault.

Conversations between members of the research team and university officials indicated that the prevalence of reported sexual assaults by athletes was dramatic in some instances following changes in coaching staffs. This suggests that coaches may have a significant impact on the team's social milieu and thus on athletes' behavior outside of sport. A qualitative approach to this topic might prove most beneficial.

There is also a need to explore factors influencing rates of reporting. The disparity between the data sets (police and judicial affairs) not only confirms our speculation about the differences between these two reporting sites but also reinforces our earlier cautions about official reports not producing representative samples. This disparity also suggests a new avenue of research: Under what conditions do women report sexual assaults committed by athletes? One possible explanation for the disparity is that women believe that the university will provide swifter recourse while significantly reducing the amount of public humiliation that accompanies a criminal trial. In addition, victims may anticipate an extremely negative response from the broader community if they were to press criminal charges against a Division I athlete. Conversely, women may perceive more severe retribution from other male groups (e.g., fraternity members) with whom they socialize on a regular basis (Martin and Hummer 1989) than they do from athletes, who are less likely to be a part of their daily lives. Clearly, more research is needed in this area.

Finally, if sexual aggression is a form of behavior that is influenced by social and group cultural factors, subject to control and change, intervention and education may reduce the frequency of sexually aggressive behavior among men, including athletes. Recently, educators have developed sexual assault prevention programs specifically designed to reach athletes (Parrot 1994). Social researchers must go beyond describing the problem; they must document the relative success of these programs and make recommendations for more effective interventions.

NOTES

1. Of the 24 campus gang rapes analyzed by O'Sullivan (1991), 54 percent were committed by fraternities, 38 percent by athletes, and 8 percent by other groups.

2. In general, the term *judicial affairs* refers to a department with jurisdiction over university and college code of conduct violations. Every institution has a method of disciplining students who violate university rules. Although there is not a universal protocol for establishing a judicial affairs office, schools typically have either a dean or judicial affairs director who is responsible for overseeing any alleged violations of the student code of conduct. Most institutions have either a student court or a body of administrators that hears complaints and determines appropriate sanctions.

3. It should be noted that the original data set included two gang rapes, one of which was committed by a group of student–athletes. Due to the focus of our research, we excluded this data from our sample.

4. The dependent variable for this analysis was the difference between the incident rates for student–athletes and those for other male students. Two dummy variables, coded for year (1991, 1992, 1993), were the independent variables. The regression results showed that neither of the coefficients for the independent variables was statistically significant, $t = 1.44$, $p = .16$; $t = .49$, $p = .63$. Thus the differences between the incident rates were not statistically related to the year of data collection. Therefore, it was determined that combining the 3 years of judicial affairs data for analysis purposes would be appropriate.

5. Although a more representative sample might have been gathered through self-reports, the reliability of this form of data has been the subject of considerable attack in the popular press. Admittedly, there are some limitations inherent with research based on self-reported data. They are nowhere near as pronounced as they appear in the press (see, e.g., Rophie 1993). The most public attacks have been authored by academics and students who do not have training in statistical research. The willingness of the media to publish these attacks speaks to the level of hostility gender researchers face in these rather reactionary times (Faludi 1991).

6. Based on a personal conversation with Mary Koss.

REFERENCES

Bohmer, C., and A. Parrot. 1993. *Sexual Assault on Campus: The Problem and the Solution.* Lexington, MA: Lexington.

Brownmiller, S. 1975. *Against Our Will.* New York: Simon and Schuster.

Bryson, L. 1987. "Sport and Maintenance of Masculine Hegemony." *Women's Studies International Forum* 10: 349–360.

Curry, T. 1991. "Fraternal Bonding in the Locker Room: A Profeminist Analysis of Talk about Competition and Women." *Sociology of Sport Journal* 8: 119–135.

Deford, F. 1993. "Does Team Sports Culture Encourage Prospect of Rape?" National Public Radio, March 24.

Dershowitz, A. 1994. "When Women Cry Rape—Falsely." *Boston Herald,* August 6, 13.

Ehrhart, J., and D. Sandler. 1992. *Campus Gang Rape: Party Games?* Washington, DC: Center for Women Policy Studies.

Eskanazi, G. 1990. "The Male Athlete and Sexual Assault." *New York Times,* June 3, 1, 4.

Faludi, S. 1991. *Backlash: The Undeclared War against American Women.* New York: Crown.

Hofmann, R. 1986. "Rape and the College Athlete." *Philadelphia Daily News,* March 17, 102.

Kane, M. J., and L. Disch. 1993. "Sexual Violence and the Reproduction of Male Power in the Locker Room: The 'Lisa Olson Incident.'" *Sociology of Sport Journal* 10: 4.

Kidd, B. 1990. "The Men's Cultural Center: Sports and the Dynamic of Women's Oppression/ Men's Repression." In M. Messner and D. Sabo, eds., *Sport, Men and the Gender Order: Critical Feminist Perspectives.* Champaign, IL: Human Kinetics.

Kirshenbaum, J. 1989. "An American Disgrace: A Violent and Unprecedented Lawlessness Has Arisen among College Athletes in All Parts of the Country." *Sports Illustrated* (February 27): 16.

Koss, M., and J. Gaines. 1993. "The Prediction of Sexual Aggression by Alcohol Use, Athletic Participation and Fraternity Affiliation." *Journal of Interpersonal Violence* 8: 94–108.

Larimer, T. 1991. "Under Pressure to Produce Winners, Some College Coaches Turn to Risky Recruits." *Sporting News* (December 16): 8.

MacKinnon, C. 1987. *Feminism Unmodified: Discourses on Life and Law.* Cambridge, MA: Harvard University Press.

Malamuth, N., R. Sockloskie, P. Koss, and T. Tanaka. 1991. "Characteristics of Aggressors against Women: Testing a Model Using a National Sample of College Students." *Journal of Consulting and Clinical Psychology* 50: 670–681.

Martin, P., and R. Hummer. 1989. "Fraternities and Rape on Campus." *Gender and Society* 3: 457–473.

Melnick, M. 1992. "Male Athletes and Sexual Assault." *Journal of Physical Education, Recreation, and Dance* 63, no. 5: 32–35.

Messner, M. 1992. *Power at Play: Sports and the Problems of Masculinity.* Boston: Beacon.

Messner, M., and D. Sabo. 1994. *Sex, Violence, and Power in Sports: Rethinking Masculinity.* Freedom, CA: Crossing.

Muehlenhard, C., and M. Linton. 1987. "Date Rape and Sexual Aggression in Dating Situations: Incidence and Risk Factors." *Journal of Counseling Psychology* 34: 186–196.

National Victim's Center. 1992. *Rape in America: Report to the Nation,* April 23. Arlington, VA: National Victim's Center.

Nelson, M. B. 1991. *Are We Winning Yet? How Women Are Changing Sports and Sports Are Changing Women.* New York: Random House.

———. 1994. *The Stronger Women Get, the More Men Love Football: Sexism and the American Culture of Sports.* New York: Harcourt Brace.

O'Sullivan, C. 1991. "Acquaintance Gang Rape on Campus." Pp. 120–156 in A. Parrot and L. Bechhofer, eds., *Acquaintance Rape: The Hidden Crime.* New York: Wiley.

Parrot, A. 1994. "A Rape Awareness and Prevention Model for Male Athletes." *Journal of American College Health* 42 (January): 179–184.

Parrot, A., and L. Bechhofer. 1991. *Acquaintance Rape: The Hidden Crime.* New York: Wiley.

Rophie, K. 1993. "Date Rape's Other Victim." *New York Times Magazine* (June 13): 26.

Russell, D. 1975. *The Politics of Rape: The Victim's Perspective.* New York: Stein and Day.

Sabo, D. 1980. "Best Years of My Life?" Pp. 74–78 in D. Sabo and R. Runfola, eds., *Jock: Sports and Male Identity.* Englewood Cliffs, NJ: Prentice-Hall.

Sabo, D., and R. Runfola. 1980. *Jock: Sports and Male Identity.* Englewood Cliffs, NJ: Prentice-Hall.

Sanday, P. 1981. "The Socio-Cultural Context of Rape: A Cross-Cultural Study. *Journal of Social Issues* 37, no. 4: 5–27.

———. 1990. *Fraternity Gang Rapes: Sex, Brotherhood, and Privilege on Campus.* New York: New York University Press.

Toufexis, A. 1990. "Sex in the Sporting Life: Do Athletic Teams Unwittingly Promote Assaults and Rapes?" *Time* (August 6): 76.

Whitson, D. 1990. "Sport and the Social Construction of Masculinity." Pp. 19–30 in M. Messner and D. Sabo, eds., *Sport, Men, and the Gender Order: Critical Feminist Perspectives.* Champaign, IL: Human Kinetics.

18

Crime and Athletes

New Racial Stereotypes

Richard E. Lapchick

It is ironic that as we begin a new millennium, hopeful that change will end the ills such as racism that have plagued our society throughout past centuries, more subtle forms of racism in sport may be infecting American culture.

Polite white society can no longer safely express the stereotypes that so many believe about African Americans. Nonetheless, surveys show that the majority of whites still believe that most African Americans are less intelligent, are more likely to use drugs and be violent, and are more inclined to be violent against women.

However, sport as it is currently being interpreted, now provides whites with the chance to talk about athletes in a way that reinforces those stereotypes about African Americans. With African Americans dominating the sports we watch most often (77 percent of the players in the National Basketball Association, 65 percent in the National Football League, 15 percent in Major League Baseball—another 25 percent are Latino). African Americans comprise 57 percent of the students playing National Collegiate Athletic Association (NCAA) Division I basketball and 47 percent of those playing NCAA Division IA football. Whites tend to "think black" when they think about the major sports.

Many athletes and community leaders believe that the public has been unfairly stereotyping athletes all across America. The latest, and perhaps most dangerous,

Source: Richard E. Lapchick, "Crime and Athletes: New Racial Stereotypes," *Society* 37 (March–April 2000): 14–20. Copyright © 2000 Springer Science and Business Media. Used by permission.

stereotype, is that playing sport makes athletes more prone to being violent and, especially, gender violent.

Rosalyn Dunlap, an eight-time All-American sprinter who now works on social issues involving athletes, including gender violence prevention, said, "perpetrators are not limited to any category or occupation. The difference is that athletes who rape or batter will end up on TV or in the newspapers. Such images of athletes in trouble create a false and dangerous mindset with heavy racial overtones. Most other perpetrators will be known only to the victims, their families, the police and the courts."

On our predominantly white college campuses, student athletes are being characterized by overwhelmingly white student bodies and faculties while they are being written about by a mostly white male media for a preponderance of white fans.

At an elite academic institution, I asked members of the audience to write down five words they would use to describe American athletes. In addition to listing positive adjectives, not one missed including one of the following words: dumb, violent, rapist, or drug user!

In the past two years, I have met with NBA and NFL players as well as college-student athletes on more than a dozen campuses. There are a lot of angry athletes who are convinced the public is characterizing them because of the criminal acts of a few.

Tom "Satch" Sanders helped the Boston Celtics win eight world championships. Sanders noted, "If they aren't angry about their broad brush depiction, they should be. The spotlight is extremely bright on athletes; their skills have made them both famous and vulnerable. Their prominence means they will take much more heat from the media and the public for similar situations that befall other people with normal lives."

He is now vice president for player programs for the NBA. That office helps guide players off the court to finish their education, prepares them for careers after basketball, and helps those that may have problems adjusting to all the attention that goes to NBA stars.

Many American men have grown to dislike athletes. Given the choice, a typical man might want the money and the fame but knows it is unattainable for him. After reading all the negative stories about athletes, he doesn't want to read about Mike Tyson complaining about being treated unfairly when Tyson has made a reported $100 million in his post-release rehabilitation program; or about the large number of professional athletes signing contracts worth more than $10 million a year.

The anger of some white men extends to people who look or act differently than themselves. They are a mini-thought away from making egregious stereotypes about the "other groups" they perceive as stealing their part of the American pie.

Big-time athletes fit the "other groups." Whether it is an African American athlete or coach, or a white coach of African American athletes, when something goes wrong with a player, the national consequences are likely to be immediate.

Sanders expanded on this. "Everyone feels that athletes have to take the good with the bad, the glory with the negative publicity. However, no one appreciates the broad brush application that is applied in so many instances. Of the few thousand that play sport on the highest level, if four or five individuals in each sport—particularly if they are black—have problems with the law, people won't have long to wait before some media people are talking about all those athletes."

Here is the equation we are dealing with as stereotypes of our athletes are built. Fans, who are mostly white, observe sport through a media filter which is overwhelmingly made up of white men. There are 1,600 daily newspapers in America. There are only four African American sports editors in a city where there are professional franchises and 19 African American columnists. Both numbers, as reported at the recent conference of the National Association of Black Journalists, have almost doubled since 1998 and represent a positive sign. Nonetheless, there are no African American sports writers on 90 percent of the 1,600 papers!

I do not, nor would I ever, suggest that most or even many of the white writers are racist. However, they were raised in a culture in which many white people have strong beliefs about what it means to be African American.

The obvious result is the *reinforcement* of white stereotypes of athletes, who are mostly African American in our major sports.

According to the National Opinion Research Center Survey, sponsored by the National Science Foundation for the University of Chicago, whites share the following attitudes:

- 56 percent of whites think African Americans are more violent;
- 62 percent think African Americans are not as hard working as whites;
- 77 percent of whites think most African Americans live off welfare;
- 53 percent think African Americans are less intelligent.

It can be expected that some white writers learned these stereotypes in their own upbringing. When they read about an individual or several athletes who have a problem, it becomes easy to leap to the conclusion that fits the stereotype. Sanders said, "Blacks in general have been stereotyped for having drugs in the community as well as for being more prone to violence. However, now more than ever before, young black athletes are more individualistic and they resist the 'broad brush.' They insist on being judged as individuals for everything." But even that resistance can be misinterpreted by the public and writers as merely being off-the-court trash-talking.

SPORTS' SPECIFIC PROBLEMS

There are, of course, problems in college and professional sports. For the purposes of this chapter, I will only deal with those that involve problems and perceptions of athletes.

Our athletes are coming from a generation of despairing youth cut adrift from the American dream. When the Center for the Study of Sport in Society started in 1984, one of its primary missions was helping youth balance academics and athletics. Now, the issue for youth is balancing life and death.

We are recruiting athletes:

- who have increasingly witnessed violent death. If one American child under the age of 16 is killed every two hours with a handgun, then there is a good chance that our athletes will have a fallen family member or friend. More American children have died from handguns in the last ten years than all the American soldiers who died in Vietnam. Tragedies in places like Paducah, Kentucky, and Littleton, Colorado, have shown us that violent deaths are not limited to our cities.
- who are mothers and fathers when they get to our schools. There are boys who helped 900,000 teenage girls get pregnant each year so we are increasingly getting student-athletes who will leave our colleges after four years with one or more children who are 4–5 years old.
- who have seen friends or family members devastated by drugs.
- who have seen battering in their home.
- who were victims of racism in school. Three-quarters (75 percent) of all students surveyed by Lou Harris reported seeing or hearing about racially or religiously motivated confrontations with overtones of violence very or somewhat often.
- who come home alone: 57 percent of all American families, black and white alike, are headed by either a single parent or two working parents.

We desperately need professionals on our campuses who can deal with these nightmarish factors. The reality is that few campuses or athletic departments have the right people to help guide these young men and women into the 21st century. So what are our problems?

ACADEMIC ISSUES IN COLLEGE SPORT

Academically, we get athletes who have literacy problems. The press discusses that student-athletes have literacy problems extensively throughout the year as if it were a problem unique to athletes. However, it is rarely reported—and never in the sports pages—that 30 percent of *all entering freshmen* must take remedial English or math.

Academically, we get athletes who will not graduate. It is—and always should be—an issue for college athletics to increase the percentages of those who graduate from our colleges. However, the demographics of college have now changed to the point where only 14 percent of entering freshmen graduate in four years. If an athlete does not graduate in four years, some call him dumb; others say the school failed him. Few note that he may be typical of college students.

Don McPherson nearly led Syracuse to a national championship when he was their quarterback in the 1980s. After seven years in the NFL and CFL, McPherson worked until recently directing the Mentors in Violence Prevention (MVP) Program.

MVP is the nation's biggest program using athletes as leaders to address the issue of men's violence against women.

McPherson reflected on the image of intelligence and athletes. "When whites meet an uneducated black athlete who blew opportunities in college or high school, they think he is dumb. They don't question what kind of school he may have had to attend if he was poor, or how time pressures from sport may have affected him. If they don't make it as a professional athlete, they're through without a miracle.

"I met lots of 'Trust Fund Babies' at Syracuse. They blew opportunities. No one called them dumb, just rich. We knew they would not need a miracle to get a second chance.

"I played at Syracuse at a time when being a black quarterback had become more acceptable. But the stereotypes still remained. As a player, people still remember me as a great runner and scrambler. I had not dented their image of the physical vs. intelligent black athlete."

This was in spite of the fact that McPherson led the nation in passing efficiency over Troy Aikman and won the Maxwell Award. He won many awards but Don McPherson was most proud of being the nation's passing efficiency leader. "I should have shattered the image of the athletic and mobile black quarterback and replaced it with the intelligent black quarterback. Unfortunately, stereotypes of football players, mostly black, still prevail. They make me as angry as all the stereotypes of black people in general when I was growing up."

McPherson wore a suit to class and carried the *New York Times* under his arm. He was trying to break other images of African American men and athletes. But McPherson said that those whites who recognized his style were both "surprised and said I was 'a good black man' as if I was different from other black men. Most students assumed I was poor and that football was going to make me rich. Like many other blacks on campus, I was middle class. My father was a detective and my mother was a nurse."

There is a common belief that student-athletes, especially those in the revenue sports, have lower graduation rates than students who are not athletes. The facts do not bear this out. Yet it is difficult to get accurate reporting.

- Irrespective of color or gender, student-athletes graduate at higher rate than non-student-athletes.
- White male Division I student-athletes graduate at a rate of 58 percent vs. 57 percent for white male nonathletes. African American male Division I student-athletes graduate at a rate of 42 percent vs. 34 percent for African American male nonathletes.
- White female Division I student-athletes graduate at a rate of 70 percent while 61 percent of white female nonathletes graduate. African American female Division I student-athletes graduate at a rate of 58 versus only 43 percent of the African American female nonathletes.

The disparities, however, remain when we compare white to African American student athletes:

- White male Division I basketball student-athletes graduate at a rate of 52 percent versus a 38 percent graduation rate for African American male Division I basketball student-athletes, still higher than the 34 percent grad rate for African American male nonathletes.
- White female Division I basketball student athletes graduate at a rate of 71 percent while only 57 percent of African American female Division I basketball student-athletes graduate.

College sport does not own these problems. They belong to higher education in general and its inheritance of the near bankruptcy of secondary education in some communities. The publication of graduation rates, long feared by athletic administrators, at once revealed those scandalous rates, but also showed what poor graduation rates there were for all students of color. It turned out that our predominantly white campuses were unwelcoming environments for all people of color.

African American student-athletes arrive on most campuses and see that only seven percent of the student body, three percent of the faculty, and less than five percent of top athletics administrators and coaches look like them. Unless there is a Martin Luther King Center or Boulevard, all of the buildings and streets are named after white people.

In many ways, the publication of graduation rates for student-athletes helped to push the issue of diversity to the forefront of campus-wide discussions of issues of race, ethnicity, and gender. Educators finally recognized what a poor job they were doing at graduating all students of color.

DRUGS AND ALCOHOL IN SPORT

We will get athletes who use drugs. CNN Headline News will understandably run footage of every name athlete who is arrested with drugs. It has become a common belief that athletes have a particular problem with drug and alcohol abuse. Reoccurring problems of athletes like Darryl Strawberry reinforce this image but facts do not bear this out.

According to an extensive *Los Angeles Times* survey of athletes and crime committed in 1995, a total of 22 athletes and three coaches were accused of a drug-related crime in 1995. That means that, on average, we read about a new sports figure with a drug problem every two weeks! Anecdotally, those numbers have seemed to continue in succeeding years. Each new story reinforces the image from the last one.

Their stories are and surely should be disturbing. But those stories are rarely, if ever, put in the context of the 1.9 million Americans who use cocaine each month or the 2.1 million who use heroin throughout their lives. A total of 13 million people (or a staggering 6 percent of the American population) use some illicit drug each month. When you look at the 18–25 male age group in general, the percentage leaps to 17 percent. Twenty-two athletes represent a small fraction of a single percent of the more than 400,000 who play college and professional sports in America.

The NBA's drug policy with the potential of a lifetime ban is generally recognized as a model for sports. The policy may have stopped a substance abuse problem that existed before its inception.

Now players recognize that using so-called "recreational" drugs can seriously hurt their professional abilities in one of America's most competitive professions. Don McPherson emphasized the point that "our personal and professional lives have to be clean and sharp. We cannot afford to lose the competitive edge or our careers will be cut short. There are too many talented young men waiting to step in our shoes."

The NBA's Sanders insists that African American athletes are still being stereotyped as drug users because "blacks in general have been stereotyped for having drugs in the community.... I know they [athletes] are hurt by the broad brush" used by the public when it come to African American athletes.

In the same *Los Angeles Times* survey, 28 athletes and 4 coaches had charges related to alcohol. None of these 32 cases were put in the context of the 13 million Americans who engage in binge drinking at least 5 times per month. Yet we read about a new athlete with an alcohol problem every 11 days. Such images can surely create a building sense of problems in athletics if they are not viewed in the context of society.

McPherson remembered being "shocked" when he arrived on Syracuse's campus to see how much drinking went on each night among students in general. He felt compelled to call football players he knew on other campuses. "It was the same everywhere. Now when I go to speak on college campuses I always ask. It is worse today. Athletes are also part of that culture, but insist that practice and academics crowd their schedules too much to be in bars as often as other students."

ATHLETES AND VIOLENCE

We are getting athletes who have fights during games, in bars, and on campus. Is there a link between the violence of a sport and one's actions away from that sport? There is certainly a growing body of public opinion that assumes that there is. Media reports regularly imply that the violence of sport makes its participants more violent in society.

Are sports any more violent today than 20 years ago when no one would have made such an assertion? Or is it the fact that our streets and our schools surely are more violent. According to the National Education Association, there are 2,000 assaults *in our schools every hour of every day!* It is an ugly phenomenon that is neither bound by race, class, geography, nor by athlete vs. nonathlete.

We do have athletes who are the perpetrators in cases of gender violence. In the wake of the O.J. Simpson case, any incident involving an athlete assaulting a woman has received extraordinary publicity. The individual cases add up to the mindset stereotype of 1999: athletes, especially basketball and football players, are more inclined to be violent towards women than nonathletes.

Joyce Williams-Mitchell is the executive director of the Massachusetts Coalition of Battered Women's Service Groups. As an African American woman, she abhors the imagery of athletes being more prone to be violent against women. "It is a myth. The facts do not bear this out. All the studies of patterns of batterers; defined by occupation point to men who control women through their profession. We hear about police, clergy, dentists, and judges. I only hear about athletes as batterers when I read the paper. They are in the public's eye. Men from every profession have the potential to [be] batterers."

There have been, of course, too many cases of athletes committing assaults on girls and women.

However, there has never been a thorough, scientific study conclusively showing that athletes are more inclined than others to commit assaults. The only study that comes close was written by Jeffrey Benedict, Todd Crossett, and Mark McDonald. It was based on 65 cases of assault against women over three years on 10 Division I campuses. Thirteen of the cases involved athletes; seven were basketball or football players.

In spite of the authors pointing out the limitations of both the small numbers and the fact that they did not control for use of alcohol, tobacco, and the man's attitude toward women (the three main predictors of a male's inclination to gender violence), the press regularly quotes their study without qualification. Media reports never state that it is a study that came up with 13 athletes over three years. They simply say that the study concluded that nearly 20 percent of all campus assaults are committed by student-athletes and most are committed by basketball or football players. Rosalyn Dunlap underlines that "This is a racially loaded conclusion. When I was a student-athlete at the University of Missouri, I never thought of keeping myself safe from a 260-pound football player anymore than any other man on the street. In fact, male athletes on campus protected me."

Here is some critical data usually missing in the debate about athletes and violence against women.

- In 1994, 1,400 men killed their significant others. O.J. Simpson was the only athlete accused of murder.
- In 1998, an estimated three million women were battered and close to one million were raped. According to various reports in the press over the past five years, between 70 and 100 athletes and coaches have been accused of assault against a woman each year.
- In data released in 1999 in *The Chronicle of Higher Education*'s annual campus crime survey, there were 1,053 forcible sex offenses in 1997. Less than 35 student-athletes were arrested.

Gender violence is a serious problem of men in America. The cost of crime to America is pegged at $500 billion per year according to a National Institute for Justice research report for the Justice Department released in March 1996. Gender assault and child abuse account for $165 billion—more than one-third of that total! Men who beat their significant others are statistically also likely to beat their children.

Dunlap, who works with McPherson to create more awareness about the issue, said, "There are no men who should be exempted from being educated about the issue of gender violence although many believe they are. It is a problem for naval commanders, day care providers, fraternities, guys at a bar, in corporations, in halls of higher education and, yes, on athletic teams. But no more so on athletic teams."

There have been numerous cases in corporations in which women brought suits against the corporation for harassment and/or assault. The *Boston Globe* gave extensive coverage to the case in which there were 16 formal legal complaints for incidents from sexual harassment to rape at Astra USA, Inc., a chemical company. Mitsubishi had a suit against it placed by 29 women for the same reasons. No stories about Astra suggested that working in a chemical company produced this climate. At Mitsubishi, no one suggested that any relationship to the manufacturing process is a link to gender assault. So why do stories about athletes imply such a linkage to athletics? Does it fit white America's racial imagery?

McPherson believes it does.

> Football and basketball mean black. When the public talks about gender violence and athletes, it talks black. No one discusses the problems of golfer John Dailey or Braves manager Bobby Cox. Warren Moon was another story altogether.
>
> Problems about athletes hit the papers and people think they detect a pattern because of the seeming frequency. But no one else's problems get in the papers. How do we make legitimate comparisons?
>
> With Astra and Mitsubishi, we look at the corporate climate and don't generalize about individuals. But with athletes, especially black athletes, we look at players and look for patterns to add up.

Some observers say athletes are trained to be violent and we can expect that to carry over into our homes. If this is true about training, then what about the training we give to police, the Army, Air Force, Navy, and Marines to use lethal force. Will they come home and kill? McPherson adds, "There is no logic to connect these cases but we do fit our stereotypes of African Americans with such images when we carry through the implication for athletes."

With all the recent publicity about the horrors of gender violence, it would be easy to forget that it was America's big, dirty secret until the notoriety surrounding the O.J. Simpson case. Few were willing to talk about gender violence. But we can never change if we do not confront this disease that is devouring our communities. The same unwillingness to confront racism diminishes society's ability to eradicate it.

Neither were being realistically discussed on college campuses nor in corporate board rooms. We are paying a horrible human price as we realize that society rarely told men that their dominating and controlling actions against women have helped create a climate in which there is a seemingly uncontrollable tidal wave of men's brutality against women.

Athletes should take a leadership role on this, just as they have on drug abuse and educational opportunities. In 1990, Louis Harris completed a landmark study which showed that our children desire to participate in changing their society and viewed athletes as their first choice in terms of who they wanted to give them socially relevant messages.

The MVP Program, organized in 1992 by Northeastern University's Center for the Study of Sport in Society, has been on more than 55 campuses over the last seven years training male athletes to be spokespeople on the issue of gender violence. Each of those schools has become proactive on an issue that has hurt so many women and their families. Don McPherson worked full-time for MVP for several years.

Our society is unraveling at a breakneck pace and McPherson insists "we have to do more to help our youth survive by including our athletes rather than excluding them in helping our youth. The stereotyping of our athletes does not help. We need to be ready with facts to dispute the easy labels."

McPherson and Sanders both argue vigorously that America's athletes not only don't fit the emerging stereotypes about athletes and crime but that the vast majority of professional athletes are extremely positive individuals. Sanders said, "When I look at the many NBA players who have their own foundations and who are very involved with giving back to the communities where they play and where they came from, I know they are hurt by the stereotypes." McPherson asserts that "most of the players in the NFL are deeply religious, family-centered men who are constantly giving back to their communities with time and money."

Rosalyn Dunlap wonders when the public and the media will stop being cynical about athletes.

> I hear so many people say that if athletes do some thing in the community that they do it for publicity. Why can't we accept that athletes want to help?
>
> Sport and those who play it can help educate us and sensitize us. While we can't ignore the bad news, we should also focus on the overwhelming good news of what athletes do to make this a better world.

What is the power of sport? Lin Dawson, a ten-year NFL veteran who has spent much his post-playing career in efforts to improve race relations, said,

> Sports can bring good news that can lift the weight of the world. That is a powerful gift to possess, one we all share when we use it in the most noble way we can—to lift the spiritual poverty that hovers over our children. That spirit is the antidote to the loneliness and the feeling of being unwanted that so many young people are burdened with.
>
> We can give them the richness of spirit that comes with being part of a real team, being interdependent and being able to count on a brother or a sister in a time of need.

Sports figures are in a unique position to affect change. Among them are a few who have dramatically hurt the image of the vast majority. Dawson, who is now the chief operating officer of the National Consortium for Academics and Sport, added, "the community needs positive role models now more than ever. They can help young people to believe in what they cannot yet see. Our children need faith considering what they do see in their communities."

The distortions about our athletes and the crimes that a few of them commit need to be put in their real social context. The misleading perceptions need to be corrected so we can focus on the truth and what is really necessary. In that way, we can help America live up to the dream that Jackie Robinson created for us more than 50 years ago.

* FOR FURTHER STUDY *

Benedict, Jeff. 2004. *Out of Bounds: Inside the NBA's culture of Rape, Violence, and Crime.* New York: HarperCollins.

Coakley, Jay. 2007. *Sports in Society: Issues and Controversies.* 9th ed. New York: McGraw-Hill.

Eitzen, D. Stanley. 2000. "Sport and Social Control." Pp. 370–381 in Jay Coakley and Eric Dunning, eds., *Handbook of Sport Studies.* London: Sage.

Eitzen, D. Stanley, and George H. Sage. 2009. *Sociology of North American Sport.* 8th ed. Boulder, CO: Paradigm.

Horrow, Rick. 2006. "You Can Still Bet on It: Gambling and March Madness." Available at http://cbs.sportsline.com (September 26).

Nack, William, and Don Yaeger. 1999. "Every Parent's Nightmare." *Sports Illustrated* (September 13): 40–53.

Nixon, Howard L. II. 2008. *Sport in a Changing World.* Boulder, CO: Paradigm.

Palmer, Catherine. 2001. "Outside the Imagined Community: Basque Terrorism, Political Activism, and the Tour de France." *Sociology of Sport Journal* 18 (2): 143–161.

Young, Kevin. 2000. "Sport and Violence." Pp. 382–407 in Jay Coakley and Eric Dunning, eds., *Handbook of Sport Studies.* London: Sage.

Zaichkowsky, Leonard D. 2000. "The Dark Side of Youth Sports: Coaches Sexually Abusing Children." *USA Today* 128 (January): 56–58.

PART SEVEN

Problems of Excess: Performance-Enhancing Drugs in Sports

Athletes have long used artificial means to enhance performance. These practices raise many questions: Is it fair to have competitions where some athletes compete against those who have used artificial means to improve upon their natural abilities? If you feel that it is unfair, then where do you draw the line? Should any athlete that uses a stimulant be disqualified? Then what about the caffeine in coffee? Should athletes who sleep in parabolic chambers to simulate the conditions of high altitude be disqualified but not those endurance athletes who train at high altitudes? What about vitamins? Bee pollen? Is it all right for wrestlers and boxers to use over-the-counter diuretics to lose weight in order to compete at lower weight classes? Should access to the wonders of the pharmaceutical world trump training, hard work, and strategy? Or is that cheating?

The first chapter in this section provides the background information on anabolic steroids—the most commonly abused drug used by athletes for strength. Included are what the drug does, the extent of usage, and the short- and long-term health effects for users.

The second chapter looks to the future of performance enhancement—gene doping. That is, permanently inserting strength- or endurance-boosting genes into DNA. The final selection by sportswriter Robert Lipsyte shows the role of drugs in society by athletes and nonathletes alike. The issues and contradictions are complex. So, too, are the answers.

19

Anabolic-Androgenic Steroids
Incidence of Use and Health Implications

Charles E. Yesalis and Michael S. Bahrke

"The use of performance-enhancing drugs like steroids in baseball, football and other sports is dangerous, and it sends the wrong message—that there are shortcuts to accomplishment, and that performance is more important than character."
—President George W. Bush, State of the Union address, January 20, 2004

NOTE FROM THE EDITORS

In recent months there have been more than a few stories in the national media related to the use of anabolic-androgenic steroids among athletes. Because of this attention, and because steroid abuse is not limited to athletes, the editors felt that the time was right for an issue of the *Research Digest* devoted to steroids. As the reference list for this article attests, Charles Yesalis and Michael Bahrke, the authors of this issue of the *Research Digest,* are widely published experts on steroid use and abuse. Yesalis and Bahrke were charged with presenting the evidence about steroid use, something that they did quite well. The authors were not asked to dwell on the legal and ethical issues associated with the use of steroids. For this reason, the editors wish to make it

Source: Charles E. Yesalis and Michael S. Bahrke, "Anabolic-Androgenic Steroids: Incidence of Use and Health Implications," *President's Council on Physical Fitness and Sports Research Digest* ser. 5, no. 5 (March 2005).

clear to readers, especially youth who might read this paper, that anabolic-androgenic steroids are illegal drugs when used for performance enhancement and attempting to increase muscle mass. In addition most sports organizations, including the Olympics, the NCAA, high school athletic groups, and professional sports, ban the use of these substances. These bans are based on the notion that the use of performance-enhancing drugs is not only illegal, but unethical. More importantly, as the authors of this issue point out, there are many negative health consequences associated with the inappropriate use of steroids.

INTRODUCTION

Testosterone is the primary natural male hormone (produced primarily by the testes). Though testosterone is considered to be the "male" hormone, it is also present in females in lesser amounts. Testosterone has androgenic or masculinizing effects such as growth of facial and body hair and deepening of the voice. In addition, testosterone has anabolic or tissue-building effects such as increases in muscle cell size. Because males produce more testosterone as they mature, both masculinizing and tissue-building changes are observed during adolescence and into adulthood. Tissue building is increased in females as well, but not to the same extent as for males.

By 1935, testosterone had been isolated and chemically characterized, and the nature of its anabolic effects elucidated (Kochakian and Yesalis, 2000). Anabolic-androgenic steroids, as discussed in this paper, are synthetic derivatives of testosterone. A pure anabolic steroid has yet to be discovered, but many different forms of derivatives of this drug (with many different names) are now in distribution (see Table 19-1), all properly referred to as anabolic-androgenic steroids. The more common term "anabolic steroid" is used here for convenience. Related substances include prohormones, such as androstenedione ("Andro") and dehydroepiandrosterone (DHEA), which are steroids in the biosynthesis pathway.

Most commonly, anabolic steroids are taken orally or by intra-muscular injection (see Table 19-2). More recently, gels and creams are being used by elite athletes as delivery mechanisms in an attempt to circumvent drug testing.

Table 19-1 **Examples of Anabolic Agents Identified by the 31 IOC/WADA Accredited Laboratories in 2003**

Testosterone	Nandrolone	Stanozolol
Methandienone	Mesterolone	Boldenone
Tetrahydrogestrinone (THG)	Methyltestosterone	Methenolone
Oxandrolone	Androstenedione (Andro)	Clostebol
Fluoxymesterone	Danazol	Oxymetholone
DHEA	Norethandrolone	Drostanolone
Oxymesterone	Trenbolone	

Source: World Anti-Doping Agency, http://www.wada-ama.org/en/tl.asp, WADA Statistics, 2003.

Table 19-2 Examples of Oral and/or Injectible Anabolic Steroids

Steroid	Oral*	Injectible**
Testosterone cypionate		X
Nandrolone decanoate		X
Stanozolol	X	X
Methandienone	X	
Mesterolone	X	
Boldenone undecylenate		X
Tetrahydrogestrinone (THG) (may also be a gel or injectible)	X	X
Methyltestosterone	X	
Methenolone acetate	X	
Methenolone enanthate		X
Oxandrolone	X	
Androstenedione (Andro)	X	
Clostebol acetate	X	X
Fluoxymesterone	X	
Danazol	X	
Oxymetholone	X	
DHEA	X	
Norethandrolone	X	
Drostanolone proprionate	X	X
Oxymesterone	X	
Trenbolone acetate		X

*Adverse effects of oral steroids-liver disease, decreased HDL, increased LDL.

**Adverse effects of injecting anabolic steroids (i.e., "needle sharing"): infections, AIDS, hepatitis.

Sources: Adapted from Llewellyn, W. *Anabolics* 2000. Aurora, CO: Anabolics.com, Inc., 2000: Grunding, P. and Bachmann, M. *World Anabolic Review* 1996, Houston, TX; *MB Muscle Books,* 1995; and Phillips, W. N. *Anabolic Reference Guide Sixth Issue,* Golden, CO: Mile High Publishing, 1991.

As will be discussed in greater detail later in this paper, as many as one million young people have used steroids even though they are illegal and banned by most sports organizations. Health concerns are the principal reason for prohibiting the sales of anabolic steroids while sporting organizations have banned their use for ethical reasons.

WHY DO PEOPLE USE ANABOLIC STEROIDS?

There are many different reasons why people choose to use steroids. Use was initially most prevalent among athletes with goals of enhancing performance. However, in recent years use by non-athletes has become more prevalent. Now an increasing number of anabolic steroid users simply want to "look good"—which to many people means being big and muscular.

The goals of individuals who use anabolic steroids in sport and exercise are dependent on the activity in which they participate. Bodybuilders desire more lean body mass and less body fat. Weight lifters desire to lift the maximum amount of weight possible. Field athletes want to put the shot, or throw the hammer, discus, or javelin, farther than their competitors or holders of previous records. Swimmers and runners hope to be able to perform their frequent, high-intensity, long-duration workouts without physical breakdown. Football players want to increase their lean body mass and strength so they can be successful at the high school, college, or professional level.

Anabolic steroids have traditionally been taken in "cycles," which are episodes of use lasting 6 to 12 weeks or more (Llewellyn, 2000). Athletes often take more than one steroid at a time; this is referred to as '"stacking." In an attempt to avoid developing a tolerance to a particular anabolic steroid ("plateauing"), some users stagger their drugs, taking the anabolic steroids in an overlapping pattern, or stop one drug and start another (Duchaine, 1989; Gallaway, 1997). Often steroid users will "pyramid" their administration patterns, moving from a low daily dose at the beginning of the cycle to a higher dose and then tapering down the dose toward the end of their cycle (Grunding and Bachmann, 1995; Wright, 1982). In addition, individuals may use other drugs concurrently with anabolic steroids to counteract the common adverse effects of steroids. These drugs include diuretics, antiestrogens, human chorionic gonadotrophin, and anti-acne medications. This polypharmacy is termed an "array" (Duchaine, 1989). The frequency of concurrent drug use or the frequency or efficacy of each of these administration patterns is poorly documented.

The dosage of anabolic steroids depends on the sport as well as on the particular needs of the athlete. Endurance athletes use steroids primarily for their alleged catabolism-blocking effects, i.e., to forestall the occurrence of "overtraining" (decreased natural testosterone levels, fatigue, muscle atrophy and soreness, etc.) (Friedl, 2000a). These athletes, for the most part, are trying to maintain their testosterone levels in the "normal" range. Thus, they use dosages at or slightly below physiological replacement levels, that is, about 7 mg/day of testosterone (Yen and Jaffe, 1978). Participants in the traditional strength sports, seeking to "bulk up," have generally used dosages that exceed physiological replacement levels by 10 to 100 times or more (Kerr, 1982; Wright, 1982). Administration patterns also vary among athletes within a particular sport, based on each athlete's training goals and response to the drugs, as well as on the biological activity of different anabolic steroids (Kochakian and Yesalis, 2000; Wright, 1982). Women, regardless of sport, are generally thought to use lower dosages of anabolic steroids than men (Elliot and Goldberg, 2000).

While it appears that many *elite* athletes obtain pharmaceutical-grade drugs from medical professionals, the large majority of anabolic steroid users are not elite athletes and use black market steroids produced by clandestine labs in the United States and by companies outside the U.S. that do not adhere to the rigid industry standards that ensure each dosage form contains a predictable and consistent amount of active ingredient(s) (see Table 19-3). These products may be contaminated and/or may not be what they are purported to be. Regardless of the source, the use of anabolic steroids for purposes of performance enhancement is illegal and unethical.

Table 19-3 Sources of Anabolic Steroids

Countries	Medical Professionals	Sports Personnel
United States	Physicians	Sport Coaches
Mexico	Pharmacists	Conditioning Coaches
Russia	Veterinarians	Nutrition Consultants
Poland	Dentists	
Hungary	Athletic Trainers	
Spain	Physical Therapists	
Italy		
Greece		
Canada		
Netherlands		
Thailand		

Source: Adapted from Bahrke, M. S., and Yesalis, C. E. *Performance-Enhancing Substances in Sport and Exercise.* Champaign, IL: Human Kinetics, 2002.

HOW PREVALENT IS ANABOLIC STEROID USE?

High levels of use of anabolic steroids have been attributed to professional football players, weight lifters, power lifters, bodybuilders, and throwers in track and field events since the 1960s (Yesalis, Courson, and Wright, 2000). Use by high school athletes was rumored as early as 1959 (Frazier, 1973; Gilbert, 1969a, 1969b, 1969c). However, until the mid-1970s, information on the incidence of non-medical use of steroids was based on anecdotes, testimonials, and rumors (Yesalis and Bahrke, 1995). Although rumors still abound, estimates of the incidence of steroid use are now based on the results of systematic surveys. Surveys of steroid use are categorized here as those of (1) adolescent school-age students, (2) college students, and (3) athletes not falling into categories 1 or 2.

Use among Adolescent School-Age Students

In 1987 the first U.S. national study of anabolic steroid use at the high school level was conducted by Buckley and associates (Buckley et al., 1988). The investigators found that 6.6 percent of male high school seniors reported having used these drugs. There was no difference in the level of reported steroid use between urban and rural areas, but there was a small, yet significant, difference by size of enrollment: students at larger high schools had a higher rate of reported steroid use. In addition, among the self-reported steroid users, 38 percent had initiated use before 16 years of age; and more than one-third of the steroid users did not intend to participate in inter-scholastic sports.

During the early to mid-1990s, multiple U.S. local-, state-, and national-level studies confirmed the findings of Buckley et al. (1988), and showed that 4 percent to 6 percent (with a range of 3 percent to 12 percent) of high school males admit

Table 19-4 Trends in Lifetime Prevalence of Use of
Anabolic Steroids for Eighth, Tenth, and Twelfth Graders

						Year							
Grade	91	92	93	94	95	96	97	98	99	00	01	02	03
8th	1.9	1.7	1.6	2.0	2.0	1.8	1.8	2.3	2.7	3.0	2.8	2.5	2.5
10th	1.8	1.7	1.7	1.8	2.0	1.8	2.0	2.0	2.7	3.5	3.5	3.5	3.0
12th	2.1	2.1	2.0	2.4	2.3	1.9	2.4	2.7	2.9	2.5	3.7	4.0	3.5

Source: Monitoring the Future Study, the University of Michigan.

to using anabolic steroids at some time in their life (Yesalis, Barsukiewicz, Kopstein, and Bahrke, 1997). Some of these studies also examined the use of anabolic steroids among high school females, generally showing that 1 percent to 2 percent reported having used anabolic steroids (Yesalis, Bahrke, Kopstein, and Barsukiewicz, 2000). Likewise, several of the studies confirmed that substantial percentages of steroid users do not participate in traditional school-sponsored sports.

Since 1991, steroid use by males as measured by U.S. national surveys has generally increased (Grunbaum et al., 2004; Hewitt, Smith-Akin, Higgins, and Jenkins, 1998; Johnston, Bachman, O'Malley, and Schulenberg, 2004; Kann, Warren, Harris, Collins, Douglas, et al., 1995; Feyrer-Melk, Corbin, and Lewis, 1994) (Table 19-4). Furthermore, since 1991, data from these U.S. national surveys point to an increase in anabolic steroid use among adolescent females as well as a sharp drop in the perceived dangers of using steroids (Johnston, Bachman, O'Malley, and Schulenberg, 2004). What is more troubling is that the 2003 Youth Risk and Behavior Surveillance System data (Grunbaum et al., 2004) showed that among 9th- to 12th-grade students (ages 13–19) in public and private high schools in the United States, 6.8 percent of males and 5.3 percent of females (up from 4.1 percent and 2.0 percent respectively in 1997) had used anabolic steroids at least once in their lives. Based on 2000 Census estimates of high school students, these period prevalence rates translate to well over one million young people in the United States who have used (cycled) anabolic steroids at least once during their lifetime.

We should also note that the use of anabolic steroids by adolescents is not limited to the U.S. (Newman, 1994; Yesalis, Ortner, and Bahrke, 1996). Three Canadian studies (Adalf and Smart, 1992; Canadian Centre for Drug-Free Sport, 1993; Killip and Stennett, 1990), four Swedish surveys (Kindlundh, Isacson, Berglund, and Nyberg, 1999; Nilsson, 1995; Nilsson, Baigi, Marklund, and Fridlund, 2001a and b), two South African investigations (Lambert, Titlestad, and Schwellnus, 1998; Schwellnus, Lambert, and Todd, 1992), one British study (Williamson, 1993), and one Australian investigation (Handelsman and Gupta, 1997) have reported overall prevalence rates for high school–aged students to range between 1.2–5.9 percent for males and 0.0–1.5 percent for females. Although these rates are slightly lower, they approximate those reported for the U.S., and reflect the cross-cultural impact of anabolic steroids on performance and physical appearance.

Use among College Athletes

Since 1985, Anderson et al. (1985, 1991, 1993) and the National Collegiate Athletic Association (NCAA) (1997, 2001) have conducted five surveys of male and female student athletes at selected NCAA member colleges and universities regarding substance abuse, including anabolic steroids. In the five surveys, the heaviest anabolic steroid use (defined as use in the past 12 months) was reported in 1985–4.9 percent among all athletes. Thereafter, steroid use decreased to its lowest level in 1997 (1.1 percent); in 2001 the level of use increased to 1.4 percent. In all five surveys, the pattern of self-reported use was fairly consistent among Division I-III schools. In the 2001 survey, there was no striking difference in anabolic steroid use by race. The level of use in men's sports ranged from 0.2 percent in swimming to 3.0 percent in football and a high of 5.0 percent among water polo participants. In women's sports, self-reported steroid use was highest in lacrosse (1.6 percent): there were five women's sports that reported no steroid use in the 2001 survey. Of the student athletes who acknowledged use of anabolic steroids, over half reported first using these drugs in junior high or high school. Not surprisingly, the predominant reason (42.7 percent) given for their use of anabolic steroids was the improvement of athletic performance.

Yesalis, Buckley, Anderson, Wang, Norwig, Ott, Puffer, and Strauss (1990) employed projected response survey techniques with collegiate athletes, using indirect questions. Thus, respondents were asked to estimate the level of their competitors' anabolic steroid use. Over 1600 male and female athletes at five NCAA Division I institutions participated in this study during the 1989–1990 academic year. The mean overall projected rate of any prior use of anabolic steroids across all sports surveyed was 14.7 percent for male and 5.9 percent for female athletes. Among men's sports, football showed the highest projected lifetime steroid use rates with 29.3 percent, followed by track and field events with 20.6 percent. The greatest projected use rate for women's sports was 16.3 percent for track and field events. The reported overall projected rate of anabolic steroid use during the past 12 months was approximately three times greater than the rate obtained from self-reports in the 1991 NCAA survey (NCAA Research Staff, 2001).

The true level of steroid use among athletes probably lies between the lower-bound estimates from self-reports and the upper-bound estimates obtained from the projective response techniques (Yesalis, Buckley, Anderson, Wang, Norwig, Ott, Puffer, and Strauss, 1990). While the response of adolescents to anonymous surveys of drug use is considered generally valid, the results of this projective response study as well as those of other validation studies of elite athletes (Yesalis, Bahrke, Kopstein, and Barsukiewicz, 2000) call into question the validity of surveys of elite athletes and argue that there is a substantial underreporting bias.

Use by Olympic Athletes

Track and field event athletes who participated in the 1972 Olympics were surveyed (Silvester, 1973): and 68 percent of the participants reported prior steroid use, with

61 percent having used steroids within six months of the Games. In 1975, Ljungqvist surveyed elite Swedish male track and field event athletes and found that 31 percent admitted prior anabolic steroid use. None of the middle- or long-distance runners admitted to anabolic steroid use, but 75 percent of the throwers did.

In a survey of 155 U.S. Olympians who participated in the 1992 Winter Games, 80 percent of the athletes classified steroid use among Olympic competitors as a very serious or somewhat serious problem: just 5 percent thought that it was not a problem (Pearson and Hansen, 1992). When asked to estimate the level of steroid use in their own sport, 43 percent of the respondents estimated use by 10 percent or more of competitors, while 34 percent estimated use at 1 percent to 9 percent. Only 23 percent of the athletes surveyed believed that there was no steroid use in their sport. In another survey of former Olympians (Pearson, 1994), 75 percent of the medalists and 63 percent of the nonmedalists stated that more athletes were using performance-enhancing drugs than when they themselves had competed.

An intensive two-year investigation of doping in Olympic sport conducted for the U.S. Office of National Drug Control Policy concluded that while estimates of the magnitude of the doping epidemic vary widely (from 10 percent to 90 percent of athletes), there exists an atmosphere in our society that fosters drug use by athletes: "The high financial stakes for Olympic athletes, corporate sponsors, the TV broadcast and cable industries and sport governing bodies, coupled with the pharmacopoeia of performance-enhancing substances, the athlete's drive to win and the absence of an effective policing mechanism, create an environment that encourages doing anything—including doping—to win" (National Center on Addiction and Substance Abuse, 2000: 2).

While testing and education programs have been in effect for some time, new efforts to reduce steroid use have recently been implemented. On October 1, 2000, the U.S. Anti-Doping Agency (USADA) was formed as the independent anti-doping agency for Olympic sports in the United States. It was created as the result of recommendations set forth by the U.S. Olympic Committee's Select Task Force on Externalization. They have full authority for testing, education, and research, as well as adjudication for U.S. Olympic, Pan Am, and Paralympic athletes.

Use by Weight Lifters

Weight trainers in three gymnasiums in the Chicago area were questioned (Frankle, Cicero, and Payne, 1984): 44 percent reported prior steroid use. In a study of amateur competitive bodybuilders (Tricker, O'Neil, and Cook, 1989), over half of the men and 10 percent of the women reported that they had used anabolic steroids at some time in their life. In 1993, of the 185 members of gymnasiums and health clubs, 18 percent of men and 3 percent of women acknowledged having used or currently using anabolic steroids (Kersey, 1993). In 1988, Yesalis et al. surveyed elite power lifters using both questionnaires and follow-up telephone interviews. One-third of the questionnaire respondents admitted prior anabolic steroid use: however, 55 percent of those interviewed later by telephone conceded steroid use.

The level of steroid use appears to have increased significantly over the past three decades (Johnston, Bachman, O'Malley, and Schulenberg, 2004; Yesalis, Anderson, Buckley, and Wright, 1990; Yesalis, Kennedy, Kopstein, and Bahrke, 1993), and is no longer limited to elite athletes or to men. Although higher rates of steroid use are reported by competitive athletes, a significant number of recreational athletes and non-athletes appears to be using these drugs, probably to "improve" their appearance. Looking at elite sport in the twentieth century through the eyes of historians and journalists as well as the athletes themselves, an unmistakable picture emerges of a *sustained* doping pandemic of huge proportions in elite sport (Yesalis and Bahrke, 2003). Of greater concern is that the use of anabolic steroids has cascaded down from the Olympic, professional, and college levels to the high schools and junior high schools, and there are significantly more adolescents using anabolic steroids than elite athletes.

ERGOGENIC EFFECTS: DO ANABOLIC STEROIDS IMPROVE PERFORMANCE?

While the vast majority of the athletic community accepts that anabolic steroids enhance exercise capacity and performance (Yesalis, Anderson, Buckley, and Wright, 1990), from 1977 to 1984, the American College of Sports Medicine (1977, 1984) regarded anabolic steroids as ineffective, sending mixed messages to the athletic community concerning the potential of anabolic steroids to enhance performance. As recently as 1992, other scientists (Celotti and Negri-Cesi, 1992) remained skeptical, also reporting that anabolic steroids were ineffective. However, a study by Bhasin and his colleagues in 1996 quelled much of the residual doubt concerning the effectiveness of anabolic steroids in humans. Using a relatively high dose of an anabolic steroid (600 mg/wk of testosterone enanthate for 10 weeks), Bhasin et al. (1996) found a 13 lb (6 kg) weight gain and 48.5 lb (22 kg) improvement in the one-repetition maximum (1-RM) bench press in experienced lifters. The results of the Bhasin study (1996) also suggested additive effects of exercise and steroids, with a bench press improvement of approximately 22 lb (10 kg) produced by exercise *or* steroid, *and* 44 lb (20 kg) produced by exercise and steroid.

Thus, anabolic steroids, as a class, produce lean mass gain in normal healthy, adult men with a reciprocal decrease in total body adipose tissue. In addition, a dose response effect has been demonstrated (Forbes, 1985; Herbst and Bhasin, 2004). Typical weight gains are 6.6 to 11 lb (3–5 kg) after several weeks of high-dose steroid use. The effects of steroids on strength performance are mostly seen with experienced weight lifters and when strength training is performed concurrently with the steroid administration. Most studies demonstrating strength gains also demonstrate weight gains.

At least one study has demonstrated a threshold response of body composition to anabolic steroids, as well as variations in response according to type of steroid (Friedl, Dettori, Hannan, Patience, and Plymate, 1991). The mechanisms of action for an effect on muscle mass have been increasingly elucidated and involve multiple mechanisms including increased protein anabolism and differentiation of pluripotent stem cells toward the myogenic lineage (Herbst and Bhasin, 2004). Furthermore, the resultant muscle hypertrophy and regeneration is associated with an increase in myoblast differentiation or the number of satellite cells (Herbst and Bhasin, 2004).

While the ergogenic effects of anabolic steroids have been established, the effects of high doses or prolonged administration of anabolic steroids on physique or physiological capacities have not been documented. Likewise, the residual effects of anabolic steroids on physiological capacities after the termination of use have not been established. Furthermore, results of any dose on physical/physiological capacities or performance in females are unknown.

Although the evidence is incomplete, anabolic steroids may also inhibit or block the catabolic effects of glucocorticoids that are released during intense training (Kuhn, 2002). Theoretically, this anti-catabolic effect would allow athletes to train more frequently and more intensely, and this may be the most important factor concerning the performance-enhancing effects of anabolic steroids. Furthermore, while there is little evidence to support a beneficial role of anabolic steroids in other types of exercise performance such as muscular endurance or aerobic endurance, anabolic steroids increase the number of red blood cells (RBCs). With the anti-catabolic effect and an increase in RBCs, endurance athletes may be able to train more frequently, for longer periods of time, and with greater intensity. In turn, this could produce improved aerobic capacity resulting in quicker running times or in more repetitions of a particular activity.

WHAT ARE THE SHORT- AND LONG-TERM HEALTH EFFECTS OF ANABOLIC STEROID USE?

Physical and Physiological Effects

The short-term health effects of anabolic-androgenic steroids have been increasingly studied, and several authors have reviewed the physiological and health effects of these drugs (Friedl, 2000b; Haupt and Rovere, 1984; Lamb, 1984; Wilson, 1988; Wright, 1980) (see Table 19-5). Although anabolic steroid use has been associated (mainly through case reports) with a number of adverse and even fatal effects, the incidence of serious effects thus far reported has been extremely low (Friedl, 2000b). However, for several decades experts have consistently stated that the long-term health effects of anabolic steroid use are unknown (Yesalis, Wright, and Bahrke, 1989). Specifically, the long-term health effects as related to type of steroid, dose, frequency of use, age at initiation, and concurrent drug use have not been elucidated. Confounding the assessment of health consequences is the fact that some individuals use large doses of anabolic steroids for prolonged periods of time, while others use therapeutic doses intermittently (Buckley et al., 1988; Duchaine, 1989; Grunding and Bachmann, 1995; Llewellyn, 2000).

Table 19-5 Potential Adverse Effects of Anabolic Steroids

Males	Females	Both Males and Females
Baldness	Breast Shrinkage	Acne
Prostate Changes	Clitoral Enlargement	Aggression
Gynecomastia	Increased Facial/Body Hair	Brittle Connective Tissue
Impotence/Sterility	Menstrual Irregularities	Cardiovascular Disease
	Premature Hair Loss	Cerebrovascular Incidents
	Deepened Voice	Dependency
	(Vocal cord thickening)	Headaches
		Hypertension
		Liver Disease
		Psyche and Behavior Changes
		Short Stature
		(Premature growth-plate closure)

Source: Adapted from M. S. Bahrke and C. E. Yesalis. *Performance-Enhancing Substances in Sport and Exercise* (Champaign, IL: Human Kinetics, 2002).

Although the role of anabolic steroids in the etiology of various diseases in both animals and humans is still uncertain, steroid use in clinical trials and in laboratory studies has been associated with numerous deleterious changes in risk factors and in the physiology of various organs and body systems, suggesting potential for subsequent health problems (American College of Sports Medicine, 1984; Kruskemper, 1968; Wright, 1980; Freidl, 2000b). The best-documented effects are those on the liver, serum lipids, and the reproductive system. Other suspected areas of concern include the psyche and behavior, coronary artery disease, cerebrovascular accidents, prostatic changes, and the immune function (Friedl, 2000b).

Steroid use has been related to cardiovascular risk factors. The most important are changes in lipoprotein fraction, increased triglyceride levels and concentrations of several clotting factors, and hyperinsulinism and diminished glucose tolerance (Friedl, 2000b; Glazer, 1991; Haupt and Rovere, 1984; Sullivan, Martinez, Gennis, and Gallagher, 1998; Wright, 1980). It should be noted, however, that although these effects vary significantly between types and doses of anabolic steroids and between individuals and situations (Kruskemper, 1968), all of the effects have been demonstrated to be fully reversible within several months after cessation of steroid use (Friedl, 2000b; Haupt and Rovere, 1984; Wright, 1980).

Anabolic steroids have been shown to be cardiotoxic in animals (Hartgens, Cherlex, and Kulpers, 2003). In addition, some studies in humans, but not all, have shown that anabolic steroid use is associated with left ventricular (LV) hypertrophy (Karila et al., 2003; Hartgens, Cherlex, and Kulpers, 2003; Urhausen, Albers, and Kindermann, 2004). Furthermore, one study demonstrated that the increases in LV mass persist several years after discontinuation of anabolic steroid use (Urhausen, Albers, and Kindermann, 2004).

Acute thrombotic risk has been linked to steroid use in 17 case reports of non-fatal myocardial infarction and stroke in athletes who were using anabolic steroids (Rockhold, 1993; Wu and Eckardstein, 2003). Although there is no direct evidence anabolic steroids are thrombogenic in humans (Ansell, Tiarks, and Fairchild, 1993), the clinical circumstances of these reports suggest a possible causal relationship. These reports further suggest that, if a causal relationship exists, anabolic steroids could have serious short-term effects.

Liver structure and function have also been altered by administration of anabolic steroids: associated conditions include cholestatic jaundice, peliosis hepatitis, hepatocellular hyperplasia, and hepatocellular adenomas (Dickerman, Pertusi, Zachariah, Dufour, and McConathy, 1999; Soe, Soe, and Gluud, 1992). Peliosis hepatitis is clearly associated with the use of 17-a-alkylated (oral) anabolic steroids, but with unknown frequency. Hepatic tumors are rare in men (1 percent to 3 percent), but nearly half of the discovered tumors rupture, and a larger proportion may remain undetected. In two cases, rupture proved fatal (Friedl, 2000b). It has not been convincingly demonstrated that anabolic steroids can cause, at least with therapeutic doses, the development of hepatocellular carcinomas. In summary, virtually all histological changes in the liver have been associated with the use of 17-a-alkylated (oral) steroids (Friedl, 2000b; Kruskemper, 1968; Wilson, 1988; Wright, 1980); and the cause-and-effect relationship between oral anabolic steroids and these conditions is strengthened by the return of normal blood values and excretory function, the regression of tumors, a general recovery, and a return toward normal liver function after cessation of steroid use (Friedl, 2000b).

The effects of anabolic-androgenic steroids on the male reproductive system include reductions in levels of endogenous testosterone, gonadotrophic hormones, and sex hormone-binding globulin (SHBG); reductions in testicle size, sperm count, and sperm motility; and alterations in sperm morphology (Friedl, 2000b; Wright, 1980). When steroid use is stopped, the testes resume sperm production and sperm quality usually recovers spontaneously within four months. However, the impact of anabolic steroids on spermatogenesis may persist for a year or more (Dohle, Smit, and Weber, 2003).

Anabolic steroids have been associated through case reports with tendon injuries and neuropathies (Friedl, 2000b). While the results of animal studies support a causal association, to date the effects of steroids on musculoskeletal injuries in humans cannot be distinguished from the risks ordinarily faced by strength athletes not using anabolic steroids.

In women, anabolic steroids have been associated with a number of adverse effects, some of which are not reversible upon discontinuation of steroid use (Elliot and Goldberg, 2000). These include menstrual abnormalities; deepening of the voice; shrinkage of the breasts; male-pattern baldness; and an increase in sex drive, acne, body hair, and clitoris size. In addition, women using steroids experience dramatically elevated testosterone levels and lowered levels of SHBG, follicle-stimulating hormone, and thyroid-binding proteins (Elliot and Goldberg, 2000; Malarkey, Strauss, and Leizman, 1991). Premature halting of growth in younger male and female users has not been systematically studied, although such effects have been described in case reports for several decades (Rogol and Yesalis, 1992).

Psychological Effects

Previous and current research studies have documented significant positive relationships between testosterone levels, dominance, and aggressive behavior in various species of animals, including nonhuman primates (Bahrke, Yesalis, and Wright, 1996). Relative to the animal literature, fewer studies have assessed the relationship of endogenous or exogenous androgens to aggression or violent behavior in humans. However, a positive pattern of association between endogenous testosterone levels and aggressive behavior in males has been increasingly established (Bahrke, 2000). Also, while random clinical trials using moderate doses of exogenous testosterone for contraceptive and other purposes reveal few adverse effects on male sexual and aggressive behavior, other investigations and case reports of athletes using higher doses suggest the possibility of affective and psychotic syndromes (some of violent proportions), psychological dependence, and withdrawal symptoms.

While several published reports support a pattern of association between the use of anabolic steroids by athletes and increased levels of irritability, aggression, personality disturbance, and psychiatric diagnoses, others do not (Bhasin et al., 1996; Millar, 1996; Yates, Perry, MacIndoe, Holman, and Ellingrod, 1999). Only a few prospective, blinded studies documenting aggression and adverse overt behavior resulting from steroid use have been reported (Hannan, Friedl, Zold, Kettler, and Plymate, 1991; Pope, Kouri, and Hudson, 2000; Kouri, Lukas, Pope, and Oliva, 1995; Su et al., 1993). As Bjorkqvist and colleagues (1994) point out, much of the psychological and behavioral effect of steroid intake may be placebo. In a double-blind experiment, human males (n = 27) were given either testosterone, placebo, or no treatment, over a one-week period. The results revealed a significant placebo effect. After treatment, the placebo group scored higher than both the testosterone and the control groups on self-estimated anger, irritation, impulsivity, and frustration. Observer-estimated mood yielded similar results. Anticipation of the aggressiveness related to steroid use may lead to actual violent acts and become, in effect, an excuse for aggression.

Although anabolic steroid dependency may be a problem, its prevalence and symptomatology are difficult to reliably establish based on the existing literature. There is some evidence that testosterone is mildly reinforcing (relative to the classic reinforcers, cocaine and heroin) in male rats and hamsters self-administering (Wood et al., 2004). Brower (2002) in his review found no evidence that anabolic steroids lead to dependence (i.e., meeting the Diagnostic and Statistical Manual of Mental Disorders criteria for dependence) with therapeutic use. However, he noted 165 instances of dependence among weightlifters and bodybuilders using supraphysiologic doses of anabolic steroids.

It is interesting to note that with a million or more steroid users in the United States (Yesalis, Kennedy, Kopstein, and Bahrke, 1993), only an extremely small percentage of users appear to experience mental disturbances that result in clinical treatment. Also, of the few individuals who do experience significant changes, most apparently recover without additional problems when the use of steroids is terminated.

CONCLUSION

Anabolic steroids are synthetic derivatives of testosterone. They are usually administered orally and by injection. Anabolic steroids are used by athletes to enhance performance and non-athletes to enhance appearance. Strong evidence now exists demonstrating that anabolic steroid use results in increased body weight and muscular strength. There is also an increasing body of evidence that anabolic steroid use is associated with a variety of health problems. While the long-term effects of anabolic steroids remain unclear, the best-documented physiological effects are those on the liver, serum lipids, and the reproductive system. A pattern of association between the use of anabolic steroids and increased levels of irritability, aggression, personality disturbance, dependence, and psychiatric diagnoses has been revealed in a number of reports.

Although anabolic steroids are illegal, and their use is banned by virtually every sport governing body, survey and drug-testing data indicate continued use by competitive athletes at all levels. The fact that the level of steroid use appears to have increased significantly over the past three decades among adolescents, women, and recreational athletes is also of growing concern. The use of anabolic steroids presents an interesting public health challenge. While these drugs are associated with deleterious physical and psychological outcomes, they are being used to achieve what many consider socially desirable ends: being physically attractive and being a winner.

REFERENCES

Adalf, E. M., and Smart, R. G. 1992. "Characteristics of Steroid Users in an Adolescent School Population." *Journal of Alcohol and Drug Education* 38, no. 1: 43–49.

American College of Sports Medicine. 1977. "Position Statement on the Use and Abuse of Anabolic-Androgenic Steroids in Sports." *Medicine and Science in Sports* 9: 11–13.

———. 1984. "Position Stand on the Use of Anabolic-Androgenic Steroids in Sports." *Sports Medicine Bulletin* 19: 13–18.

Anderson, W., and D. McKeag. 1985. "The Substance Use and Abuse Habits of College Student-Athletes: Research Paper 2." Mission, KS: National Collegiate Athletic Association.

Anderson, W., M. Albrecht, and D. McKeag. 1993. *Second Replication of a National Study of Substance Use and Abuse Habits of College Student-Athletes: Final Report.* Overland Park, KS: National Collegiate Athletic Association.

Anderson, W., M. Albrecht, D. McKeag, D. O. Hough, and C. A. McGrew. 1991. "A National Survey of Alcohol and Drug Use by College Athletes." *Physician and Sports Medicine* 19: 91–104.

Ansell, J., C. Tiarks, and V. Fairchild. 1993. "Coagulation Abnormalities Associated with the Use of Anabolic Steroids." *American Heart Journal* 125, no. 2: 367.

Bahrke, M. S. 2000. "Psychological Effects of Endogenous Testosterone and Anabolic-Androgenic Steroids." Pp. 247–278 in C. E. Yesalis, ed., *Anabolic Steroids in Sport and Exercise,* 2nd ed. Champaign, IL: Human Kinetics.

Bahrke, M., C. Yesalis, and J. Wright. 1996. "Psychological and Behavioral Effects of Endogenous Testosterone and Anabolic-Androgenic Steroids: An Update." *Sports Medicine* 22, no. 6: 367–390.

———. 2002. *Performance-Enhancing Substances in Sport and Exercise.* Champaign, IL: Human Kinetics.

Bhasin, S., T. Storer, N. Berman, C. Callegari, B. Clevenger, J. Phillips, T. J. Bunnell, R. Tricker, A. Shirazi, and R. Casaburi. 1996. "The Effects of Supraphysiologic Doses of Testosterone on Muscle Size and Strength in Normal Men." *New England Journal of Medicine* 335, no. 1: 1–7.

Bjorkqvist, K., T. Nygren, A. C. Bjorklund, and S. E. Bjorkqvist. 1994. "Testosterone Intake and Aggressiveness: Real Effect or Anticipation." *Aggressive Behavior* 20: 17–26.

Brower, K. 2002. "Anabolic Steroid Use and Dependence." *Current Psychiatry Reports* 4: 377–387.

Buckley, W. E., C. E. Yesalis, K. E. Friedl, W. A. Anderson, A. L. Streit, and J. E. Wright. 1988. "Estimated Prevalence of Anabolic-Androgenic Steroid Use among Male High School Seniors." *Journal of the American Medical Association* 260, no. 23: 3441–3445.

Canadian Centre for Drug-Free Sport. 1993. *National School Survey on Drugs and Sport: Final Report.* Gloucester, ON: Canadian Centre for Drug-Free Sport.

Celotti, F., and P. N. Negri-Cesi. 1992. "Anabolic Steroids: A Review of Their Effects on the Muscles, of Their Possible Mechanisms of Action, and Their Use in Athletics." *Journal of Steroid Biochemistry Molecular Biology* 43, no. 5: 469–477.

Dickerman, R. D., R. M. Pertusi, N. Y. Zachariah, D. R. Dufour, and W. J. McConathy. 1999. "Anabolic Steroid-Induced Hepatotoxicity: Is It Overstated?" *Clinical Journal of Sport Medicine* 9: 34–39.

Dohle, G., M. Smit, and R. Weber. 2003. "Androgens and Male Fertility." *World Journal of Urology* 21: 341–345.

Duchaine, D. 1989. *Underground Steroid Handbook II.* Venice, CA: HLR Technical Books.

Elliot, D. L., and L. Goldberg. 2000. "Women and Anabolic Steroids." Pp. 225–246 in C. E. Yesalis, ed., *Anabolic Steroids in Sport and Exercise,* 2nd ed. Champaign, IL: Human Kinetics.

Feyrer-Melk, S. A., C. B. Corbin, and L. Lewis. 1994. "Anabolic Steroids: A Study of High School Athletes." *Pediatric Exercise Science* 6: 149–158.

Forbes, G. 1985. "The Effect of Anabolic Steroids on Lean Body Mass: The Dose Response Curve." *Metabolism* 34, no. 6: 571–573.

Frankle, M., G. Cicero, and J. Payne. 1984. "Use of Androgenic Anabolic Steroids by Athletes [Letter]." *Journal of the American Medical Association* 252: 482.

Frazier, S. 1973. "Androgens and Athletes." *American Journal of Diseases of Children* 125: 479–480.

Friedl, K. E. 2000a. "Effect of Anabolic Steroid Use on Body Composition and Physical Performance." Pp. 139–174 in C. E. Yesalis, ed., *Anabolic Steroids in Sport and Exercise,* 2nd ed. Champaign, IL: Human Kinetics.

———. 2000b. "Effect of Anabolic Steroids on Physical Health." Pp. 175–223 in C. E. Yesalis, ed., *Anabolic Steroids in Sport and Exercise,* 2nd ed. Champaign, IL: Human Kinetics.

Friedl, K. E., J. R. Dettorri, C. J. Hannan, T. H. Patience, and S. R. Plymate. 1991. "Comparison of the Effects of High-Dose Testosterone and 19-Nortestosterone to a Replacement Dose of Testosterone on Strength and Body Composition in Normal Men." *Journal of Steroid Biochemistry and Molecular Biology* 40: 607–612.

Gallaway, S. 1997. *The Steroid Bible,* 3rd ed. Sacramento, CA: BI Press.

Gilbert, B. 1969a. "Drugs in Sport, Part 1: Problems in a Turned-On World." *Sports Illustrated* (June 23): 64–72.

———. 1969b. "Drugs in Sport, Part 2: Something Extra on the Ball." *Sports Illustrated* (June 30): 30–42.

———. 1969c. "Drugs in Sport, Part 3: High Time to Make Some Rules." *Sports Illustrated* (July 7): 30–35.

Glazer, G. 1991. "Atherogenic Effects of Anabolic Steroids on Serum Lipid Levels." *Archives of Internal Medicine* 151: 1925–1933.

Grunbaum, J. A. 2004. "Youth Risk Behavior Surveillance—U.S. 2003." *MMWR CDC Surveillance Summary* 53.

Grunding, P., and M. Bachmann. 1995. *World Anabolic Review 1996.* Houston: MB Muscle Books.

Handelsman, D. J., and L. Gupta. 1997. "Prevalence and Risk Factors for Anabolic-Androgenic Steroid Abuse in Australian High School Students." *International Journal of Andrology* 20: 159–164.

Hannan, C. J., K. E. Friedl, A. Zold, T. M. Kettler, and S. R. Plymate. 1991. "Psychological and Serum Homovanillic Acid Changes in Men Administered Androgenic Steroids." *Psychoneuroendrocrinology* 16: 335–342.

Hartgens, F., E. Cherlex, and H. Kulpers. 2003. "Prospective Echocardiographic Assessment of Androgenic-Anabolic Steroids' Effects on Cardiac Structure and Function in Strength Athletes." *International Journal of Sports Medicine* 24: 344–351.

Haupt, H., and G. Rovere. 1984. "Anabolic Steroids: A Review of the Literature." *American Journal of Sports Medicine* 12, no. 6: 469–484.

Herbst, K., and S. Bhasin. 2004. "Testosterone Action on Skeletal muscle." *Current Opinions in Clinical Nutrition and Metabolic Care* 7: 271–277.

Hewitt, S. M., C. K. Smith-Akin, M. M. Higgins, and P. M. Jenkins. 1998. "Youth Risk Behavior Surveillance: United States, 1997." *MMWR CDC Surveillance Summary* 47: 61.

Johnston, L., P. Bachman, J. O'Malley, and J. Schulenberg. 2004. *Monitoring the Future: National Results on Adolescent Drug Use—Overview of Key Findings 2003.* NIH Publication No. 04–5506. Washington, DC: National Institute on Drug Abuse, U. S. Department of Health and Human Services.

Kann, L., C. W. Warren, W. A. Harris, J. L. Collins, K. A. Douglas, M. E. Collins, B. I. Williams, J. G. Ross, and L. J. Kolge. 1995. "Youth Risk Behavior Surveillance: United States, 1993." *MMWR CDC Surveillance Summary* 44: 1–55.

Karila, T., et al. 2003. "Anabolic-Androgenic Steroids Produce Dose-Dependent Increase in Left Ventricular Mass in Power Athletes, and This Effect Is Potentiated by Concomitant Use of Growth Hormone." *International Journal of Sports Medicine* 24: 237–343.

Kerr, R. 1982. *The Practical Use of Anabolic Steroids with Athletes.* San Gabriel, CA: Kerr.

Kersey, R. 1993. "Anabolic-Androgenic Steroid Use by Private Health Club/Gym Athletes." *Journal of Strength and Conditioning* 7: 118–126.

Killip, S. M., and R. G. Stennett. 1990. "Use of Performance-Enhancing Substances by London Secondary School Students." London, ON: Board of Education for the City of London.

Kindlundh, A. M. S., D. G. L. Isacson, L. Berglund, and F. Nyberg. 1999. "Factors Associated with Adolescent Use of Doping Agents: Anabolic-Androgenic Steroids." *Addiction* 94, no. 4: 543–553.

Kochakian, C. D., and C. E. Yesalis. 2000. "Anabolic-Androgenic Steroids: A Historical Perspective and Definition." Pp. 17–49 in C. E. Yesalis, ed., *Anabolic Steroids in Sport and Exercise*, 2nd ed. Champaign, IL: Human Kinetics.

Kouri, E. M., S. E. Lukas, H. G. Pope, and P. S. Oliva. 1995. "Increased Aggressiveness Responding in Male Volunteers Following the Administration of Gradually Increasing Doses of Testosterone Cypionate." *Drug and Alcohol Dependence* 40, no. 1: 73–79.

Kruskemper, H. L. 1968. *Anabolic Steroids.* New York: Academic Press.

Kuhn, C. 2002. "Anabolic Steroids." *Recent Progress in Hormone Research* 57: 411–434.

Kruskemper, H. L. 1968. *Anabolic Steroids.* New York: Academic Press.

Lamb, D. 1984. "Anabolic Steroids in Athletics: How Well Do They Work and How Dangerous Are They?" *American Journal of Sports Medicine* 12, no. 1: 31–38.

Lambert, M. I., S. D. Titlestad, and M. P. Schwellnus. 1998. "Prevalence of Androgenic-Anabolic Steroid Use in Adolescents in Two Regions of South Africa." *South African Medical Journal* 88, no. 7: 876–880.

Ljungqvist, A. 1975. "The Use of Anabolic Steroids in Top Swedish Athletes." *British Journal of Sports Medicine* 9: 82.

Llewellyn, W. 2000. *Anabolics 2000.* Aurora, CO: Anabolics.com.

Malarkey, W., R. Strauss, and D. Leizman. 1991. "Endocrine Effects in Female Weight Lifters Who Self-Administer Testosterone and Anabolic Steroids." *American Journal of Obstetrics and Gynecology* 165, no. 5: 1385–1390.

Millar, A. P. 1996. "Anabolic Steroids: A Personal Pilgrimage." *Journal of Performance Enhancing Drugs* 1, no. 1: 4–9.

National Center on Addiction and Substance Abuse. 2000. *Winning at Any Cost: Doping in Olympic Sport.* Report by the CASA National Commission on Sports and Substance Abuse. New York: National Center on Addiction and Substance Abuse.

National Collegiate Athletic Association Research Staff. 1997. *NCAA Study of Substance Use Habits of College Student-Athletes.* Indianapolis: National Collegiate Athletic Association Research.

———. 2001. *NCAA Study of Substance Use Habits of College Student-Athletes.* Indianapolis: National Collegiate Athletic Association Research.

Newman, S. 1994. "Despite Warnings, Lure of Steroids Too Strong for Some Young Canadians." *Canadian Medical Association Journal* 151: 844–846.

Nilsson, S. 1995. "Androgenic Anabolic Steroid Use Among Male Adolescents in Falkenberg." *European Journal of Clinical Pharmacology* 48, no. 1: 9–11.

Nilsson, S., A. Baigi, B. Marklund, and B. Fridlund. 2001a. "The Prevalence of the Use of Androgenic Steroids by Adolescents in a County of Sweden." *European Journal of Public Health* 11, no. 2: 195–197.

———. 2001b. "Trends in the Misuse of Anabolic Steroids Among Boys 16–17 Years Old in a Primary Health Care Area in Sweden." *Scandinavian Journal of Primary Health Care* 19: 181–182.

Pearson, B. 1994. "Olympic Survey: Olympians of Winters Past." *USA Today,* February 7, C5.

Pearson, B., and Hansen, B. 1992. Survey of U.S. Olympians. *USA Today,* February 5, 10C.

Phillips, W. N. 1991. *Anabolic Reference Guide Sixth Issue.* Golden, CO: Mile High Publishing.

Pope, H. G., E. M. Kouri, and J. I. Hudson. 2000. "Effects of Supraphysiologic Doses of Testosterone on Mood and Aggression in Normal Men." *Archives of General Psychiatry* 57: 133–140.

Rockhold, R. 1993. "Cardiovascular Toxicity of Anabolic Steroids." *Annual Review of Pharmacology and Toxicology* 33: 497–520.

Rogol, A., and C. Yesalis. 1992. "Anabolic-Androgenic Steroids and the Adolescent." *Pediatrics Annual* 21, no. 3: 175–188.

Schwellnus, M., M. Lambert, and M. Todd. 1992. "Androgenic-Anabolic Steroid Use in Matric Pupils." *South African Medical Journal* 82: 154–158.

Silvester, L. 1973. "Anabolic Steroids at the 1972 Olympics." *Scholastic Coach* 43: 90–92.

Soe, K., M. Soe, and C. Gluud. 1992. "Liver Pathology Associated with the Use of Anabolic Steroids." *Liver* 12: 73–79.

Su, T. P., M. Pagliaro, P. J. Schmidt, D. Pickar, O. Wolkowitz, and D. R. Rubinow. 1993. "Neuropsychiatric Effects of Anabolic Steroids in Male Normal Volunteers." *Journal of the American Medical Association* 269: 2760–2764.

Sullivan, M. L., C. M. Martinez, P. Gennis, and E. J. Gallagher. 1998. "The Cardiac Toxicity of Anabolic Steroids." *Progress in Cardiovascular Diseases* 41, no. 1: 1–15.

Tricker, R., M. O'Neil, and D. Cook. 1989. "The Incidence of Anabolic Steroid Use among Competitive Bodybuilders." *Journal of Drug Education* 19: 313–325.

Urhausen, A., T. Albers, and W. Kindermann. 2004. "Are the Cardiac Effects of Anabolic Steroid Abuse in Strength Athletes Reversible?" *Heart* 90: 496–501.

Williamson, D. J. 1993. "Anabolic Steroid Use among Students at a British College of Technology." *British Journal of Sports Medicine* 27, no. 3: 200–201.

Wilson, J. 1988. "Androgen Abuse by Athletes." *Endocrine Reviews* 9(2): 181–199.

Wood, R., L. Johnson, L. Chu, C. Schad, and D. Self. 2004. "Testosterone Reinforcement: Intravenous and Intraocerebroventricular Self-Administration in Male Rats and Hamsters." *Psychopharmacology* 171: 298–305.

Wright, J. E. 1980. "Steroids and Athletics." *Exercise and Sports Sciences Reviews* 8: 149–202.

———. 1982. *Anabolic Steroids and Sport II.* Natick, MA: Sports Science Consultants.

Wu, F., and A. von Eckardstein. 2003. "Androgens and Coronary Artery Disease." *Endocrine Reviews* 24, no. 2: 183–217.

Yates, W. R., P. J. Perry, J. MacIndoe, T. Holman, and V. L. Ellingrod. 1999. "Psychosexual Effects of Three Doses of Testosterone Cycling in Normal Men." *Biological Psychiatry* 45: 254–260.

Yen, S., and R. Jaffe. 1978. *Reproductive Endocrinology.* Philadelphia: Saunders.

Yesalis, C., W. Anderson, W. Buckley, and J. Wright. 1990. "Incidence of the Non-Medical Use of Anabolic-Androgenic Steroids." Pp. 97–112 in G. Lin and L. Erinoff, eds., *Anabolic Steroid Abuse.* National Institute on Drug Abuse Research Monograph Series No. 102. Rockville, MD: U.S. Department of Health and Human Services, Public Health Service, and Alcohol, Drug Abuse, and Mental Health Administration.

Yesalis, C. E., and M. S. Bahrke. 1995. "Anabolic-Androgenic Steroids: Current Issues." *Sports Medicine* 19: 326–340.

Yesalis, C., M. and Bahrke. 2003. "History of Doping in Sport." *International Sports Studies* 24, no. 1: 42–76.

Yesalis, C. E., M. Bahrke, A. N. Kopstein, and C. K. Barsukiewicz. 2000. "Incidence on Anabolic Steroid Use: A Discussion of Methodological Issues." Pp. 73–115 in C. E. Yesalis, ed., *Anabolic Steroids in Sport and Exercise,* 2nd ed. Champaign, IL: Human Kinetics.

Yesalis, C. E., C. K. Barsukiewicz, A. N. Kopstein, and M. S. Bahrke. 1997. "Trends in Anabolic-Androgenic Steroid Use Among Adolescents." *Archives of Pediatric and Adolescent Medicine* 151: 1197–1206.

Yesalis, C., W. Buckley, W. Anderson, M. O. Wang, J. H. Norwig, G. Ott, J. C. Puffer, and R. H. Strauss. 1990. "Athletes' Projections of Anabolic Steroid Use." *Clinical Sports Medicine* 2: 155–171.

Yesalis, C. E., S. P. Courson, and J. E. Wright. 2000. "History of Anabolic Steroid Use in Sport and Exercise." Pp. 51–71 in C. E. Yesalis, ed., *Anabolic Steroids in Sport and Exercise,* 2nd ed. Champaign, IL: Human Kinetics.

Yesalis, C., R. Herrick, W. Buckley, K. Friedl, D. Brannon, and J. Wright. 1988. "Self-Reported Use of Anabolic-Androgenic Steroids by Elite Power Lifters." *Physician and Sportsmedicine* 16: 91–100.

Yesalis, C. E., N. Kennedy, A. Kopstein, and M. S. Bahrke. 1993. "Anabolic-Androgenic Steroid Use in the United States." *Journal of the American Medical Association* 270: 1217–1221.

Yesalis, C. E., C. K. Ortner, and M. S. Bahrke. 1996. "Steroidi anabolizzanti mascolinizzanti: Dal si dice al quanto: Uno sguardo alla situazione internationale." *Sport e Medicina* 5: 27–35.

Yesalis, C., J. Wright, and M. Bahrke. 1989. "Epidemiological and Policy Issues in the Measurement of the Long Term Health Effects of Anabolic-Androgenic Steroids." *Sports Medicine* 8, no. 3: 129–138.

20

Finding the Golden Genes

Patrick Barry

In early August—8/8/08, to be precise—the curtain will rise on what many experts believe could prove to be the first genetically modified Olympics.

For the unscrupulous or overdriven Olympic athlete, the banned practice of "doping" by taking hormones or other drugs to enhance athletic prowess may seem so last century. The next thing in doping is more profound *and* more dangerous. It's called gene doping: permanently inserting strength- or endurance-boosting genes into DNA.

"Once you put that gene in, it's there for the rest of that person's life," says Larry Bowers, a clinical chemist at the U.S. Anti-Doping Agency in Colorado Springs, Colo "You can't go back and fish it out."

Scientists developed the technology behind gene doping as a promising way to treat genetic diseases such as sickle-cell anemia and the "bubble boy" immune deficiency syndrome. This experimental medical technology—called gene therapy—has begun to emerge from the pall of early failures and fatalities in clinical trials. As gene therapy begins to enjoy some preliminary successes, scientists at the World Anti-Doping Agency, which oversees drug testing for the Olympics, have started to worry that dopers might now see abuse of gene therapy in sport as a viable option, though the practice was banned by WADA in 2003.

"Gene therapy has now broken out from what seemed to be too little progress and has now shown real therapies for a couple diseases, and more coming," says

Source: Patrick Barry, "Finding the Golden Genes," *Science News* (August 2, 2008): 16, 18, 20–21. Reprinted with permission of *Science News*.

Theodore Friedmann, a gene therapy expert at the University of California, San Diego and chairman of WADA's panel on gene doping.

While gene therapy research has begun making great strides, the science of detecting illicit use of gene therapy in sport is only now finding its legs. To confront the perceived inevitability of gene doping, Friedmann and other scientists have started in recent years to explore the problem of detecting whether an athlete has inserted a foreign gene—an extra copy that may be indistinguishable from the natural genes—into his or her DNA.

It's proving to be a formidable challenge. Genetic makeup varies from person to person, and world-class athletes are bound to have some natural genetic endowments that other people lack. Somehow, gene-doping tests must distinguish between natural genetic variation among individuals and genes inserted artificially—and the distinction must stand up in court.

Scientists are fighting genetics with genetics, so to speak, enlisting the latest technologies for gene sequencing or for profiling the activity of proteins to find the telltale signs of gene doping. Some techniques attempt the daunting search for the foreign gene itself, like looking for a strand of hay in an enormous haystack.

But new research could also lead to an easier and more foolproof approach: detecting the characteristic ways that an inserted gene affects an athlete's body as a whole.

RESURGENCE OF GENE THERAPY

In 1999, 18-year-old Jesse Gelsinger died during a gene therapy trial for a rare liver disease. Investigators later attributed his death to a violent immune reaction to the delivery virus rather than to the therapeutic gene. His death was a major setback for the field. It also may have scared away early would-be gene dopers.

In recent years, safety and efficacy of gene therapy have shown signs of progress in numerous clinical trials for conditions ranging from early-onset vision loss to erectile dysfunction. As scientists develop ways to use safer, weaker viruses for delivery, and as gene therapies wind their way through clinical trials, athletes and coaches might start to see gene doping as even more viable than they already do.

In the courtroom during the 2006 trial of Thomas Springstein, a German track coach accused of giving performance-enhancing drugs to high-school-age female runners, prosecutors read aloud an e-mail Springstein had written that would shock the sports world.

"The new Repoxygen is hard to get," the e-mail read, according to press reports. "Please give me new instructions soon so that I can order the product before Christmas."

Repoxygen isn't merely another doping drug such as a hormone or the latest designer steroid—it's an experimental virus designed to deliver a therapeutic gene and insert it into a person's DNA.

British pharmaceutical company Oxford BioMedica developed Repoxygen in 2002 as a treatment for severe anemia. The therapy "infects" patients with a harmless virus carrying a modified gene that encodes erythropoietin, a protein that boosts red blood cell production. This protein, often called EPO, is itself a favorite among dopers seeking to increase their oxygen capacity, and hence their endurance.

Viruses have the natural ability to inject genetic material into their host's DNA. The host's cells can translate that gene into active proteins as if the foreign gene were the cells' own. So by delivering the gene for EPO within a virus, Repoxygen could potentially increase the amounts of EPO protein—and the change would be permanent.

Athletes might also be tempted by perhaps the most tantalizing gene therapy experiment of all: the "mighty mouse." In 1998, H. Lee Sweeney and his colleagues at the University of Pennsylvania School of Medicine injected mice with a virus carrying a gene that boosted production of insulin-like growth factor 1, or IGF-1, a protein that regulates muscle growth. As a result, the mice had 15 percent more muscle mass and were 14 percent stronger than untreated mice—without ever having exercised. The treatment also prevented the decline of muscle mass as the mice grew older.

Other genetic paths to increase muscle strength and volume could include the gene for human growth hormone or segments of DNA that block a protein called myostatin, which normally limits muscle growth.

Endurance might also be boosted by the gene encoding a protein called peroxisome proliferator-activated receptor delta, or PPAR-delta. Mice engineered to have extra copies of this gene hopped onto a treadmill and, without ever having trained, ran about twice as far as unaltered mice. The extra PPAR-delta improved the ability of the mice's muscles to use fat molecules for energy, and it shifted the animals' ratio of muscle fiber types from fast-twitch toward slow-twitch fibers—a change that would improve muscle endurance in people as well. Ronald Evans and his colleagues at the Salk Institute for Biological Studies in La Jolla, Calif., published the research in 2004.

Since then, Evans says, he has been routinely approached by curious coaches and athletes. "I've had athletes come to my lectures and go to the microphone and say, 'If I took this drug, would it work with EPO and growth hormone?' I mean, they would ask this publicly," Evans says.

"Based on athletes I've talked with, I'd say that it's a reasonable possibility that gene doping will be used in this Olympics, and I think there's a very high probability that it will be used in the next Olympics," he says.

ELUSIVE SIGNS

Around the time that Evans was announcing his "marathon mouse" results, WADA kicked off a funding program to focus scientific research on strategies for detecting gene doping.

"A key part of our project is to try to define what we call signatures of doping," says Olivier Rabin, a biomedical engineer and director of science for WADA. "We are looking at the impact of those kinds of genetic manipulations at different levels."

The first and most obvious approach is simply to look for the inserted gene among the roughly 6 billion "letters" of genetic code in both sets of a person's chromosomes.

For clinical gene therapy trials, finding the inserted gene is fairly easy. Scientists know the exact sequence of the gene they inserted, and often they know where on the person's chromosomes the gene should have ended up. Standard DNA sequencing techniques can reveal the genetic code for that region on the chromosomes, and the unique sequence of the inserted gene will be in plain view. With gene doping, the situation is much trickier.

"In sport, you don't know where that gene will be put, what virus was used or even what particular variety of gene was used," Friedmann says. "You don't have the advantage of knowing where to look and for what, so the argument is to look everywhere."

Another difficulty is that copies of the foreign gene wouldn't be in all of a person's cells. The gene-carrying viruses selectively target certain tissues such as muscle or liver (the liver helps to regulate muscle metabolism). Some blood cells might also take in the viruses' genetic payloads, but it's questionable whether a standard blood sample from an athlete would contain the gene. Instead, anti-doping officials would have to sample muscle tissue directly using punch biopsies, a procedure that is mildly painful.

"No one's expecting that an athlete will agree to a muscle biopsy," Friedmann says. "That's a nonstarter."

Still, direct detection of inserted genes could work in some cases. Evans points out that an artificially inserted gene for PPAR-delta would be much smaller than the natural gene. That's because the natural gene is far too big to hitch a ride on the carrier virus. Fitting the gene onto a virus means only a trimmed down version of the gene can be used. This distinctive genetic pattern would only exist in a person who had undergone gene doping.

In other cases, genes would end up in tissues where they're not normally active, making detection more straightforward. For example, the liver and kidneys normally produce the protein EPO, which makes red blood cells, but gene doping could deliver the EPO-coding gene directly to muscle tissues. The trick, then, is to find a noninvasive way to detect where EPO production is occurring inside the body.

One solution is to use medical imaging techniques such as PET scans. In research funded by WADA, Jordi Segura and his colleagues at the Municipal Institute for Medical Research in Barcelona, Spain, attached slightly radioactive "flags" to molecules made during EPO production. A standard PET scan can spot this radioactivity, revealing where EPO was being made in the bodies of mice injected with gene-doping viruses, the team reported in the October 2007 *Therapeutic Drug Monitoring*. The researchers showed that production of EPO in muscle tissue was a telltale sign of gene doping.

With radioactivity that is relatively mild, the labels are routinely used in medical imaging to diagnose diseases and don't pose a significant hazard. But Friedmann notes that asking athletes to undergo such a procedure could be controversial.

DETECTION BY PROXY

Another approach is to look for signs of the viral "infection," rather than for the gene itself. Even a weakened virus could trigger a mild, and specific, immune reaction that might show up in a blood test.

Perhaps the greatest challenge facing this method is that viruses aren't the only way to deliver a gene into a doper's body. "The reality is that you can just inject naked DNA directly into tissues" with a syringe, Evans says. "Direct injection could be more local and harder to detect."

This relatively crude way to insert a gene won't spread the gene as widely through a person's body as viruses injected into the bloodstream would. But many cells near the site of injection could take in the gene, perhaps enough to improve athletic performance.

Microscopic, synthetic spheres of fat molecules called liposomes can also shuttle doping genes into the body.

To prevent dopers from evading detection by simply changing delivery vehicles, scientists are also exploring a third approach to developing tests: proteomics, the detailed study of all the proteins in the human body.

Regardless of the vehicle used, adding a new gene to the body's tightly woven web of interacting genes and proteins will cause ripples of change to spread throughout that web. "There will be a body-wide response no matter what gene you use or where in the body you put it," Friedmann says, "and those changes can be used as a signature of doping."

Painful biopsies wouldn't be required. Because the cascade of changes in protein activity would be widespread, anti-doping officials could test using blood, urine, hair or even sweat. Tools developed for the burgeoning fields of genomics and proteomics allow scientists to see the activity levels of thousands of genes or proteins simultaneously.

In preliminary unpublished experiments, Friedmann and his colleagues injected a type of muscle cell with the gene for IGF-1. Activity of hundreds of genes changed as a result, including a boost in the activity of genes that control production of cholesterol, steroids and fatty acids. All of these changes might be detectable with simple blood tests.

WADA is funding half a dozen or so ongoing studies on this proteome-based detection strategy, but research in this area is still at an early stage. "There's good reason to think that's likely to work, and a number of labs are having some nice results," Friedmann says.

As for whether any tests for gene doping will be ready in time for the Beijing Olympics, anti-doping authorities aren't giving away many hints that might help dopers evade detection. "We never say when our tests are going to be in place," WADA's Rabin says.

Even if detection methods do lag behind the games, dopers may want to think twice before assuming they're in the clear, Friedmann notes. "With stored [blood and urine] samples, one always has the option of going back some months or years later and checking again with the newest tests."

Just in case the dangers of tampering with a person's genetic makeup weren't enough of a disincentive.

EXPLORE MORE

National Institutes of Health Handbook on Gene Therapy: ghr.nlm.nih.gov/handbook/therapy/genetherapy.

Gene Therapy, Athletes, and Doping

1928
IAAF, the International Association of Athletics Federations, becomes the first international sport federation to ban doping, the use of performance-enhancing substances.

1968
The International Olympic Committee approves a ban on doping, a year after British cyclist Tom Simpson collapsed and died during the Tour de France. His autopsy revealed high levels of methamphetamine.

1998
Mighty mouse: injecting mice with a virus carrying the gene for IGF-1 makes the animals 14 percent stronger, even without the benefit of exercise. This mouse is shown climbing a ladder while carrying weights.

1999
18-year-old Jesse Gelsinger becomes the first person to die during a gene therapy clinical trial, apparently because of a massive immune response to the virus used to deliver the genes.

2004
The World Anti-Doping Agency begins a program to fund scientific research on ways to detect gene doping.

2006
The first public evidence of a coach seeking gene doping substances for his athletes emerges in court during the trial of German coach Thomas Springstein.

June 10–11, 2008
The World Anti-Doping Agency holds the third Gene Doping Symposium, in Saint Petersburg, Russia.

Gene therapy could help an athlete change production of ...	And the result could be ...
Erythropoietin	Enhanced red blood cell production, thus greater oxygen delivery for endurance
Human growth factor	Increased muscle size, power and recovery from fatigue
Insulin-like growth factor	Increased number of muscle regulator cells, thus size, power and recovery from fatigue
PPAR-delta	More fat metabolism and increased muscle endurance
Myostatin	Greater muscle growth due to the inhibition of myostatin production

21

Outraged over the Steroids Outrage

Robert Lipsyte

As a longtime steroid user, I'm confused by the frenzied reaction to the juicy news coming out of baseball these days.

Why should we care what those players do, as long as they entertain us? Who wouldn't expect pro athletes, like the rest of us, to try to be the best they could be? And how has this become a chance for yet more face time for flabby moralists instead of an opportunity to gather some necessary information?

Here's what I want to know: Exactly which performances are enhanced—and how—by which anabolic steroids, androgens, human growth hormone, and whatever else athletes shoot, swallow, and sniff? What are the long-term and short-term effects? Are those enhancements and side effects different for adolescents and adults, men and women?

I have ethical questions, too. How different is steroid use from cosmetic surgery for the male TV newsies reporting these stories, from Botox for actresses, beta blockers for public speakers and all the new psychological drugs for well people with the willies—the shy, the anxious, the fidgety, and the sexually apprehensive?

Speaking of which, consider the tomcat fight between two of baseball's best-known sluggers and congressional testifiers, Jose Canseco and his childhood pal, Rafael Palmeiro. In his best seller, *Juiced,* Canseco claims he personally injected steroids

Source: Robert Lipsyte, "Outraged over the Steroids Outrage," *USA Today: The Magazine of the American Scene,* March 22, 2005. Used with permission. See http://www.robertlipsyte.com.

into Palmeiro when they both played for George W. Bush's Texas Rangers. Palmeiro denies it. Of course, Palmeiro, as baseball's most famous pitchman for Viagra, is no stranger to performance-enhancing drugs.

"Performance-enhancement is in a gray area," says Robert Klitzman, codirector of Columbia University's Center for Bioethics. "Would you include new technologies to improve cognitive abilities? How about access to SAT prep coaching? Assisted pregnancies?"

Meanwhile, athletes certainly have no ethical dilemma about using steroids, says Michael Miletic, a psychiatrist whose Detroit-based practice includes high school, college, and professional athletes. "Steroids are totally embedded in the sports culture. We need to get past the finger-pointing. There's been a wholesale abandonment of critical analysis."

MY STEROID USE

Analyze this: I've been shooting steroids for almost 15 years, since a third cancer operation left me unable to produce testosterone naturally. Once a month, I nail one of my quadriceps with a 22-gauge needle and pump in the oily yellow fluid. Without it, my prescribing surgeon tells me, I would be physically fatigued and mentally sluggish, lose my sex drive, be achy and depressed. No question, I'm taking a performance-enhancing drug.

Yet, even with it, I can't hit a major-league fastball, sack a moving NFL quarterback, or bench-press 500 pounds. Using steroids, most people can train harder and recover more quickly from breakdown and injury. But to reach all-pro you have to be what athletes call a "freak" with those potentially all-pro genes to tweak.

But chemicals also help high school boys pump themselves into beach studs, put on extra pounds for the football team, and gain strength and stamina for the campaign to win a college scholarship and a pro contract. This is the danger zone, says Miletic, who is far less concerned with the middle-aged Barry Bonds's possible career choices than with unsupervised drug use by kids.

"This is where we should be paying attention," Miletic says. "First of all, there is adult complicity here. Some parents and coaches are actively helping kids get drugs, others are looking the other way. How could you not notice the dramatic changes in your child's body?

"I don't believe kids are taking steroids because they think it helped Mark McGwire. They're taking it because teammates, opponents, a strength coach, a gym owner is telling them it will make them better," he says.

Performance-enhancers have been around for a long time, and as our games, from Little League to Super Bowl, became less classrooms for character building and more stages for spectaculars, the pressure to enhance performance swelled like Popeye's biceps (his drug was spinach, remember?). We expect our sports heroes to do anything to win for us, to find the edge, to take risks, even to play hurt. If they don't, they're replaced by those who will.

"WHERE DOES CHEATING BEGIN?"

At the same time, the self-help movement made the concept of improvement, of reinvention, of taking charge of body and psyche, a kind of mandate for everybody. To refuse to at least try to find a way to feel better, look better, do better was regarded as almost a crime. Is self-help from a mind-numbing mantra more moral than self-help from the tip of a needle?

"It's going to get even more complicated," says Klitzman, the Columbia bio-ethicist, "as techniques for screening embryos and scanning brains become more sophisticated. Scientists will be looking for stupidity genes and smart pills. Cosmetic psycho-pharmacology is an area where people with money will have advantages over people who don't. Is that fair? In an ideal world, there would be a level playing field. Exactly where does cheating begin?"

I'll be watching baseball this season for guys who look less bulked-up than they did last season. How many are using newer, riskier, test-proof drugs? That's probably not fair.

The pundits and politicians will declare a moral victory and move on, leaving our questions unanswered. That's cheating.

✳ FOR FURTHER STUDY ✳

Bee, Peta. 2005. "This One Will Help Me Run and Run: The World of Sport Is Full of Performance-Enhancing Fads." *Guardian,* August 30. Available at http://sport.guardian.co.uk/news/story/0,10488,1558931.00.html.

Begley, Sharon, and Martha Brant. 1999. "The Real Scandal in International Sport: Doping." *Newsweek* (February 15): 48–54.

Bjerklie, David, and Alice Park. 2004. "How Doctors Help the Dopers." *Time* (August 16): 58–62.

Dixon, Patrick. 2006. "Steroids: The Truth about Steroids." *Global Change* (January 3). Available at http://www.globalchange.com/steroids/htm.

Hoberman, John M. 2004. *Testosterone Dreams: Rejuvenation, Aphrodisia, Doping.* Berkeley: University of California Press.

Jendrick, Nathan. 2006. *Dunks, Doubles, Doping: How Steroids Are Killing American Athletes.* Guilford, CT: Lyons.

Mehlman, Maxwell J. 2004. "What's Wrong with Using Drugs in Sports? Nothing." *USA Today* (August 11). Available at http://www.usatoday.com/news/opinion/editorials/2004–08–11-mehlman_w.htm.

Pound, Richard W. 2006. *Inside Dope: How Drugs Are the Biggest Threat to Sports, Why You Should Care, and What Can Be Done about Them.* New York: Wiley.

PART EIGHT

Problems of Excess:
Big-Time College Sport

Interschool sports are found in almost all American schools and at all levels. There are many reasons for this universality. Sports unite all segments of a school and the community or neighborhood they represent. School sports remind constituents of the school, which may lead to monetary and other forms of support. School administrators can use sport as a useful tool for social control. But the most important reason for the universality of school sports is the widespread belief that the educational goals are accomplished through sport. There is much merit to this view; sports do contribute to physical fitness, to learning the value of hard work and perseverance, and to being goal-oriented. There is some evidence that sports participation leads to better grades, higher academic aspirations, and positive self-concept.

However, there also is a negative side to school sports. They are elitist, since only the gifted participate. Sports often overshadow academic endeavors (e.g., athletes are disproportionately rewarded and schools devote too much time and money to athletics that could be diverted to academic activities). Where winning is paramount—and where is this not the case?—the pressure becomes intense. This pressure has several negative consequences, the most important of which is that participants are prevented from fully enjoying sport. The pressure is too great for many youngsters. The game is work. It is a business.

The pressure to win also contributes to abuse by coaches, poor sportsmanship, dislike of opponents, intolerance of losers, and cheating. Most significant, although not usually considered so, is that while sport is a success-oriented activity, it is fraught with failure (losing teams, bench warmers, would-be participants cut from teams, the humiliation of letting down your teammates and school, and so on). For every ego enhanced by sport, how many have been bruised?

While this description fits all types of schools, big-time college sports deserve special attention, for they have unique problems. Athletes in these settings are athletes first and students second; thus they are robbed of a first-class education. They are robbed by the tremendous demands on their time and energy. This problem is further enhanced by athletes being segregated from the student body (in classes, majors, and in eating and living arrangements); thus they are deprived of a variety of influences that college normally facilitates.

Another problem of college sports is that they tend to be ultraelitist. The money and facilities go disproportionately to the male athletes in the revenue-producing sports rather than to intramurals, minor sports, and club sports.

The greatest scandal involving college sports is the illegal and immoral behavior of overzealous coaches, school authorities, and alumni in recruiting athletes. In the quest to bring the best athletes to a school, players have been given monetary inducements, sexual favors, forged transcripts, and surrogates to take their entrance exams. In addition to the illegality of these acts, two fundamental problems exist with these recruiting violations: (1) Such behaviors have no place in an educational setting, yet they are done by some educators and condoned by others, and (2) these illicit practices by so-called respected authorities transmit two major lessons—that greed is the ultimate value and that winning supersedes how one wins.

Finally, the win-at-any-cost ethic that prevails in many of America's institutions of higher learning puts undue pressure on coaches. They must win to keep their jobs. Hence, some drive their athletes too hard or too brutally. Some demand total control over their players on and off the field. Some use illegal tactics to gain advantage (not only in recruiting but also in breaking the rules regarding the allowed number of practices, ineligible players, and unfair techniques). But coaches are not the problem. They represent a symptom of the process by which school sports are big business and where winning is the only avenue to achieve success.

The chapters of part 8 reflect on these problems and offer solutions. The first is by sports administration professor John R. Gerdy, who demythologizes the value of college athletics. The second, by journalist Stewart Mandell, discusses cheating in big-time athletic programs. The final chapter, by D. Stanley Eitzen, uses the metaphor of slavery to show how big-time college athletes are exploited.

22

An Experiment Justified

John R. Gerdy

> I love fools' experiments; I am always making them.
>
> —Charles Darwin

Elite athletics was incorporated into our educational system for several reasons. It was believed that involvement in athletics was educational for, and built the "character" of, participants. Further, athletics could also provide entertainment and serve a unifying function for the school and surrounding communities, generating positive school and community spirit. Finally, it was believed that participation in athletics would not only be healthy for the athletes but would serve an important public health function by promoting awareness of the value of being fit.

These justifications applied to athletics at both the high school and college levels. But high schools and colleges each had additional, unique reasons for embracing elite athletics. Despite idealized notions to the contrary, the most significant reason athletics was incorporated into our high schools had little to do with education in the traditional sense. The driving force behind the development of such programs was the great industrialists of the early 1900s. But rather than having an interest in educating through sport, these business leaders looked upon organized athletics as a means to train, socialize, and control a workforce. Industrial America required workers to be loyal, dependable, physically fit, team oriented, and, above all else, obedient. Sport, it was believed, instilled these characteristics. In the minds of Andrew

Source: John R. Gerdy, *Air Ball* (Jackson: University Press of Mississippi, 2006), excerpt from pp. 11–23.

Carnegie, J. D. Rockefeller, and the like, there was little room for lofty thinking on the assembly line. Factory owners of that time did not want their line workers to be great thinkers, preferring them to passively conform: "The leaders of American industry felt that their workers needed to be loyal and punctual, but not necessarily good academically" (Miracle and Rees, 1994, p. 178).

In the case of higher education, it was believed that athletics could contribute to institutional mission through resource acquisition in the form of money, widespread visibility, increased student enrollment, and enhanced alumni support. Until the late 1800s, university athletics were operated by student-run associations. Students were responsible for arranging travel, securing equipment, and generally administrating the teams. Athletics was simply an institutional afterthought, an activity to keep students amused, but certainly not critical to the educational mission of the university. It was the constant search for resources, coupled with the rapidly growing public interest in athletics and their resultant capability to generate revenue, that convinced presidents and boards to formally incorporate athletics into the structure of their institutions.

Incorporating elite athletics programs into our educational system represents one of the most significant experiments in the history of American education. It can be categorized as an experiment because, at the time, there was no solid empirical evidence to support the reasons used to justify athletics' place in the academy. While the justifications used were certainly plausible and, indeed, desirable, they were guesses, with no research or track record to substantiate them.

Looming over all of these justifications was a basic assumption regarding the role that athletics would play in the institution. It was assumed that the benefits of elite athletics could be achieved in a way that would supplement rather than undermine the academic values and the educational mission of institutions. While some faculty members warned that the marriage of highly competitive, elite athletics with academe was fraught with danger, it was taken largely as a matter of faith that, on balance, athletics would be a positive contributor to an institution's mission. This was an enormous leap because there were no examples in other countries where the responsibility for developing elite athletes and teams rested with the educational system. The marriage of highly competitive, elite athletics and the educational system was a uniquely American experiment.

It has been an experiment that has had an impact far beyond the walls of the academy, greatly influencing our culture and societal values. Virtually every American has been impacted or influenced by high school or college athletics. Whether as a participant, fan, or student, high school and college sports have influenced our attitudes regarding the role that athletics should play in our lives, families, communities, and country.

Now, more than a century later, has the experiment been successful? How effective have our athletics programs been in fulfilling the long-held justifications for their incorporation into our educational system? Sadly, not very effective at all. American education's experiment with elite athletics has been a failure.

THE PRICE HIGHER EDUCATION PAYS

From the involvement of the president of St. Bonaventure University in academic fraud to the murder of a Baylor University basketball player by a teammate and subsequent attempt by the head coach to mislead investigators, there is no shortage of examples of how athletics undermines academic values and educational mission. These transgressions are symptomatic of a larger problem—the alienation of athletics from the university's mission and this trend's impact on public trust in higher education. As the Knight Foundation Commission on Intercollegiate Athletics stated in its 2001 report titled *A Call to Action: Reconnecting College Sports and Higher Education,* "[T]he cultural sea change is now complete. Big-time college football and basketball have been thoroughly professionalized and commercialized" (p. 23).

When the hypocrisy of big-time, NCAA Division I football and basketball being justified on educational grounds is revealed, athletics' negative impact on American higher education is apparent. The effect of this hypocrisy is particularly pernicious because athletics is the clearest window through which the public views higher education. Athletics, particularly big-time NCAA Division I athletics, is extremely popular. Media coverage through newspapers, television, and the internet is extensive. Athletics scandals receive an unprecedented amount of attention and coverage. The result is that college athletics' profile within our national consciousness has risen to an extraordinary level.

In short, the consequences for higher education of sponsoring this highly visible hypocrisy are enormous. If the public sees athletics departments with little integrity, how can that same public have faith in higher education's ability to effectively address more pressing societal problems?

The purpose of this book, however, is not to dwell on, sensationalize, or revel in the failure of the current model of elite athletics in America, with its now all-too-extensive and familiar laundry list of examples of academic fraud, uncontrolled spending, institutional lies and cover-ups, recruiting scandals, illiterate athletes, lack of institutional control and integrity, and out-of-control boosters, coaches, and fans. Such examples have become a part of the college athletics landscape and there is simply no need to repeat here what has been written about so extensively elsewhere. That said, however, the current model's shortcomings must be articulated and a few long-held and widely accepted beliefs regarding the value of college athletics must be considered briefly because they relate directly to the fundamental purposes on which the athletics enterprise is founded.

SHATTERING MYTHS

Despite the fact that economics was the primary reason athletics was formally in-corporated into American higher education institutions, the NCAA continues to promote the education of athletes and athletics' effectiveness in supplementing the academic mission of the institution as its fundamental purposes. Unfortunately, the gulf between the athletics and academic cultures on our college campuses has become so wide that we can simply no longer pretend that athletics is effectively accomplishing these goals.

Institutions recruit athletes who are not prepared for college work and then place athletic demands upon them that allow little time for academics. Many are placed in "crib" courses and/or "bogus" majors. Far too many coaches are more interested in winning games, making money, and being media personalities than in meeting their responsibilities as educators. Consistently low graduation rates for athletes, particularly black athletes, in football and men's basketball offer evidence of this disconnect. Athletics scandals severely damage the reputation of an institution and erode public trust in higher education. And skewed institutional priorities are on display for all to see when palatial arenas and athletics offices are built while classrooms and laboratories lack basic amenities and coaches are paid more than university presidents. As these trends continue, it becomes more difficult to make the case that elite college athletics supplements the educational process of the athlete and the academic mission of the institution.

Another widely held belief regarding athletics departments is that they generate money and resources for the institution. A first glance would suggest that, from an economic standpoint, college athletics is booming. Basketball and football games can be seen on television virtually every night of the week. CBS paid the NCAA more than $6.2 billion for the rights to telecast the NCAA men's basketball tournament for eleven years. Conference championship, football bowl, and basketball tournament games generate millions of dollars for participating institutions and their conferences. Corporations pay millions of dollars for event sponsorship rights and stadium skyboxes. There are now two twenty-four-hour college sports cable networks (ESPN-U and College Sports Television). Colleges also rake in millions from the sale of sports apparel and related merchandise. Corporate logos are plastered on fields, courts, equipment, and uniforms, while coaches are paid hundreds of thousands of dollars to hawk products. Athletics department budgets are bigger, as are stadiums and arenas.

Despite this apparent bonanza, only 18 percent of Division I athletics departments generate more revenue than they expend (Fulks, 2001, pp. 28, 46, 64). Of Division II institutions, less than 6 percent reported a profit (Fulks, 2001, pp. 81, 99). And department costs, as high as they are, may not yet be telling the entire financial story, as many indirect or overhead athletics costs (for example, buildings and grounds maintenance, security, coaches salaries, athletic scholarships) are often paid through the institutional budget. So, the idea that athletics departments are financial engines for universities is misguided. While the profitability of an athletics department may not be a major concern at those schools where athletics is an institutional budget item (largely NCAA Division III institutions), it does raise concerns at institutions that have established programs intended to produce revenue.

It is unfair, however, to evaluate an athletics department's performance on dollars alone. Thus, we have come to accept another major assumption regarding athletics' institutional impact. Athletics, it is said, generates resources in the form of student enrollment, alumni giving, visibility, and public relations. While it is logical that athletics would contribute to the institution in these ways, it is becoming increasingly clear that even in these areas athletics is simply not delivering on its promise.

For example, recent data contradicts one of the strongest myths about college athletics—that winning teams, and especially winning football teams, have a large, positive impact on rates of philanthropic giving at universities that operate big-time programs. Further, when asked which institutional priorities they would like emphasized more and which they would like emphasized less, alumni "voted" for placing *less* emphasis, not more, on intercollegiate athletics. Those who made the biggest donations assigned lower priority to intercollegiate athletics than to nearly every other aspect of college or university life they were asked to rank (Shulman and Bowen, 2001, pp. 220, 201, 226).

The idea that athletics positively impacts a potential student's choice of institution is also a myth. According to a study of college-bound seniors in the spring of 2000 by the Art and Science Group, a research company in Baltimore, most students' awareness of intercollegiate athletics was extremely superficial. Neither the quality nor divisional affiliation of a school's sports program was important to them. Intramural and recreational sports offerings, for example, had a much greater influence on college choice than the intercollegiate athletics program. Students rated jobs, internships, student clubs and organizations, and intramural sports as activities that are more important to them in choosing a college (Suggs, 2001, p. A-51). The fact is most institutions will continue to attract quality students who, when they graduate, will donate money to their alma maters with little regard to the quality or even existence of a big-time athletics program.

The claim that athletics programs serve a unifying function for an educational institution also can be disputed. There are just as many students, faculty, parents, and taxpayers who would rather see institutional resources and energy devoted to improving their school's art, science, theater, or English departments than to renovating a football stadium to include skyboxes that will be utilized less than ten games a year. Furthermore, there are risks in relying on athletics teams to unify educational communities. Schools that use athletics to solve the problems of a fragmented community run the risk of making athletics, not educational and academic excellence, the primary purpose of the institution. Although a football or basketball program can unite a school in a way that an English department cannot, the primary purpose of the institution remains, as it always has been, educational. In short, a winning football team does not make a quality educational institution.

Another justification for the use of athletics is that it generates important resources for the university in the form of visibility and public relations. While there is no denying that athletics can generate significant public exposure and visibility for universities, the larger question is what message is higher education sending to the public through its sponsorship of elite athletics programs? Is it a message that promotes positive academic ideals and principles or rather one that reeks of the hypocrisy of pursuing athletics glory and money at any cost?

The most obvious example of the negative visibility associated with our current elite model of college athletics is the national media coverage that accompanies an athletic scandal. Beyond that, however, there are indications that the public views athletics and the NCAA in ways harmful to higher education. For example, a 2002 NCAA study found that education is not strongly linked with the NCAA image and that most of the public believes that for the NCAA assuring student-athletes get a degree is a low priority. Further, the image of the NCAA is directly linked with connotations of big business and money and the assumption that schools "cheat all the time" (p. 22).

One needs only to watch a televised college football or basketball game to realize that Division I athletics visibility does little to promote educational values or higher education's mission. College sports is packaged, marketed, and projected purely as entertainment with the promotion of educational themes, values, and information an afterthought at best. It is easy to see why televised college sports are overwhelmingly geared to promote athletics. The management of this aspect of athletics programs has always been left to coaches, athletics directors, conference commissioners, and television executives, the very people who are most personally vested in the current model. As a result, televised college athletics has never been considered an opportunity to interface with the public in an educational context. Instead, it is simply one game after another, all devoid of any larger educational purpose or vision—just like the pros.

In short, the use of the elite, professional model of athletics as a commercial vehicle to increase visibility and public relations comes at a high cost to higher education. This cost comes in the repeated failures to promote education and the pervasive negative public opinion regarding the hypocrisy of universities and the NCAA claiming to be about education while operating professional sports franchises.

Another long-held assumption regarding college athletics is that they are a problem only at big-time NCAA Division I institutions. This belief has been particularly harmful because it provides an easy excuse for presidents, faculty, and students at all but the one hundred or so schools at the NCAA Division I-A level to turn a blind eye to athletics' impact on campus values. "Athletics isn't a problem at my school," they say. Meanwhile, the public has come to accept the idea that athletics abuses occur only at a very small percentage of our nation's colleges and universities.

We now know that notion is a myth as well. Two important books, *The Game of Life: College Sports and Educational Values* by James Shulman and William Bowen, along with a follow-up book by Bowen and Sarah Levin entitled *Reclaiming the Game: College Sports and Educational Values,* document the fact that the gap between sport and education is widening not only at Division I institutions but at virtually every institution sponsoring intercollegiate athletics, including Ivy League and select liberal arts colleges. These books, released in 2001 and 2003, respectively, analyze data on ninety thousand students who attended thirty selective colleges and universities over the course of forty years. Combining their research with other historical research and data on alumni giving and budgetary spending on athletics, the authors shatter some very basic assumptions regarding the impact of athletics on institutional culture and academic values.

Specifically, the authors maintain that despite the almost universal acceptance of the notion that issues of college athletic reform apply to big-time football and basketball only, a distinct "athletic culture" is appearing in essentially *all* sports at *all* levels of play, including Division III coed liberal arts colleges. This culture tends to separate athletes from other students and exacerbates the problem of poor academic performance, raising even more difficult questions of educational policy for small private colleges and highly selective universities than for big-time scholarship-granting schools (Shulman and Bowen, 2001, p. 82).

It is particularly noteworthy that these findings apply to schools at all levels of play. In fact, sports' impact on admissions and academic performance may be more significant at small liberal arts colleges and Ivy League institutions because athletes make up a larger percentage of the student population. "The impact of sports programs at places like these may not be as visible on national television, but it can, nevertheless, end up being more consequential" (Shulman and Bowen, 2001, p. 203). This revelation broadens the debate about the potential pitfalls of sponsoring competitive intercollegiate athletics from one concerning major college, full-scholarship programs such as the University of Michigan's to one including nonscholarship, Division III programs such as Williams College's.

Perhaps most disturbing is that in virtually every category, these negative effects are becoming greater. This is so because the intensity of everything connected to the athletics experience, from recruiting, to individual commitment to the sport, to the level of play, has increased at every level, from peewee to professional leagues, all driven by the increasingly professionalized nature of the entire sports system. The result is that the chasm between athletics values and priorities and those of the academic community, always apparent, is becoming greater.

Herein lies the conundrum. At a time when college athletics appears to be more popular than ever, do institutions continue to sponsor their programs as currently structured, despite the fact that their alleged benefits are not being realized and that most of the rationales upon which these programs have been built are not being met?

Again, the purpose of this short review was not to dwell on the scandals and hypocrisies that have become an accepted part of college athletics. It is clear that these highly visible incidents inflict tremendous damage on the integrity of the institution and erode public trust in higher education. But the point must be made: higher education's sponsorship of elite athletics has been a failure. What other conclusion can be drawn when virtually all of its alleged benefits are not being realized and all of the fundamental justifications for its incorporation into academe have, for the most part, been proven to be myths?

23

Everybody Cheats—Just Not My School

Stewart Mandel

In November 2004, I wrote a column on SI.com suggesting that Ohio State president Dr. Karen Holbrook take the unprecedented step of shutting down the university's scandal-plagued athletic department for a year. Earlier that week, *ESPN The Magazine* had published a multipart investigative feature in which several former football players told of receiving phony jobs and academic favors. The most salacious allegations came from former star runningback Maurice Clarett, previously dismissed from the program for lying to NCAA investigators about extra benefits he'd received. Clarett alleged that Buckeyes head coach Jim Tressel introduced him to boosters who lavished him with cash, free cars, and do-nothing jobs. Mind you, when I wrote my column I didn't actually expect the school to voluntarily shut down a $90 million enterprise beloved by hundreds of thousands of fans. My point was that Ohio State—which was already facing major sanctions against its men's basketball program at the time—had allowed its athletic culture to spin out of control and that a serious response from the school was in order. (To its credit, Ohio State has since made numerous progressive changes to its athletic department under new director Gene Smith).

Obviously, I realized Ohio State fans would not be overly pleased with my proposal—no one likes to see their favorite team portrayed in a negative fashion. What was most startling about the e-mails I received from Buckeyes' fans, however, was not their anger over the death-penalty suggestion or their creative use of profanities, but

Source: Stewart Mandel, *Bowls, Polls, and Tattered Souls* (New York: John Wiley and Sons, 2007), excerpts from pp. 232–234, 238–239, and 242–244.

the seemingly universal belief that despite overwhelming evidence to the contrary, their school had done nothing wrong, that the disreputable Clarett had fabricated his entire story, and that writers like myself and those at *ESPN* had committed egregious journalistic sins. "If it weren't for a pathetic, egomaniacal street punk masquerading as a viable pro football prospect, there would be no issue with Ohio State athletics," wrote one. "Everything that has happened at OSU has happened at every school in the Top 25, don't kid yourself, and my school will not take the fall," wrote another. And those were the nicer ones.

We'll never know whether or not Clarett was telling the truth. Shaken by the fallout from his *ESPN* interview, which some harebrained adviser suggested might help his sagging NFL stock, he refused to cooperate with NCAA investigators, and eventually the matter was dropped.[1] What we do know, however, is that six weeks after Clarett's allegations became public, Ohio State's star quarterback, Troy Smith, a close friend of Clarett's at the time, was suspended for the Buckeyes' 2004 bowl game after an attorney for a Columbus-area health care company notified the university that the player had come into its office and walked out with an envelope allegedly filled with $500 cash from CEO Robert Q. Baker, an OSU booster—a scene exactly like the type Clarett described in the article. We also know that at Tressel's former school, Youngstown State, the coach introduced Ray Isaac, his star quarterback at the time, to a prominent booster who lavished him with more than $10,000 in illegal benefits. Ohio State officials even bolstered Clarett's claims when they admitted he had been seen around campus driving a different car nearly every week. It didn't take a rocket scientist to conclude that bad things went down during Clarett's brief career as a Buckeye, and that they probably involved more players than just him. Yet in Columbus, OSU fans believe to this day that the program was "vindicated" by the NCAA and that their school was the innocent victim of a venomous media crusade.

USC, Miami, Tennessee, and Colorado, on the other hand—now *those* guys are dirty.

When it comes to stories about malfeasance in college football, it never ceases to amaze me how fans suddenly morph into full-fledged political operatives. Anyone not directly affiliated with their program, from reporters to NCAA officials, is considered an enemy with a potential agenda, while anyone within their gates can do no wrong. As soon as a negative rumor hits the message boards about one of their players, someone invariably posts the obligatory, "let's wait for the facts to come out" admonition. Such caution gets thrown to the wind, however, when a similar headline surfaces about a rival team or generally hated program. The fangs come out, and the natives become bloodthirsty. They want nothing more than to see the other team go down in a flame of rolling heads and NCAA sanctions. Of course, if the same exact headline were to be written about their own team, they'd likely accuse the author of initiating a witch-hunt.

Cheating in college football is a tradition nearly as old as tailgating and letter sweaters. Tales of hundred-dollar handshakes, duffle bags, and shiny new cars date back to at least the days of legendary coach Bear Bryant, whose Texas A&M teams were placed on NCAA probation in the 1950s as a result of the coach soliciting the help of a few deep-pocketed oil men in the Aggies' recruiting efforts. Though the sport is monitored much more closely today than it was in its Wild West days, new scandals emerge on a near-annual basis, causing no shortage of shock and outrage among pundits, observers, and academics. In turn, fans of the teams involved mostly get angry at the outraged pundits, observers, and academics. "Fans would rather win a championship and later get busted for cheating than finish 8–4 or 9–3 every year with an upright program of student-athletes," wrote Ted Miller, the *Seattle Post-Intelligencer's* college football columnist. "Media rants about the hypocrisy of college sports no longer raise hackles; they're just part of the background noise." Indeed, when allegations first come to light about a program, the most pressing concern among fans isn't the possibility of corruption at their revered institution but the potential impact the negative publicity might have on recruiting.

. . .

The NCAA's most severe football sanctions since SMU were dealt to Alabama in 2002, when the revered southern powerhouse was banned from participating in a bowl game for two seasons, stripped of twenty-one scholarships over three seasons, and placed on five years' probation for multiple recruiting violations involving payments by boosters. In one of the biggest bombshells ever to hit the sport, it was revealed that Logan Young, a wealthy Alabama booster in Memphis who for years had bragged to associates about his connections to Crimson Tide recruiting, paid $150,000 to Lynn Lang, a crooked Memphis high school coach, to assure the signature of the nation's top defensive line prospect in 2000, Albert Means. While the greasing of palms in the recruiting game occurs far more frequently than gets reported, $150,000 for one player is a downright staggering sum. Young's involvement was uncovered when Lang's bitter ex-assistant, Milton Kirk, blew the whistle on the scheme the two coaches had concocted to shop Means to the highest bidder, with Lang asking for as much as $200,000 and SUVs for both himself and Kirk. The plan hit a snag when Kirk never received his ride. Apparently, Lang must not have watched enough mafia movies to know what happens when you try to keep all the loot for yourself.

In all the annals of college football cheating, rarely has there been a case more cut-and-dried than this one. During the course of the NCAA's investigation, Kirk's version of events was corroborated by ten other individuals. Young (who died in April 2006 in what police described as an accident at his home) was eventually convicted of federal racketeering after both his and Lang's bank records confirmed many of the alleged transactions. Because Alabama was considered a "repeat violator," having been banned from the postseason in 1995 for another booster-related scandal, and because Means was not the only player involved in the latest go-round (another recruit, Kenny Smith, received $20,000 from Young and another booster, while linebacker Travis Carroll received a free SUV from a third booster), the Crimson Tide's sanctions could easily have been even worse.

. . .

In the fall of 1999, less than a year after the Vols won their first national championship in forty-seven years,[2] ESPN.com obtained an internal memo written by a Tennessee academic administrator alleging that five members of the title team had schoolwork completed for them by athletic tutors. Complicating matters, the allegations had never been properly reported to the appropriate people or sent through the proper channels. The report caused quite an uproar at the time, but the school launched an internal probe and, a month later, proudly declared itself devoid of any impropriety. "We have no evidence that the student athletes or tutors acted improperly. There's no pattern," university president J. Wade Gilley told the *New York Times*. "We are confident we have a very sound system with seasoned people of integrity in place." The NCAA concurred, even though it never launched a full-blown investigation of its own.

Frustrated by the lack of response and appalled by what she called "a system tantamount to institutionalized slavery," UT English professor Linda Bensel-Myers decided to conduct her own personal investigation of the athletic department's academic practices. In reviewing thirty-nine football players' transcripts, she found what she considered an unmistakable pattern of academic abuse, including questionable grade changes, phantom majors, and athlete-friendly teachers. Once again, the charges were largely brushed under the rug, subject only to a cursory internal probe. In fact, the only party to suffer from the mess was the whistleblower herself, Bensel-Myers, who became the subject of hate mail, death threats, and a divorce. "Give it a rest," wrote the author of one e-mail Bensel-Myers shared with the *Florida Times-Union*. "The taxpayers of Tennessee like winning teams. The players pay your salary. Go to Harvard, Yale, Stanford, or some private college and teach if you want a perfect institution." Wrote another: "'Do yourself a favor. Do the state of Tennessee a favor. Do the entire NCAA a favor and shut the hell up!!!!" You know the old cliché, "Don't shoot the messenger?" College football fans aren't big on the "don't" part.

Considering that college football players are, at least in theory, supposed to be students first and foremost, one could easily make the argument that manipulating a player's academic standing is no less a breach of ethics than handing him cash under the table. So why, then, did Alabama pay the price for its misdeeds while Tennessee skated? Because paying $150,000 for a recruit is a textbook violation of NCAA bylaws; steering players toward easy classes is not. Sure, NCAA president Myles Brand likes to talk tough when it comes to academic integrity, going so far as to adopt a new metric, the Academic Progress Rate (APR), in 2005, that takes away scholarships from schools that fail to graduate and retain their players at an acceptable standard. But the NCAA is still, at its core, a sports organization, one that lacks the authority to tell the University of Tennessee what its students should be majoring in or what criteria a teacher must follow before changing a student's grade. If Tennessee is willing to let half its football team major in urban studies, or if Ohio State, as was disclosed in the *ESPN The Magazine* articles, is willing to award credits for a course called "Officiating Tennis," well, that's up to the schools' own deans and provosts.

The reality is, these sorts of academic farces take place at nearly every school in the country with powerhouse football programs, and will continue to do so as long as the schools feel they're necessary to field winning teams. A 2006 *New York Times* exposé revealed that an Auburn sociology professor awarded high grades to eighteen members of Auburn's undefeated 2004 team (including star runningback Carnell

Williams) for directed-reading courses in which the players did not have to attend class and did little to no work. The professor wound up losing his title as department chair, but there were zero repercussions for the football program. There are in fact NCAA bylaws regarding academic fraud, under which the alleged writing of players' papers by tutors at Tennessee would certainly fall, but it's a tough charge to prove. In nearly all major cases where such violations have been found (Minnesota and Fresno State basketball come to mind), the people committing the fraud confessed to it; because no such volunteers were present at Tennessee or Auburn, it's not like the NCAA was going to send in homework experts to start examining the veracity of players' philosophy papers. Unfortunately, academic unseemliness will likely remain a largely overlooked staple of most major college football programs. But at least those Ohio State players who aced "Officiating Tennis" will be able to get a job one day as a line judge at the U.S. Open.

NOTES

1. The troubled Clarett, his football career ruined, eventually turned to crime and was incarcerated following an attempted armed robbery.
2. One of the amazing "coincidences" of college football is how these things always seem to come to light after a team wins the national championship. Such was the case for Miami, Florida State, and Tennessee in the 1990s and Ohio State and USC in the 2000s.

24

The Big-Time College Sports Plantation and the Slaves Who Drive It

D. Stanley Eitzen

The plantation owner of old couldn't stay in business were he to divest himself of slaves. Slaves were the production engines of production.
    —Walter Mosley in *Workin' on the Chain Gang*

Many youths dream of playing football or basketball for a university with a big-time sports program. They want to be part of the pageantry, glory, excitement of intense competition, shared sacrifice, commitment to excellence, bonding with teammates, and to be the object of adoring fans. Not incidentally, they would also receive an all-expenses-paid college education, which, if a professional sports career does not work out, would open other lucrative career opportunities. Many observers of big-time college sports accept this idealized version, but just how glamorous is participation in athletics at this level? Are the athletes as privileged as it appears?

There is a dark side to big-time college sports. To show this, let me use the metaphor of big-time college sports as a plantation system. I admit at the outset that this metaphor is overdrawn. Big-time college sports is not the same as the brutalizing, inhumane, degrading, and repressive institution of slavery found in the antebellum South. Nevertheless, there are significant parallels with slavery that highlight the seri-

Source: D. Stanley Eitzen, "Slaves of Big-Time College Sports" (revised and updated), *USA Today: The Magazine of the American Scene* 120 (September 2000): 26–30. Used with permission.

ous problems plaguing collegiate athletics. Thus, the plantation/slavery metaphor is useful for understanding the reality of the big-time college sports world.

There is the organization—the National Collegiate Athletic Association (NCAA)—that preserves the plantation system, making and enforcing the rules to protect the interest of the individual plantation owners. The plantations are the football and men's basketball factories within the universities with big-time programs. The overseers are the coaches who extract the labor from the workers. The workers are owned by the plantation and, much like the slaves of the antebellum South, produce riches for their masters while receiving a meager return on the plantation's profits.

Many observers of big-time college sports, most certainly the coaches and players, would argue vehemently with this assertion that big-time college athletes are slaves in a plantation environment. After all, the athletes not only choose to participate, they want desperately to be part of big-time sport. Moreover, they have special privileges that separate them from other students (much like what house slaves received, when compared to field slaves of the Old South), such as more and better food, special housing arrangements, favorable handling in registration for classes, and, sometimes, generous treatment when they cross the line. Also, the athletes, unlike slaves, can leave the program if they wish.

If participation is voluntary and the athletes want to be part of the system, what is the problem? My argument that these athletes are slaves in a plantation system, whether they realize it or not, involves several dimensions: The athletes (slaves) are exploited economically, making millions for their masters but provided only with a subsistence wage of room, board, tuition, and books; they are controlled with restricted freedoms; they are subject to physical and mental abuse by overseers; and the master-slave relationship is accepted by the athletes as legitimate. I begin my argument with demonstrating that big-time college football and men's basketball bring in large sums to the "plantations" while severely limiting the wages of the workers.

THE PLANTATION PROFITS FROM THE WORK OF SLAVES

The governing body of big-time college sports, the NCAA, is caught in a huge contradiction—trying to reconcile a multibillion-dollar industry while claiming that it is really an amateur activity. That it is a huge money-making industry is beyond dispute.

- The major conferences have an eight-year package (ending in 2006) worth $930 million with ABC to televise the Bowl Championship Series (BCS) at the conclusion of the football season. Each team playing in a BCS game now receives about $15 million and with this new contract, each team will receive about $17 million in the final years of the agreement. Since the teams share these monies with their conference members, the 62 schools involved will share approximately $116 million annually.

- The NCAA has signed a $6.2 billion, 11-year deal giving CBS the rights to televise its men's basketball championship (that's $545 million a year). The NCAA also, of course, makes money from advertising and gate receipts for this tournament. To enhance gate receipts the finals are always scheduled in huge arenas with seating capacities of at least 30,000, rather than normal basketball-sized venues.
- Universities sell sponsorships to various enterprises for advertising. The athletic department of the University of Colorado, for example, has 50 corporate sponsors. Its major sponsor is Coors Brewing Company, which has a $300,000 advertising package for scoreboard, radio and TV advertising, and a sign on the mascot's trailer. That university also named its basketball arena the Coors Events Center in return for a $5 million gift.
- Several football and basketball coaches are paid in excess of $2 million in overall compensation (base salary, television and radio, shoe company stipends).
- An estimated $2.5 billion a year in college merchandise is sold under license, generating about $100 million to the schools in royalties. The University of Michigan receives the most income from this source—about $6 million annually.
- The dominant schools have lucrative deals with shoe companies (Nike, Reebok, Adidas) worth millions to each school in shoes, apparel, and cash. For example, in 2001 the University of North Carolina at Chapel Hill signed an eight-year agreement with Nike worth about $3.2 million annually.
- The top programs have annual athletic budgets from $60 to $80 million. At Ohio State in 2002–03, the football team cleared a profit of $22 million and men's basketball made $9 million, and also made over $4 million from the sale of merchandise.
- In 2003 Ohio State played at the University of Michigan before more than 112,000 spectators. If those fans paid an average of $30 a ticket (doubtless a low estimate), that single game brought in $3.36 million not counting money from parking, concessions, and television rights.

Obviously, big-time athletic programs are commercial enterprises. The irony is that while the sports events generate millions for each school, the workers are not paid. Economist Andrew Zimbalist has written that: "Big-time intercollegiate athletics is a unique industry. No other industry in the United States manages not to pay its principal producers a wage or a salary." The universities and the NCAA claim that their athletes in big-time sports programs are amateurs and that, despite the money generated, the NCAA and its member schools are amateur organizations promoting an educational mission. This amateur status is vitally important to the plantation owners in two regards. First, by schools *not* paying the athletes what they are worth their expenses are minimized, thus making the enterprises more profitable. And, second, since athletic departments and the NCAA are considered part of the educational mission, they do not pay taxes on their millions from television, sponsorships, licensing, the sale of sky boxes and season tickets, and gate receipts. Moreover, contributions by individuals and corporations to athletic departments are tax deductible.

THE INJUSTICE OF AMATEURISM

To keep big-time college sports "amateur," the NCAA has devised a number of rules that eliminate all economic benefits to the athletes: They may receive only educational benefits (i.e., room, board, tuition, fees, and books); cannot sign with an agent and retain their eligibility; cannot do commercials; cannot receive meals, clothing, transportation, or other gifts from individuals other than family members; and their relatives cannot receive gifts of travel to attend games or other forms of remuneration.

These rules reek with injustice. Athletes can make money for others, but not for themselves. Their coaches have agents as may students engaged in other extracurricular activities but the athletes cannot. Athletes are forbidden to engage in advertising, but their coaches can readily endorse products for generous compensation. Corporate advertisements are displayed in the arenas where they play but with no payoff to the athletes. The shoes and equipment worn by the athletes bear very visible corporate logos, for which the schools are compensated handsomely. The athletes make public appearances for their schools and their photographs are used to publicize the athletic department and sell tickets, but they cannot benefit.

The schools sell memorabilia and paraphernalia that incorporate the athletes' likenesses, yet only the schools pocket the royalties. The athletes cannot receive gifts but coaches and other athletic department personnel receive the free use of automobiles, country club memberships, housing subsidies, etc.

Most significantly, coaches receive huge deals from shoe companies (e.g., Duke coach Mike Krzyzewski, has a fifteen-year shoe endorsement deal with Adidas, which includes a $1 million bonus plus $375,000 annually), while the players are limited to wearing that corporation's shoes and apparel. An open market operates when it comes to the pay for coaches resulting in huge pay packages for the "golden glamour coaches but not so for star players. When a coach is fired or resigns he often receives a parachute," which sometimes is in the multimillion dollar category, while players who leave a program early receive nothing but vilification for being disloyal. When a team is invited to a bowl game it means an extra month of practice for the athletes while head coaches, depending on the bowl venue, receive generous bonuses. A university entourage of administrators and their spouses accompany the team to the bowl game with all expenses paid while the parents and spouses of the athletes have to pay their own way.

As an extreme example of the discrepancy in pay for college athletes, an analysis of the economic impact of basketball star Patrick Ewing to Georgetown University during his four years there shows that he brought more than $12 million to the university (a tripling of attendance, increased television revenues, and qualifying for the NCAA tournament each year). Meanwhile the cost to Georgetown for Ewing's services totaled only $48,600—providing a tidy profit of $11,951,400 for the university. A study by an economist over a decade ago found that top-level college football players at that time generated a net gain (subtracting room, board, tuition, and books) of more than $2 million over a four-year period.

What exactly are the wages of average college athletes in the big-time sports? The answer is a bit complicated since athletes who do not graduate have not taken advantage of their tuition, so they have played only for their room and board. Also, there is a significant difference in tuition costs between state and private universities. Economist Richard G. Sheehan has calculated the hourly wage of big-time college players taking these considerations into account and assuming a workload of 1,000 hours per year. The best pay received, he found, occurred at private schools with high graduation rates for the athletes; the lowest pay at state schools with low graduation rates. Duke, for example paid an equivalent of $20.37 an hour for its football players, while Texas–El Paso paid $3.51. The median wage at all big-time schools for basketball players was $6.82 an hour and $7.69 an hour for football players. Now compare these wages with their coaches, assuming they also work 1,000 hours annually. A coach with a $1 million package makes $1,000 an hour; a coach with a $250,000 package only $250 an hour. Meanwhile, the workers—whose health is jeopardized by participation in hazardous sports—make a relative pittance and even then not in the form of money but in "free" room, board, and tuition. So it is, that the work of the big-time college athletes, just like the slaves on the antebellum plantations, allows the masters to accumulate wealth at their expense.

RESTRICTIONS ON THE RIGHTS AND FREEDOMS OF THE SLAVES

Slaves, by definition, are not free. The slaves of the antebellum era did not have the right to assemble or to petition. They did not have the right to speak out or freedom of movement. Those conditions characterize today's college athletes as well. The NCAA, the schools, and the coaches restrict the freedom of the athletes in many ways. By NCAA fiat, once athletes sign a contract to play for a school, they are bound to that school. They make a four-year commitment to that college, yet the school makes only a one-year commitment to them. If an athlete wishes to play for another big-time school, he is ineligible for one year (two years if their former coach refuses to release the athlete from his contract). Yet if a coach wants to get rid of an athlete, the school is only bound to provide the scholarship for the remainder of that academic year. Coaches, on the other hand, can break their contracts, and immediately coach another school. Richard Sheehan illustrates how unfair this rule is for athletes, when they are compared with nonathlete students: "Suppose you accept a scholarship from Harvard to study under a Nobel laureate who then takes a position at Yale. Are you under any obligation to attend Harvard and not attempt to matriculate at Yale? This NCAA regulation, like many others, gives schools options and gives athletes nothing."

The right to privacy is invaded routinely when it comes to athletes. College athletes—but not their coaches, teachers, administrators, or other students—are subject to mandatory drug testing. Personnel from the athletic department watch athletes in their dorms and locker rooms, either in person or on closed-circuit television, for "deviant behaviors." Bed checks are not uncommon. Sometimes there are "spies" who watch and report on the behaviors of athletes in local bars and other places of amusement.

Freedom of choice is violated when athletes are red-shirted (i.e., held from play for a year) without their consent. Athletes may have little or no choice in what position they play. They may be told to gain or lose weight, with penalties for noncompliance. Coaches may demand mandatory study halls. They may determine what courses the athletes will take and their majors. Robert Smith, formerly a running back for the Minnesota Vikings, was a pre-med student and star athlete at Ohio State University. To meet his pre-med requirements Smith needed a laboratory course that conflicted with football practices twice a week. The coaches insisted that football take precedence and that he must drop the course. To Smith's credit, he took the course and did not play football that year.

A number of coaches insist that their athletes avoid political protest. Some paternalistic coaches prohibit their athletes from associating with individuals or groups that they feel will have a negative influence on their players. Certain coaches demand dress codes and may even organize leisure-time activities that everyone must attend. University of Colorado basketball coach Ricardo Patton, for example, has included among his mandatory team activities: touring a prison, attending church services, sleeping together on cots in the gym for a week, and practicing at six in the morning. During slavery, the masters imposed their religious beliefs on to their slaves. In today's sports world, team chaplains, chapel services, Bible study, and team prayers are commonplace. Ricardo Patton, coach at a public university, for example, concludes each practice with the players holding hands in a circle while Patton or a player he calls upon leads the team in prayer. He claims that participation is voluntary. Sportswriter Mike Littwin of the *Denver Rocky Mountain News* argues that the practice is anything but voluntary: "According to the argument, players, whose playing time and scholarship are dependent upon the coach's whim, are free to pray or not to pray with him. Here's what I believe: Anyone who thinks that when the coach says it's time to pray that it's somehow voluntary ought to pray for more wisdom. It is inherently coercive. It's about as voluntary as when the coach tells you to run laps. You're not the coach for 60 minutes of practice and then not the coach once you kneel on the floor."

OPPRESSION, BRUTALITY, AND TERROR: KEEPING SLAVES IN THEIR PLACE

Although not a universal trait of coaches, instances of physical and mental cruelty toward players occur all too frequently. Bob Knight, the highly successful basketball coach at Indiana University and now Texas Tech once stopped the videotape of a game to say to one of his players: "Daryl, look at that. You don't even run back down the floor hard. That's all I need to know about you, Daryl. All you want to be out there is comfortable. You don't work, you don't sprint back. Look at that! You never push yourself. You know what you are Daryl? You are the worst f____ pussy I've ever seen play basketball at this school. The absolute worst pussy ever. You have more goddamn ability than 95 percent of the players we've had here but you are pussy from the top of your head to the bottom of your feet. An absolute f____ pussy."

When University of South Carolina football coach Lou Holtz was at Notre Dame University, one of his players, Chet Lacheta, made several mistakes in practice. In Lacheta's words: "[Holtz] started yelling at me. He said that I was a coward. He said that I should find a different sport to play and that I shouldn't come back in the fall. He was pretty rough.... First he grabbed me by my face mask and shook it. Then he spit on me."

On the return trip from a road game coaches may punish their players by having the bus driver let them off several miles from the school. Another tactic is to schedule practices at inconvenient times such as 2 a.m. or on holidays. Coach Bob Knight schedules some holiday practices, without telling the players when to report for the next practice. Consequently, they must wait by their phones to hear from the manager about the practice schedule. If not, they will incur the wrath of their autocratic boss. These acts of control are similar to those used by the military to train recruits. As sociologist Philip Slater has observed: "Exposure to random punishment, stress, fatigue, personal degradation and abuse, irrational authority, and constant assertions of one's worthlessness as a human being [are] all tried-and-true techniques of 'reeducation' used by totalitarian regimes." In effect, these are powerful means to create and maintain obedient slaves.

THE SLAVE MENTALITY

Historians George Fredrickson and Christopher Lasch have stated that the real horror of slavery was that many of the slaves "mentally identified with the system that bound and confined them." This is an especially troubling aspect of the plantation system that is big-time college sport. Jerry Farber's description of students in his classic 1960s critique of higher education, "The Student as Nigger," aptly describes athletes as well: "They're pathetically eager to be pushed around. They're like those old grey-headed house niggers you can still find in the South who don't see what all the fuss is about because Mr. Charlie 'treats us real good.'"

Sport sociologist George H. Sage provides some of the reasons why athletes rarely resist the authoritarian and unjust regime under which they labor:

> A question may be raised about the lack of protest from intercollegiate athletes about the prevailing conditions under which they labor. In one way it can be expected that the athletes would not find anything to question: they have been thoroughly conditioned by many years of organized sport involvement to obey athletic authorities. Indeed, most college athletes are faithful servants and spokespersons for the system

of college sport. They tend to take the existing order for granted, not questioning the status quo because they are preoccupied with their own jobs or making the team and perhaps gaining national recognition. As a group, athletes tend to be politically passive and apathetic, resigned to domination from above because, at least partly, the institutional structure of athletics is essentially hostile to independence of mind. Hence, athletes are willing victims whose self-worth and self-esteem have largely become synonymous with their athletic prowess. Their main impulse is to mind their own business while striving to be successful as athletes.

Another reason for the docility and submissiveness of athletes is that they are politically disenfranchised. Athletes who challenge the athletic power structure risk losing their scholarships and eligibility. Athletes who have a grievance are on their own. They have no union and no arbitration board. The coaches, athletic directors, and ultimately the NCAA have power over them as long as they are scholarship athletes. Their only option is to leave the plantation. If they do quit, they are often viewed by others as the problem. After all, most accept the system. Those who quit are not seen as victims but as losers. So powerful is the socialization of athletes, even those who quit are likely to turn their anger inward, regarding themselves as the problem.

Others may tolerate the oppressive system because they see it as the only vehicle for becoming a professional athlete. If they were to become professional athletes, the rewards are substantial. However, making it to the pros is just a dream except for the most-talented few. Of the thousands of players eligible for the National Football League draft each year, only 336 are drafted and about 160 actually make a final roster. Fewer than one-half of 1 percent of all Division I male basketball players make it to the National Basketball Association.

DISMAL GRADUATION RATES

Since most college athletes never play at the professional level, the attainment of a college degree is a crucial determinant for their upward mobility, and thus a rationale for tolerating the unjust plantation system. But graduation from college, while not the long shot of becoming a professional athlete, is also a bad bet.

The 1999 report on graduation rates compiled by the National Collegiate Athletic Association (NCAA), examined Division I athletes who enrolled as freshmen in 1996 to determine how many had graduated after six years (athletes who left school in good academic standing were not counted in the results). The data show that while the overall graduation rate for all male students at Division I schools was 56 percent, the rate for football players was 54 percent and 44 percent for male basketball players. While some programs are exemplary (Notre Dame graduated 81 percent of its football players, and Stanford graduated 100 percent of its men's basketball players over the six-year period); others are not. Among top-rated basketball programs, Arizona graduated only 23 percent, while Connecticut and Maryland graduated 27 percent.

There are several reasons for the relatively low graduation rates for big-time college athletes. Compared to nonathletes they are less prepared for college. On average, they enter college in the bottom quarter of the freshman class (based on SAT scores). Football and men's basketball players in big-time sports programs are more than six times as likely as other students to receive special treatment in the admissions process, that is, they are admitted *below* the standard requirements for their universities. Second, athletes spend 30 to 40 hours a week on their sport, which is demanding, as well as physically and mentally fatiguing. Third, an anti-intellectual atmosphere is common within the jock subculture. Finally, some athletes attend college, not for the education, but because they believe it will lead to a professional career. In this regard, Iowa State football coach Jim Walden has said: "Not more than 20 percent of the football players go to college for an education."

Not only do typical athletes in big-time sports enter at an educational disadvantage, they often encounter a diluted educational experience while attending their schools. Coaches, under the intense pressure to win, tend to diminish the student side of their athletes by counseling them to take easy courses, to choose easy majors, and to enroll in easy courses from professors friendly to the athletic department. Some of the more unscrupulous have altered transcripts, given athletes answers to tests, staged phantom courses, and hired surrogate test takers. In one infamous case of academic fraud, a tutor for the University of Minnesota athletic department wrote more than 400 papers for basketball players over five years. Even with that help only 23 percent of the players recruited since 1986 to play basketball at that university have graduated, the worst rate of any Big Ten basketball team during that period.

Some ill-prepared and/or unmotivated athletes manage to stay eligible without being educated. Dexter Manley, for example, testified before a Senate committee that he had played football four years at Oklahoma State University only to leave illiterate. As Cynthia Tucker, editor of the *Atlanta Constitution* editorial page, writing about exploited basketball players but applicable to football players as well, said: "So those college basketball players you're watching on the court desperately need to earn degrees. If they don't, they'll be left with little more than shattered 'hoop dreams.'" When less than 40 percent of the black basketball players do not leave college with a degree something is drastically amiss. The uneducated have been exploited by their schools and when used up, the schools turn to another crop to exploit. As columnist George Will has argued: "College football and basketball are, for many players, vocations, not avocations, and academics are unsubstantiated rumors."

Reexamining the plantation/slave metaphor, athletes voluntarily enter into an unjust arrangement. Nevertheless, there are important similarities that college sport shares with slavery. The plantation system as represented by the NCAA and the individual (school) plantations benefit handsomely from the work of the athletes. The athletes, meanwhile, like slaves, are bound to the plantation by the plantation's rules. They are dominated, managed, and controlled. They take orders. They do not receive a wage commensurate with their contribution to the economic return. They are sometimes mistreated physically and mentally by their overseers. They are denied the rights and freedoms of other citizens and they have no real democratic recourse to right an unjust system.

CHANGING THE PLANTATION SYSTEM

The obvious starting point for changing the "plantation" system is to pay athletes in the revenue-producing sports fair compensation for the revenues they generate. Athletes should receive a monthly stipend for living expenses, insurance coverage, and paid trips home during holidays and for family emergencies. Media basketball commentator Dick Vitale suggests a modest plan to make the system somewhat fairer. He says that the NCAA should invest a billion of its $6.2 billion deal to broadcast the NCAA men's basketball tournament and pay the athletes $250 a month. *Sports Illustrated* writer E. M. Swift responded: "Is Vitale right on the money? You make the call. For now, as the NCAA continues to treat its athletes with supercilious contempt while reaping GNP-sized windfalls from their labor, you can at least say this for scholarship athletes: They're getting a free education in no-holds-barred capitalism."

The time has come to end the pretense that players in big-time college sports are amateurs. They are paid through a scholarship but far from a just or living wage in this world of big-time sports megabucks.

Second, maximize the probability that athletes receive a legitimate education and graduate. The late Ernest L. Boyer, former president of the Carnegie Foundation for the Advancement of Teaching, said: "I believe that the college sports system is one of the most corrupting and destructive influences on higher education. It is obscene, and there is no way to put an educational gloss on this enterprise." In short, as currently structured, big-time sports are not compatible with education.

To emphasize education and replace athlete-student with student-athlete, I suggest the following: Do not admit athletes who do not meet the minimum entrance requirements for admission and retention. Eliminate freshman eligibility so that incoming students have time to adjust to the demanding and competitive academic environment. Provide remedial classes and tutoring as needed. Reduce the time demands on athletes by eliminating spring football practice, starting the basketball season at the beginning of second semester, and holding the weekly time devoted to sport at 20 hours. Include among the criteria for evaluating coaches, the humane treatment of players, and, most critically, the proportion of their athletes who graduate in six years.

Third, establish a comprehensive athletes' Bill of Rights to ensure a nonexploitive context. At a minimum these "Rights" should include:

- The right to transfer schools. Athletes who transfer should be eligible to play the next school year, not the current stipulation that they must wait a year with no athletic scholarship aid.
- The right to a four-year scholarship, not the one-year renewable at the option of the coach as is the current NCAA policy. Those athletes who compete for three years should be given an open-ended scholarship guaranteeing that they will receive aid as long as it takes to graduate.
- The rights that other college students have (freedom of speech, privacy rights, protections from the physical and mental abuse of authorities, and

the fair redress of grievances). There should be an impartial committee on each college campus, separate from the athletic department, that monitors the behavior of coaches and the rules imposed by them on athletes to ensure that individual rights are guaranteed.

- The right of athletes to consult with agents concerning sports career choices.
- The right of athletes to make money from endorsements, speeches, and the like. Walter Byers, former executive director of the NCAA, has stated that athletes should have the same financial opportunities as other students, arguing that "The athlete may access the marketplace just as other students exploit their own special talents, whether they are musicians playing on weekends, journalism students working piecemeal for newspapers, or announcers for the college radio station filing reports for CNN radio."

Big-time college sport presents us with a fundamental dilemma. We like the festival, pageantry, exuberance, excitement, and the excellence, but are we then willing to accept the hypocrisy, scandal, and exploitation that go with them? To date, the plantation system is not challenged as the college presidents and various NCAA committees make timid and tepid cosmetic changes. As a beginning to the real reform of the oppressive system, we need to understand who benefits and who is exploited. The plantation/slave metaphor illuminates the injustices of the system in stark reality. Seeing it this way should create an urgency among educators to make real changes. The time is ripe for bold action to transform big-time college athletics so that it can be part of the educational vision of the university *without* the shame and the sham that characterize it now.

* FOR FURTHER STUDY *

Bower, William G., and Sarah A. Levin. 2003. *Reclaiming the Game: College Sports and Educational Values.* Princeton, NJ: Princeton University Press.

Burke, Monte. 2008. "The Most Powerful Coach in Sports." *Forbes* (September 1): 92–96.

Coakley, Jay. 2007. *Sports in Society: Issues and Controversies.* 9th ed. New York: McGraw-Hill.

Eitzen, D. Stanley. 2007. "Sport, College." Pp. 4665–4668 in *Blackwell Encyclopedia of Sport.* Vol. 9.

Eitzen, D. Stanley. 2009. *Fair and Foul: Beyond the Myths and Paradoxes of Sport.* 4th ed. Lanham, MD: Rowman and Littlefield.

Eitzen, D. Stanley, and George H. Sage. 2009. *Sociology of North American Sport.* 8th ed. Boulder, CO: Paradigm.

Feldman, Bruce. 2007. *Meat Market: Inside the Smash-Mouth World of College Football Recruiting.* New York: ESPN Books.

Gerdy, John R. 2006. *Air Ball: American Education's Failed Experiment with Elite Athletics.* Jackson: University Press of Mississippi.

Lewis, Michael. 2007. *The Blind Side.* New York: W. W. Norton.

Meggyesy, David. 2000. "Athletes in Big-Time College Sports." *Society* 37 (March–April): 24–28.

Shulman, James L., and William G. Bowen. 2001. *The Game of Life: College Sports and Educational Values.* Princeton, NJ: Princeton University Press.

Sokolove, Michael. 2002. "Football Is a Sucker's Game." *New York Times Magazine* (December 22): 36–41, 64, 68–71.

Solomon, Alisa. 2002. "Guys and Dollars: Women Still Trail the Greed Game of College Sports." *Village Voice* (April 11). Available at http://villagevoice.com/issues/0215/solomon.php.

Walton, Teresa. 2001. "The Sprewell/Carlesimo Episode: Unacceptable Violence or Unacceptable Victim?" *Sociology of Sport Journal* 18 (3): 345–357.

Young, Kevin. 2002. "Standard Deviations: An Update on North American Sports Crowd Disorder." *Sociology of Sport Journal* 19 (3): 237–275.

Zimbalist, Andrew. 1999. *Unpaid Professionals: Commercialism and Big-Time College Sports.* Princeton, NJ: Princeton University Press.

PART NINE

Problems of Excess: Sport and Money

A dilemma that characterizes professional sport and much of what is called amateur sport in the United States has been described by journalist Roger Kahn: "Sport is too much a game to be a business and too much a business to be a game."[1] The evidence indicating a strong relationship between sport and money is overwhelming.

Some recent facts demonstrate this relationship.

- The estimated size of the entire sports industry in 2006 in the United States was $390 billion.[2]
- In the 1960s, the prize money for the entire Professional Golf Association (PGA) tour was about $7 million. In 2007 it was $266 million, with the winner of the FedEx Cup earning an additional $10 million.
- The National Football League (NFL) has total revenues of $6 billion a year.
- The Osca de la Hoya/Floyd Mayweather Jr. boxing match in 2007 generated $120 million in pay-per-view revenue.
- Tiger Woods is the first $100 million-a-year athlete, making $111,941,827 in 2007 (about $100 million is from endorsements).
- More than $8 billion is bet illegally on the annual Super Bowl. Another $100 million is bet legally in Nevada on this game.
- Sports video games represent a $1 billion industry, accounting for more than 30 percent of all video game sales.

There is no longer any question that corporate sport is a business, although the owners and certainly big-time sport universities would like to perpetuate the myth that it is not. In this part of the book we will examine the intimate interrelationship between money and sport and the consequences of this trend.

Money is often the key motivator of athletes. Players and owners give their primary allegiance to money rather than to the sport or to the fans. Modern sport, whether professional, big-time college, or Olympic, is "corporate sport." The original purpose of sport—pleasure in the activity—has been lost in the process. Sport has become work. Sport has become the product of publicity agents using superhype methods. Money has superseded the content as the ultimate goal. Illicit tactics are commonplace, because winning translates into more revenues. In short, U.S. sport is a microcosm of the values of U.S. society. Journalist Roger Angell has said of baseball what is applicable to all forms of corporate sport. "Professional sports now form a noisy and substantial, if irrelevant and distracting, part of the world, and it seems as if baseball games taken entirely—off the field as well as on it, in the courts and in the front offices as well as down on the diamonds—may now tell us more about ourselves than they ever did before."[3]

The chapters in part 9 illustrate the problems and issues involving the impact of money on sports. The first, by D. Stanley Eitzen, examines the role of money in the 2008 Beijing Olympic Games. Journalist Ted Evanoff demonstrates how professional teams make huge profits in the public financing of stadiums. Although he focuses on the Indianapolis Colts, he also lists the lucrative arrangements for each of the NFL franchises. The next chapter is by investigative journalist Tom Farry. He looks at the cost of youth sports to parents of potential elite athletes. Included is a list of the odds by sport of playing at the collegiate level. The final chapter, by journalist Pablo S. Torre, looks at the consequences of the expensive stadiums—how the increasing cost of sports is changing the face of the sports fan.[4]

NOTES

1. Roger Kahn, quoted in CBS Reports, "The Baseball Business," television documentary narrated by Bill Moyers (1977).

2. D. Stanley Eitzen and George H. Sage, Sociology of North American Sport, 8th ed. (Boulder, CO: Paradigm Publishers, 2008), p. 314.

3. Roger Angell, "The Sporting Scene: In the Counting House," *New Yorker* (May 10, 1976): 107.

4. See David Epstein, "Money Changes Everything," *Sports Illustrated* (October 13, 2008): 18–19, for examples of how an economic crisis affects sports negatively.

25

The Commercial Beijing Olympic Games

D. Stanley Eitzen

The Olympic movement has two overt objectives. The first is found in the motto of the Olympics: "Citius, Altius, Fortius" ("Faster, Higher, Stronger"). The emphasis, obviously, is on exceptional performance by athletes. The second objective of the Olympic movement is to foster international communication and peace. The Olympics, however, involve much more than these efforts, much of it economic and self-serving. The focus of this essay is on the economics of the Olympics[1] limiting the discussion to the costs and benefits to the International Olympic Committee, the host nation, corporations, and athletes.

THE INTERNATIONAL OLYMPIC COMMITTEE AND OTHER ORGANIZATIONAL TIERS

The International Olympic Committee (IOC) owns the Olympic logos, the design of the Olympic flag, the motto, creed, and anthem. The rights to these intangible properties are sold to corporations for their use in advertising, generating almost $1 billion in revenue. Control of Olympic symbols and the granting of official status to corporations requires that the IOC conduct sweeps to determine if there are violations. When nonsanctioned corporate logos are found within the Olympic venues, the IOC's enforcement team literally covers them with duct tape.[2] Also, the police arrest vendors selling items with "bogus" Olympic logos.

Source: This essay was written expressly for the eighth edition of *Sport in Contemporary Society.*

According to economist Robert Weissman, the IOC and the various tiers of Olympic organizational committees "have auctioned off virtually every aspect of the Games to the highest bidder.... A record 63 companies have become sponsors or partners of the Beijing Olympics and Olympics-related advertising in China alone could reach $4 billion to $6 billion [in 2008].... Well over 100 corporations are sponsoring the U.S. Olympic Committee or U.S. national teams."[3]

The IOC also sells the broadcast rights to the Olympic events. Some 220 countries and territories aired the Games in 2008, generating revenue amounting to $1.74 billion to the IOC. The U.S. rights, purchased by NBC, cost $894 million.

The IOC generated revenue of over $3 billion for the Beijing Olympics. Some 92 percent of this is distributed to the host nation, National Olympic Committees, and to house and feed the Olympic athletes and their administrators.[4]

THE HOST NATION: CHINA

China was overjoyed to be selected by the IOC in 2001 to host the 2008 Games. This was an opportunity to showcase China worldwide to billions in this 17-day festival. The intended message was to be that China had re-emerged as a global economic force and that it was a country that the rest of the world should treat with admiration and respect.[5] As *USA Today* editorialized: "These Games are a perfect metaphor for China's emerging competitiveness in areas beyond athletics. For centuries, it was focused on keeping the world out. Not anymore. Beijing is aggressively engaged in the world."[6]

The economic cost to produce the Games, however, was high. There were a total of 10,500 athletes from 204 nations competing in 302 events in 28 sports, and another 4,000 athletes with disabilities competed in the Paralympics the next month. New venues had to be constructed, most notably the Beijing National Stadium (the "Bird's Nest") with a seating capacity of 90,000. To prepare for all of the visitors, Beijing's transportation infrastructure was expanded (highways, subways, railways, and an expansion of the airport). The overall cost of the Beijing Olympics project was $43 billion.

This is a huge expenditure that likely will haunt China for a long time. In 1988 Canada's hosting of the Games resulted in a thirty-year debt. In 2004 Athens spent $15 billion, a debt that will not be repaid until 2014. The Chinese economy did benefit from the money spent for the Beijing Games adding an estimated 0.8 percent to annual Gross Domestic Product. There was considerable job creation in the four years prior to the Games. Tourism during and after the Olympics increased. The sports venues constructed for the Games were converted into places to be used by locals and tourists. For example, the Bird's Nest will hold up to 60 soccer matches and concerts a year to cover its annual maintenance cost of $7 million to $10 million.[7] And, much of the $43 billion would have been necessary anyway, since Beijing needed improved transportation and infrastructure with or without the Olympics.[8]

The $43 billion does not include the cost of running the 3,000 state-run athletics academies that train nearly 400,000 youngsters, some as young as three (the annual budget exceeds $700 million). The most talented of these youngsters are funneled to the National Training Center. The goal is to use the sports prowess of their athletics to win gold medals at the Olympics and international respect in the process. The program is working. In 1988 China won five golds at the Seoul Olympics. In Athens (2004) China won 32 gold medals and in Beijing it won 51 golds (the United States, by the way, won 36).[9] While successful at one level, there is a human cost resulting from this policy. "After all, for every Olympic champion the sports academies produce, hundreds of thousands of other children fail. Most of these kids miss out on the education provided in regular schools. The *China Sports Daily* estimates that about 80 percent of the country's retired athletes are plagued by unemployment, poverty or chronic health problems resulting from overtraining."[10]

Another downside of the Beijing Olympics was the displacement of people to make room for Olympic venues and city beautification schemes. The Center on Housing Rights and Evictions estimated that while eviction is increasingly a normal practice by countries hosting the Olympics, the scale of displacement in China was unprecedented—the uprooting of 1.5 million (the 1988 Games in Seoul, Korea held the previous record of 720,000 evictions).[11]

CORPORATIONS

The Beijing Olympics were a special attraction to transnational corporations, because of the "opportunity to appeal to the roughly 300 million middle-class Chinese consumers with significant disposable income."[12] The *Economist* argued that the Olympics is a festival of global business. "For companies, the games are a golden marketing opportunity. Sportswear manufacturers have no better showcase. For almost anyone selling anything, the Beijing Olympics are a chance to reach 1.3 billion people in an economy with double-digit growth, not to mention billions more watching around the world."[13]

Global companies such as Nike, Visa, Coca-Cola, Johnson & Johnson, Kodak, and Panasonic clearly are eager to tap the Chinese market, with its growing middle class and expanded consumer spending. The global corporations, noted above, are among the twelve granted rights by the IOC for a combined cost of $866 million, to be the exclusive suppliers and the official Olympic sponsors for four years, ending with the 2008 Games.

Of special interest is General Electric, which supplied many of the Beijing venues with electronic surveillance equipment, including 300,000 closed circuit cameras. Not only was General Electric one of the official Olympic sponsors and crucial suppliers of goods and services to the Games, it is also the parent company of NBC, which paid $894 million for the exclusive rights to telecast the Beijing Olympics in the United States. NBC advertising sales for the Olympic telecasts exceeded $1 billion. GE claims that its official Beijing Olympic sponsorship created $700 million in China revenue. General Electric's projected 2010 revenue from China is $10 billion, up from $4.4 billion in 2007.[14]

ATHLETES

The IOC does not award prize money but it does not prohibit members from paying incentives to the athletes. Some examples from the Beijing Olympics: Singapore offered $708,381 (U.S. dollars) for a gold medal; the Chinese winner of a gold received $150,000; Russian gold medalists received $25,000 from the government and an unspecified amount from a $12 million fund created by ten of the wealthiest tycoons in Russia; and Canadians achieving a gold received $20,000. The U.S. Olympic Committee awarded U.S. gold medal winners $25,000, $15,000 for a silver, and $10,000 for a bronze medal. The first Afghan to ever win an Olympic medal (bronze) was given a new house by the President of Afghanistan, and a new Toyota sedan and $20,000 from the owner of the country's main cell phone network.

If Michael Phelps, winner of eight gold medals, had been swimming for Singapore he would have received $5.6 million from the government. As is, he collected $200,000 from the U.S. Olympic Committee and another $480,000 from USA Swimming. In addition, Phelps makes millions from endorsements. Before Beijing, Phelps was making between $3 million and $5 million in endorsements (Visa, Speedo, Omega, Hilton, and AT&T). For winning the eight gold medals Speedo (suppliers of his swimsuit) gave him a bonus of $1 million. Companies are lined up to secure future endorsements and his agent estimates that he will make as much as $50 million in the year following the Olympics. In addition, there is a book deal worth a $1.6 million advance. Even Phelps's mother, Deborah Phelps, who was the darling of the media in Beijing, signed endorsement contracts with Johnson & Johnson and Chicos.

Other American Olympic champions who captured the imagination of the public such as Nastia Liukin, winner of the gold for all-around gymnastics, Shawn Johnson, second in the all-around and first on the beam, and Dara Torres, who at age 41 won a gold and three silvers in swimming, were able to capitalize on their Olympic achievements. Torres, for example, signed a $3 million contract to write two books, one a memoir, the other a health and fitness guide. Similarly, a few stars from other countries also benefitted economically from their Olympic achievements.

In short, for a few celebrated Olympic athletes the Olympic motto of "Faster, Higher, Stronger" also includes "Richer." For most participants, however, economic gains are missing. Only 9 percent of the participants (958 out of 10,500) won a gold, silver, or bronze medal and will not benefit much economically from their Olympic participation. Their reward was intrinsic, in participation rather than economic gain. For them, the reward was in the journey not the destination.

In sum, while the Olympic Games, in the words of Beijing organizing committee head Liu Qi, were "a grand celebration of sport, of peace and friendship."[15] The Olympics were also a huge commercial marketplace, which undermines the professed ideals of the Olympic Movement.

NOTES

1. For a discussion of the political side of the Olympics, see D. Stanley Eitzen and George H. Sage, *Sociology of North American Sport,* 8th ed. (Boulder, CO: Paradigm, 2009). For specific discussions of the politics of the Beijing Games, see for example, Dave Zirin, "China's Olympic Trials," *Nation* (August 18, 2008); and Naomi Klein, "The Olympics: Unveiling Police State 2.0," *Huffington Post* (August 7, 2008), available at http://www.commondreams.org/archive/2008/08/07/10862;print.

2. Rod Mickleburgh, "Sticking to Official Olympic Brands—with Duct Tape," *Toronto Globe and Mail* (August 15, 2008), available at http://www.theglobeandmail.com/servlet/story/RTGAM.20080815. wolymduct15/BNStory/beijing 2008/home.

3. Robert Weissman, "Commercial Games," *Progressive Populist* (September 15, 2008), 19; see also Jennifer Wedekind, "The Commercial Games: Selling Off the Olympic Ideals," *Multinational Monitor* 29 (September–October 2008), 47–53.

4. Tara Kalwarski, "The Beijing Olympics: Follow the Gold," *Business Week* (August 11, 2008), 15.

5. *Economist,* "Fun, Games, and Money" (August 2, 2008): 3–4.

6. *USA Today,* "Olympic Games Display Lessons in Competition," August 8, 2008, 8A.

7. Calum MacLeod, "Olympic Venues Will Have Afterlife," *USA Today,* August 22, 2008, 6A.

8. *Economy Watch,* "Sports Industry: The Economics of the Olympics" (August 8, 2008), available at http://www.economywatch.com/economy-business-and-finance-news.

9. Calculated a different way, the number of gold medals by the population of the country, Jamaica ranked first in Beijing (one gold per 452,333 people), the United States ranked 32nd (one gold per 13,790,000), and China ranked 47th (one gold per 25,991,431 people). See *Symworld,* "Beijing 2008 Olympic Medal Tally" (August 25, 2008), available at http://www.symworld.com/medals/index.php.

10. Hanna Beech, "Crazy for Gold," *Time* (June 23, 2008), 50.

11. Erica Bulman, "Rights Group: 1.5 Million People Displaced by Preparations for 2008 Beijing Olympics," *USA Today,* June 5, 2007, available at http://www.usatoday.com/sports/olympics/2007–06–05–343105549_x.htm.

12. Wedekind, p. 49.

13. *Economist,* "Fun, Games, and Money," 3.

14. Michael Hiestand, "Beijing is Rich Feather for NBC Peacock," *USA Today,* August 7, 2008, 3C.

15. Quoted in Dave Zirin, "The 2008 Olympics: Subterranean Rot," *Nation* (August 24, 2008), available at http://www.thenation.com/blogs/notion/348214.

26

New Deal Lets Colts Rake in Cash

Financial Terms of Team's Pact with Indy Are among the Most Lucrative in NFL

Ted Evanoff

Show up on game day, grab a hot dog and a beer, and the club takes a cut. Tickets, hats, jerseys, food, stadium parking, even the advertising on the wall—if its sold in the stadium, the Colts make money.

Sales of suites and club seats to corporations and the well-heeled will mean more dollars rolling in—and the club keeps every dime.

Altogether, the Colts could pocket at least $41 million in new annual revenue above and beyond the $150 million or more a year the club has made in recent years at the RCA Dome, according to an Indianapolis Star estimate.

The bottom line? The Colts could reap $1.4 billion over the next three decades in one of the sweeter stadium deals in the National Football League.

Professional sports teams long have raked in money from sales of tickets, food, drinks and apparel. The Indiana Pacers do it at Conseco Fieldhouse. And the Colts did it in the RCA Dome. But the Colts' deal at Lucas Oil Stadium is much richer.

"The Colts have gotten a really good deal, but then they would have to," said University of Indianapolis sports marketing expert Laurence DeGaris. "They're playing in one of the smaller cities in the league."

Source: Ted Evanoff, "New Deal Lets Colts Rake in Cash," *Indianapolis Star,* August 24, 2008.

Smaller cities such as Indianapolis tend to shell out more for new stadiums because they fear the team will move away—something club owners often threaten to do. To make sure the team stayed put, the city's negotiators agreed that taxpayers would cover 87 percent of the cost of building the $720 million stadium. That's a much larger burden on taxpayers here than in all but a handful of other NFL cities.

Colts owner Jim Irsay and city officials who hammered out the deal say the new stadium will deliver big dividends to the public as well as the team.

Above all, the new stadium means area football fans can root for their Colts for at least the next 30 years.

WHERE THE MONEY'S COMING FROM

Of the $41 million a year, drinks and meals will bring the Colts at least $6.3 million—a figure based on the assumption that 63,000 fans each spend $25 per game at this year's 10 regular-season and preseason home games. That adds up to $15.7 million, and the Colts get to keep 40 percent of the total.

But where Lucas Oil Stadium offers the Colts real entree to the NFL big leagues falls outside the typical fan's pocketbook. According to the deal:

- About $6 million a year for 20 years will come from California-based Lucas Oil for the stadium naming rights.
- Other companies will pay the Colts a total of $14 million a year for the right to put up ads inside the stadium and in some cases name entire interior sections, such as the Bud Light Blue Zone, a bar.
- And then there's the special seating. Luxury suites and club seats will fetch at least $25 million a year for the club—almost as much cash as 60,000 ordinary seats produce in ticket sales to 10 NFL games.

The Colts benefit in other ways:

- The team will get to keep all stadium revenue on game days.
- Playing in the stadium will be free for the Colts—there's no rent to pay. And the team won't have to employ ticket takers, ushers, security guards or janitors. Those chores and their expenses will be left to the city taxpayer-supported Capital Improvement Board.
- The team won't need to set aside money for potential repairs to the retractable roof or any part of the stadium. Fixing and keeping the stadium in good condition are the CIB's jobs.
- When rodeos or rock concerts or other non-NFL events are held at the stadium, the Colts get half the ticket and concession revenue—up to $3.5 million a year.

AND WHERE MUCH OF IT WILL GO

Indianapolis benefits from the deal, too.

Keeping the team in Indianapolis lends the city a certain prestige bestowed on few American cities.

The new stadium also made it possible for the city to win the bidding competition for the 2012 Super Bowl, which is expected to bring millions of dollars to the city.

Razing the dome made way for expansion of the Indiana Convention Center, now under way. Once complete, it promises to draw more and bigger conventions.

A new stadium also wiped away the potential of up to $160 million in subsidies that the city would have had to pay the team if ticket sales to games at the dome dropped below a certain point.

"My goal was to take the risk off the city. I thought, 'You (the Colts) can have the revenue'" from game days in the new stadium, said Fred Glass, the former CIB president who helped negotiate the deal. "'If you do, I hope you do well. If you don't, then it's your problem.'"

Irsay hopes people don't get the wrong idea about where all of that money ends up.

The team owner, a Carmel resident who inherited the club in 1998, said he built the Colts into a respected contender, but that doing so cost more than $100 million borrowed from lenders and family funds.

Thanks to luxury suites and other amenities, Irsay said, clubs in modern stadiums out-earned the Colts in their dome years.

The league's $4.2 billion in TV revenues helps keep owners in the black. The Colts' share of those revenues came to $109 million last year, better than ever. But expenses have been rising, too.

Since he took over, Irsay said, Colts coaching salaries have risen 400 percent. The club also employs 130 people who are not players, more than any other NFL club.

"I said: 'I'm going to spend money. I'm going to lose money,'" Irsay said of the years when he took over the club. "But I'm going to invest in the brand and hope a new day comes.'"

That day arrived when the Colts won their first Super Bowl in decades in 2007.

In the same year, the Colts ran an operating loss of $17.4 million on $184 million in revenue, according to an estimate by Forbes magazine.

Now, with at least $41 million more a year flowing in from its operations at Lucas Oil Stadium, the Colts should be able to easily reverse those losses.

"What's going to bail out the Colts is the new stadium," said Kurt Badenhausen, an NFL finance expert for Forbes. "They're probably going to move into the top half of revenue producers in the NFL."

Better yet, according to Irsay, the extra cash will help pay off debts incurred to build the club into a contender.

"Where most of the money is going to go is to pay off debts and pay off the ... family accounts we shifted money out of" to get the stadium built, he said.

After that, whatever is left is Irsay's.

STADIUM DEALS

How the Colts' deal compares to others around the NFL

Arizona Cardinals

Name: University of Phoenix Stadium
Built: 2006
Cost: $455 million
Public portion: 76 percent
Terms: Team contributes $109 million
plus land.

Baltimore Ravens

Name: M&T Stadium at Camden
Yards
Built: 1998
Cost: $229 million
Public portion: 87 percent
Terms: M&T pays club $75 million for
naming rights.

Carolina Panthers

Name: Bank of America Stadium
Built: 1996
Cost: $248 million
Public portion: None
Terms: City donated land for stadium.
Investors sold seat licenses to finance
construction. Bank of America paid
$140 million for naming rights.

Chicago Bears

Name: Soldier Field II
Renovated: 2003
Cost: $660 million
Public portion: 62 percent
Terms: Bank One pays club $48
million as sponsor.

Cincinnati Bengals

Name: Paul Brown Stadium
Built: 2000
Cost: $453 million
Public portion: 89 percent
Terms: Team pays rent to defray
building cost.

Cleveland Browns

Name: Cleveland Browns Stadium
Built: 1999
Cost: $315 million
Public portion: 77 percent
Terms: Club borrowed $50 million
from NFL for construction.

Dallas Cowboys

Name: Cowboys Stadium
Built: Under construction
Cost: $1.1 billion
Public portion: 30 percent
Terms: Club sells ad rights to four
sections of stadium, gets cash from
billboards, concourse and portal signs,
gates, tickets, parking passes.

Denver Broncos

Name: INVESCO Field at Mile High
Built: 2001
Cost: $364 million
Public portion: 73 percent
Terms: Club split the $120 million in
name rights paid by INVESCO with
the city.

Detroit Lions

Name: Ford Field
Built: 2002
Cost: $430 million
Public portion: 36 percent
Terms: Ford Motor paid $20 million
for name rights.

Green Bay Packers

Name: Lambeau Field
Renovated: 2003
Cost: $295 million
Public portion: 100 percent
Terms: Sale of seat licenses ($92.5
million), public stock ($20.5 million)
and NFL loan ($13 million) went to
construction.

Houston Texans

Name: Reliant Stadium
Built: 2002
Cost: $352 million
Public portion: 73 percent
Terms: Club sold Reliant naming rights
for $300 million.

Indianapolis Colts

Name: Lucas Oil Stadium
Built: 2008
Cost: $760 million
Public portion: 87 percent
Terms: Club sold naming rights for
$121.5 million. NFL loaned club $50
million for building; city kicked in $48
million to break RCA Dome lease.

Jacksonville Jaguars

Name: Alltel Stadium
Renovated: 1995
Cost: $130 million
Public portion: 100 percent
Terms: Club split $62 million naming
rights payment with city.

Kansas City Chiefs

Name: Arrowhead Stadium
Renovated: Under way.
Cost: $575 million includes Kauffman
Stadium renovation
Public portion: less than 50 percent
Terms: State OK'd $50 million in tax
credits.

New England Patriots

Name: Gillette Stadium
Built: 2002
Cost: $325 million
Public portion: None
Terms: Club sold stadium name rights
for reported $114 million.

Philadelphia Eagles

Name: Lincoln Financial Field
Built: 2003
Cost: $512 million
Public portion: 39 percent
Terms: Club sold name rights for $140
million.

Pittsburgh Steelers

Name: Heinz Field
Built: 2001
Cost: $281 million
Public portion: 69 percent
Terms: Club sold stadium name rights
for $57 million.

Seattle Seahawks

Name: Qwest Field
Built: 2003
Cost: $360 million
Public portion: 83 percent
Terms: Sports lottery raised $127
million for building.

St. Louis Rams

Name: Edward Jones Dome
Built: 1995
Cost: $280 million
Public portion:100 percent
Terms: Club sold stadium name rights
for $74 million.

Tampa Bay Buccaneers

Name: Raymond James Stadium
Built: 1998
Cost: $169 million
Public portion: 100 percent
Terms: Club sold stadium name rights
for $32.5 million.

Tennessee Titans

Name: LP Field
Built: 1999
Cost: $292 million
Public portion: 100 percent
Terms: Louisiana-Pacific paid club $30
million for stadium name rights.

Washington Redskins

Name: FedEx Field
Built: 1997
Cost: $250 million
Public portion: 28 percent
Terms: Club sold stadium name rights
for $205 million.

Source: Marquette University Law School; National Sports Law Institute; Sports Economics LLC, *Fort Worth Star-Telegram.*

27

Follow the Money

The Cost of Youth Sports

Tom Farrey

When Karly gets a couple of years older, she'll get to take the Carl Gray Aggression Test. It's his personal tool for figuring out who has what it takes to excel at the next level. He'll hold two quarters in one of his steely fists and tell the girl she can do whatever she wants to try and pry it loose—scratch, punch, spit, bite, kick him in the groin—no act is too uncivil so long as she does not break eye contact. If the girl doesn't retrieve the coins, she gets a rating on a scale of 1 to 10. "I want to find out how they are going to be in a competitive situation," he says. "A few of them have taken a piece of meat out." None have gotten the quarters, though. Or a score higher than an 8.

Karly is Gray's kind of prospect. She's a sweetheart at elementary school, everyone's playmate because she's so inclusive. Her teacher can't believe this little girl who stuffs Rico the Penguin into her backpack every day plays the sport associated with missing teeth. But get Karly on the ice, and those soft, brown eyes harden, especially when the disc is anywhere near the end of her stick. Gray swears she skates faster with the puck than without it. In a one-on-one practice drill near the front of the net, her shot gets trapped in the crease by the square-faced girl tending the net today, Amanda Reilly. Karly whacks away at her teammate's oversize glove anyway, determined to pry the black pearl loose from its closed-up oyster shell.

Source: From *Game On: The All-American Race to Make Champions of Our Children* by Tom Farrey, copyright © 2008 by Tom Farrey. Used by permission of Ballantine Books, a division of Random House, Inc.

"Okay, enough Karly," an assistant coach says. He shakes his head, looks at me, and chuckles. "Karly's a madwoman," he says.

An athlete gets nowhere without a passion for the game. It's an asset of Karly's. But she's handicapped, too. At bedtime, she and her three preteen siblings lay their heads down in the happy, modest home of her grandmother, a Salvadoran immigrant who helps 33-year-old Karla make ends meet. An office assistant in the financial aid division of nearby Bentley College, Karla is the only single mother among the Assabet Valley team parents—Karly has no contact with her father—and meeting commitments is a stretch, both financially and logistically. Just with transportation, Karla needs ample help from her mother, who often makes the 30-minute drive to Valley Arena two or three days a week, as well as to the games 50 minutes away at a different arena.

Youth hockey has become an expensive sport. Gray's registration fee of $1,000 a season is less than that of comparable clubs. But there's the expense of gas, tolls, and hotel rooms for the occasional out-of-state tournament. This year, the team is signed up for one weekend event in Vermont, which the Aguirres plan to make their big vacation for the year, "since we don't go to Disney" and other faraway theme parks, Karla says. To avoid breaking the family budget, she starts saving for Karly's hockey six months before the start of the next season. New blades make old skates last longer, and as Karly gets older, she'll wear hand-me-down boots from siblings. Still, the cost of select-level hockey will grow measurably in the coming years. Some parents on the 12 Reds will easily drop $10,000 on one child's hockey involvement during the year, between nationals in California, their town team, and other commitments.

These costs won't be an issue for Amanda Reilly, the girl in goal, and her fraternal twin, Shannon, who also plays on the Assabet Valley team. They live in an exclusive neighborhood of million-dollar homes several suburban towns over from Karly's working-class enclave. Dad's a Harvard-educated chemical engineer who's taking time off to "play the market" with his investments, and mom is a whip-smart civil prosecutor in the state attorney general's office. The Tudor home in which they will lay their heads down tonight doesn't qualify as a mansion, but it's large enough to comfortably accommodate five children, one sheep dog, and a backyard ice rink (which, in the present clement weather, is just a large puddle).

In short, it's a home with everything except a maid.

"This is our locker room," Kristen, the mother, jokes, nodding at a family room that is more stylistically frat house than Martha Stewart. Scattered everywhere are socks, jerseys, helmets, sticks, pads, bags, and skates—she says the family has 58 pairs. A tennis-racket-stringing machine sits in the corner. In an adjacent room (ostensibly the library), a pyramid of children's books rises from the carpet in the shape of a campus bonfire. Academics are important in this home, but so too are sports, and with all the kids' scheduled activities, something's got to give. It's tidiness.

Kristen's organizational efforts go into the making of the daily youth sports schedule, printed out from a Microsoft Word document and distributed the night before. She hands me a copy of today's grid, which, she insists, is relatively light for a Saturday:

5:55 a.m.	Leave for twins' Mite A 6:50 a.m. game at Hockeytown.
6:40	Leave to get Karen to her 7:40 a.m. Squirt game at Fessenden.
7:30	Leave for Barry (8 to 10).
10:00	Leave to get twins to their 11:00 a.m. Mite A game at Wilmington rink.
10:15	Leave with Karen for her 11 to 1 Igor skate.
1:35 p.m.	Karen has U10 White game at Northboro (miss).
1:45	Leave with Jimmy for his singles match at home at Win. Bld. No. 1 ag. Woburn Red.
2:30	Leave with twins for their 3:00 Assabet dryland and 4:00 Assabet practice. Leave there by 4:45 at the latest due to 5:40 Top Gun game.
3:15	Leave with Josh for his doubles match at home at Win. Bld No. 2 ag. Woburn Red w/Ross.
5:40	Twins have Top Gun game at New England Sports Center ag. Eagles (big game!).

So, to translate and recap: The 7-year-old twins played two games today with their town team and one more with their (otherwise) all-boys select team based in New Hampshire, in between two hours of practice with Assabet Valley, at four separate rinks. Eldest daughter Karen, 9, played one game with her town team and also got two hours of group instruction with Igor, the $4,000-a-season former Soviet Red Army skater whom the twins also see on Saturdays when not booked solid with commitments to their three teams. The eldest boy, 13-year-old Josh, a nationally ranked tennis player, and little brother, Jimmy, 11, whose main sports are hockey and football, got a lesson and played some club tennis, but that's all—they were done in time to go see the new Bond movie, *Casino Royale,* with their dad/chauffeur, Mark. "I was home for two hours today," Mark says with a wry smile, scarfing down a Whopper he picked up on the way home from the Cineplex. (The family usually eats its fast food in transit.) "It was great."

The Reillys already spend more than $10,000 a year per twin on hockey, if you include the $2,500 in figure skating lessons they use to sharpen their edges. Amanda and Shannon also have twice-weekly lessons at the Harvard courts in tennis, a sport in which both are ranked in the New England region. But Josh's private tennis instruction, for eight hours with a couple of different pros, is the big ticket there. He and Joey also see a $60-an-hour personal trainer, who works with them on speed, strength, and balance. ("The best investment, because it's injury prevention," Kristen says.) Kasey, who has yet to specialize in a sport, takes private lessons in tennis and figure skating in between games for her two soccer and two hockey teams. Throw in fees and miscellaneous costs for gymnastics, golf, baseball, lacrosse, skiing, cross country, and Pop Warner football, and it wouldn't surprise me if the Reillys are dropping a hundred grand a year on their five kids' athletic endeavors.

And none of them are even in high school.

So over the 10 years leading to college, that's conceivably a bill of ... $1 million on youth sports? "Hey," Mark says, "it's not like we go out to a lot of fancy dinners."

He and Kristen are coy with the actual figures. They understand how ridiculous this all sounds. But they also understand that they are in an arms race of sorts. They hear the stories: Of the girl who gets $900 in tennis lessons *a day;* of the fifth grader whose father moved into a rented trailer in Florida with her so that she could train at a top sports academy; of the parents of a New York club hockey team who reward its blue-chip coach with a $2,000 gift each Christmas. (This isn't out of line with other people's efforts in other parts of the country: Some families drop $70,000 a year, soup to nuts, to get *one* kid professionally groomed in golf or tennis at the famed IMG Academies in Bradenton, Fla.) In the land of plenty, it's pay or perish in some sports.

Since she has the resources, Kristen sees it as her duty to seek out the best sport training for her children. "Parents believe they're supporting their kids by showing up for games," she says, "but I think it's cruel to ask a kid to entertain you and not prepare him or her to do well. It's like you're going to the game to *watch* them? When you've done little to support them? And they might not be on team next year because they're no longer good enough? I don't know. I guess they're showing emotional support."

Sometimes the prosecutor gets put on the defense for this stance. A few years ago one of her boys had a hockey game that made them late to a friend's birthday party. When they arrived, she apologized and explained the circumstances. It was like walking into a bear trap. One of the parents in attendance happened to be Bob Bigelow, a former NBA player who co-wrote the 2001 book, *Just Let the Kids Play: How to Stop Other Adults From Ruining Your Child's Fun and Success in Youth Sports,* which argues for, among other things, the elimination of travel teams before grade seven. Bigelow, who happens to live across town from the Reillys, has railed for a decade about the intensification of kids' games, firing away from lecterns and television talk shows. And now the 6-foot-7 hometown hero was about to breathe fire on the red-haired, red-faced Kristen, 16 inches shorter and surrounded by kids.

"You're apologizing for being late because you missed half of this party for a hockey game? In September?"

He asked for the team schedule. She handed it to him.

"Why are you playing a team 30 miles away from here?"

"It's the schedule I got," she responded meekly, not wanting to create a scene.

The counselor has done a lot of thinking about Bigelow and his sermon since that night. And here's what she's decided: Nice guy, good intentions, outdated message. Like Bigelow, she enjoyed the more casual youth sports environment of the 1960s and '70s. She won two Virginia state championships playing high school soccer, a sport she didn't even pick up until sixth grade. She went on to participate as a gymnast on the club team at the University of Virginia. But she believes modern reality is that without focused training when her children are young, they might not have the chance to play even high school sports. "Let kids be kids? Is that possible anymore?" she says. "Can you develop an athlete that way these days? I don't care about winning. It's just the price of being on a team.

"I'm way past Bob Bigelow."

When I call Bigelow later and remind him of the party and relay Kristen's thoughts, he at first remains on the offensive. "What does she know about child development?" he says. "She only knows more, more, more—the code of the West. She's swallowed the Kool-Aid and swallowed it early." He grudgingly concedes, though, that she's "probably right" in surmising that a kid can no longer wait until his teenage years to take up hockey and hope to play in high school. "But that's only because of the clueless idiots who are ruining the system by insisting on getting their kids on the right team early," he adds.

Bigelow or no Bigelow, hockey season keeps the Reilly family from getting to Mass as much as they would like—not that the twins complain about that. More hockey + less church = win/win. They *do* miss the play dates that are sacrificed. We're sitting at the kitchen table now, and Amanda smiles shyly when her mother, who is stroking her shoulder-length brown locks, mentions the absence of down time with town friends.

"Yeah, that's all we think about," Amanda says, glass half empty.

"Sometimes they come to our house," Shannon says, glass half full.

"They know so many kids from New Hampshire, from their Top Gun team," Kristen says, reconciling. "Those are their play dates."

Kristen says their goal in hockey is ambitious: To make the Assabet Valley U12 Reds. Once that happens, everything else falls in place.

I ask the twins what their goal is, just 'cause I want to hear it from them. There's silence for a moment. Amanda fiddles with a painted toy soldier among the Christmas decorations on the table. Shannon looks at her mom for guidance. "I know what *her* goal is," Kristen says, filling in the blank. "It's to take the puck. And the harder you work in practice"—she's now talking directly to Shannon—"the easier it is to take the puck. So if you don't have it, you go get it. You steal it. Even if someone is taller than you." The twins listen intently.

The truth, of course, is that most 7-year-olds don't have long-term goals. They're still in the moment. Kristen, in no small measure, is inserting her ambition for theirs. But again, you could call it an act of love, as every kid wants to be good at what she or he does, and no 7-year-old could find the pathway to the U12 Reds without ample amounts of planning, sacrifice, and financial investment by parents such as Mark and Kristen. At practice, I had asked the U12 Reds as a group when each of them first played hockey. Six of the girls were on skates at age 2. All but two were on teams by age 5. The player who started at the latest age, 7, raised her hand meekly, in embarrassment. They are Massachusetts girls. In most states where hockey is popular, girls usually join teams somewhere between the ages of 9 and 14. On a chart, youth-participation levels through high school are shaped like the classic bell curve, with a bulge in the middle school middle. But in Massachusetts, home to some of America's leading prep schools and universities, where the scent of educational advantage is omnipresent, the largest chunk of girls registered with USA Hockey is in the youngest category—6 and under. The participation rate tapers off gradually from there, as girls quit their town teams. "The stakes are higher, sooner here in Massachusetts," says Ben Smith, who coached the 1998 U.S. women's team to the Olympic gold medal.

Hockey is a game that could take the twins far—if they make the commitment. The greatest barrier to entry is ice time, which is scarce and thus expensive. Pond hockey, the pick-up form of the game that launched the career of many NHL old-timers, is all but dead, the casualty of residential development, global warming, and jittery parents. Opportunity now runs almost exclusively through rinks like Valley Arena, which opens at 4:30 a.m. and keeps the lights on through midnight to accommodate demand. Inevitably, it's a not a game accessible to much of society. Only one percent of Americans pick up a stick even once a year, and among females, just one percent of those come from a household with less than $25,000 in annual income. Fully 85 percent come from families that take in more than $50,000. The demographics are more blue collar on the boys' side, but not by much. Nearly a quarter of all frequent players, of both genders, are drawn from households with incomes of at least $100,000.

These are the kids who will have first dibs on college hockey. Up-by-the-bootstrap success stories like those of Jack Welch, who started with no family wealth and went on to play for the University of Massachusetts, are now rare. In fact, college athletics in general are more the province of the privileged than the poor.

The images that dominate media coverage of college sports are of basketball and football, with more than a few of the players coming from distressed families. In his 2006 letter to Congress justifying the NCAA's tax-exempt status, Myles Brand went out of his way to mention that the $1.5 billion in athletic scholarships that gets doled out annually helps "many low-income students who would otherwise have to forgo the college experience." But a decade earlier, a survey by the U.S. Department of Education debunked the notion of college sports as a tool of broad social uplift. Tracking students from eighth grade through college, it found that children with a high socioeconomic status (those in the top 25 percent on a measure that considers their parents' occupations, education, and income) were 10 times as likely to play Division I sports as those with low socioeconomic status (those in the bottom 25 percent). Even among elite high school athletes—defined as those who were MVPs or captains on their team—only four percent of kids from disadvantaged backgrounds went on to play at the D1 level.

Look at the list of sports that offer the best odds of playing on the collegiate level (see Table 27-1). Most of those at the top—rowing, equestrian events, fencing, gymnastics, lacrosse, swimming, water polo, golf—draw athletes from or are popular in suburbs that are wealthy or at least middle class. Not surprisingly, two-thirds of all D1 athletes are Caucasian.

Down the Norman Rockwell zone of Division III, by far the largest NCAA grouping, with 443 schools, there are no athletic scholarships. Of course, the affluent have less need for athletic scholarships. Admission to a small, prestigious college such as Amherst or Williams can be a bigger prize, and a coach's nod may be reward enough for a sizable investment in youth sports. (Schools in the New England Small College Athletic Conference accepted just under two-thirds of the athletes they recruited as compared with only 31 percent of other applicants.) All told Division III appears to pull from poor or minority homes even less frequently than D1. "We certainly don't

Table 27-1 The Odds of Playing College Sports
The probability of a high school athlete going on to play in college, both in Division I and all levels, broken down by sport and sex.

Sport	D1 Teams	Odds of Making D1	All Teams	Odds of Making Any
Men				
Rowing	24	1 in 2	59	1 in 1
Fencing	21	1 in 5	36	1 in 3
Gymnastics	17	1 in 8	19	1 in 7
Rifle	22	1 in 15	35	1 in 9
Ice hockey	58	1 in 22	133	1 in 9
Lacrosse	56	1 in 28	214	1 in 9
Swimming	141	1 in 30	381	1 in 14
Water polo	21	1 in 33	46	1 in 18
Football	234	1 in 42	614	1 in 18
Div. 1-A football	117	1 in 77		
Skiing	14	1 in 47	35	1 in 21
Baseball	286	1 in 48	873	1 in 17
X-Country	299	1 in 48	865	1 in 18
Golf	289	1 in 53	762	1 in 20
Track	261	1 in 56	656	1 in 24
Tennis	265	1 in 59	742	1 in 21
Soccer	197	1 in 67	737	1 in 19
Wrestling	86	1 in 100	224	1 in 42
Basketball	326	1 in 111	1,000	1 in 35
Volleyball	22	1 in 111	79	1 in 37
Women				
Rowing	85	2 in 1	141	3 in 1
Equestrian	13	1 in 2	39	1 in 1
Fencing	27	1 in 4	45	1 in 2
Rifle	27	1 in 4	36	1 in 4
Ice hockey	29	1 in 11	74	1 in 4
Gymnastics	63	1 in 16	85	1 in 12
Lacrosse	80	1 in 26	264	1 in 9
Water polo	31	1 in 26	61	1 in 15
Swimming/diving	188	1 in 30	489	1 in 14
Golf	228	1 in 31	483	1 in 16
X-Country	321	1 in 33	940	1 in 14
Field hockey	77	1 in 37	257	1 in 11
Skiing	16	1 in 39	39	1 in 19
Soccer	301	1 in 42	913	1 in 15
Track	295	1 in 42	704	1 in 22
Tennis	309	1 in 62	876	1 in 20
Softball	264	1 in 72	911	1 in 23
Bowling	28	1 in 83	45	1 in 50
Volleyball	311	1 in 91	982	1 in 29
Basketball	323	1 in 100	1,025	1 in 31

have those stories here at Ithaca, and really at many of the private schools," says Ellen Staurowsky, a sports management professor and the former director of athletics at Division III Ithaca College (N.Y.). "College athletics caters to the upper economic strata. There's a big mythology out there that these opportunities are going to inner-city kids. But that's not our clientele." Even in men's hoops, only one in five D3 players is black, some of whom of course are from middle-class, suburban areas.

So, beneath the thin layer of sports entertainment that makes its way onto television are the bulk of college athletes: Well off and white. That's not to say these athletes and their families don't have their own struggles; but they are, frankly, more Shannon and Amanda Reilly than Karly Aguirre.

28

The Changing Face of the Sports Fan

Pablo S. Torre

If you're a typical sports fan—you know, the kind who worries about gas prices, tuition and the trade deadline—New York's new stadiums might look as if they belong behind a boutique window.

In the Bronx looms the skeleton of Yankee Stadium 2.0, a coliseum with half as many bleacher seats as its predecessor but more than three times the luxury boxes. In Queens, the Mets traded Shea's 20,420-seat hull of an upper deck for Citi Field and its 54 suites, burnished by leases priced firmly in the six figures. Even the Barclays Center in Brooklyn, future home of the Nets, will have 118 luxury suites in a venue designed by the Pritzker Prizewinning architect Frank Gehry. And across the Hudson River? The Jets' and Giants' new Meadowlands Stadium, opening in 2010, has incorporated personal seat licensing—the process by which fans pay somewhere between $1,000 and $25,000 for the sheer right to buy season tickets. (It's an investment opportunity!)

So what about this economic downturn, you ask? How can these teams upgrade their arenas so strikingly amid government bailouts and a subprime mortgage crisis and the declining dollar?

The tough economic times are affecting the different leagues in different ways. The NBA and NHL have been proactive in trying to keep ticket prices affordable. College football fans have remained fiercely loyal to their teams, but schools are taking a hit with higher travel costs. Meanwhile, NASCAR and high school sports have

Source: Pablo S. Torre, "The Changing Face of the Sports Fan," SportsIllustrated.com, October 8, 2008.

felt the economic downturn the most. (How will the economy affect your sports experience? Weigh in with your thoughts here.)

Sports aren't recession-proof anymore, but all in all, the major pro sports have flourished while other sectors have atrophied. Last season, the multibillion-dollar NFL set an all-time attendance record for the sixth-consecutive year, while baseball also enjoyed its highest spring training numbers in '08. Impressively, MLB and the NBA then followed up their '07 figures—the leagues' third- and fourth-consecutive attendance records, respectively—by effectively holding constant, dipping this past year by statistically insignificant marks of between one and two percent.

"If we look throughout history," Clemson economist Raymond Sauer said, "the relationship between attendance and the economy does not appear to be cyclical."

What makes these milestones even more historic is tickets cost more than ever. Team Marketing Report calculates that it now takes $396.36 for a typical family of four to attend an NFL game, $281.90 for the NBA and $191.92 for MLB—each mark an all-time high. (Gas not included, naturally.) And economists tell SI.com that the gate will continue to boom.

Why? A rise in popularity is only one reason. Despite today's wilting economy, the reality is that our most popular sports are also climbing the social ladder. Higher-end customers are gladly paying more and more to take middle class consumers' old seats at the game—and for the time being, at least, they have the disposable income to keep the turnstiles spinning. Said Temple economist Mike Leeds, "Joe Sixpack is becoming a thing of the past."

A LOOK IN THE STANDS

If you've recently heard a native Bostonian lament "Fenway isn't Fenway anymore," you're not alone. Though the charming 96-year-old edifice has survived amid rumors of a Yankee Stadium–type reconstruction (and yes, the prospective blueprint, abandoned in 2005, included twice as many luxury boxes), the atmosphere nowadays still seems palpably different from a decade ago. Less authentic, even.

At Fenway—as elsewhere around the country—surging ticket prices and the team's success have seemingly drained institutional memory, bringing in wealthier fair-weather fans and ushering out the diehards. The addition of Green Monster seats in 2005 was an endearing gesture, to be sure, but it also created some of the priciest tickets in the house. That's no accident: Ever since Baltimore's Camden Yards ignited the stadium-building revolution in 1992, the architectural designs of arenas have precisely targeted a demographic that wears pinstripes—and not the ones on a replica jersey.

"If this downturn continues to have less of an impact on sports than previous periods," Leeds said, "its in part because in terms of gate attendance, the business has hitched its wagon to the higher-end customer."

All of it adds up to a skewing of fans we might have expected to see at games. At law firms and banks, the pro sporting event has become a full-on social and networking experience that signals class and cultural currency. No franchise would eliminate the bleachers altogether, of course; that would be a public relations nightmare. But in replacing the multi-purpose, municipal ballpark with a breed of compact, single-use arenas, teams can raise prices and make cheap seats less plentiful all at once.

Consider the NFL season-ticket holder. For many teams, waiting lists for season tickets stretch for miles, ready to be bequeathed from generation to generation. But thanks to the one-two-three punch of tighter incomes, surging ticket prices and personal seat licenses, lifers like Jim Merritt, 45, now have a decision to make. The 23-year Jets season-ticket holder has been tailgating for decades, but now he wonders if he should buy the one-time PSLs (in his case, a projected $5,000 for each of his three seats) just so he can buy his tickets (for a projected increase to $120 per seat, per game, up from $80 this year) and required parking pass (another $20 per game).

"I'm not affluent—I mean, I do fine—but at what cost do I want to see these games?" Merritt said. "At some point, do I want to put that money toward something else? Should my family go to Europe on vacation for a month instead? My conscience may not let me buy these things. And what they're doing is pricing out the people who really care if the team wins or loses."

Merritt has yet to make his decision, which speaks, at the very least, to the singular love of sports that still drives this country. But for the middle class, the strategy behind season tickets has permanently evolved. If you keep them, you're being handicapped more than ever before; and with the institution of PSLs, which can also be sold off at their owner's whim, the net effect is to raise prices for everyone else in the primary and secondary markets.

"At first, I used to go to as many games as possible and take my friends for pure enjoyment, and I never looked to sell tickets or make a profit," Merritt said. "Now the Jets are essentially telling me that a PSL is an 'investment opportunity for the future.'" Do I even want to worry about making money like that? Do I want to worry about needing to sell off certain tickets and boosting them to a certain price?"

WHAT IT TAKES TO GET THERE

Adding further to the pressure on fans is another cost on the rise: transportation. The peripherals surrounding sports, particularly in non-metropolitan areas, are becoming more and more expensive, from the climbing cost of gasoline to the price of food.

It's no coincidence that a number of baseball teams like the Texas Rangers responded to this reality in 2008, offering promotions such as $5 gas cards with the purchase of a ticket, all-you-can-eat seats and two-for-one specials. "It's a recognition by owners and league heads that sports for certain people is not really recession-proof—even though it may be recession-resistant," said Leo Kahane, editor of the *Journal of Sports Economics.*

Economists say you should thus expect to see fewer families of four at the stadium. More people who are single and more fans who will go out with a group of eight-to-ten friends, spending more than $100 each and treating the game as a one-off experience.

"Already, if you turn on the television today, I don't think you're seeing the same families from 10 or 15 years ago," Colorado College economist Aju Fenn said. "With all the costs involved, they just may not go to as many games as before."

And if you can't afford to go? Good news. Luckily for the health of the teeming sports-industrial complex, fans priced out of the stadium might still spend to follow the action, whether it's on HD television, through a special cable package, on satellite radio, via cell phone or online. From the hot-stove to the preseason, corporations presently have more opportunities than ever to deploy tentacles that draw fans into the game and generate revenue, without ever giving them a seat. MLB's Advanced Media subsidiary, which runs its online and digital operations, is reportedly worth $450 million alone.

"People across the country are seeing their disposable income being whittled away," said UNC Charlotte economist Craig Depken. "So they're beginning to ask themselves: Do I really need to go? My guess is that if you stand out on some street corner and asked average people how many games they physically traveled to last year versus this year, you'd see a real difference."

PREMIER ENTERTAINMENT

We are far removed from the $6 tickets of Super Bowl I in 1967, a game played in front of 31,054 empty seats at the L.A. Coliseum and from the Yankees playing the Red Sox at Fenway in front of 11,000 people, as happened more than once in 1960. Nowadays, such scenes are unimaginable.

Last NFL season, for instance, advertisers competed to fork over $2.7 million for 30 seconds of Super Bowl commercial airtime. This year, with five months remaining until Super Bowl XLIII, NBC has already one-upped itself, selling 85 percent of its advertising inventory at a record-high $3 million per 30-second slot. Said NBC's head of ad sports sales, Seth Winter: "We see the end zone right now."

Regrettably, most fans can't say the same. The price for a seat at Super Bowl XLII was $700. On the online reseller StubHub.com, one customer actually traded $90,000 in February for 14 seats to watch the Patriots and Giants in Glendale, a markup of 918 percent per ticket. As Michael Hershfield, founder of the competing site LiveStub.com, once quipped, "You gotta mortgage your home to get into the game."

In that spirit, eBay bought StubHub for $310 million in early 2007 ($74 million more than J.P. Morgan paid for Bear Stearns in March and $60 million more than Barclays paid for Lehman Brothers' North American investment banking and trading unit in September). On StubHub's Web site, the World Series (average secondary ticket price: $1,036), BCS Championship ($1,362) and Super Bowl ($3,540) each sparked traffic in excess of 1,000 seats sold, with the latter two events setting all-time company records for sheer dollar volume moved. This July, StubHub moved its 15 millionth ticket (a Red Sox–Yankees ticket for July 4, if you were wondering).

But there's more. In perfect synergy, the Jets announced an unprecedented partnership with StubHub last month, wherein the best seats at the new stadium—

dubbed the "Coaches Club," complete with "private 20,000 square foot bar and lounge designed by Nobu architect David Rockwell"—will be awarded via auction. It takes $5,000 per PSL to have the chance to bid.

THE BOTTOM LINE

The harsh truth is that only when those precious luxury suites start to go unclaimed—thus portending a loss of corporate windfall—will leagues truly begin to worry. For the time being, they have the audience, the revenue and an ever-visible, ever-popular product.

"A lot of us behave like we're addicted to sports. We live our lives through it," Southern Utah economist Dave Berri said. "Just think about the things we support with bumper stickers. No one has a car that declares that they're a fan of Starbucks or Tom Cruise."

Recently, NFL commissioner Roger Goodell warned of a potential slowdown in an internal memo. While he stressed that individual teams' bottom-line budget projections will be secure for the coming fiscal year, he conspicuously observed a simple detail that has long been true for other American businesses: "Costs are rising and ... revenues are under pressure."

If the economy doesn't recover soon, sports executives fear corporations will ultimately scrutinize shrinking margins and decide how important it is to have a physical presence at games, whether it be through advertising, naming rights, luxury boxes or corporate season tickets.

"While we have seen dramatic growth in recent years for things like corporate hospitality and sponsorships, we are worried about that continuing," Red Sox executive vice president Sam Kennedy told the *Sports Business Journal.* "We haven't seen any dramatic cut, although we have had some 2009 planning with sponsors who have told us stories about their business that aren't pretty."

For the time being, the turnstiles will continue to spin—even if it's no longer the average fan who's coming through the gate.

✳ FOR FURTHER STUDY ✳

Armstrong, Jim. 1999. "Money Makes the Sports Go 'Round,'" *Denver Post,* July 25, 1C, 12C.

Atkinson, Michael. 2002. "Fifty Million Viewers Can't Be Wrong: Professional Wrestling, Sports-Entertainment, and Mimesis." *Sociology of Sport Journal* 19 (1): 1–24.

Badenhausen, Kurt. 2008. "Where the Money Is." *Forbes* (June 30): 114.

Barney, Robert K., Stephen R. Wenn, and Scott G. Martyn. 2002. *Selling the Five Rings: The International Olympic Committee and the Rise of Olympic Commercialism.* Salt Lake City: University of Utah Press.

Beamish, Rob. 2007. "Sport and Capitalism." Pp. 4660–4662 in *Blackwell Encyclopedia of Sociology.* Vol. 9.

Brown, Clyde, and David M. Paul. 2002. "The Political Scorecard of Professional Sports Facility Referendums in the United States, 1984–2000." *Journal of Sport and Social Issues* 26 (August): 248–267.

Coakley, Jay. 2007. *Sports in Society: Issues and Controversies.* 9th ed. New York: McGraw-Hill.

Crapeau, Richard. 2007. "The *Flood* Case." *Journal of Sport History* 34 (Summer): 183–191.

Delaney, Kevin J., and Rick Eckstein. 2003. *Public Dollars, Private Stadiums: The Battle over Building Sports Stadiums.* New Brunswick, NJ: Rutgers University Press.

Eckstein, Rick, and Kevin Delaney. 2002. "New Sports Stadiums, Community Self-Esteem, and Community Collective Conscience." *Journal of Sport and Social Issues* 26 (August): 235–247.

Eitzen, D. Stanley. 2009. *Fair and Foul: Beyond the Myths and Paradoxes of Sport.* 4th ed. Lanham, MD: Rowman and Littlefield.

Eitzen, D. Stanley, and George H. Sage. 2009. *Sociology of North American Sport.* 8th ed. Boulder, CO: Paradigm.

Harvey, Jean, Alan Law, and Michael Cantelon. 2001. "North American Professional Sport Franchises Ownership Patterns and Global Entertainment Conglomerates." *Sociology of Sport Journal* 18 (4): 435–457.

Hudson, Ian. 2001. "The Use and Misuse of Economic Impact Analysis: The Case of Professional Sports." *Journal of Sport and Social Issues* 25 (February): 20–39.

Lewis, Michael. 2001. "Franchise Relocation and Fan Allegiance." *Journal of Sport and Social Issues* 25 (February): 6–19.

Malcolm, Dominic. 2007. "Sports Industry." Pp. 4713–4717 in *Blackwell Encyclopedia of Sport.* Vol. 9.

Nixon, Howard L. II. 2008. *Sport in a Changing World.* Boulder, CO: Paradigm.

Zimbalist, Andrew. 2006. *The Bottom Line: Observations and Arguments on the Sports Business.* Philadelphia, PA: Temple University Press.

Zimmer, Martha Hill, and Michael Zimmer. 2001. "Athletes as Entertainers: A Comparative Study of Earnings Profiles." *Journal of Sport and Social Issues* 25 (May): 202–215.

PART TEN

Structured Inequality:
Sport and Race/Ethnicity

By definition, a minority group is one that (1) is relatively powerless compared with the majority group, (2) possesses traits that make it different from others, (3) is systematically condemned by negative stereotyped beliefs, and (4) is singled out for differential and unfair treatment (that is, discrimination). Race (a socially defined category on the basis of a presumed genetic heritage resulting in distinguishing social characteristics) and ethnicity (the condition of being culturally distinct on the basis of race, religion, or national origin) are two traditional bases for minority group status and the resulting social inequality. Sociologists of sport are interested in the question: Is sport an area of social life where performance counts and race or ethnicity is irrelevant? The three selections in this section examine four racial or ethnic minorities—Native Americans, Asian Americans, Latinos, and African Americans—to answer this question.

The first chapter, by journalist Kevin Simpson, seeks an answer to the dilemma posed by the typical behaviors of excellent Native American athletes from reservations: Why do so many who are given scholarships either refuse them or return quickly to the reservation? These responses do not make sense to Anglos because the reservation has high unemployment, a life of dependency, and disproportionate alcohol abuse. Simpson points to these young men being "pulled" by the familiar, by the strong bonds of family, and by their unique culture. They are also "pushed" back to the reservation by social isolation, discrimination, poor high school preparation for college, and little hope for a return on their investment in a college education.

The second chapter is an excerpt from the 2008 *Racial and Gender Report Card* by Richard Lapchick and his associates at the Institute for Diversity and Ethics in

Sport. It summarizes and evaluates various dimensions of inequality in the National Football League.

Finally, Dave Zirin provides a brief account of the surge in Latinos in Major League Baseball along with various issues of discrimination.

29

Sporting Dreams Die on the "Rez"

Kevin Simpson

Last season, basketball fans followed Willie White everywhere through the unforgiving South Dakota winter. Mesmerized by smooth moves, and spectacular dunks, they watched the most celebrated product of the state's hoop-crazy Indian tribes secure his status as local legend by leading his high school to an undefeated season and state championship.

They would mob him after games in an almost frightening scene of mass adulation, press scraps of paper toward him, and beg for an autograph preferably scribbled beneath some short personal message. White would oblige by scrawling short, illegible phrases before signing. He made certain they were illegible for fear someone would discover that the best prep basketball player in South Dakota could barely read or write.

As the resident basketball hero on the impoverished Pine Ridge Reservation, where there was precious little to cheer about before the state title rekindled embers of Indian pride, White was allowed to slip undisturbed through the reservation school system, until, by his senior year, he could read at only the sixth-grade level. Ironically, the same hero status moved him to admit his problem and seek help. The constant humiliation at the hands of autograph-seekers proved more than he could take.

"I had to face up to it," says White, a soft-spoken 6-foot–4 Sioux who looks almost scholarly behind his wire-rimmed glasses. "I couldn't go on forever like that. In school I didn't study. I cheated on every test they gave me. I couldn't read good enough to answer the questions."

Source: Kevin Simpson, "Sporting Dreams Die on the 'Rez,'" Denver Post, September 6, 1987, 1C, 19C. Copyright 1987 The Denver Post. Reprinted by permission.

After some intense individual help with his reading and writing, this fall White enrolled at Huron (South Dakota) College, where he intends to continue his basketball career and take remedial reading courses. If he manages to play four years and complete his degree, he'll be the first schoolboy athlete from Pine Ridge to do so.

Other than his close friends, nobody thinks he stands a chance. Indians usually don't.

Every year, all over the western United States, promising native American athletes excel in high school sports only to abandon dreams of college, return to economically depressed reservations, and survive on their per capita checks, welfare-like payments from the tribal government, or the goodwill of more fortunate relatives. They waste away quietly, victims of alcohol, victims of inadequate education, victims of boredom, victims of poverty, but nearly always victims of their own ambivalence, caught between a burning desire to leave the reservation and an irresistible instinct to stay.

"We've had two or three kids get scholarships in the eight years I've been here," says Roland Bradford, athletic director and basketball coach at Red Cloud High School, just a few miles down the highway from Pine Ridge. "None have lasted. It's kind of a fantasy thing. In high school they talk about going to college, but it's not a reality. They have no goals set. They start out, things get tough and they come home."

At 6-foot–7 and 280 pounds, Red Cloud's Dave Brings Plenty inspired enough comparisons to the Refrigerator to lure a photographer from *People* magazine out to the reservation. He went to Dakota Wesleyan to pursue his football career, but returned home after suffering a mild concussion in practice. He never played a game. Brings Plenty says he might enroll at a different school sometime in the future, but his plans are vague. For now, he's content to hang out on the reservation and work as a security guard at a bingo parlor.

Some of the athlete-dropouts have squandered mind-boggling potential. Jeff Turning Heart, a long-distance legend on South Dakota's Cheyenne River Reservation, enrolled at Black Hills State College in Spearfish, South Dakota, on a Bureau of Indian Affairs grant in 1980 amid great expectations. He left eight days later.

In 1982, he wound up at Adams State College in Alamosa, Colorado. Longtime Adams State coach Joe Vigil, the U.S. men's distance coach for the 1988 Olympics, says that as a freshman Turning Heart was far more physically gifted than even Pat Porter, the Adams State graduate who now ranks as the premier U.S. runner at 10,000 meters. Both Porter and Vigil figured Turning Heart was on a course to win the national cross-country title—until he left school, supposedly to tend to his gravely ill father in North Dakota. He promised to return in a few days. The story was bogus and Turning Heart never went back.

At Black Hills State, where in 19 years as athletic director and track coach, David Little has seen only one Indian track athlete graduate, Turning Heart wasn't the first world-class, Native American runner to jilt him. Myron Young Dog, a distance man from Pine Ridge who once won 22 straight cross-country races in high school, came to Black Hills after dropping out of Ellendale (North Dakota) Junior College in 1969. Although he was academically ineligible for varsity sports and hadn't trained, Young

Dog stepped onto the track during a physical conditioning class and ran two miles in 9:30 "like it was a Sunday jog," according to Little. Three weeks later he entered a 15-km road race and ran away from all the collegiate competition.

It was a tantalizing glimpse of talent ultimately wasted. Little still rates Young Dog as one of the top 10 athletes ever to come out of South Dakota, but in the spring of 1970 he returned to the reservation, never to run competitively again.

It doesn't take many heartbreaks before the college coaches catch on to the risky business of recruiting off the reservations. Although Indian athletes often are immensely talented and given financial backing from the tribe and the BIA—a budgetary boon to small schools short on scholarship funds—they suffer from a widespread reputation as high-risk recruits who probably won't stick around for more than a few weeks.

That's part of the reason so many schools backed off Willie White—that and his reading deficiency. Huron College coach Fred Paulsen, who made White his first in-state recruit in four years, thought the youngster's potential made him worth the risk.

"I hate to stereotype," says Paulsen, "but is he the typical Indian? If Willie comes and doesn't make it, nobody will be surprised. My concern is that he'll go home for the weekend and say he'll be back on Monday. Which Monday?"

Talented Indians are diverted from their academic and athletic career courses for many reasons, but often they are sucked back to subsistence-level life on the reservation by the vacuum created by inadequate education and readily available escapes like drugs and alcohol.

Ted Little Moon, an all-state basketball player for Pine Ridge High School in 1984 and '85, still dominates the asphalt slab outside the school. At 6-foot–6, he roams from baseline to baseline jamming in rebounds, swatting away opponents' shots, and threading blind passes to teammates beneath the basket. He is unmistakable small-college talent.

But Little Moon missed his first opportunity to play ball in college when he failed to graduate from high school. By the following August, though, he had passed his high school equivalency exam and committed to attend Huron College. But when the basketball coach showed up at his house to pick him up and drive him to school, Little Moon said he couldn't go because he had gotten his girlfriend pregnant and had to take care of a newborn son.

He played independent basketball, a large-scale Indian intramural network, until last fall, when he planned to enroll at Haskell Junior College, an all-Indian school in Lawrence, Kansas. He and some friends drank heavily the night before he was to take the bus to Kansas. Little Moon was a passenger in a friend's car when they ran a stop sign and hit another vehicle. He spent four days in jail, missed his bus, and missed out on enrolling at Haskell.

Now he talks of going back to school, of playing basketball again, but there's ambivalence in his voice. He has become accustomed to cashing his biweekly per capita check for $28.50, drinking beer, and growing his own marijuana at a secret location on the reservation. He distributes it free to his friends.

"I guess I'm scared to get away," Little Moon admits. "But also I'm afraid I'll be stuck here and be another statistic. You grow old fast here. If I get away, I have a chance. But I'm used to what I'm doing now. Here, your mom takes care of you, the BIA takes care of you. You wait for your $28.50 and then party. It's something to look forward to.

"I started drinking as a freshman in high school, smoking dope as a sophomore. I used to get high before practice, after practice. I still do it, on the average, maybe every other day. After I play, I smoke some. It makes you forget what you're doing on the reservation."

At home, alcohol offers whatever false comfort family ties cannot. Then it kills. Two years ago, Red Cloud's Bradford tallied all the alcohol-related deaths he had known personally and came up with some sobering statistics. In 13 years of teaching, 18 of his former students have died in alcohol-related tragedies. Aside from students, he has known an incredible 61 people under the age of 22 who have lost their lives in one way or another to the bottle.

Many died along a two-mile stretch of Highway 407 that connects Pine Ridge with Whiteclay, Nebraska, a depressing cluster of bars and liquor stores that do a land-office business. Three years ago, South Dakota's highway department began erecting metal markers at the site of each alcohol-related fatality. Locals say that if they'd started 10 years ago, the signs would form an unbroken chain along the road. They'd have run out of signs before they ran out of death.

Among Indians nationwide, four of the top 10 causes of death are alcohol-related: accidents, suicides, cirrhosis of the liver, and homicide. Alcohol mortality is nearly five times higher among Indians, at 30 per 100,000 population, than for all other races. According to Dr. Eva Smith of the Indian Health Service in Washington, D.C., between 80 and 90 percent of all Indian accidents, suicides, and homicides are alcohol-related.

Fred Beauvais, a research scientist at Colorado State University, points out that Indians not only start using drugs and alcohol earlier than the general population, but the rate of use also tends to be higher. According to a 1987 study of 2,400 subjects in eight western tribes Beauvais conducted with funding from the National Institute on Drug Abuse, 50 percent of Indian high school seniors were classified as "at risk" of serious harm because of drug and alcohol use. An amazing 43 percent are at risk by the seventh grade. The figure for seniors probably is too low, Beauvais explains, because by 12th grade many Indian students already have dropped out.

He attributes these phenomena not to racial or cultural idiosyncrasies, but to socioeconomic conditions on the reservations.

"Once it becomes socially ingrained, it's a vicious cycle," Beauvais says. "The kids see the adults doing it and they see no alternatives. It's a real trap. For some Indian kids to choose not to drink means to deny their Indianness. That can be a powerful factor."

Even those athletes who excel in the classroom are not necessarily immune to the magnetic pull of alcohol. Beau LeBeau, a 4.0 student at Red Cloud High who has started for the varsity basketball team since he was in eighth grade, recognizes the dangers but speaks of them as if they are elements quite out of his control. He estimates that 90 percent of his friends abuse alcohol.

"I'm going to the best academic school on the reservation," he says. "I should get a good education if I don't turn to drugs and alcohol in the next few years and ruin it for myself. In my room before I go to sleep I think, 'Is this how I'm going to spend the rest of my life? On the reservation?' I hope not."

For all the roadside signs that stand as chilling monuments to death around Pine Ridge, the drinking continues, a false and addictive cure for boredom and futility.

"If they win they want to celebrate," offers Bryan Brewer, athletic director at Pine Ridge High School. "If they lose, that's another excuse to drink. People who didn't make it want to drag the good athletes down with them."

Consequently, the road to a college athletic career sometimes ends before it even begins.

"I'm not opposed to recruiting the Indian athlete," offers Black Hills State athletic director Little. "I'm selective about who I recruit, though. I don't have the answer to the problem and don't know [if] I totally understand the situation. I do know that what's going on now is not working."

Something definitely isn't working in Towoac (pronounced TOI-ahk), in southwestern Colorado, where Indian athletes don't even wait until after high school to see their careers disintegrate. There, on the Ute Mountain Reservation, a multitude of Indian athletes compete and excel up to eighth grade and then quit rather than pursue sports at Montezuma-Cortez High, a mixed-race school 17 miles north of the reservation in the town of Cortez.

They drop out at the varsity level sometimes for academic reasons but often because of racial tension—or what they feel is bias on the part of white coaches. Pressed for particulars, current and former athletes make only vague accusations of negative attitudes and rarely cite specific instances. But how much of the discrimination is real and how much imagined is academic. The perception of discrimination remains, passed down among the athletes almost as an oral tradition.

For instance, today's athletes hear stories like those told by former Cortez High athlete Hanley Frost, who in the mid-1970s felt the wrath of the school administration when he was a sophomore on the basketball team and insisted on wearing his hair long, braided in traditional Indian style. He played four games with it tucked into his jersey but then was told school policy demanded that he cut it off. Eventually, he quit the team and began experimenting with drugs and alcohol.

Frost stated, "Really, it was the townspeople who didn't enjoy having a long-haired Indian on the team. There were a lot of people out there who would rather see their kids in a position on the team an Indian kid has."

"There's something about Towoac that just doesn't sit right." Adds reservation athletic director Doug Call, a Mormon who came to the Ute Mountain Reservation from Brigham Young University. "I don't know if people are afraid or what, but there's a stigma if you live out here."

Those Indians who do participate in sports at the high school level tend to live in Cortez, not on the reservation. An invisible wall of distrust seems to surround

Towoac, where most of the young athletes play what is known on reservations as "independent ball," a loosely organized kind of intramural basketball.

"They feel they're not getting a fair chance, I know they do," says Gary Gellatly, the Cortez High School athletic director who once served as recreation director on the reservation. "And I'm sure they have been discriminated against, directly or indirectly. It's tough to get them to compete. Yet you go out there on any weekend and watch those independent tournaments—you'll see kids playing basketball that you've never seen before. But I'm afraid if we start an overt effort to get them to participate you crowd them into a tighter corner. In a sense, not participating because they think they might be discriminated against is a cop-out, but it's been perpetuated by circumstances. Somewhere, something happened that wasn't good."

After massive turnover in the school's coaching staff, some new hires have expressed a desire to see more Indians become involved in the school's sports programs. Bill Moore, the new head football coach, heard the rumors that Indian kids wouldn't even try out for the squad and mailed tryout invitations to much of the student body including as many Indian boys as he could find addresses for. Even so, the turnout hasn't been markedly different from previous years.

"The solution," says varsity basketball coach Gordon Shepherd, "is that something has to give. Cultural groups that remain within themselves don't succeed. For Indians to succeed in white society terms, they have to give up some cultural ethnicity."

Ethnic idiosyncrasies present a whole range of problems—from students' inclination or ability to perform in the classroom to conflicts such as the one currently under way at Jemez Pueblo, a small reservation north of Albuquerque, New Mexico. There, in a hotbed of mountain running, a cross-country coach at a mixed-race school has struggled with athletes who reject modern training techniques for the less formal but highly traditional ways of their ancestors.

On some reservations, Indian student-athletes are merely ill-prepared to cope with the stringent academic demands of college. According to BIA statistics, the average Indian high school senior reads at the ninth-grade level. Of the 20 percent of high school seniors who go on to attempt college, 40 percent drop out.

And with some reservations approaching economic welfare states, students considering college confront a serious question about the value of an education: Why spend four years pursuing a college degree only to return to a reservation that has few or no private sector jobs?

Indians often find themselves without any real ethnic support system in college and become homesick for reservation life and the exceptionally strong bonds of an extended family in which aunts, uncles, and grandparents often live under the same roof. In some tribal cultures, 18- or 19-year olds still are considered mere children and haven't been pressed to formulate long-term goals. It's no coincidence, says an education administrator for the Arapahoe tribe on central Wyoming's Wind River Reservation, that most successful Indian students are in their mid- to late 20s—when, incidentally, athletic eligibility has gone by the board.

Even the basic incentive of athletics tends to evaporate in a more intense competitive climate far removed from the reservation.

Myron "The Magician" Chavez, a four-time all-state guard from Wyoming Indian High School on the Wind River Reservation, enrolled at Sheridan (Wyoming) College last fall but left school during preseason workouts when he was asked to redshirt. He felt he had failed because he didn't step immediately into a starting position. Jeff Brown, who preceded Chavez at WIHS, had a scholarship offer from the University of Kansas in 1982 but turned it down because he feared he would fail—academically if not athletically.

Dave Archambault, a Sioux who started the athletic program at United Tribes Junior College in Bismarck, North Dakota, has found the fear of failure to be a familiar theme among talented Indian athletes. On the reservations, he points out, athletes become heroes, modern extensions of the old warrior society that disappeared after defeat at the hands of the white man.

"They're kicking butt on the reservation," Archambault explains, "and then all of the sudden they're working out with juniors and seniors in college and getting their butts kicked. They're not held in that high regard and esteem. But they can go back to the reservation any time and get it."

They recapture their high school glory through independent ball, the intramural network among reservations that quenches an insatiable thirst for basketball competition among all age groups. There are tournaments nearly every weekend and an all-Indian national tournament each spring, where the best teams often recruit talent from a wide area by offering modest incentives like cash and expenses. At most levels, though, independent ball resembles extremely organized pickup basketball.

For most Indian athletes, it represents the outer limits of achievement, caught though it is in a void between the reservation and the outside world. It's in that limbo—socially as well as athletically—that most Indians play out their careers.

"There's no way to return to the old way, spiritually and economically," observes Billy Mills, the 1964 Olympic gold medalist at 10,000 meters who grew up on the Pine Ridge Reservation. "It's like walking death—no goals, no commitment, no accomplishment. If you go too far into society, there's a fear of losing your Indianness. There's a spiritual factor that comes into play. To become part of white society you give up half your soul. Society wants us to walk in one world with one spirit. But we have to walk in two worlds with one spirit."

30

The 2008 Racial and Gender Report Card
National Football League

Richard Lapchick with Eric Little and Colleen Lerner

EXECUTIVE SUMMARY

The National Football League maintained a B+ grade on racial hiring practices in the 2008 NFL Racial and Gender Report Card.

However, the NFL slipped slightly from the previous report from a score for race of 88.6 points out of 100 to 87.1. Once again, The Institute did not issue a grade for gender in this report card for reasons explained below. The NFL's last gender grade was a D+ in the 2004 Report Card.

Using data from the 2007 season, The Institute conducted an analysis of racial breakdowns of the players, managers and coaches. In addition, the Report includes a racial and gender breakdown of the top team management, senior administration, professional administration, physicians, head trainers, and broadcasters. Coaches, general managers, presidents and owners were updated as of August 15, 2008.

The biggest breakthroughs have been the fact that two African American head coaches faced each other in the 2007 Super Bowl for the first time and an African American general manager helped lead his team to a win in the 2008 Super Bowl.

Source: Richard Lapchick with Eric Little and Colleen Lerner, *The 2008 Racial and Gender Report Card: National Football League,* August 27, 2008 (Orlando, FL: Institute for Diversity and Ethics in Sports, University of Central Florida, 2008).

The Report shows sustained progress in the key positions of head coach (seven in 2006, six in 2007 and 2008), general manager (four in 2006, five in 2007 and 2008) and assistant coach where the NFL reached all-time highs.

The NFL League Office is the only one of the professional leagues that does not participate in the Racial and Gender Report Card. It neither provides League Office data nor chooses to review and corroborate the data that we submit to each league prior to publication in order to try to achieve the most accurate analysis. This is the fourth time the NFL took this position. Without League Office data, The Institute was left with less than sufficient data on gender and, therefore, we did not issue a grade on gender. The record of NFL teams regarding the hiring of women remained poor, especially compared to the significant progress on race.

Tables for the report are included in the Appendix.

It is imperative that sports teams play the best athletes they have available to win games. The Institute strives to emphasize the value of diversity to sports organizations when they choose their team on the field and in the office. Diversity initiatives such as diversity management training can help change attitudes and increase the applicant pool for open positions. It is clearly the choice of the organization regarding which applicant is the best fit for their ball club, but The Institute wants to illustrate how important it is to have a diverse organization involving individuals who happen to be of a different race or gender. This element of diversity can provide a different perspective, and possibly a competitive advantage for a win in the board room as well as on the field.

The Report Card asks, "Are we playing fair when it comes to sports? Does everyone, regardless of race or gender, have a chance to score a touchdown and operate the business of professional football?"

The Institute for Diversity and Ethics in Sport (TIDES) located at the University of Central Florida publishes the *Racial and Gender Report Card* to indicate areas of improvement, stagnation and regression in the racial and gender composition of professional and college sports personnel and to contribute to the improvement of integration in front office and college athletics department positions. The publication of the 2008 NFL Racial and Gender Report Card follows the publication of the reports on MLB, the NBA, the WNBA, and the Associated Press Sports Editors. The remaining reports for this year will be for Major League Soccer and college sport.

REPORT HIGHLIGHTS

- The Rooney Rule helped the NFL to increase the number of African American head coaches from two in 2001 to six in 2005. There were seven African American head coaches in 2006 and six in both 2007 and 2008.
- In addition, an African American head coach and an African American general manager led their teams to Super Bowl victories in 2007 and 2008. Tony Dungy led the Colts to victory in the Super Bowl for the first time in 2007. The game was the first in which two African American head coaches

faced off for the Championship. New York Giants general manager, Jerry Reese helped put together the team that won the Super Bowl in 2008.

- There are six African American head coaches in 2008. No African American head coaches were fired after the 2007 season. Four new head coaches were hired prior to the 2008–09 season and they were all white. However, it was announced that when Indianapolis Colts head coach, Tony Dungy, retires then Colts assistant head coach, Jim Caldwell, will take over. Caldwell is African American.
- In 2006, the NFL had four African American general managers. As the 2007 season started, there were five after Jerry Reese was named by the New York Giants as GM. They all were at the helm as the 2008 season began.
- There were a record number of people of color in assistant coaching positions in the 2007 season with 172 assistant coaches of color, or 38 percent, matching the percentage of the last Report Card.
- In the 2007 NFL season, the percentage of white players remained constant at 31 percent while the percentage of African American players decreased slightly from 67 to 66 percent.
- Amy Trask of the Oakland Raiders remained the only female President/CEO of a team in the NFL, a position she has held since 2005. There has never been a person of color serving as president or CEO in the history of the NFL.
- There were 12 African American vice presidents in 2007, one less than reported in last year's Report Card.
- People of color increased slightly in both team senior administration positions and in professional administration.
- In general, the record of NFL teams regarding gender hiring practices remained poor although the percentage of women did increase slightly in the categories of team senior administration and in professional administration positions. Overall, it was very close to the results in the previous Racial and Gender Report Card.

OVERALL GRADES

The NFL received an overall B+ grade for race (87.1 out of 100). That was down slightly from 88.6 in the previous Racial and Gender Report Card. Once again, no grade was issued for gender.

The percentages for people of color increased for team senior administrators, professional administration, and physicians from 2006 to the 2007 season. It also increased for general managers from 2007 to the 2008 season. The percentages for people of color decreased only for radio and TV broadcasters while remaining the same for players, head and assistant coaches, team presidents, vice presidents, and head trainers.

The percentages for women increased for team senior administrators and professional administration. They decreased as team vice presidents and radio and TV broadcasters in 2007 and as owners in 2008.

For race, the NFL received an A+ for players and assistant coaches and a B+ for head coaches and team senior administrators.

The NFL had received a D+ for gender in the 2004 Report. The percentages of women have increased slightly between 1–3 percent since then in the categories of team vice presidents, team senior administration positions and in professional administration. Overall, there was little change on gender in the last three reports.

GRADES BY CATEGORY

Players

In the NFL's 2007 season, the percentage of African Americans was 66 percent, a decrease of one percentage point from 2006. The all-time high for African American players was in 2003 at 69 percent. The percentage of whites remained constant at 31 percent from 2006. The percentages of Latinos increased to just over one percent (up from 0.5 percent in 2006) and Asians in the NFL increased slightly from 1.5 to 2 percent. Of all professional leagues in the United States, the NFL continues to have the smallest percentage of international players at two percent in 2007 (up from one percent in 2006).

NFL Grade for Players: A+

See Table 30-1.

NFL League Office

The NFL did not report league office data so it could not be evaluated.

NFL Grade for League Office: None issued

See Table 30-2.

Ownership

There has never been a majority owner of color in the NFL. The NFL appeared to take a giant step in 2005 when it was announced that Red McCombs was selling the Minnesota Vikings to Reggie Fowler, an African American. That would have meant that, for the first time, all four major sports in the United States had a majority owner of color. However, the sale was not approved and Fowler became a minority owner of the Vikings.

There has never been a majority owner of color in the NFL.

There were three women who held ownership of an NFL team during the 2007 season.

See Table 30-3.

Head Coaches

The efforts of the Commissioner's Office, as well as the diversity groups appointed by the NFL in the last five years, have brought about a dramatic change in head coaches. Former players formed the Fritz Pollard Alliance to add pressure and create more momentum for change.

Nothing highlighted this more than when the Indianapolis Colts and Chicago Bears faced off in the 2007 Super Bowl with Tony Dungy and Lovie Smith, two African Americans, leading their respective teams. It was the first time this happened in the NFL. It had only happened once in the NBA and it has never happened in Major League Baseball.

The Rooney Rule, which requires that people of color be interviewed as part of the search process for head coaches, has helped to more than double the number of African American head coaches in the NFL from two in 2001 to six in 2005. There were seven African American head coaches in 2006 and six in both 2007 and 2008. The Rooney Rule was named after Steelers' owner Dan Rooney, who is the head of the league's diversity committee. The NFL's policy is similar to the approach adopted earlier by Major League Baseball in 1999 under Bud Selig, which helped triple the number of managers of color in MLB in the first few years after implementation.

In 2003, with the hiring of Marvin Lewis by the Cincinnati Bengals, the number of head coaches of color in the NFL increased to three. The percentage of African American head coaches grew to 16 percent before the start of the 2004 season when the NFL added two more African American head coaches: Dennis Green of the Arizona Cardinals and Lovie Smith of the Chicago Bears. After the 2005 Super Bowl, Romeo Crennel was hired as head coach of the Cleveland Browns, giving the NFL six African American head coaches, two times the previous high of three African American NFL head coaches.

After the 2005 NFL season, Herman Edwards was released of his contract with the New York Jets and subsequently hired by the Kansas City Chiefs. Art Shell was hired as the head coach of the Oakland Raiders. Shell was the first African American coach in the NFL when he was hired by the Raiders in 1989, and continued in this position until 1994.

Dennis Green and Art Shell were let go after the 2006 season and Mike Tomlin was hired by the Pittsburgh Steelers prior to the start of the 2007 NFL season. Four new head coaches were hired prior to the 2008 NFL season and all were white. This leaves six African American head coaches.

NFL Grade for Head Coaches: B+

See Table 30-4.

Assistant Coaches

The 2007 season saw a record number of people of color in assistant coaching positions in the NFL when there were 172 assistant coaches of color, or 38 percent. This was up from 165 assistant coaches of color, while matching the 38 percent in the last Report Card.

In the 2007 NFL season, the number of white assistant coaches remained constant with the 2006 season at 62 percent, while African Americans increased by one percentage point to 36 percent. Latinos moved down one percentage point to one percent, and Asian assistant coaches remained at one percentage point. Seven African Americans held coordinator positions in the NFL, up from six in the last Report Card.

Nine African Americans held coordinator positions in the NFL, up from six in the last Report Card.

NFL Grade for Assistant Coaches: A+

See Table 30-5.

Top Management

CEOs/Presidents

Amy Trask of the Oakland Raiders is the only woman president/CEO in the NFL, a position she has held since 2005.

There has never been a president/CEO of color in the NFL.

See Table 30-6.

Stacking

Most observers agree that the issue of stacking in the NFL is no longer a major concern. In the 2007 NFL season, the percentage of African American quarterbacks increased three percentage points to 19 percent. Quarterback is football's central "thinking" position. Historically, the positions of running back, wide receiver, cornerback and safety have had disproportionately high percentages of African Americans. The latter positions rely a great deal on speed and reactive ability. The quarterback position was the primary concern since it was so central to the game and now that African Americans have broken down that barrier, concern about other positions has been greatly diminished.

While the positions of running back (89 percent), wide receiver (89 percent), cornerback (97 percent) and safety (84 percent) continued to be disproportionately held by African Americans, these are of less concern. That is also true for the position of center, considered to be the anchor of the offensive line, which was still dominated (77 percent) by whites.

See Tables 30-7 and 30-8.

APPENDIX

Table 30-1 Players

	%	#			%	#
2007			*1997*			
White	31%	730		White	33%	x
African American	66%	1566		African American	65%	x
Latino	1%	30		Latino	<1%	x
Asian	2%	44		Other	1%	x
Other	<1%	1	*1996*			
International	2%	43		White	31%	x
2006				African American	66%	x
White	31%	532		Latino	<1%	x
African American	67%	1131		Other	2%	x
Latino	0.5%	8	*1995*			
Asian	1.5%	25		White	31%	x
Other	0%	0		African American	67%	x
International	1%	24		Latino	0%	x
2005				Other	<2%	x
White	31.50%	537	*1994*			
African American	65.50%	1116		White	31%	x
Latino	<1%	10		African American	68%	x
Asian	2%	34		Latino	0%	x
Other	<1%	1		Other	1%	x
International	1%	18	*1993*			
2003				White	35%	x
White	29%	516		African American	65%	x
African American	69%	1228		Latino	0%	x
Latino	1%	9	*1992*			
Asian	1%	22		White	30%	x
Other	0%	0		African American	68%	x
2000				Latino	<1%	x
White	x	x		Other	1%	x
African American	x	x	*1991*			
Latino	x	x		White	36%	x
Other	x	x		African American	62%	x
1999				Latino	2%	x
White	32%	x	*1990*			
African American	67%	x		White	39%	x
Latino	<1%	x		African American	61%	x
Other	<1%	x		Latino	0%	x
1998				White	40%	x
White	32%	x		African American	60%	x
African American	66%	x		Latino	0%	x
Latino	<1%	x				
Other	1%	x				

x = Data not recorded.

Table 30-2 League Office: NFL

	Office Management %	#	Support Staff Personnel %	#
2003-2006				
White	NFL DID NOT SUPPLY DATA			
African American				
Latino				
Asian				
Other				
Women				
Total				
2002				
White	74%	150	51%	42
African American	14%	28	25%	21
Latino	4%	9	19%	16
Asian	8%	16	5%	4
Other	0%	0	0%	0
Women	26%	53	54%	45
Total		203		83
2000				
White	77%	140	57%	31
African American	14%	25	22%	12
Latino	<3%	5	19%	10
Asian	7%	12	2%	1
Other	0%	0	0%	0
Women	29%	53	56%	30
Total		182		54
1998				
White	79%	131	70%	40
African American	15%	25	19%	11
Latino	2%	3	9%	5
Asian	4%	6	2%	1
Other	0%	0	x	x
Women	26%	43	75%	43
Total		165		57
1997				
White	80%	119	68%	34
African American	15%	22	22%	11
Latino	2%	3	8%	4
Asian	3%	4	2%	1
Other	0%	0	x	x
Women	26%	39	84%	42
Total		148		50
1996				
White	82%	93	81%	56
African American	14%	16	12%	8
Latino	<1.0%	1	4%	3
Asian	2%	2	3%	2
Other	<1.0%	1	x	x
Women	22%	25	64%	44
Total		113		69
1995				
White	79%	62	85%	68
African American	15%	12	8%	6
Latino	<2%	1	5%	4
Asian	3%	2	3%	2
Other	<2.0%	1	x	x
Women	21%	16	58%	46
Total		75		80

Note: Data provided by the NFL league office.

x = Data not recorded.

Table 30-3   Majority Owners

	%			%
2008			*2003*	
White	100%		White	100%
African American	0%		African American	0%
Latino	0%		Latino	0%
Asian	0%		Asian	0%
Other	0%		Women	10%
Women	6%		*2001*	
2007			White	100%
White	100%		African American	0%
African American	0%		Latino	0%
Latino	0%		Asian	0%
Asian	0%		Women	9%
Other	0%		*1999*	
Women	8%		White	100%
2006			African American	0%
White	100%		Latino	0%
African American	0%		Asian	0%
Latino	0%		Women	6%
Asian	0%		*1998*	
Other	0%		White	100%
Women	9%		African American	0%
2005			Latino	0%
White	100%		Asian	0%
African American	0%		Women	6%
Latino	0%		*1997*	
Asian	0%		White	100%
Other	0%		African American	0%
Women	11%		Latino	0%
			Asian	0%
			Women	7%

Table 30-4 Head Coaches

	%	#			%	#
2008				**1999**		
White	81%	26		White	94%	29
African American	19%	6		African American	6%	2
Asian	0%	0		Asian	0%	0
Latino	0%	0		Latino	0%	0
Other	0%	0		Women	0%	0
Women	0%	0		**1997**		
2007				White	90%	27
White	81%	26		African American	10%	3
African American	19%	6		Asian	0%	0
Asian	0%	0		Latino	0%	0
Latino	0%	0		Women	0%	0
Other	0%	0		African American	10%	3
Women	0%	0		Latino	0%	0
2006				**1995**		
White	78%	25		White	90%	27
African American	22%	7		African American	10%	3
Asian	0%	0		Latihno	3%	1
Latino	0%	0		**1994**		
Other	0%	0		White	93%	28
Women	0%	0		African American	7%	2
2005				Latino	0%	0
White	81%	26		**1993**		
African American	19%	6		White	89%	25
Asian	0%	0		African American	7%	2
Latino	0%	0		Latino	<4%	1
Women	0%	0		**1992**		
2003				White	89%	25
White	91%	29		African American	7%	2
African American	9%	3		Latino	<4%	1
Asian	0%	0		**1991**		
Latino	0%	0		White	93%	26
Women	0%	0		African American	7%	2
2001				Latino	0%	0
White	94%	30		**1990**		
African American	6%	2		White	96%	27
Asian	0%	0		African American	4%	1
Latino	0%	0		Latino	0%	0
Women	0%	0				
2000						
White	90%	28				
African American	10%	3				
Asian	0%	0				
Latino	0%	0				
Women	0%	0				

Table 30-5 Assistant Coaches

	%	#			%	#
2007			*1997*			
White	62%	284		White	73%	311
African American	36%	162		African American	26%	113
Latino	1%	5		Latino	1%	3
Asian	1%	5		Asian	<1%	1
Other	0%	0		Other	0%	0
Women	0%	0		Women	0%	0
2006			*1996*			
White	62%	269		White	74%	307
African American	35%	151		African American	25%	102
Latino	2%	10		Latino	<1%	3
Asian	1%	4		Asian	<1%	1
Other	0%	0		Other	0%	0
Women	0%	0	*1995*			
2005				White	76%	289
White	66%	316		African American	23%	88
African American	32%	154		Latino	0%	0
Latino	1%	5		Asian	0%	0
Asian	1%	3		Other	<1%	4
Other	0%	0	*1994*			
Women	0%	0		White	77%	249
2003				African American	23%	73
White	67%	341		Latino	<1%	1
African American	30%	153		Asian	<1%	1
Latino	2%	8		Other	0%	0
Asian	0%	1	*1993*			
Other	1%	7		White	76%	217
Women	0%	0		African American	23%	73
2001				Latino	<1%	1
White	71%	333		Other	0%	0
African American	28%	132	*1992*			
Latino	<1%	6		White	80%	264
Asian	<1%	1		African American	20%	65
Other	0%	0		Latino	0%	0
Women	0%	0		Other	0%	0
1999			*1991*			
White	72%	330		White	84%	289
African American	28%	127		African American	16%	54
Latino	0%	0				
Asian	0%	0				
Other	0%	0				
Women	0%	0				

Table 30-6 CEO/President

	%	#			%	#
2008				**2003**		
White	100%	29		White	100%	32
African American	0%	0		African American	0%	0
Latino	0%	0		Latino	0%	0
Asian	0%	0		Asian	0%	0
Other	0%	0		Women	9%	3
Women	3%	1		**2000**		
2007				White	100%	x
White	100%	30		African American	0%	x
African American	0%	0		Latino	0%	x
Latino	0%	0		Asian	0%	x
Asian	0%	0		Women	3%	x
Other	0%	0		**1999**		
Women	3%	1		White	100%	x
2006				African American	0%	x
White	100%	35		Latino	0%	x
African American	0%	0		Asian	0%	x
Latino	0%	0		Women	3%	x
Asian	0%	0		**1998**		
Other	0%	0		White	100%	x
Women	3%	1		African American	0%	x
2005				Latino	0%	x
White	100%	41		Asian	0%	x
African American	0%	0		Women	3%	x
Latino	0%	0		**1997**		
Asian	0%	0		White	100%	x
Women	3%	1		African American	0%	x
				Latino	0%	x
				Other	0%	x
				Women	0%	x

x = Data not recorded.

Table 30-7 NFL Offense

	QB	RB	WR	TE	OT	OG	C
2007							
White	76%	9%	10%	56%	49%	59%	77%
African American	19%	89%	89%	42%	49%	35%	18%
2006							
White	82%	10%	8%	54%	43%	53%	70%
African American	16%	88%	91%	43%	57%	42%	26%
2005							
White	82%	9%	9%	57%	44%	54%	69%
African American	16%	89%	91%	40%	55%	39%	24%
2003							
White	77%	13%	14%	55%	44%	56%	85%
African American	22%	86%	86%	42%	55%	41%	12%
2002							
White	76%	16%	12%	56%	45%	56%	83%
African American	24%	82%	88%	41%	53%	41%	14%
2000							
White	78%	13%	10%	56%	48%	48%	70%
African American	21%	86%	90%	41%	30%	50%	25%
1999							
White	81%	13%	9%	55%	42%	55%	75%
African American	18%	86%	91%	42%	55%	42%	20%
1998							
White	91%	13%	8%	55%	39%	67%	83%
African American	8%	87%	92%	42%	55%	29%	17%
1997							
White	91%	7%	8%	52%	49%	72%	72%
African American	7%	90%	89%	48%	47%	23%	20%
1993							
White	93%	8%	10%	39%	51%	64%	79%
African American	7%	92%	90%	60%	47%	32%	18%

Note: 66% of all players in the NFL are Black. 31% of all players are White. 3% of all players in the NFL are either Pacific Islander, Latino, or Asian American. Any totals of less than 100% are due to the third category of other.

Table 30-8 NFL Defense

		CB	S	LB	DE	DT
2007						
	White	2%	13%	26%	21%	18%
	African American	97%	84%	71%	73%	76%
2006						
	White	4%	14%	24%	24%	18%
	African American	96%	85%	73%	75%	75%
2005						
	White	5%	14%	26%	24%	20%
	African American	95%	83%	71%	75%	75%
2003						
	White	2%	19%	17%	22%	20%
	African American	98%	81%	80%	77%	76%
2002						
	White	1%	13%	19%	20%	23%
	African American	98%	87%	78%	78%	78%
2000						
	White	7%	13%	22%	25%	26%
	African American	93%	87%	76%	73%	73%
1999						
	White	4%	10%	23%	21%	20%
	African American	96%	90%	74%	77%	68%
1998						
	White	1%	9%	24%	19%	31%
	African American	99%	91%	75%	79%	63%
1997						
	White	2%	10%	24%	15%	24%
	African American	98%	89%	74%	8%	71%
1993						
	White	1%	18%	27%	27%	30%
	African American	99%	80%	72%	71%	53%

Note: 66% of all players in the NFL are Black. 31% of all players are White. 3% of all players in the NFL are either Pacific Islander, Latino, or Asian American. Any totals of less than 100% are due to the third category of other.

31

Say It Ain't So, Big Leagues
The Downside for Latin American Players

Dave Zirin

In early October 30-year-old Mario Encarnación was found dead in his Taipei, Taiwan, apartment from causes unknown. His lonely death, with the lights on and refrigerator door open, ended a tragic journey that began in the dirt-poor town of Bani in the Dominican Republic and concluded on the other side of the world. In between, Encarnación, or "Super Mario," as he was known on the baseball diamond, was the most highly touted prospect in the Oakland A's organization, considered better than future American League Most Valuable Player Miguel Tejada. Tejada, also from Bani, paid the freight to bring his friend home from Taiwan. It's hard to imagine who else from their barrio could have managed to foot the bill.

Encarnación's death was not even a sidebar in the sports pages of the United States. A 30-year-old playing out his last days in East Asia might as well be invisible.

But he shouldn't be. As Major League Baseball celebrates its annual fall classic, the World Series, it is increasingly dependent on talent born and bred in Latin America. Twenty-six percent of all players in the major leagues now hail from Latin America, including some of the game's most popular stars, like David Ortiz, Pedro Martinez and Sammy Sosa. Leading the way is the tiny nation of the Dominican Republic. Just five years ago there were sixty-six Dominican-born players on baseball's Opening Day rosters. This year, there were more than 100. This means roughly one

Source: Dave Zirin, "Say It Ain't So, Big Leagues: The Downside for Latin American Players," *Nation* (November 14, 2005).

out of every seven major league players was born in the DR, by far the highest number from any country outside the United States. In addition, 30 percent of players in the US minor leagues hail from this tiny Latin American nation, which shares an island with Haiti and has a population roughly the size of New York City's.

All thirty teams now scout what baseball owners commonly call "the Republic of Baseball," and a number of teams have elaborate multimillion-dollar "baseball academies." The teams trumpet these academies. (One executive said, "We have made Fields of Dreams out of the jungle.") But unmentioned is that for every Tejada there are 100 Encarnaciós. And for every Encarnación toiling on the margins of the pro baseball circuit, there are thousands of Dominican players cast aside by a Major League Baseball system that is strip-mining the Dominican Republic for talent. Unmentioned is the overarching relationship Major League Baseball has with the Dominican Republic, harvesting talent on the cheap with no responsibility for who gets left behind. Unmentioned is what Major League Baseball is doing—or is not doing—for a country with 60 percent of its population living below the poverty line. As American sports agent Joe Kehoskie says in *Stealing Home,* a PBS documentary, "Traditionally in the Latin market, I would say players sign for about 5 to 10 cents on the dollar compared to their US counterparts." He also points out that "a lot of times kids just quit school at 10, 11, 12, and play baseball full-time. It's great, it's great for the kids that make it because they become superstars and get millions of dollars in the big leagues. But for ninety-eight kids out of 100, it results in a kid that is 18, 19, with no education."

Considering both the poverty rate and the endless trumpeting of rags-to-riches stories of those like Sosa and Tejada, it's no wonder the academies are so attractive to young Dominicans. Most young athletes in the DR play without shoes, using cut-out milk cartons for gloves, rolled-up cloth for balls, and sticks and branches for bats. The academies offer good equipment, nice uniforms and the dream of a better life.

Sacramento Bee sportswriter Marcos Breton's book *Home Is Everything: The Latino Baseball Story* highlights the appeal of the academies: "Teams house their players in dormitories and feed their prospects balanced meals. Often it's the first time these boys will sleep under clean sheets or eat nutritious meals. The firsts don't stop there: Some of these boys encounter a toilet for the first time. Or an indoor shower. They are taught discipline, the importance of being on time, of following instructions."

The competition to get into the "baseball factories," as they are often referred to, is fierce. Sports anthropologist Alan Klein describes, in *Stealing Home,* the scene in front of one of the academies:

> Every morning you would drive to the Academy, you would see fifteen, twenty kids out there, not one of them had a uniform, they all had pieces of one uniform or another, poor equipment, they would be right at the gate waiting for the security people to open up the gates and they would go in for their tryout. If they got signed, they were happy. If they didn't get signed, it didn't even deter them for a minute; they would be on the road hitchhiking to the next location. And they would eventually find one of those 20-some clubs that would eventually pick them up. And if not, then they might return to amateur baseball.

✻ FOR FURTHER STUDY ✻

Beton, Maracos, and Jose Luis Villegas. 2003. *Home Is Everything: The Latino Baseball Story from the Barrio to the Major Leagues.* El Paso, TX: Cinco Puntos Press.

Boeck, Greg. 2007. "The Native American Barrier: Group Culture and Individualism." *USA Today* (February 22): 1C-2C.

Brown, Tony N., James S. Jackson, Kendrick T. Brown, Robert M. Sellers, Shelley Keiper, and Warde J. Manuel. 2003. " 'There's No Race on the Playing Field': Perceptions of Racial Discrimination among White and Black Athletes." *Journal of Sport and Social Issues* 27 (May): 162–183.

Bryant, Howard. 2002. *Shut Out: A Story of Race and Baseball in Boston.* New York: Routledge.

Carrington, Ben. 2007. "Sport and Race" Pp. 4686–4690 in *Blackwell Encyclopedia of Sport.* Vol. 9.

Coakley, Jay. 2007. *Sports in Society: Issues and Controversies.* 9th ed. New York: McGraw-Hill.

Edwards, Harry. 1998. "An End of the Golden Age of Black Participation in Sport?" *Civil Rights Journal* 3 (Fall): 19–24.

———. 2000. "Crisis of Black Athletes on the Eve of the 21st Century." *Society* 37 (March–April): 9–13.

Eitzen, D. Stanley. 2009. *Fair and Foul: Beyond the Myths and Paradoxes of Sport.* 4th ed. Lanham, MD: Rowman and Littlefield.

Eitzen, D. Stanley, and George H. Sage. *Sociology of North American Sport.* 8th ed. Boulder, CO: Paradigm.

Goldsmith, Pat Antonio. 2003. "Race Relations and Racial Patterns in School Sports Participation." *Sociology of Sport Journal* 20 (2): 147–171.

Hanson, Sandra L. 2005. "Hidden Dragons: Asian American Women and Sports." *Journal of Sport and Social Issues* 29 (August): 259–265.

Harrison, C. Keith. 2000. "Black Athletes at the Millennium." *Society* 37 (March–April): 35–39.

Hoberman, John. 2000. "The Price of 'Black Dominance.' " *Society* 37 (March–April): 35–39.

Jamieson, Katherine M. 2003. "Occupying a Middle Space: Toward a Mestiza Sport Studies." *Sociology of Sport Journal* 20 (1): 1–16.

Jones, Robyn L. 2002. "The Black Experience within English Semiprofessional Soccer." *Journal of Sport and Social Issues* 26 (February): 47–64.

Juffer, Jane. 2002. "Who's the Man? Sammy Sosa, Latinos, and Televisual Redefinitions of the 'American' Pastime." *Journal of Sport and Social Issues* 26 (November): 337–359.

King, C. Richard. 2007. "Sport and Ethnicity." Pp. 4681–4684 in *Blackwell Encyclopedia of Sport.* Vol. 9.

King, C. Richard, and Charles Fruehling Springwood. 2001. *Beyond the Cheers: Race as Spectacle in College Sport.* Albany: State University of New York Press.

Lapchick, Richard E. 2008. "Games Could Have Lasting Impact on Asian-Americans." *Sports Business Journal* (August 25). Available at rlapchick@bus.ucf.edu.

Lapchick, Richard E. Annual Report. *Racial and Gender Report Card.* Institute for Diversity and Ethics in Sport, University of Central Florida–Orlando.

McDonald, Mary G. 2005. "Special Issue: Whiteness and Sport." *Sociology of Sport Journal* 22 (September).

Nixon, Howard L. II. 2008. *Sport in a Changing World*. Boulder, CO: Paradigm.

Rhoden, William C. *Forty-Million-Dollar Slaves: The Rise, Fall, and Redemption of the Black Athlete*. New York: Crown.

Segura, Melissa. 2008. "The Latino Athlete Now." *Sports Illustrated* (October 6, 2008): 52–55.

Verducci, Tom. 2003. "Blackout: The African-American Baseball Player Is Vanishing. Does He Have a Future?" *Sports Illustrated* (July 7): 56–66.

PART ELEVEN

Structured Inequality: Sport and Gender

Traditionally, gender role expectations have encouraged girls and women to be passive, gentle, delicate, and submissive. These cultural expectations clashed with those traits often associated with sport, such as assertiveness, competitiveness, physical endurance, ruggedness, and dominance. Thus, young women past puberty were encouraged to bypass sports unless the sport retained the femininity of participants. These "allowable" sports had three characteristics: (1) they were aesthetically pleasing (e.g., ice skating, diving, and gymnastics); (2) they did not involve bodily contact with opponents (e.g., bowling, archery, badminton, volleyball, tennis, golf, swimming, and running; and (3) the action was controlled to protect the athletes from overexertion (e.g., running short races, basketball where the offense and defense did not cross half-court).

In effect, these traditional expectations for the sexes denied women equal access to opportunities, not only to sports participation but also to college and to various occupations. Obviously, girls were discriminated against in schools by woefully inadequate facilities—compare the "girls' gym" with the "boys' gym" in any school—and in the budgets. The consequences of sexual discrimination in sport were that: (1) the femininity of those who defied the cultural expectations was often questioned, giving them marginal status; (2) approximately one-half of the population was denied the benefits of sports participation; (3) young women learned their "proper" societal role (i.e., to be on the sidelines supporting men who do the actual achieving); and (4) women were denied a major source of college scholarships.

Currently, quite rapid changes are occurring. Unquestionably, the greatest change in contemporary sport is the dramatic increase in and general acceptance of sports participation by women. These swift changes have occurred for several related reasons. Most prominent is the societal-wide women's movement that has gained increasing momentum since the mid-1960s. Because of the consciousness raising resulting from the movement and the organized efforts to break down the cultural tyranny of gender roles, court cases were initiated to end sexual discrimination in a number of areas. In athletics, legal suits were successfully brought against various school districts, universities, and even the Little League.

In 1972 Congress passed Title IX of the Education Amendments Act. The essence of this law, which has had the greatest single impact on the move toward sexual equality in all aspects of schools, is: "No person in the United States shall, on the basis of sex, be excluded from taking part in, be denied the benefits of, or be subjected to discrimination in any educational program or activity receiving federal financial assistance."

Although the passage of Title IX and other pressures have led to massive changes, discrimination continues. The first chapter, by D. Stanley Eitzen, provides an overview of gender issues in sport. The second, by John Cheslock, using data compiled by the Women's Sports Foundation, examines current trends in participation by gender in college sports. The final chapter, by sociologist Michael A. Messner, answers the question "What is the relationship between participation in organized sports and a young male's developing sense of himself as a success or failure?"

32

Sport and Gender

D. Stanley Eitzen

Sport in its organization, procedures, and operation serves to promote traditional gender roles, thus keeping order (order, however, is not always positive). Sport advances male hegemony in practice and ideology by legitimating a certain dominant version of social reality. From early childhood games to professional sports, the sports experience is "gendered." Boys are expected to participate in sports, to be aggressive, to be physically tough, to take risks, and to accept pain. Thus sport, especially aggressive physical contact sport, is expected for boys and men but not for girls and women. These expectations reproduce male domination in society.[1]

Lois Bryson has argued that sport reproduces patriarchal relations through four minimalizing processes: definition, direct control, ignoring, and trivialization.[2] "When we take a critical look at dominant sport forms in many societies around the world, we see that they often involve actions highlighting masculine virility, power, and toughness—the attributes associated with dominant ideas about masculinity in those societies."[3] Male standards are applied to female performance, ensuring female inferiority and even deviance. As sport sociologist Paul Willis has observed, "[The ideal description of sport] is a male description concerning males. Where women become at all visible, then the terms of reference change. There is a very important thread in popular consciousness which sees the very presence of women in sport as bizarre."[4]

Source: D. Stanley Eitzen, *Fair and Foul: Beyond the Myths and Paradoxes of Sport,* 2nd ed. (Lanham, MD: Rowman and Littlefield, 2003), excerpts from pp. 81–83, 97–100.

Sports participation is expected for men. Sport is strongly associated with male identity and popularity. For women, however, the situation is entirely different. As Willis has stated, "Instead of confirming her identity, [sports] success can threaten her with a foreign male identity.... The female athlete lives through a severe contradiction. To succeed as an athlete can be to fail as a woman, because she has, in certain profound symbolic ways, become a man."[5] Superior women athletes are suspect because strength and athletic skill are accepted as "masculine" traits.

Women's sport is minimized when it is controlled by men. This is demonstrated in the gender composition of leadership positions on the International Olympic Committee, various international and national sports bodies, the National Collegiate Athletic Association, and the administrative and coaching roles in schools and professional leagues.

Women in sport are minimized (and men maximized) when women's activities are ignored. The mass media in the United States have tended to overlook women's sports. When they are reported, the stories, photographs, and commentary tend to reinforce gender role stereotypes. Women's sports are also ignored when cities and schools disproportionately spend enormous amounts on men's sports. As writer Mariah Burton Nelson has noted,

> We live in a country in which the manly sports culture is so pervasive we may fail to recognize the symbolic messages we all receive about men, women, love, sex, and power. We need to take sports seriously—not the scores or the statistics, but the process. Not to focus on who wins, but on who's losing. Who loses when a community spends millions of dollars in tax revenue to construct a new stadium and only men get to play in it, and only men get to work there? Who loses when football and baseball so dominate the public discourse that they eclipse all mention of female volleyball players, gymnasts, basketball players, and swimmers?[6]

Women are also minimized when they are trivialized in sport. As noted earlier, the media framing of the female athlete reinforces gender stereotypes. Considering photographs of women and men athletes, scholar Margaret Carlisle Duncan[7] found that these images emphasized gender differences: (1) female athletes who are sexy and glamorous are most common; (2) female athletes are often photographed in sexual poses; (3) in the framing of photos, male athletes are more likely to be photographed in dominant positions and female athletes in submissive positions; (4) camera angles typically focus up to male athletes and focus down on female athletes; and (5) female athletes are more likely to be shown displaying emotions. As sociologist Michael A. Messner has argued, "The choices, the filtering, the entire mediation of the sporting event, is based upon invisible, taken-for-granted assumptions and values of dominant social groups, as such the presentation of the event tends to support corporate, white, and male-dominant ideologies."[8]

Another example of the trivialization of women's sports activities is the naming of their teams. A study comparing the unifying symbols of women's and men's teams found that more than half of colleges and universities in the United States employ names, mascots, and/or logos that demean and derogate women's teams.[9] Some schools name their men's teams the Wildcats and their women's teams the Wildkittens. Or the men are the Rams and the women, the Lady Rams (an oxymoron if there ever was one). Thus the naming of women's teams tends to define women athletes and women's athletic programs as second class and trivial.

The secondary treatment of women in sport that defines and characterizes them as inferior also defines them, by extension, as less capable than men in many other areas of life. Scholar Lois Bryson asserts that "each cultural message about sport is a dual one, celebrating the dominant at the same time as inferiorizing the 'other,'"[10] in this case, celebrating the masculine and inferiorizing the feminine.

Although this dominant ideology is perpetuated in many ways, it is also challenged and contested with some success in all institutional areas, including sport.[11] Pioneering women have broken down the "men-only" rules in such traditionally unlikely areas as automobile racing (Janet Guthrie became the first woman to race in the Indianapolis 500 in 1977; Danica Patrick became the first woman in history to win an Indy-style race in 2008), men's locker rooms (women sportswriters now routinely conduct interviews there), high school wrestling against boys, and refereeing men's games (in 1997 the NBA hired two women, Dee Kantner and Violet Palmer, as referees, the first women to officiate in a major professional all-male sports league). In 2002, we witnessed the first woman to referee in the NCAA's men's basketball championship tournament.

The traditional conception of femininity as passive and helpless is challenged today by the fit, athletic, and even muscular appearance of women athletes. Women now engage in pumping iron to sculpt their bodies toward a new standard of femininity that combines beauty with taut, developed muscles. Similarly, women are now rejecting traditional notions of femininity by pushing the limits in endurance events in running, cycling, swimming, and mountain climbing and by engaging freely in strength sports such as bodybuilding, weight lifting, and throwing weights.

GENDER INEQUITIES

Until the 1970s high school, college, and professional sports in the United States were, with few exceptions, male activities. The barriers were breached finally by court cases (for example, a legal decision to open Little League baseball to girls) and by federal legislation (Title IX in 1972). With these changes, sports opportunities for girls and women have increased greatly. "However, prejudices are not altered by courts and legislation, and culturally conditioned responses to gender ideology are ubiquitous and resistant to sudden changes. Therefore, laws may force compliance in equality of opportunity for females in the world of sport, but inequities in sport continue, albeit in more subtle and insidious forms, as has been the case with racism."[12] Major gender inequities remain, despite the tremendous gains generated by Title IX. An assessment of the situation at big-time schools discloses the following disparities by gender:

- Viewed as a group, only 17.7 percent of head coaches of men's and women's teams were women. Fewer than 2 percent of coaching positions in men's programs are held by women, and most of those were coaches of combined men's and women's teams in cross-country, tennis, and swimming.
- Men outnumber women (57 percent to 42.4 percent) as coaches of women's teams.
- Only 18.6 percent of women's intercollegiate programs are administered by women.
- At the Division IA level, women hold less than 8 percent of athletic director positions. There are more female college presidents of Division IA schools than there are female athletic directors.
- The higher the level of competition and the better paying the positions, the more likely men will be head coaches and top administrators of women's teams and programs.
- African American women, facing the double jeopardy of minority race and gender, are underrepresented among coaches and administrators.
- Women's collegiate sports are controlled by the NCAA, a male-dominated organization.
- In 2007, although female students comprised 57 percent of the college student population, female athletes received only 43 percent of participation opportunities. Despite being a majority of college students, women received only 45 percent of the athletic scholarships.
- In 2007 Division IA, head coaches for woen's teams received an average salary of $850,400 while head coaches for men's teams average $1,783,100, a difference of $932,700.
- It is not uncommon for a school with a big-time football program to spend *twice as much on its football team as it spent on all women's sports.*[13]

At the professional level, women have many fewer opportunities than men, and the monetary rewards are considerably less (with the exceptions of ice skating and women's tennis). In professional basketball, for example, there are more teams for men within the United States and abroad. Moreover, the pay is highly skewed with top men receiving in excess of $20 million a year, while only a few women superstars approach $100,000. The women's professional basketball league is the WNBA, operating under the auspices of the NBA. In 2007, women with four or more years of experience in the WNBA received $49,134, and a maximum salary was $93,000 (with few endorsement opportunities. Compare this with the average player salary in excess of $5 million in the NBA, with the highest paid, Shaquile O'Neal, making $200,000 in salary and another $15 million in endorsements. The prize money for PGA tournaments (for male professional golfers) is about five times more than for women professionals playing in the LPGA (the L stands for Ladies, by the way, which connotes elegance, a decidedly unathletic trait). Very few women have been able to make it in automobile racing. Most significant, while men have the chance for careers as relatively well-paid professional athletes in a number of sports, women do not have these opportunities in sports such as baseball, hockey, and football.

For ancillary positions in sport, women again have many fewer opportunities than men. Some examples of positions where women are disproportionately underrepresented include team physicians, head trainers, referees and umpires, radio and television announcing positions, and sports information directors.

Historically, the International Olympic Committee (IOC) has restricted the number and type of women's sports that were part of the Olympic Games. For example, there were no women athletes at the 1896 Games, and only 14 percent of the athletes in the 1968 Summer Games were women. By 2000 women had gained in participation but were still only 38 percent of the athletes at the Games in Sydney (there were 168 men's events, 120 women's events, and 12 events where women and men competed). The gender composition of the IOC was exclusively male until the 1980s and now only about 10 percent of this powerful administrative body is women. Between 1990 and 1996, forty of the forty-two new appointments went to men.[14] The U.S. Olympic Committee is better represented by women, but they are still a decided minority.

The data show that women in sport are second-class citizens. Women have fewer sports participation and career opportunities, fewer resources devoted to their programs, and they are given less media attention than men's sports. Added to this is the discrediting of women athletes by trivializing or marginalizing their accomplishments, focusing on their sexiness or the possibility of their deviant sexuality (the whisper charge of lesbianism). Sport sociologist Mary Jo Kane puts it this way:

> Sport is one of the most powerful institutions in this culture, because of its status and economic and political clout. There's a great deal at stake in sports participation, and the group that has monopolized sport doesn't want to give that up. They know that the best way to maintain control is to trivialize or marginalize their accomplishments.... After all, if females are great athletes, then it's harder to say as a society that they shouldn't get press coverage, money, scholarships. But if they are portrayed as people who do sports in their spare time, or as merely pretty girls, it's much easier to deny them access and to maintain the status quo.... [The University of Minnesota's Tucker Center for Research on Girls and Women in Sport] 1998 research found that because of the notion that sport belongs to men, there remain deep-seated and persistent barriers to girls in sport: gender stereotyping, sexism, and homophobia.[15]

NOTES

1. Michael A. Messner, *Taking the Field: Women, Men, and Sports* (Minneapolis: University of Minnesota Press, 2002).

2. Lois Bryson, "Sport and the Maintenance of Masculine Hegemony," *Women's Studies International Forum* 10 (1987): 349–360.

3. Jay J. Coakley, *Sport in Society: Issues and Controversies,* 7th ed. (New York: McGraw-Hill, 2001), 227.

4. Paul Willis, "Women in Sport Ideology," in Jennifer Hargreaves, ed., *Sport, Culture, and Ideology*, (London: Routledge and Kegan Paul, 1982), 121.

5. Willis, "Women in Sport Ideology," 123.

6. Mariah Burton Nelson, *The Stronger Women Get, the More Men Love Football: Sexism and the American Culture of Sports* (New York: Harcourt Brace, 1994), 8.

7. Margaret Carlisle Duncan, "Sports Photographs and Sexual Difference: Images of Women and Men in the 1984 and 1988 Olympic Games," *Sociology of Sport Journal* 7 (March 1990): 22–43.

8. Michael A. Messner, "Sports and Male Domination," 204–205.

9. D. Stanley Eitzen and Maxine Baca Zinn, "The De-Athleticization of Women: The Naming and Gender Marking of Collegiate Sport Teams," *Sociology of Sport Journal* 6 (1989): 362–370.

10. Bryson, "Sport," 349–360.

11. Messner, "Sports and Male Domination."

12. D. Stanley Eitzen and George H. Sage, *Sociology of North American Sport,* 7th ed. (New York: McGraw-Hill, 2002), 282.

13. R. Vivian Acosta and Linda J. Carpenter, *Women in Intercollegiate Sport: A Longitudinal Study—Twenty-Nine Year Update* (West Brookfield, MA: Carpenter/Acosta, 2006), available at http://webpages.charter.net/womeninsport; Donna Lopiano, "Pay Inequity in Athletics," Women's Sports Foundation, 2007, available at http://www.womenssportsfoundation.org/cgi-bin/iowa/issues/article/html?record=1136.

14. Jay J. Coakley, *Sport in Society: Issues and Controversies,* 7th ed. (New York: McGraw-Hill, 2001), 214, 219.

15. Mary Jo Kane, "Can Women Save Sports? An Interview by Lynette Lamb," *Utne Reader* 97 (January–February 2000): 57.

33

Who's Playing College Sports?
Trends in Participation

John Cheslock

EXECUTIVE SUMMARY

The 35th anniversary of Title IX is an excellent time to consider men's and women's participation in intercollegiate athletics. This study provides the most accurate and comprehensive examination of participation trends to date. We analyze data from almost every higher education institution in the country and utilize data and methods that are free of the shortcomings present in previous research on this subject. A 10-year NCAA sample containing 738 NCAA colleges and universities is examined over the 1995–1996 to 2004–2005 period. In addition, a complete four-year sample containing 1,895 higher education institutions is examined over the 2001–2002 to 2004–2005 period.

The results demonstrate that women continue to be significantly underrepresented among college athletes. At the average higher education institution, the female share of undergraduates is 55.8 percent while the female share of athletes is 41.7 percent. Women did enjoy a substantial increase in participation opportunities in the late 1990s, but this progress slowed considerably in the early 2000s. In fact, the increase in women's participation levels was roughly equal to the increase in men's participation levels between 2001–2002 and 2004–2005. Progress towards more equitable participation numbers for men and women has stalled.

Source: Cheslock, J., 2007, *Who's Playing College Sports? Trends in Participation* (East Meadow, NY: Women's Sports Foundation), pp. 3–4.

Debates over Title IX have focused more on maintaining the numerous athletic opportunities that men have historically enjoyed rather than ensuring that women gain access to the opportunities they have been historically denied. In other words, the significant underrepresentation of women among college athletes often receives relatively little attention. Instead, the debate focuses on whether or not men have maintained their high participation levels, and many claim that men's athletic participation has seriously declined over time. The results of this study clearly refute this claim and instead indicate small overall increases in men's participation in intercollegiate athletics. Men's participation levels grew slightly between 1995–1996 and 2001–2002, a period containing the *Cohen vs. Brown* decision that encouraged colleges and universities to take Title IX more seriously. Furthermore, men's participation levels continued to increase between 2001–2002 and 2004–2005, a moment of tough financial times for many higher education institutions.

This report demonstrates the importance of providing a complete portrait of participation trends. Examination of specific sports or sets of institutions can produce misleading results. For example, participation in men's wrestling and tennis declined substantially over time, but other men's sports (football, baseball, lacrosse and soccer) experienced much larger gains. While it is true that men's participation levels fell slightly among Division I-A institutions, no other set of institutions experienced declines and many saw their men's participation levels increase.

MAJOR FINDINGS

1. Women's athletic participation levels substantially increased during the late 1990s, but this growth slowed considerably in the early 2000s.
   - For the 10-year/738 NCAA institutions sample, female participation grew by almost 26,000 athletes between 1995–96 and 2004–05, but only 15 percent of this increase came during the 2001–02 to 2004–05 period.
   - For the complete four-year/1,895 institutions sample, female participation grew by 11,000 athletes between 2001–02 and 2004–05, an increase similar to that experienced by men.
2. Women's participation still lags far behind men's participation levels.
   - For the average higher education institution in the complete four-year/1,895 institutions sample, the female share of undergraduate enrollment in 2004–05 was 55.8 percent while the female share of athletes was only 41.7 percent.
   - For the complete four-year/1,895 institutions sample, the reported number of men's participants in 2004–05 was 291,797, while the corresponding number for women was 205,492. In combination, these figures demonstrate that as of 2004–05, only 41 percent of athletic participants were women and 151,149 female athletes would need to have been added (assuming no reduction in male participants) to reach a share of 55 percent, the female share of full-time undergraduates in the fall of 2004.

3. Men's overall athletic participation levels increased over time.
   - For the 10-year/738 NCAA institutions sample, male participation grew by around 7,000 athletes between 1995–96 and 2004–05, an average of almost 10 athletes per institution.
   - For the complete four-year/1,895 institutions sample, male participation grew by almost 10,000 athletes between 2001–02 and 2004–05, an average of slightly over five athletes per institution.
4. While a few men's sports suffered substantial declines, a larger number of men's sports enjoyed increases that far outnumbered those losses.
   - For the 10-year/738 NCAA institutions sample, only tennis (–678) and wrestling (–488) experienced declines of more than 80 athletes between 1995–96 and 2004–05. In contrast, four men sports grew by much larger amounts: football grew by more than 4,000 participants while baseball (+1,561), lacrosse (+1,091) and soccer (+758) also rose sharply.
   - For the complete four-year/1,895 institutions sample, only two men's sports (tennis and volleyball) experienced declines of more than 60 athletes between 2001–02 and 2004–05, while 12 men's sports had increases of at least that amount. Men's football, baseball, lacrosse and soccer again enjoyed the largest increases.
   - For some of the growing men's sports (especially football),the participation increases were primarily due to growth in the average roster size. As a result, the total number of men's teams essentially remained the same over the period of study.
5. The only subset of higher education institutions that experienced declines in men's participation levels was NCAA Division I-A schools, the institutions that spend the most on intercollegiate athletics.
   - For the 10-year/738 NCAA institutions sample between 1995–96 and 2004–05, men's participation grew in Divisions II and III, remained mostly the same in Divisions I-AA and I-AAA, and fell only in Division I-A.
   - For the complete four-year/1,895 institutions sample between 2001–02 and 2004–05, all six of the major intercollegiate athletic organizations (NCAA, NAIA, NCCAA, NJCAA, COA, NWAAC) experienced overall increases in men's participation levels.

POLICY IMPLICATIONS

Many of the arguments against Title IX in intercollegiate sports are not supported by the data presented in this comprehensive report. The findings in this study have implications for the ways that policymakers think about how Title IX has shaped the lives and opportunities of female and male athletes on American campuses.

1. Further weakening of Title IX, as represented by the March 2005 policy clarification, is unjustified.
2. Title IX does not need to be reformed to stop large overall decreases in men's

athletic participation because such decreases have not occurred.

3. The debate over Title IX should not be based on the experience of a few individual sports.

4. Efforts to analyze and stem reductions in men's sports should focus on Division I-A institutions, the only set of institutions that experienced declines. Future attempts to explain the declines of men's athletic participation at Division I-A institutions should consider institutional policies and practices associated with the "arms race" in athletic spending.

34

The Meaning of Success

The Athletic Experience and the Development of Male Identity

Michael A. Messner

Vince Lombardi supposedly said, "Winning isn't everything; it's the only thing," and I couldn't agree more. There's nothing like being number one.

—Joe Montana

The big-name athletes will get considerable financial and social remuneration for their athletic efforts. But what of the others, the 99% who fail? Most will fall short of their dreams of a lucrative professional contract. The great majority of athletes, then, will likely suffer disappointment, underemployment, anxiety, or perhaps even serious mental disorders.

—Donald Harris and D. Stanley Eitzen

What is the relationship between participation in organized sports and a young male's developing sense of himself as a success or failure? And what is the consequent impact on his self-image and his ability to engage in intimate relationships with others? Through the late 1960s, it was almost universally accepted that "sports builds character" and that "a winner in sports will be a winner in life." Consequently, some liberal feminists argued that since participation in organized competitive sports has served as a major source of socialization for males' successful participation in the public world, girls and young women should have equal access to sports. Lever, for instance, concluded that if women were ever going to be able to develop the proper competitive values and orientations toward work and success, it was incumbent on them to participate in sports.[1]

In the 1970s and 1980s, these uncritical orientations toward sports have been questioned, and the "sports builds character" formula has been found wanting. Sabo points out that the vast majority of research does *not* support the contention that success in sports translates into "work success" or "happiness" in one's personal life.[2] In fact, a great deal of evidence suggests that the contrary is true. Recent critical analyses of success and failure in sports have usually started from assumptions similar to those of Sennett and Cobb and of Rubin:[3] the disjuncture between the *ideology* of success (the Lombardian Ethic) and the socially structured *reality* that most do not "succeed" brings about widespread feelings of failure, lowered self-images, and problems with interpersonal relationships.[4] The most common argument seems to be that the highly competitive world of sports is an exaggerated reflection of advanced industrial capitalism. Within any hierarchy, one can actually work very hard and achieve a lot, yet still be defined (and perceive oneself) as less than successful. Very few people ever reach the mythical "top," but those who do are made ultravisible through the media.[5] It is tempting to view this system as a "structure of failure" because, given the definition of *success,* the system is virtually rigged to bring about the failure of the vast majority of participants. Furthermore, given the dominant values, the participants are apt to blame themselves for their "failure." Schafer argues that the result of this discontinuity between sports values/ideology and reality is a "widespread conditional self-worth" for young athletes.[6] And as Edwards has pointed out, this problem can be even more acute for black athletes, who are disproportionately channeled into sports, yet have no "social safety net" to fall back on after "failure" in sports.

Both the traditional "sports builds character" and the more recent "sports breeds failures" formulas have a common pitfall: Each employs socialization theory in an often simplistic and mechanistic way. Boys are viewed largely as "blank slates" onto which the sports experience imprints values, appropriate "sex-role scripts," and orientations toward self and the world. What is usually not taken into account is the fact that boys (and girls) come to the sports experience with an *already gendered* identity that colors their early motivations and perceptions of the meaning of games and sports. As Gilligan points out, observations of young children's game-playing show that girls bring to the activity a more pragmatic and flexible orientation toward the rules—they are more prone to make exceptions and innovations in the middle of the game in order to make the game more "fair" and maintain relationships with others.[7] Boys tend to have a more firm, even inflexible orientation to the rules of a game—they are less willing to change or alter rules in the middle of the game; to them, the rules are what protects any "fairness." This observation has profound implications for sociological research on sports and gender: The question should not be *simply* "how does sports participation affect boys [or girls]?" but should add "what is it about a developing sense of male identity that *attracts* males to sports in the first place? And how does this socially constructed male identity develop and change as it interacts with the structure and values of the sports world?" In addition to being a social-psychological question, this is also a *historical* question: Since men have not at all times and places related to sports the way they do at present, it is important to explore just what kinds of men exist today. What are their needs, problems, and dreams? How do these men relate to the society they live in? And how do organized sports fit into this picture?

THE "PROBLEM OF MASCULINITY" AND ORGANIZED SPORTS

In the first two decades of this century, men feared that the closing of the frontier, along with changes in the workplace, the family, and the schools, was having a "feminizing" influence on society.[8] One result of the anxiety men felt was the creation of the Boy Scouts of America as a separate sphere of social life where "true manliness" could be instilled in boys *by men.*[9] The rapid rise of organized sports in roughly the same era can be attributed largely to the same phenomenon. As socioeconomic and familial changes continue to erode the traditional bases of male identity and privilege, sports became an increasingly important cultural expression of traditional male values— organized sports became a "primary masculinity-validating experience."[10]

In the post–World War II era, the bureaucratization and rationalization of work, along with the decline of the family wage and women's gradual movement into the labor force, have further undermined the "breadwinner role" as a basis for male identity, thus resulting in a "problem of masculinity" and a "defensive inse-curity" among men.[11] As Mills put it, the ethic of success in postwar America "has become less widespread as fact, more confused as image, often dubious as motive, and soured as a way of life. [Yet] there are still compulsions to struggle, to 'amount to something.'"[12]

How have men expressed this need to "amount to something" within a social context that seems to deny them the opportunities to do so? Again, organized sports play an important role. Both on a personal-existential level for athletes and on a symbolic-ideological level for spectators and fans, sports have become one of the "last bastions" of traditional male ideas of success, of male power and superiority over—and separation from—the perceived "feminization" of society. It is likely that the rise of football as "America's number-one game" is largely the result of the comforting clarity it provides between the polarities of traditional male power, strength, and violence and the contemporary fears of social feminization.

But these historical explanations for the increased importance of sports, despite their validity, beg some important questions: Why do men fear the (real or imagined) "feminization" of their world? Why do men appear to need a separate male sphere of life? Why do organized sports appear to be such an attractive means of express-ing these needs? Are males simply "socialized" to dominate women and to compete with other men for status, or are they seeking (perhaps unconsciously) something more fundamental? Just what is it that men really *want*? To begin to answer these questions it is necessary to listen to athletes' voices and examine their lives with a social-psychological perspective.

Daniel Levinson's concept of the "individual life structure" is a useful place to begin to construct a gestalt of the life of the athlete.[13] Levinson demonstrates that as males develop and interact with their world, they continue to change throughout their lives. A common theme during developmental periods is the process of individuation, the struggle to separate, to "decide where he stops and where the world begins." "In successive periods of development, as this process goes on, the person forms a clearer boundary between self and world.... Greater individuation allows him to be more separate from the world, to be more independent and self-generating. But it also gives him the confidence and understanding to have more intense attachments in the world and to feel more fully a part of it."[14]

This dynamic of separation and attachment provides a valuable social-psychological framework for examining the experiences and problems faced by the athlete as he gropes for and redefines success throughout his life course. In what follows, Levinson's framework is utilized to analyze the lives of 30 former athletes interviewed between 1983 and 1984. Their *interactions* with sports are examined in terms of their initial boyhood attraction to sports; how notions of success in sports connect with a developing sense of male identity; and how self-images, relationships to work and other people, change and develop after the sports career ends.

BOYHOOD: THE PROMISE OF SPORTS

Given how very few athletes actually "make it" through sports, how can the intensity with which millions of boys and young men throw themselves into athletics be explained? Are they simply pushed, socialized, or even *duped* into putting so much emphasis on athletic success? It is important here to examine just what it is that young males hope to get out of the athletic experience. And in terms of *identity*, it is crucial to examine the ways in which the structure and experience of sports activity meet the developmental needs of young males. The story of Willy Rios sheds light on what these needs are. Rios was born in Mexico and moved to the United States at a fairly young age. He never knew his father, and his mother died when he was only 9 years old. Suddenly he felt rootless, and at this time he threw himself into sports, but his initial motivations do not appear to be based upon a need to compete and win. "Actually, what I think sports did for me is it brought me into kind of an instant family. By being on a Little League team, or even just playing with all kinds of different kids in the neighborhood, it brought what I really wanted, which was some kind of closeness."

Similar statements from other men suggest that a fundamental motivational factor behind many young males' sports strivings is a need for connection, "closeness" with others. But why do so many boys see *sports* as an attractive means of establishing connection with others? Chodorow argues that the process of developing a gender identity yields insecurity and ambivalence in males.[15] Males develop "rigid ego boundaries" that ensure separation from others, yet they retain a basic human need for closeness and intimacy with others. The young male, who both seeks and fears attachment with others, thus finds the rulebound structure of games and sports to be a psychologically "safe" place in which he can get (nonintimate) connection with others within a context that maintains clear boundaries, distance, and separation from others. At least for the boy who has some early successes in sports, some of these ambivalent needs can be met, for a time. But there is a catch: For Willy Rios, it was only after he learned that he would get attention (a certain kind of connection) from other people for being a good athlete—indeed, that this attention was *contingent on* his *being good*—that narrow definitions of success, based on performance and winning, became important to him. It was years before he realized that no matter how well he performed, how successful he became, he would not get the closeness that he craved through sports. "It got to be a product in high school. Before, it was just fun, and having acceptance, you know. Yet I had to work for my acceptance in high school that way, just being a jock. So it wasn't fun any more. But it was my self-identity, being a good ballplayer. I was realizing that whatever you excel in, you put out in front of you. Bring it out. Show it. And that's what I did. That was my protection.... It was rotten in high school, really."

This conscious striving for successful achievement becomes the primary means through which the young athlete seeks connections with other people. But the irony of the situation, for so many boys and young men like Willy Rios, is that the athletes are seeking to get something from their success in sports that sports cannot deliver—and the *pressure* that they end up putting on themselves to achieve that success ends up stripping them of the ability to receive the one major thing that sports really *does* have to offer: fun.

ADOLESCENCE: YOU'RE ONLY AS GOOD AS YOUR LAST GAME

Adolescence is probably the period of greatest insecurity in the life course, the time when the young male becomes most vulnerable to peer expectation, pressures, and judgments. None of the men interviewed for this study, regardless of their social class or ethnicity, seemed fully able to "turn a deaf ear to the crowd" during their athletic careers. The crowd, which may include immediate family, friends, peers, teammates, as well as the more anonymous fans and media, appears to be a crucially important part of the process of establishing and maintaining the self-images of young athletes. By the time they were in high school, most of the men interviewed for this study had found sports to be a primary means through which to establish a sense of manhood in the world. Especially if they were good athletes, the expectations of the crowd became very powerful and were internalized (and often *magnified*) within the young man's own expectations. As one man stated, by the time he was in high school, "it was *expected* of me to do well in all of my contests—I mean by my coach and my peers, and my family. So I in turn expected to do well, and if I didn't do well, then I'd be very disappointed."

When so much is tied to your performance, the dictum that "you are only as good as your last game" is a powerful judgment. It means that the young man must continually prove, achieve, and then *re*prove, and *re*achieve his status. As a result, many young athletes learn to seek and *need* the appreciation of the crowd to feel that they are worthy human beings. But the internalized values of masculinity along with the insecure nature of the sports world mean that the young man does *not* need the crowd to feel *bad* about himself. In fact, if one is insecure enough, even "success" and the compliments and attention of other people can come to feel hollow and meaningless. For instance, 48-year-old Russ Ellis in his youth shared the basic sense of insecurity common to all young males, and in his case it was probably compounded by his status as a poor black male and an insecure family life. Athletics emerged early in his life as the primary arena in which he and his male peers competed to establish a sense of self in the world. For Ellis, his small physical stature made it difficult to compete successfully in most sports, thus feeding his insecurity—he just never felt as though he belonged with "the big boys." Eventually, though, he became a top middle-distance runner. In high school, however: "Something began to happen there that later plagued me quite a bit. I started doing very well and winning lots of races and by the time the year was over, it was no longer a question for me of *placing*, but *winning*. That attitude really destroyed me ultimately. I would get into the blocks with worries that I wouldn't do well—the regular stomach problems—so I'd often run much less well than my abilities—that is, say, I'd take second or third."

Interestingly, his nervousness, fears, and anxieties did not seem to be visible to "the crowd": "I know in high school, certainly, they saw me as confident and ready to run. No one assumed I could be beaten, which fascinated me, because I had never been good at understanding how I was taken in other people's minds—maybe because I spent so much time inventing myself in their regard in my own mind. I was projecting my fear fantasies on them and taking them for reality."

In 1956 Ellis surprised everyone by taking second place in a world-class field of quarter-milers. But the fact that they ran the fastest time in the world, 46.5, seemed only to "up the ante," to increase the pressures on Ellis, then in college at UCLA.

> Up to that point I had been a nice zippy kid who did good, got into the *Daily Bruin* a lot, and was well-known on campus. But now an event would come up and the papers would say, "Ellis to face so-and-so." So rather than my being in the race, I *was* the race, as far as the press was concerned. And that put a lot of pressure on me that I never learned to handle. What I did was to internalize it, and then I'd sit there and fret and lose sleep, and focus more on not winning than on how I was doing. And in general, I didn't do badly—like one year in the NCAA's I took fourth—you know, in the *national finals*. But I was focused on winning. You know, later on, people would say, "Oh wow, you took fourth in the NCAA?—you were *that good?*" Whereas I thought of these things as *failures*, you know?

Finally, Ellis's years of training, hopes, and fears came to a head at the 1956 Olympic trials, where he failed to qualify, finishing fifth. A rival whom he used to defeat routinely won the event in the Melbourne Olympics as Ellis watched on television. "That killed me. Destroyed me.... I had the experience many times after that of digging down and finding that there was infinitely more down there than I ever got—I mean, I know that more than I know anything else. Sometimes I would really feel like an eagle, running. Sometimes in practice at UCLA running was just exactly like flying—and if I could have carried that attitude into events, I would have done much better. But instead, I'd worry. Yeah, I'd worry myself sick."

As suggested earlier, young males like Russ Ellis are "set up" for disappointment, or worse, by the disjuncture between the narrow Lombardian definition of success in the sports world and the reality that very few ever actually reach the top. The athlete's sense of identity established through sports is therefore insecure and problematic, *not simply* because of the high probability of "failure," but also because *success* in the sports world involves the development of a personality that *amplifies* many of the most ambivalent and destructive traits of traditional masculinity. Within the hierarchical world of sports, which in many ways mirrors the capitalist economy, one learns that if he is to survive and avoid being pushed off the ever-narrowing pyramid of success, he must develop certain kinds of relationships—to himself, to his body, to other people, and to the sport itself. In short, the successful athlete must develop a highly goal-oriented personality that encourages him to view his body as a tool, a machine, or even a weapon utilized to defeat an objectified opponent. He is likely to have difficulty establishing intimate and lasting friendships with other males because of low self-disclosure, homophobia, and cut-throat competition. And he is likely to view his public image as a "success" as far more basic and fundamental than any of his interpersonal relationships.

For most of the men interviewed, the quest for success was not the grim task it was for Russ Ellis. Most men did seem to get, at least for a time, a sense of identity (and even some happiness) out of their athletic accomplishments. The attention of the crowd, for many, affirmed their existence as males and was thus a clear motivating force. Gary Affonso, now 42 years old and a high school coach, explained that when he was in high school, he had an "intense desire to practice and compete." "I used to practice the high jump by myself for hours at a time—only got up to 5'3"—scissor! [*Laughs.*] But I think part of it was, the track itself was in view of some of the classrooms, and so as I think back now, maybe I did it for the attention, to be seen. In my freshman year, I chipped my two front teeth in a football game, and after that I always had a gold tooth, and I was always self-conscious about that. Plus I had my glasses, you know. I felt a little conspicuous." This simultaneous shyness, self-consciousness, and conspicuousness *along with* the strongly felt need for attention and external validation (attachment) so often characterize athletes' descriptions of themselves in boyhood and adolescence. The crowd, in this context, can act as a distant, and thus nonthreatening, source of attention and validation of self for the insecure male. Russ Ellis's story typifies that what sports seem to *promise* the young male—affirmation of self and connection with others—is likely to be *undermined* by the youth's actual experience in the sports world. The athletic experience also "sets men up" for another serious problem: the end of a career at a very young age.

DISENGAGEMENT TRAUMA:
A CRISIS OF MALE IDENTITY

For some, the end of the athletic career approaches gradually like the unwanted house-guest whose eventual arrival is at least *known* and can be planned for, thus limiting the inevitable inconvenience. For others, the athletic career ends with the shocking suddenness of a violent thunderclap that rudely awakens one from a pleasant dream. But whether it comes gradually or suddenly, the end of the playing career represents the termination of what has often become the *central aspect* of a young male's individual life structure, thus initiating change and transition in the life course.

Previous research on the disengagement crises faced by many retiring athletes has focused on the health, occupational, and financial problems frequently faced by retiring professionals.[16] These problems are especially severe for retiring black athletes, who often have inadequate educational backgrounds and few opportunities within the sports world for media or coaching jobs.[17] But even for those retiring athletes who avoid the pitfalls of financial and occupational crises, substance abuse, obesity, and ill health, the end of the playing career usually involves a crisis of identity. This identity crisis is probably most acute for retiring *professional* athletes, whose careers are coming to an end right at an age when most men's careers are beginning to take off. As retired professional football player Marvin Upshaw stated, "You find yourself just scrambled. You don't know which way to go. Your light, as far as you're concerned, has been turned out. You miss the roar of the crowd. Once you've heard it, you can't get away from it. There's an empty feeling—you feel everything you wanted is gone. All of a sudden you wake up and you find yourself 29, 35 years old, you know, and the one thing that has been the major part of your life is gone. It's gone."

High school and college athletes also face serious and often painful adjustment periods when their career ends. Twenty-six-year-old Dave Joki had been a good high school basketball player, and had played a lot of ball in college. When interviewed, he was right in the middle of a confusing crisis of identity, closely related to his recent disengagement from viewing himself as an athlete.

> These past few months I've been trying a lot of different things, thinking about different careers, things to do. There's been quite a bit of stumbling—and I think that part of my tenuousness about committing myself to any one thing is I'm not sure I'm gonna get strokes if I go that way. *[Embarrassed, nervous laugh.]* It's scary for me and I stay away from searching for those reasons.... I guess you could say that I'm stumbling in my relationships too—stumbling in all parts of life. *[Laughs.]* I feel like I'm doing a lot but now knowing what I want.

Surely there is nothing unusual about a man in his mid-20s "stumbling" around and looking for direction in his work and his relationships. That is common for men of his age. But for the former athlete, this stumbling is often more confusing and prob-lematic than for the other men precisely because he has lost the one activity through which he had built his sense of identity, however tenuous it may have been. The "strokes" he received from being a good athlete were his major psychological foundation. The interaction between self and other through which the athlete attempts to solidify his identity is akin to what Cooley called "the looking-glass self." If the athletic activity and the crowd can be viewed as the *mirror* into which the athlete gazes and, in Russ Ellis's words, "invents himself," we can begin to appreciate how devastating it can be when that looking-glass is suddenly and permanently *shattered,* leaving the young man alone, isolated, and disconnected. And since young men often feel comfortable exploring close friendships and intimate relationships only *after* they have established their separate work-related (or sports-related) positional identity, relationships with other people are likely to become more problematic than ever during disengagement.

WORK, LOVE, AND MALE IDENTITY AFTER DISENGAGEMENT

Eventually, the former athlete must face reality: At a relatively young age, he has to start over. In the words of retired major-league baseball player Ray Fosse, "Now I gotta get on with the rest of it." How is "the rest of it" likely to take shape for the athlete after his career as a player is over? How do men who are "out of the limelight" for a few years come to define themselves as men? How do they define and redefine success? How do the values and attitudes they learned through sports affect their lives? How do their relationships with friends and family change over time?

Many retired athletes retain a powerful drive to reestablish the important relationship with the crowd that served as the primary basis for their identity for so long. Many men throw themselves wholeheartedly into a new vocation—or a confusing *series* of vocations—in a sometimes pathetic attempt to recapture the "high" of athletic competition as well as the status of the successful athlete in the community. For instance, 35-year-old Jackie Ridgle is experiencing what Daniel Levinson calls a "surge of masculine strivings" common to men in their mid-30s.[18] Once a professional basketball player, Ridgle seems motivated now by a powerful drive to be seen once again as "somebody" in the eyes of the public. When interviewed, he had recently been hired as an assistant college basketball coach, which made him feel like he again had a chance to "be somebody."

> When I say "successful," that means somebody that the public looks up to just as a basketball player. Yet you don't have to be playing basketball. You can be anybody: You can be a senator or a mayor, or any number of things. That's what I call successful. Success is recognition. Sure, I'm always proud of myself. But there's that little goal there that until people respect you, then—[*Snaps fingers.*] Anybody can say, "Oh, I know I'm the greatest thing in the world," but *people* run the world, and when *they* say you're successful, then you *know* you're successful.

Indeed men, especially men in early adulthood, usually define themselves primarily in terms of their position in the public world of work. Feminist literature often criticizes this establishment of male identity in terms of work-success as an expression of male privilege and ego satisfaction that comes at the expense of women and children. There is a great deal of truth to the feminist critique: A man's socially defined need to establish himself as "somebody" in the (mostly) male world of work is often accompanied by his frequent physical absence from home and his emotional distance from his family. Thus, while the man is "out there" establishing his "name" in public, the woman is usually home caring for the day-to-day and moment-to-moment needs of her family (regardless of whether or not she also has a job in the paid labor force). Tragically, only in midlife, when the children have already "left the nest" and the woman is often ready to go out into the public world, do some men discover the importance of connection and intimacy.

Yet the interviews indicate that there is not always such a clean and clear "before-after" polarity in the lives of men between work-success and care-intimacy. The "breadwinner ethic" as a male role *has* most definitely contributed to the perpetuation of male privilege and the subordination and economic dependence of women as mothers and housekeepers. But given the reality of the labor market, where women still make only 62 cents to the male dollar, many men feel very responsible for providing the majority of the income and financial security for their families. For instance, 36-year-old Ray Fosse, whose father left his family when he was quite young, has a very strong sense of commitment and responsibility as a provider of income and stability in his own family.

> I'm working an awful lot these days, and trying not to take time away from my family. A lot of times I'm putting the family to sleep, and working late hours and going to bed and getting up early and so forth. I've tried to tell my family this a lot of times: The work that I'm doing now is gonna make it easier in a few years. That's the reason I'm working now, to get that financial security, and I feel like it's coming very soon ... but, uh, you know, you go a long day and you come home, and it's just not the quality time you'd like to have. And I think when that financial security comes in, then I'm gonna be able to forget about everything.

Jackie Ridgle's words mirror Fosse's. His two jobs and striving to be successful in the public world mean that he has little time to spend with his wife and three children. "I plan to someday. Very seldom do you have enough time to spend with your kids, especially nowadays, so I don't get hung up on that. The wife does sometimes, but as long as I keep a roof over their heads and let 'em know who's who, well, one day they'll respect me. But I can't just get bogged down and take any old job, you know, a filling station job or something. Ah, hell they'll get more respect, my kids for me, right now, than they would if I was somewhere just a regular worker."

Especially for men who have been highly successful athletes (and never have had to learn to "lose gracefully"), the move from sports to work-career as a means of establishing connection and identity in the world is a "natural" transition. Breadwinning becomes a man's socially learned means of seeking attachment, both with his family and, more abstractly, with "society." What is salient (and sometimes tragic) is that the care that a woman gives her family usually puts her into direct daily contact with her family's physical, psychological, and emotional needs. A man's care is usually expressed more abstractly, often in his absence, as his work removes him from day-to-day, moment-to-moment contact with his family.

A man may want, even *crave,* more direct connection with his family, but that connection, and the *time* it takes to establish and maintain it, may cause him to lose the competitive edge he needs to win in the world of work—and that is the arena in which he feels he will ultimately be judged in terms of his success or failure as a man. But it is not simply a matter of *time* spent away from family which is at issue here. As Dizard's research shows clearly, the more "success oriented" a man is, the more "instrumental" his personality will tend to be, thus increasing the psychological and emotional distance between himself and his family.[19]

CHANGING MEANINGS OF SUCCESS IN MIDLIFE

The intense, sometimes obsessive, early adulthood period of striving for work and career success that we see in the lives of Jackie Ridgle and Ray Fosse often begins to change in midlife, when many men experience what Levinson calls "detribalization." Here, the man "becomes more critical of the tribe, the particular groups, institutions, and traditions that have the greatest significance for him, the social matrix to which he is most attached. He is less dependent upon tribal rewards, more questioning of tribal values.... The result of this shift is normally not a marked disengagement from the external world but a greater integration of attachment and separateness."[20]

Detribalization—putting less emphasis on how one is defined by others and becoming more self-motivated and self-generating—is often accompanied by a growing sense of *flawed* or *qualified* success. A man's early adulthood dream of success begins to tarnish, appearing more and more as an illusion. Or, the success that a man *has* achieved begins to appear hollow and meaningless, possibly because it has not delivered the closeness he truly craves. The fading, or the loss, of the dream involves a process of mourning, but, as Levinson points out, it can also be a very liberating process in opening the man up for new experiences, new kinds of relationships, and new dreams.

For instance, Russ Ellis states that a few years ago he experienced a midlife crisis when he came to the realization that "I was never going to be on the cover of *Time.*" His wife had a T-shirt made for him with the message *Dare to Be Average* emblazoned on it.

> And it doesn't really *mean* dare to be average—it means dare to take the pressure off yourself, you know? Dare to be a normal person. It gets a funny reaction from people. I think it hits at that place where somehow we all think that we're going to wind up on the cover of *Time* or something, you know? Do you have that? That some day, somewhere, you're gonna be *great,* and everyone will know, everyone will recognize it? Now, I'd rather be great because I'm *good*—and maybe that'll turn

into something that's acknowledged, but not at the headline level. I'm not racing so much; I'm concerned that my feet are planted on the ground and that I'm good.

[It sounds like you're running now, as opposed to racing?]

I guess—but running and racing have the same goals. *[Laughs, pauses, then speaks more thoughtfully.]* But maybe you're right—that's a wonderful analogy. Pacing myself. Running is more intelligent—more familiarity with your abilities, your patterns of workouts, who you're running against, the nature of the track, your position, alertness. You have more of an internal clock.

Russ Ellis's midlife detribalization—his transition from a "racer" to a runner"— has left him more comfortable with himself, with his abilities and limitations. He has also experienced an expansion of his ability to experience intimacy with a woman. He had never been comfortable with the "typical jock attitude" toward sex and women,

but I generally maintained a performance attitude about sex for a long time, which was not as enjoyable as it became after I learned to be more like what I thought a woman was like. In other words, when I let myself experience my own body, in a delicious and receptive way rather than in a power, overwhelming way. That was wonderful! *[Laughs.]* To experience my body as someone desired and given to. That's one of the better things. I think I only achieved that very profound intimacy that's found between people, really quite extraordinary, quite recently. *[Long pause.]* It's quite something, quite something. And I feel more fully inducted into the human race by knowing about that.

TOWARD A REDEFINITION OF SUCCESS AND MASCULINITY

"A man in America is a failed boy," wrote John Updike in 1960. Indeed, Updike's ex-athlete Rabbit Angstrom's struggles to achieve meaning and identity in midlife reflect a common theme in modern literature. Social scientific research has suggested that the contemporary sense of failure and inadequacy felt by many American males is largely the result of unrealistic and unachievable social definitions of masculinity and success.[21] This research has suggested that there is more to it than that. Contemporary males often feel empty, alienated, isolated, and as failures because the socially learned means through which they seek validation and identity (achievement in the public worlds of sports and work) do not deliver what is actually craved and needed: intimate connection and unity with other human beings. In fact, the lure of sports becomes a sort of trap. For boys who experience early success in sports, the resulting attention they receive becomes a convenient and attractive means of experiencing attachment with other people within a social context that allows the young male to maintain his "firm ego boundaries" and thus his separation from others. But it appears that, more often than not, athletic participation serves only to exacerbate the already problematic, insecure, and ambivalent nature of males' self-images, and thus their ability to establish and maintain close and intimate relationships with other people. Some men, as they reach midlife, eventually achieve a level of individuation—often through a midlife crisis—that leads to a redefinition of success and an expansion of their ability to experience attachment and intimacy.

Men's personal definitions of success often change in midlife, but this research, as well as that done by Farrell and Rosenberg,[22] suggests that only a *portion* of males experience a midlife crisis that results in the man's transcending his instrumental personality in favor of a more affective generativity. The midlife discovery that the achievement game is an unfulfilling rat race can as easily lead to cynical detachment and greater alienation as it can to detribalization and expanded relational capacities. In other words, there is no assurance that Jackie Ridgle, as he ages, will transform himself from a "racer" to a "runner," as Russ Ellis has. Even if he does change in this way, it is likely that he will have missed participating in the formative years of his children's lives.

Thus the fundamental questions facing future examinations of men's lives should focus on building and understanding of just what the keys are to such a shift at midlife. How are individual men's changes, crises, and relationships affected, shaped, and sometimes contradicted by the social, cultural, and political contexts in which they find themselves? And what *social* changes might make it more likely that boys and men might have more balanced personalities and needs at an *early* age?

An analysis of men's lives that simply describes personal changes while taking social structure as a given cannot adequately *ask* these questions. But an analysis that not only describes changes in male identity throughout the life course but also critically examines the socially structured and defined meaning of "masculinity" can and must ask these questions.

If many of the problems faced by all men (not just athletes) today are to be dealt with, class, ethnic, and sexual preference divisions must be confronted. This would necessarily involve the development of a more cooperative and nurturant ethic among men, as well as a more egalitarian and democratically organized economic system. And since the sports world is an important cultural process that serves, partly to socialize boys and young men to hierarchical, competitive, and aggressive values, the sporting arena is an important context in which to begin to confront the need for a humanization of men.

Yet, if the analysis presented here is correct, the developing psychology of young boys is predisposed to be attracted to the present structure and values of the sports world, so any attempt *simply* to infuse cooperative and egalitarian values into sports is likely to be an exercise in futility. The need for equality between men and women, in the public realm as well as in the home, is a fundamental prerequisite for the humanization of men, sports, and society. One of the most important changes that men could make would be to become more equally involved in parenting. The development of early bonding between fathers and infants (in addition to that between mothers and infants), along with nonsexist child rearing in the family, schools, and sports would have far-reaching effects on society: Boys and men could grow up more psychologically secure, more able to develop balance between separation and attachment, more able at an earlier age to appreciate intimate relationships with other men without destructive and crippling competition and homophobia. A young male with a more secure and balanced personality might also be able to *enjoy* athletic activities for what they really have to offer: the opportunity to engage in healthy exercise, to push oneself toward excellence, and to bond with others in a challenging and fun activity.

NOTES

1. J. Lever, "Sex Differences in the Games Children Play," *Social Problems* 23 (1976).

2. D. Sabo, "Sport Patriarchy and Male Identity: New Questions about Men and Sport," *Arena Review* 9, no. 2, 1985.

3. R. Sennett and J. Cobb, *The Hidden Injuries of Class* (New York: Random House, 1973); and L. B. Rubin, *Worlds of Pain: Life in the Working Class Family* (New York: Basic Books, 1976).

4. D. W. Ball, "Failure in Sport," *American Sociological Review* 41 (1976); J.J. Coakley, *Sports in Society* (St. Louis: Mosby, 1978); D. S. Harris and D. S. Eitzen, "The Consequences of Failure in Sport," *Urban Life* 7 (July 1978): 2; G. B. Leonard, "Winning Isn't Everything: It's Nothing," in *Jock: Sports and Male Identity*, ed. D. Sabo and R. Runfola (Englewood Cliffs, NJ: Prentice Hall, 1980); W. E. Schafer, "Sport and Male Sex Role Socialization," *Sport Sociology Bulletin* 4 (Fall 1975); R. C. Townsend, "The Competitive Male as Loser," in Sabo and Runfola, eds., *Jock*; and T. Tutko and W. Bruns, *Winning Is Everything and Other American Myths* (New York: Macmillan, 1976).

5. In contrast with the importance put on success by millions of boys, the number who "make it" is incredibly small. There are approximately 600 players in major-league baseball, with an average career span of 7 years. Approximately 6–7% of all high school football players ever play in college. Roughly 8% of all draft-eligible college football and basketball athletes are drafted by the pros, and only 2% ever sign a professional contract. The average career for NFL athletes is now 4 years, and for the NBA it is only 3.4 years. Thus the odds of getting anywhere *near* the top are very thin—and if one is talented and lucky enough to get there, his stay will be brief. See H. Edwards, "The Collegiate Athletic Arms Race: Origins and Implications of the 'Rule 48' Controversy," *Journal of Sport and Social Issues* 8, no. 1 (Winter–Spring 1984); Harris and Eitzen, "Consequences of Failure"; and P. Hill and B. Lowe, "The Inevitable Metathesis of the Retiring Athlete," *International Review of Sport Sociology* 9, nos. 3–4 (1978).

6. Schafer, "Sport and Male Sex Role," p. 50.

7. C. Gilligan, *In a Different Voice: Psychological Theory and Women's Development* (Cambridge: Harvard University Press, 1982); J. Piaget, *The Moral Judgement of the Child* (New York: Free Press, 1965); and Lever, "Games Children Play."

8. P. G. Filene, *Him/Her/Self: Sex Roles in Modern America* (New York: Harcourt Brace Jovanovich, 1975).

9. J. Hantover, "The Boy Scouts and the Validation of Masculinity," *Journal of Social Issues* 34 (1978): 1.

10. J. L. Dubbert, *A Man's Place: Masculinity in Transition* (Englewood Cliffs, NJ: Prentice Hall, 1979).

11. A. Tolson, *The Limits of Masculinity* (New York: Harper and Row, 1977).

12. C. W. Mills, *White Collar* (London: Oxford University Press, 1951).

13. D. J. Levinson, *The Seasons of a Man's Life* (New York: Ballantine, 1978).

14. Ibid., p. 195.

15. N. Chodorow, *The Reproduction of Mothering* (Berkeley: University of California Press, 1978).

16. Hill and Lowe, "Metathesis of Retiring Athlete," pp. 3–4; and B. D. McPherson, "Former Professional Athletes' Adjustment to Retirement," *Physician and Sports Medicine* (August 1978).

17. Edwards, "Collegiate Athletic Arms Race."

18. Levinson, *Seasons of a Man's Life.*

19. J. E. Dizard, "The Price of Success," in *Social Change and the Family,* ed. J. E. Dizard (Chicago: Community and Family Study Center, University of Chicago, 1968).

20. Levinson, *Seasons of a Man's Life,* p. 242.

21. J. H. Pleck, *The Myth of Masculinity* (Cambridge: MIT Press, 1982); Sennett and Cobb, *The Hidden Injuries of Class;* Rubin, *Worlds of Pain;* and Tolson, *Limits of Masculinity.*

22. M. P. Farrell and S. D. Rosenberg, *Men at Midlife* (Boston: Auburn House, 1981).

✲ FOR FURTHER STUDY ✲

Acosta, R. Vivian, and Linda Jean Carpenter. Annual report. "Women in Intercollegiate Sport." Department of Physical Education and Exercise Science, Brooklyn College.

Anderson, Deborah, John J. Cheslock, and Ronald G. Ehrenberg. 2006. "Gender Equity in Intercollegiate Athletics: Determinants of Title IX Compliance." *Journal of Higher Education* 77: 225–250.

Burstyn, Varda. 1999. *The Rites of Men: Manhood, Politics, and the Culture of Sport.* Toronto: University of Toronto Press.

Chronicle of Higher Education. 2002. "Gender Equity in College Sports: 6 Views." (December 6): B7–B10.

Coakley, Jay. 2007. *Sports in Society: Issues and Controversies.* 9th ed. New York: McGraw-Hill.

Conniff, Ruth. 1998. "The Joy of Women's Sports." *Nation* (August 10–17): 26–30.

Eitzen, D. Stanley. 2009. *Fair and Foul: Beyond the Myths and Paradoxes of Sport.* 4th ed. Lanham, MD: Rowman and Littlefield.

Eitzen, D. Stanley, and George H. Sage. 2009. *Sociology of North American Sport.* 8th ed. Boulder, CO: Paradigm.

Hargreaves, Jennifer. 2000. *Heroines of Sport: The Politics of Difference and Identity.* London: Routledge.

Higgs, Catriona T., Karen H. Weiller, and Scott B. Martin. 2003. "Gender Bias in the 1996 Olympic Games: A Comparative Analysis." *Journal of Sport and Social Issues* 27 (February): 52–64.

Hogan, Jackie. 2003. "Staging a Nation: Gendered and Ethnicized Discourses of National Identity in Olympic Opening Ceremonies." *Journal of Sport and Social Issues* 27 (May): 100–123.

Huffman, Suzanne C., A. Tuggle, and Dana Scott Rosengard. 2004. "How Campus Media Cover Sports: The Gender-Equity Issue, One Generation Later." *Mass Communication and Society* 7: 475–489.

Juffer, Jane. 2002. "Who's the Man? Sammy Sosa, Latinos, and Televisual Redefinitions of the 'American' Pastime." *Journal of Sport and Social Issues* 26 (November): 337–359.

Lapchick, Richard E. Annual Report: *Racial and Gender Report Card.* Institute for Diversity and Ethics in Sport, University of Central Florida–Orlando.

McDonagh, Eileen, and Laura Pappano. 2008. *Playing with the Boys: Why Separate Is Not Equal in Sports.* New York: Oxford University Press.

Messner, Michael A. 2002. *Taking the Field: Women, Men, and Sports.* Minneapolis: University of Minnesota Press.

Nylund, David. 2003. "Taking a Slice at Sexism: The Controversy over the Exclusionary Membership Practices of the Augusta National Golf Club." *Journal of Sport and Social Issues* 27 (May): 195–202.

O'Reilly, Jean, and Susan K. Cahn eds. 2007. *Women and Sports in the United States: A Documentary Reader.* Boston: Northeastern University Press.

Suggs, Welch. 2005. *A Place on the Team: The Triumph and Tragedy of Title IX.* Princeton, NJ: Princeton University Press.

Tucker, Lori W., and Janet B. Parks. 2001. "Effects of Gender and Sport Type on Intercollegiate Athletes' Perceptions of the Legitimacy of Aggressive Behaviors in Sport." *Sociology of Sport Journal* 18 (4): 403–413.

Wachs, Faye Linda. 2002. "Leveling the Playing Field: Negotiating Gendered Rules in Coed Softball." *Journal of Sport and Social Issues* 26 (August): 300–316.

Weistart, John. 1998. "Title IX and Intercollegiate Sports: Equal Opportunity?" *Brookings Review* 16 (Fall): 39–43.

Zimbalist, Andrew. 2000. "Backlash against Title IX: An End Run around Female Athletes." *Chronicle of Higher Education* (March 3): B9–B10.

PART TWELVE

Structured Inequality: Sport and Sexuality

Previous sections on structured inequality examined categories of people designated as minorities in society because of their race/ethnicity or gender. The members of these social categories suffer from powerlessness, negative stereotypes, and discrimination. This unit looks at another type of minority group. Unlike the other three minorities, which are disadvantaged because of economic circumstances or ascribed characteristics, the distinguishing feature of the minority examined in this section—homosexuality—is the object of discrimination because it is defined by the majority as different and, therefore, deviant. It is important to underscore a crucial point: *Homosexuality is not inherently deviant, but it is defined and labeled as deviant.*[1] Put another way, "Variance from the societal norm of heterosexuality is not a social problem; *the societal response to it is.*"[2]

An estimated 14 million adults in the United States identify themselves as gay or lesbian. Among these are former elite athletes: Glenn Burke (major-league baseball), David Kopay (professional football), Greg Louganis and Tom Waddell (Olympians), and Martina Navratilova (tennis). Athletes who publicly acknowledge their homosexuality, however, are rare because of the extent of homophobia among athletes, coaches, fans, and the sports media. "The extent of homophobia in the sports world is staggering: manifestations range from eight-year-old boys who put each other down with taunts of 'queer,' 'faggot,' or 'sissy' to high-school locker-room boasting (and, often, lying) about sexual conquests of females, and to college athletes bonding together with a little Saturday night "queer-bashing." To be suspected of being gay, and to be unable to prove one's heterosexual status in the sports world, is clearly not acceptable—indeed, it can be downright dangerous."[3]

Women in sport, more than men, endure intense scrutiny about their sexual identities.[4] This is the subject of the first selection, by Pat Griffin, as she discusses (1) the political functions of homophobia in a sexist and heterosexist culture, (2) the manifestations of homophobia in women's sport, (3) the beliefs that support homophobia in women's sport, and (4) strategies for confronting homophobia in women's sport.

The second selection, by journalist Anthony Cotton, describes the dilemmas that gay athletes face. The final chapter, by journalist John Ireland, provides the story of *Los Angeles Times* sportswriter Michael Daniel Penner, who became Christine Michelle Daniels. Ms. Daniels wrote what she considered the toughest article of her career. It was entitled, "I am a transsexual sportswriter."

NOTES

1. D. Stanley Eitzen, Maxine Baca Zinn, and Kelly Eitzen Smith, *Social Problems,* 11th ed. (Boston: Allyn and Bacon, 2007), p. 288.

2. Ibid., p. 296.

3. Michael A. Messner. "AIDS, Homophobia, and Sports." In Michael A. Messner and Donald F. Sabo, *Sex, Violence, and Power in Sports: Rethinking Masculinity* (Freedom, CA: Crossing Press, 1994), p. 121.

4. See Debra E. Blum, "College Sports' L-Word," *Chronicle of Higher Education* (March 9, 1994): A35–A36.

35

Changing the Game

Homophobia, Sexism, and Lesbians in Sport

Pat Griffin

Throughout the history of Western culture, restrictions have been placed on women's sport participation. These restrictions are enforced through sanctions that evolved to match each successive social climate. Women caught merely observing the male athletes competing in the early Greek Olympic Games were put to death. When Baron DeCoubertin revived the Olympic tradition in 1896, women were invited as spectators but barred from participation. Even in the present-day Olympic Games, women may compete in only one-third of the events.

Although the death penalty for female spectators was too extreme for the late 19th and early 20th centuries, an increasingly influential medical establishment warned white upper-class women about the debilitating physiological effects of vigorous athleticism, particularly on the reproductive system. Women were cautioned about other "masculinizing effects" as well, such as deeper voices, facial hair, and overdeveloped arms and legs. The intent of these warnings was to temper and control women's sport participation and to keep women focused on their "natural" and "patriotic" roles as wives and mothers (Lenskyj, 1986).

During the 1920s and 1930s, as the predicted dire physical consequences proved untrue, strong social taboos restricting female athleticism evolved. Instead of warnings about facial hair and displaced uteruses, women in sport were intimidated by fears of

Source: Reprinted by permission from P. Griffin, "Changing the Game: Homophobia, Sexism, and Lesbians in Sport" *Quest* 44, no. 2 (1992): 251–265.

losing social approval. Close female friendships, accepted and even idealized in the 19th century, became suspect when male sexologists like Freud "discovered" female sexuality sexuality in the early 20th century (Faderman, 1981, 1991; Katz, 1976). In the 1930s, as psychology and psychiatry became respected subfields in medicine, these doctors warned of a new menace. An entire typology was created to diagnose the "mannish lesbian," whose depraved sexual appetite and preference for masculine dress and activity were identified as symptoms of psychological disturbance (Newton, 1989). Social commentators in the popular press warned parents about the dangers of allowing impressionable daughters to spend time in all-female environments (Faderman, 1991; Smith-Rosenberg, 1989).

As a result, women's colleges and sports teams were assumed to be places where mannish lesbians lurked. Women in sport and physical education especially fit the profile of women to watch out for: they were in groups without men, they were not engaged in activities thought to enhance their abilities to be good wives and mothers, and they were being physically active in sport, a male activity. Because lesbians were assumed to be masculine creatures who rejected their female identity and roles as wives and mothers, athletic women became highly suspect.

The image of the sick, masculine lesbian sexual predator and her association with athleticism persists in the late 20th century. The power of this image to control and intimidate women is as strong today as it was 60 years ago. What accounts for the staying power of a stereotype that is so extreme it should be laughable except that so many people believe it to be accurate? Whose interests are served by stigmatizing lesbians and accusing women in sport of being lesbians? Why does sport participation by women in the late 20th century continue to be so threatening to the social order? How have women in sport responded to associations with lesbians? How effective have these responses been in defusing concern about lesbians in sport?

The purpose of this chapter is to discuss the issue of lesbians in sport from a feminist perspective that analyzes the function of socially constructed gender roles and sexual identities in maintaining male dominance in North American society. I share the perspective taken by other sport feminists that lesbian and feminist sport participation is a threat to male domination (Bennett, Whitaker, Smith, and Sablove, 1987; Birrell *and* Richter, 1987; Hall, 1987; Lenskyj, 1986; Messner *and* Sabo, 1990). In a sexist and heterosexist society (in which heterosexuality is reified as the only normal, natural, and acceptable sexual orientation), women who defy the accepted feminine role or reject a heterosexual identity threaten to upset the imbalance of power enjoyed by white heterosexual men in a patriarchal society (Bryson, 1987). The creation of the mannish lesbian as a pathological condition by early 20th-century male medical doctors provided an effective means to control all women and neutralize challenges to the sexist status quo.

To understand the social stigma associated with lesbian participation in sport, the function of homophobia in maintaining the sexist and heterosexist status quo must be examined (Lenskyj, 1991). Greendorfer (1991) challenged the traditional definition of homophobia as an irrational fear and intolerance of lesbians and gay men. In questioning how irrational homophobia really is, Greendorfer highlighted the systematic and pervasive cultural nature of homophobia. Fear and hatred of lesbians and gay men is more than individual prejudice (Kitzinger, 1987). Homophobia is a powerful political weapon of sexism (Pharr, 1988). The lesbian label is used to define the boundaries of acceptable female behavior in a patriarchal culture: When a woman is called a lesbian, she knows she is out of bounds. Because lesbian identity carries the extreme negative social stigma created by early 20th-century sexologists, most women are loathe to be associated with it. Because women's sport has been labeled a lesbian activity, women in sport are particularly sensitive and vulnerable to the use of the lesbian label to intimidate.

HOW IS HOMOPHOBIA MANIFESTED IN WOMEN'S SPORT?

Manifestations of homophobia in women's sport can be divided into six categories: (a) silence, (b) denial, (c) apology, (d) promotion of a heterosexy image, (e) attacks on lesbians, and (f) preference for male coaches. An exploration of these manifestations illuminates the pervasive nature of prejudice against lesbians in sport and the power of the lesbian stigma to control and marginalize women's sport.

Silence

Silence is the most consistent and enduring manifestation of homophobia in women's sport. From Billie Jean King's revelation of a lesbian relationship in 1981 to the publicity surrounding Penn State women's basketball coach Rene Portland's no-lesbian policy (Lederman, 1991; Longman, 1991), the professional and college sports establishment responds with silence to eruptions of public attention to lesbians in sport. Reporters who attempt to discuss lesbians in sport with sport organizations, athletic directors, coaches, and athletes are typically rebuffed (Lipsyte, 1991), and women in sport wait, hoping the scrutiny will disappear as quickly as possible. Women live in fear that whatever meager gains we have made in sport are always one lesbian scandal away from being wiped out.

Even without the provocation of public scrutiny or threat of scandal, silent avoidance is the strategy of choice. Organizers of coaches' or athletic administrators' conferences rarely schedule programs on homophobia in sport, and when they do, it is always a controversial decision made with fear and concern about the consequences of public dialogue (Krebs, 1984; Lenskyj, 1990). Lesbians in sport are treated like nasty secrets that must be kept locked tightly in the closet. Lesbians, of course, are expected to maintain deep cover at all times. Not surprisingly, most lesbians in sport choose to remain hidden rather than face potential public condemnation. Friends of lesbians protect this secret from outsiders, and the unspoken pact of silence is maintained and passed on to each new generation of women in sport.

Silence has provided some protection. Keeping the closet door locked is an understandable strategy when women in sport are trying to gain social approval in a sexist society and there is no sense that change is possible. Maintaining silence is a survival strategy in a society hostile to women in general and lesbians in particular. How effectively silence enhances sport opportunities for women or defuses homophobia, however, is open to serious question.

Denial

If forced to break silence, many coaches, athletic directors, and athletes resort to denial. High school athletes and their parents often ask college coaches if there are lesbians in their programs. In response, many coaches deny that there are lesbians in sport, at least among athletes or coaches at *their* schools (Fields, 1983). These denials only serve to intensify curiosity and determination to find out who and where these mysterious women are. The closet, it turns out, is made of glass: People know lesbians are in sport despite these denials.

In some cases, parents and athletes who suspect that a respected and loved coach is a lesbian either deny or overlook her sexual identity because they cannot make sense of the apparent contradiction: a lesbian who is competent, loved, and respected. In other instances, a respected lesbian coach is seen as an exception because she does not fit the unflattering lesbian stereotype most people accept as accurate. The end result in any case is to deny the presence of lesbians in sport.

Apology

The third manifestation of homophobia in sport is apology (Felshin, 1974). In an attempt to compensate for an unsavory reputation, women in sport try to promote a feminine image and focus public attention on those who meet white heterosexual standards of beauty. Women in sport have a tradition of assuring ourselves and others that sport participation is consistent with traditional notions of femininity and that women are not masculinized by sport experiences (Gornick, 1971; Hicks, 1979; Locke and Jensen, 1970). To this end, athletes are encouraged, or required in some cases, to engage in the protective camouflage of feminine drag. Professional athletes and college teams are told to wear dresses or attend seminars to learn how to apply makeup, style hair, and select clothes ("Image Lady," 1987). Athletes are encouraged to be seen with boyfriends and reminded to act like ladies when away from the gym (DePaul University's 1984 women's basketball brochure).

The Women's Sports Foundation (WSF) annual dinner, attended by many well-known professional and amateur female athletes, is preceded by an opportunity for the athletes to get free hairstyling and makeup applications before they sit down to eat with the male corporate sponsors, whose money supports many WSF programs. The men attending the dinner are not offered similar help with their appearance. The message is that female athletes in their natural state are not acceptable or attractive and therefore must be fixed and "femmed up" to compensate for their athleticism.

Femininity, however, is a code word for heterosexuality. The underlying fear is not that a female athlete or coach will appear too plain or out of style; the real fear is that she will look like a dyke or, even worse, is one. This intense blend of homophobic and sexist standards of feminine attractiveness remind women in sport that to be acceptable, we must monitor our behavior and appearance at all times.

Silence, denial, and apology are defensive reactions that reflect the power of the lesbian label to intimidate women. These responses ensure that women's sport will be held hostage to the *L* word. As long as questions about lesbians in sport are met with silence, denial, and apology, women can be sent scurrying back to our places on the margins of sport, grateful for the modicum of public approval we have achieved and fearful of losing it.

NEW MANIFESTATIONS OF HOMOPHOBIA IN WOMEN'S SPORT

In the past 10 years, three more responses have developed in reaction to the persistence of the association of sport with lesbians. These manifestations have developed at the same time that women's sport has become more visible, potentially marketable, and increasingly under the control of men and men's sport organizations. Representing an intensified effort to purge the lesbian image, these new strategies reflect a new low in mean-spirited intimidation.

Promotion of a Heterosexy Image

Where presenting a feminine image previously sufficed, corporate sponsors, professional women's sport organizations, some women's college teams, and individual athletes have moved beyond presenting a feminine image to adopting a more explicit display of heterosex appeal. The Ladies Professional Golf Association's 1989 promotional material featured photographs of its pro golfers posing pin-up style in swimsuits (Diaz, 1989). College sport promotional literature has employed double entendres and sexual innuendo to sell women's teams. The women's basketball promotional brochure from Northwestern State University of Louisiana included a photograph of the women's team dressed in Playboy bunny outfits. The copy crowed "These girls can play, boy!" and invited basketball fans to watch games in the "Pleasure Palace" (Solomon, 1991). Popular magazines have featured young, professional female athletes, like Monica Seles or Steffi Graf, in cleavage-revealing heterosexual glamour drag (Kiersh, 1990).

In a more muted attempt to project a heterosexual image, stories about married female athletes and coaches routinely include husbands and children in ways rarely seen when male coaches and athletes are profiled. A recent nationally televised basketball game between the women's teams from the University of Texas and the University of Tennessee featured a half-time profile of the coaches as wives and mothers. The popular press also brings us testimonials from female athletes who have had children claiming that their athletic performance has improved since becoming mothers. All of this to reassure the public, and perhaps ourselves as women in sport, that we are normal despite our athletic interests.

Attacks on Lesbians in Sport

Women in sport endure intense scrutiny of our collective and individual femininity and sexual identities. Innuendo, concern, and prurient curiosity about the sexual identity of female coaches and athletes come from coaches, athletic directors, sports reporters, parents of female athletes, teammates, fans, and the general public (South, Glynn, Rodack, and Capettini, 1990). This manifestation of homophobia is familiar to most people associated with women's sport. Over the last 10 to 12 years, however, concern about lesbians in sport has taken a nasty turn.

Though lesbians in sport have always felt pressure to stay closeted, coaches and athletic directors now openly prohibit lesbian coaches and athletes (Brownworth, 1991; Figel, 1986; Longman, 1991). In a style reminiscent of 1950s McCarthyism, some coaches proclaim their antilesbian policies as an introduction to their programs. Athletes thought to be lesbian are dropped from teams, find themselves benched, or are suddenly ostracized by coaches and teammates (Brownworth, 1991). Coaches impose informal quotas on the number of lesbians, or at least on the number of athletes they think look like lesbians, on their teams (Brownworth, 1991). At some schools, a new coach's heterosexual credentials are scrutinized as carefully as her professional qualifications (Fields, 1983). Coaches thought to be lesbians are fired or intimidated into resigning. These dismissals are not the result of any unethical behavior on the part of the women accused but happen simply because of assumptions made about their sexual identity.

Collegiate and high school female athletes endure lesbian-baiting (name-calling, taunting, and other forms of harassment) from male athletes, heterosexual teammates, opposing teams, spectators, classmates, and sometimes their own coaches (Brownworth, 1991; Fields, 1983; Spander, 1991; Thomas, 1990). Female coaches thought to be lesbians endure harassing phone calls and antilesbian graffiti slipped under their office doors. During a recent National Collegiate Athletic Association (NCAA) women's basketball championship, it was rumored that a group of male coaches went to the local lesbian bar to spy on lesbian coaches who might be there. Another rumor circulated about a list categorizing Division I women's basketball coaches by their sexual identity so that parents of prospective athletes could use this information to avoid schools where lesbians coach. Whether or not these rumors are true doesn't matter: The rumor itself is intimidating enough to remind women in sport that we are being watched and that if we step out of line, we will be punished.

Negative recruiting is perhaps the most self-serving of all the attacks on lesbians in sport. Negative recruiting occurs when college coaches or athletic department personnel reassure prospective athletes and their parents not only that there are no lesbians in this program but also that there *are* lesbians in a rival school's program (Fields, 1983). By playing on parents' and athletes' fear and ignorance, these coaches imply that young women will be safe in their programs but not at a rival school where bull dykes stalk the locker room in search of fresh young conquests.

Fears about lesbian stereotypes are fueled by a high-profile Christian presence at many national championships and coaches' conferences. The Fellowship of Christian Athletes, which regularly sponsors meal functions for coaches at these events, distributed a free antihomosexual booklet to coaches and athletes. Entitled *Emotional Dependency: A Threat to Close Friendships,* this booklet plays into all of the stereotypes of lesbians (Rentzel, 1987). A drawing of a sad young woman and an older woman on the cover hints at the dangers of close female friendships. Unencumbered by any reasonable factual knowledge about homosexuality, the booklet identifies the symptoms of emotional dependency and how this "leads" to homosexual relationships. Finally, the path out of this "counterfeit" intimacy through prayer and discipline is described. The booklet is published by Exodus, a fundamentalist Christian organization devoted to the "redemption" of homosexuals from their "disorder."

By allowing the active participation of antigay organizations in coaches' meetings and championship events, sport governing bodies like the NCAA and the Women's Basketball Coaches' Association are taking an active role in the perpetuation of discrimination against lesbians in sport and the stigmatization of all friendships among women in sport. In this intimidating climate, all women in sport must deal with the double burden of maintaining high-profile heterosexual images and living in terror of being called lesbians.

Preference for Male Coaches

Many parents, athletes, and athletic administrators prefer that men coach women's teams. This preference reflects a lethal mix of sexism and homophobia. Some people believe, based on gender and lesbian stereotypes, that men are better coaches than women. Although a recent NCAA survey of female athletes (NCAA, 1991) indicated that 61 percent of the respondents did not have a gender preference for their coaches, respondents were concerned about the images they thought male and female coaches had among their friends and family: 65 percent believed that female coaches were looked upon favorably by family and friends whereas 84 percent believed that male coaches were looked on favorably by family and friends.

Recent studies have documented the increase in the number of men coaching women's teams (Acosta *and* Carpenter, 1988). At least part of this increase can be attributed to homophobia. Thorngren (1991), in a study of female coaches, asked respondents how homophobia affected them. These coaches identified hiring and job retention as problems. They cited examples where men were hired to coach women's teams specifically to change a tarnished or negative (read *lesbian)* team image. Thorngren described this as a "cloaking" phenomenon, in which a team's lesbian image is hidden or countered by the presence of a male coach. Consistent with this perception, anecdotal reports from other female head coaches reveal that some believe it essential to hire a male assistant coach to lend a heterosexual persona to a women's team. The coaches in Thorngren's study also reported that women (married and single) leave coaching because of the pressure and stress of constantly having to deal with lesbian labels and stereotypes. Looking at the increase in the number of men coaching women's teams over the last 10 years, it is clear how male coaches have benefitted from sexism and homophobia in women's sport.

SUSPICION, COLLUSION, AND BETRAYAL AMONG WOMEN IN SPORT

The few research studies addressing homophobia or lesbians in sport, as well as informal anecdotal information, have revealed that many women have internalized sexist and homophobic values and beliefs (Blinde, 1990; Griffin, 1987; Guthrie, 1982; Morgan, 1990; Thorngren, 1990, 1991; Woods, 1990). Blinde interviewed women athletes about the pressures and stress they experienced. Many talked about the lesbian image women's sport has and the shame they felt about being female athletes because of that image. Their discomfort with the topic was illustrated by their inability to even say the word *lesbian*. Instead, they made indirect references to it as a problem. Athletes talked in ways that clearly indicated they had bought into the negative images of lesbians, even as they denied that there were lesbians on their teams. These athletes also subscribed to the importance of projecting a feminine image and were discomforted by female athletes who didn't look or act feminine.

Quotes selected to accompany the NCAA survey and the Blinde study illustrate the degree to which many female athletes and coaches accept both the negative stigma attached to lesbian identity and the desirability of projecting a traditionally feminine image:

> The negative image of women in intercollegiate sport scares me. I've met too many lesbians in my college career. I don't want to have that image. (NCAA, 1991)

> Well, if you come and look at our team, I mean, if you saw Jane Doe, she's very pretty. If she walks down the street, everybody screams, you know, screams other things at her. But because she's on the field, it's dykes on spikes. If that isn't a stereotype, then who knows what is. (Blinde, p. 12)

> Homosexual females in this profession [coaching] definitely provide models and guidance in its worst for female athletes. I'd rather see a straight male coach females than a gay women. Homosexual coaches are killing us. (NCAA, 1991)

> I don't fit the stereotype. I mean the stereotype based around women that are very masculine and strong and athletic. I wouldn't say I'm pretty in pink, but I am feminine and I appear very feminine and I act that way. (Blinde, p. 12)

These attempts to distance oneself from the lesbian image and to embrace traditional standards of femininity set up a division among women in sport that can devastate friendships among teammates, poison coach-athlete relationships, and taint feelings about one's identity as an athlete and a woman. Some women restrict close friendships with other women to avoid the possibility that someone might think they are lesbians. Other women consciously cultivate high-profile heterosexual images by talking about their relationships with men and being seen with men as often as possible. As long as our energy is devoted to trying to fit into models of athleticism, gender, and sexuality that support a sexist and heterosexist culture, women in sport can be controlled by anyone who chooses to use our fears and insecurities against us.

UNDERLYING BELIEFS THAT KEEP WOMEN IN SPORT FROM CHALLENGING HOMOPHOBIA

The ability to understand the staying power of the lesbian stigma in sport is limited by several interconnected beliefs. An examination of these beliefs can reveal how past responses in dealing with lesbians in sport have reinforced the power of the lesbian label to intimidate and control.

A Woman's Sexual Identity Is Personal

This belief is perhaps the biggest obstacle to understanding women's oppression in a patriarchal culture (Kitzinger, 1987). As long as a women's sexual identity is seen as solely a private issue, how the lesbian label is used to intimidate all women and to weaken women's challenges to male-dominated institutions will never be understood. The lesbian label is a political weapon that can be used against any woman who steps out of line. Any woman who defies traditional gender roles is called a lesbian. Any woman who chooses a male-identified career is called a lesbian. Any woman who chooses not to have a sexual relationship with a man is called a lesbian. Any woman who speaks out against sexism is called a lesbian. As long as women are afraid to be called lesbians, this label is an effective tool to control all women and limit women's challenges to sexism. Although lesbians are the targets of attack in women's sport, all women in sport are victimized by the use of the lesbian label to intimidate and control.

When a woman's lesbian identity is assumed to be a private matter, homophobia and heterosexism are dismissed. The implication is that these matters are not appropriate topics for professional discussion. As a result, the fear, prejudice, and outright discrimination that thrive in silence are never addressed. A double standard operates, however, for lesbians and heterosexual women in sport. Although open acknowledgment of lesbians in sport is perceived as an inappropriate flaunting of personal life (what you do in the privacy of your home is none of my business), heterosexual women are encouraged to talk about their relationships with men, their children, and their roles as mothers.

Magazine articles about such heterosexual athletes as Chris Evert Mill, Florence Griffiths Joyner, Jackie Joyner Kersey, Joan Benoit, Nancy Lopez, and Mary Decker Slaney have often focused on their weddings, their husbands, or their children. Heterosexual professional athletes are routinely seen celebrating victories by hugging or kissing their husbands, but when Martina Navratilova went into the stands to hug *her* partner after winning the 1990 Wimbledon Championship, she was called a bad role model by former champion Margaret Court. Although heterosexual athletes and coaches are encouraged to display their personal lives to counteract the lesbian image in sport, lesbians are intimidated into invisibility for the same reason.

Claiming to Be Feminist Is Tantamount to Claiming to Be Lesbian

Claiming to be feminist is far too political for many women in sport. To successfully address the sexism and heterosexism in sport, however, women must begin to understand the necessity of seeing homophobia as a political issue and claim feminism as the unifying force needed to bring about change in a patriarchal culture. Part of the reluctance to embrace the feminist label is that feminists have been called lesbians in the same way that female athletes have and for the same reason: to intimidate women and prevent them from challenging the sexist status quo. Women in sport are already intimidated by the lesbian label. For many women, living with the athlete, lesbian, and feminist labels is stigma overload.

By accepting the negative stereotypes associated with these labels, women in sport collude in our own oppression. Rather than seeking social approval as a marginal part of sport in a sexist and heterosexist society, we need to be working for social change and control over our sport destinies. The image of an unrepentant lesbian feminist athlete is a patriarchal nightmare. She is a woman who has discovered her physical and political strength and who refuses to be intimidated by labels. Unfortunately, this image scares women in sport as much as it does those who benefit from the maintenance of the sexist and heterosexist status quo.

The Problem Is Lesbians in Sport Who Call Attention to Themselves

People who believe this assume that as long as lesbians are invisible, our presence will be tolerated and women's sport will progress. The issue for these people is not that there are lesbians in sport but how visible we are. Buying into silence this way has never worked. Other than Martina Navratilova, lesbians in sport are already deeply closeted (Bull, 1991; Muscatine, 1991). This careful camouflage of lesbians has not made women's sport less suspect or less vulnerable to intimidation. Despite efforts to keep the focus on the pretty ones or the ones with husbands and children, women in sport still carry the lesbian stigma into every gym and onto every playing field.

Women in sport must begin to understand that it wouldn't matter if there were no lesbians in sport. The lesbian label would still be used to intimidate and control women's athletics. The energy expended in making lesbians invisible and projecting a happy heterosexual image keeps women in sport fighting among ourselves rather than confronting the heterosexism and sexism that our responses unintentionally serve.

Lesbians Are Bad Role Models and Sexual Predators

This belief buys into all the unsavory lesbian stereotypes left over from the late 19th-century medical doctors who made homosexuality pathological and the early

20th-century sexologists who made female friendships morbid. In reality, there are already numerous closeted lesbians in sport who are highly admired role models. It is the perversity of prejudice that merely knowing about the sexual identity of these admired women instantly turns them into unfit role models.

The sexual-predator stereotype is a particularly pernicious slander on lesbians in sport (South et al., 1990). There is no evidence that lesbians are sexual predators. In fact, statistics on sexual harassment, rape, sexual abuse, and other forms of violence and intimidation show that these offenses are overwhelmingly heterosexual male assaults against women and girls. If we need to be concerned about sexual offenses among coaches or athletes, a better case could be made that it is heterosexual men who should be watched carefully. Blinde (1989) reported that many female athletes, like their male counterparts, are subjected to academic, physical, social, and emotional exploitation by their coaches. When men coach women in a heterosexist and sexist culture, there is the additional potential for sexual and gender-based exploitation when the unequal gender dynamics in the larger society are played out in the coach-athlete relationship.

It is difficult to imagine anyone in women's sport, regardless of sexual identity, condoning coercive sexual relationships of any kind. Even consensual sexual relationships between coaches and athletes involve inherent power differences that make such relationships questionable and can have a negative impact on the athlete as well as on the rest of the team. This kind of behavior should be addressed regardless of the gender or sexual identity of the coaches and athletes involved instead of assuming that lesbian athletes or coaches present a greater problem than others.

Being Called Lesbian or Being Associated with Lesbians Is the Worst Thing That Can Happen in Women's Sport

As long as women in sport buy into the power of the lesbian label to intimidate us, we will never control our sport experience. Blaming lesbians for women's sports' bad image and failure to gain more popularity divides women and keeps us fighting among ourselves. In this way, we collude in maintaining our marginal status by keeping alive the power of the lesbian label to intimidate women into silence, betrayal, and denial. This keeps our energies directed inward rather that outward at the sexism that homophobia serves. Blaming lesbians keeps all women in their place, scurrying to present an image that is acceptable in a sexist and heterosexist society. This keeps our attention diverted from asking other questions: Why are strong female athletes and coaches so threatening to a patriarchal society? Whose interests are served by trivializing and stigmatizing women in sport?

Women in sport need to redefine the problem. Instead of naming and blaming lesbians in sport as the problem, we need to focus our attention on sexism, heterosexism, and homophobia. As part of this renaming process, we need to take the sting out of the lesbian label. Women in sport must stop jumping to the back of the closet and slamming the door every time someone calls us dykes. We need to challenge the use of the lesbian label to intimidate all women in sport.

Women's Sport Can Progress without Dealing with Homophobia

If progress is measured by the extent to which we, as women in sport, control our sporting destinies, take pride in our athletic identities, and tolerate diversity among ourselves, then we are no better off now than we ever have been. We have responded to questions about lesbians in sport with silence, denial, and apology. When these responses fail to divert attention away from the lesbian issue, we have promoted a heterosexy image, attacked lesbians, and hired male coaches. All of these responses call on women to accommodate, assimilate, and collude with the values of a sexist and heterosexist society. All require compromise and deception. The bargain struck is that in return for our silence and our complicity, we are allowed a small piece of the action in a sports world that has been defined by men to serve male-identified values.

We have never considered any alternatives to this cycle of silence, denial, and apology to the outside world while policing the ranks inside. We have never looked inside ourselves to understand our fear and confront it. We have never tried to analyze the political meaning of our fear. We have never stood up to the accusations and threats that keep us in our place.

What do we have to pass on to the next generation of young girls who love to run and throw and catch? What is the value of nicer uniforms, a few extra tournaments, and occasional pictures in the back of the sports section if we can't pass on a sport experience with less silence and fear?

STRATEGIES FOR CONFRONTING HOMOPHOBIA IN WOMEN'S SPORT

What, then, are the alternatives to silence, apology, denial, promoting a heterosexy image, attacking lesbians, and hiring male coaches? How can women in sport begin confronting homophobia rather than perpetuating it? If our goal is to defuse the lesbian label and to strip it of its power to intimidate women in sport, then we must break the silence, not to condemn lesbians but to condemn those who use the lesbian label to intimidate. Our failure to speak out against homophobia signals our consent to the fear, ignorance, and discrimination that flourish in that silence. If our goal is to create a vision of sport in which all women have an opportunity to proudly claim their athletic identity and control their athletic experience, then we must begin to build that future now

Institutional Policy

Sport-governing organizations and school athletic departments need to enact explicit nondiscrimination and anti-harassment policies that include sexual orientation as a protected category. This is a first step in establishing an organizational climate in which discrimination against lesbians (or gay men) is not tolerated. Most sport governing organizations have not instituted such policies and, when asked by reporters if they are planning to, avoid taking a stand (Brownworth, 1991; Longman, 1991). In addition to nondiscrimination policies, professional standards of conduct for coaches must be developed that outline behavioral expectations regardless of gender or sexual orientation. Sexual harassment policies and the procedures for filing such complaints must be made clear to coaches, athletes, and administrators. As with standards of professional conduct, these policies should apply to everyone.

Education

Everyone associated with physical education and athletics must learn more about homophobia, sexism, and heterosexism. Conferences for coaches, teachers, and administrators should include educational programs focused on understanding homophobia and developing strategies for addressing homophobia in sport.

Athletic departments must sponsor educational programs for athletes that focus not only on homophobia but on other issues of social diversity as well. Because prejudice and fear affect the quality of athletes' sport experience and their relationships with teammates and coaches, educational programs focused on these issues are appropriate for athletic department sponsorship and should be an integral part of the college athletic experience.

Visibility

One of the most effective tools in counteracting homophobia is increased lesbian and gay visibility. Stereotypes and the fear and hatred they perpetuate will lose their power as more lesbian and gay people in sport disclose their identities. Although some people will never accept diversity of sexual identity in sport or in the general population, research indicates that, for most people, contact with "out" lesbian and gay people who embrace their sexual identities reduces prejudice (Herek, 1985).

The athletic world desperately needs more lesbian and gay coaches and athletes to step out of the closet. So far only a handful of athletes or coaches, most notably Martina Navratilova, have had the courage to publicly affirm their lesbian or gay identity (Brown, 1991; Brownworth, 1991; Bull, 1991; Burke, 1991; Muscatine, 1991). The generally accepting, if not warm, reaction of tennis fans to Navratilova's courage and honesty should be encouraging to the many closeted lesbian and gay people in sport. Unfortunately, the fear that keeps most lesbian and gay sports people in the closet is not ungrounded: Coming out as a lesbian or gay athlete or coach is a risk in a heterosexist and sexist society (Brown, 1991; Brownworth, 1991; Burton-Nelson, 1991; Hicks, 1979; Muscatine, 1991). The paradox is that more lesbian and gay people need to risk coming out if homosexuality is to be demystified in North American society.

Another aspect of visibility is the willingness of heterosexual athletes and coaches, as allies of lesbian and gay people, to speak out against homophobia and heterosexism. In the same way that it is important for white people to speak out against racism and for men to speak out against sexism, it is important for heterosexual people to object to antigay harassment, discrimination, and prejudice. It isn't enough to provide silent, private support for lesbian friends. To remain silent signals consent. Speaking out against homophobia is a challenge for heterosexual women in sport that requires them to understand how homophobia is used against them as well as against lesbians. Speaking out against homophobia also requires that heterosexual women confront their own discomfort with being associated with lesbians or being called lesbian, because that is what will happen when they speak out: The lesbian label will be used to try and intimidate them back into silence.

Solidarity

Heterosexual and lesbian women must understand that the only way to overcome homophobia, heterosexism, and sexism in sport is to work in coalition with each other. As long as fear and blame prevent women in sport from finding common ground, we will always be controlled by people whose interests are served by our division. Our energy will be focused on social approval rather than on social change, and on keeping what little we have rather than on getting what we deserve.

Pressure Tactics

Unfortunately, meaningful social change never happens with tension and resistance. Every civil and human rights struggle in the United States has required the mobilization of political pressure exerted on people with power to force them to confront injustice. Addressing sexism, heterosexism, and homophobia in women's sport will be no different. Taking a stand will mean being prepared to use the media, collect petitions, lobby officials, picket, write letters, file official complaints, and take advantage of other pressure tactics.

CONCLUSION

Eliminating the insidious trio of sexism, heterosexism, and homophobia in women's sport will take a sustained commitment to social justice that will challenge much of what has been accepted as natural about gender and sexuality. Addressing sexism, heterosexism, and homophobia in women's sport requires that past conceptions of gender and sexuality be recognized as social constructions that confer privilege and normalcy on particular social groups: men and heterosexuals. Other social groups (women, lesbians, and gay men) are defined as inferior or deviant and are denied access to the social resources and status conferred on heterosexual men.

Sport in the late 20th century is, perhaps, the last arena in which men can hope to differentiate themselves from women. In sport, men learn to value a traditional heterosexual masculinity that embraces male domination and denigrates women's values (Messner and Sabo, 1990). If sport is to maintain its meaning as a masculine ritual in a patriarchal society, women must be made to feel like trespassers. Women's sport participation must be trivialized and controlled (Bennett et al., 1987). The lesbian label, with its unsavory stigma, is an effective tool to achieve these goals.

If women in sport in the 21st century are to have a sport experience free of intimidation, fear, shame, and betrayal, then, as citizens of the 20th century, we must begin to reevaluate our beliefs, prejudices, and practices. We must begin to challenge the sexist, heterosexist, and homophobic status quo as it lives in our heads, on our teams, and in our schools. A generation of young girls—our daughters, nieces, younger sisters, and students—is depending on us.

REFERENCES

Acosta, V., and L. Carpenter. 1988. "Status of Women in Athletics: Causes and Changes." *Journal of Health, Physical Education, Recreation, and Dance* 56, no. 6: 35–37.

Bennett, R., G. Whitaker, N. Smith, and A. Sablove. 1987. "Changing the Rules of the Game: Reflections Toward a Feminist Analysis of Sport." *Women's Studies International Forum* 10, no. 4: 369–380.

Birrell, S., and D. Richter. 1987. "Is a Diamond Forever? Feminist Transformations of Sport." *Women's Studies International Forum* 10, no. 4: 395–410.

Blinde, E. 1989. "Unequal Exchange and Exploitation in College Sport: The Case of the Female Athlete." *Arena Review* 13, no. 2: 110–123.

———. 1990. "Pressure and Stress in Women's College Sports: Views from Athletes." Paper presented at the annual convention of the American Alliance for Health, Physical Education, Recreation and Dance, March, New Orleans.

Brown, K. 1991. "Homophobia in Women's Sports." *Deneuve* 1, no. 2: 4–6, 29.

Brownworth, V. 1991. "Bigotry on the Home Team: Lesbians Face Harsh Penalties in the Sports World." *Advocate* (June 4): 34–39.

Bryson, L. 1987. "Sport and the Maintenance of Male Hegemony." *Women's Studies International Forum* 10, no. 4: 349–360.

Bull, C. 1991. "The Magic of Martina." *Advocate* (December): 38–40.

Burke, G. 1991. "Dodgers Wanted Me to Get Married." *USA Today,* September 18), 10C.

Burton-Nelson, M. 1991. *Are We Winning Yet?* New York: Random House.

Diaz, J. 1989. "Find the Golf Here?" *Sports Illustrated* (February 13): 58–64.

Faderman, L. 1981. *Surpassing the Love of Men: Romantic Friendship and Love Between Women from the Renaissance to the Present.* New York: Morrow.

———. 1991. *Odd Girls and Twilight Lovers: A History of Lesbian Life in Twentieth-Century America.* New York: Columbia University Press.

Felshin, J. 1974. "The Triple Option ... for Women in Sport." *Quest* 21: 36–40.

Fields, C. 1983. "Allegations of Lesbianism Being Used to Intimidate, Female Academics Say." *Chronicle of Higher Education* (October 26): 1, 18–19.

Figel, B. 1986. "Lesbians in the World of Athletics." *Chicago Sun-Times,* June 16, 119.

Gornick, V. 1971."Ladies of the Links." *Look* (May 18): 69–76.

Greendorfer, S. 1991. "Analyzing Homophobia: Its Weapons and Impacts." Paper presented at the annual convention of the American Alliance for Health, Physical Education, Recreation, and Dance, April, San Francisco.

Griffin, P. 1987. "Lesbians, Homophobia, and Women's Sport: An Exploratory Analysis." Paper presented at the annual meeting of the American Psychological Association, August, New York.

Guthrie, S. 1982. "Homophobia: Its Impact on Women in Sport and Physical Education." Unpublished master's thesis, California State University, Long Beach.

Hall, A., ed. 1987. "The Gendering of Sport, Leisure, and Physical Education" [special issue]. *Women's Studies International Forum* 10, no. 4.

Herek, G. 1985. "Beyond 'Homophobia': A Social Psychological Perspective on Attitudes Toward Lesbians and Gay Men." Pp. 1–22 in J. DeCecco, ed., *Bashers, Baiters, and Bigots: Homophobia in American Society.* New York: Harrington Park.

Hicks, B. 1979. "Lesbian Athletes." *Christopher Street* (October–November): 42–50.

"Image Lady." 1987. *Golf Illustrated* (July): 9.

Katz, J. 1976. *Gay American History.* New York: Avon.

Kiersh, E. 1990. "Graf's Dash." *Vogue* (April): 348–353, 420.

Kitzinger, C. 1987. *The Social Construction of Lesbiansim.* Newbury Park, CA: Sage.

Krebs, P. 1984. "At the Starting Blocks: Women Athletes' New Agenda." *Off Our Backs* 14, no. 1: 1–3.

Lederman, D. 1991. "Penn State's Coach's Comments About Lesbian Athletes May Be Used to Test University's New Policy on Bias." *Chronicle of Higher Education* (June 5): A27–28.

Lenskyj, H. 1986. *Out of Bounds: Women, Sport, and Sexuality.* Toronto: Women's Press.

———. 1990. "Combatting Homophobia in Sports." *Off Our Backs* 20, no. 6: 2–3.

———. 1991. "Combatting Homophobia in Sport and Physical Education." *Sociology of Sport Journal* 8, no. 1: 61–69.

Lipsyte, R. 1991. "Gay Bias Moves Off the Sidelines." *New York Times,* May 24, B1.

Locke, L., and M. Jensen. 1970. "Heterosexuality of Women in Physical Education." *Pod* (Fall): 30–34.

Longman, J. 1991. "Lions Women's Basketball Coach Is Used to Fighting and Winning." *Philadelphia Inquirer,* March 10, 1G, 6G.

Messner, M., and D. Sabo, eds. 1990. *Sport, Men, and the Gender Order: Critical Feminist Perspectives.* Champaign, IL: Human Kinetics.

Morgan, E. 1990. *Lesbianism and Feminism in Women's Athletics: Intersection, Bridge, or Gap?* Unpublished manuscript, Brown University Providence.

Muscatine, A. 1991. "To Tell the Truth, Navratilova Takes Consequences." *Women's Sports Pages* (November–December): 8–9. (Available from Women's SportsPages, P.O. Box 151534, Chevy Chase, MD 20825.)

National Collegiate Athletic Association. 1991. *NCAA Study on Women's Intercollegiate Athletics: Perceived Barriers of Women in Intercollegiate Athletic Careers.* Overland Park, KS: National Collegiate Athletic Association.

Newton, E. 1989. "The Mannish Lesbian: Radclyffe Hall and the New Woman." Pp. 281–293 in M. Duberman, M. Vicinus, and G. Chauncey, eds., *Hidden from History: Reclaiming the Gay and Lesbian Past.* New York: New American Library.

Pharr, S. 1988. *Homophobia: A Weapon of Sexism.* Inverness, CA: Chardon.

Rentzel, L. 1987. *Emotional Dependency: A Threat to Close Friendships.* San Rafael, CA: Exodus International.

Smith-Rosenberg, C. 1989. "Discourses of Sexuality and Subjectivity: The New Woman, 1870–1936." Pp. 264–280 in M. Duberman, M. Vicinus, and G. Chauncey, eds., *Hidden from History: Reclaiming the Gay and Lesbian Past.* New York: New American Library.

Solomon, A. 1991. "Passing Game." *Village Voice* (March 20): 92.

South, J., M. Glynn, J. Rodack, and R. Capettini. 1990. "Explosive Gay Scandal Rocks Women's Tennis." *National Enquirer* (July 31): 20–21.

Spander, D. 1991. "It's a Question of Acceptability." *Sacramento Bee,* September 1, D1, D14–15.

Thomas, R. 1990. "Two Women at Brooklyn College File Rights Complaint." *New York Times,* December 12, 22.

Thorngren, C. 1990. "Pressure and Stress in Women's College Sport: Views from Coaches." Paper presented at the annual convention of the American Alliance for Health, Physical Education, Recreation, and Dance, April, New Orleans.

———. 1991. "Homophobia and Women Coaches: Controls and Constraints." Paper presented at the annual convention of the American Alliance for Health, Physical Education, Recreation, and Dance, April, San Francisco.

Woods, S. 1990. "The Contextual Realities of Being a Lesbian Physical Education Teacher: Living in Two Worlds." *Dissertation Abstracts International* 51, no. 3: 788.

36

Gay Athletes' Dilemma

Anthony Cotton

This is the sports guy's favorite time, the season when grown men find themselves as giddy as children on Christmas Eve, waiting to unwrap all the goodies that await inside their widescreen televisions.

There are the Broncos, chasing the most coveted of prizes, the Super Bowl's Lombardi Trophy. There are college football bowl games, capped Wednesday by a Rose Bowl contest that features the season's final two undefeated teams, Southern California and Texas. And though the local franchises may not be title-worthy yet, the National Hockey League is back and the National Basketball Association is taking flight.

Throughout it all, men will root and cheer and agonize and despair, never once considering the psychology of so fiercely celebrating the physical prowess of other men. But as they paint their faces, don their Rod Smith jerseys and plop down onto the couch for the next month or so, former Major League baseball player Billy Bean has a question that might cause them to drop their clickers: What would happen if one of those athletic gods—a Bronco, a Miami Heat player, a USC Trojan—announced he was gay?

"If somebody famous came out, all those sports fans who love him, who run around wearing his T-shirts and jerseys, it would be something where they'd have to start asking questions about themselves," Bean said.

Which is one reason why Bean, one of only three male team-sport athletes to acknowledge being gay—and only after his playing days ended—says male sports are society's last bastion for denial. In a world where talk-show hosts and actors and

Source: Anthony Cotton, "Gay Athletes' Dilemma," *Denver Post,* January 2, 2006. Used by permission.

actresses can come out—with the public still tuning in or forking over nine bucks for their movies—or gay politicians can openly run and win elections, there has never been a gay active male athlete who has announced his sexual orientation.

Of course, Ellen DeGeneres or Nathan Lane never had to share a locker room with 50 of their entertainment peers.

"It would be very tough for someone in that situation," Broncos running back Mike Anderson said. "You're talking men, testosterone, egos.... I just think guys would find it harder to accept—if a guy came out in the locker room and said he was gay, I don't think (his teammates) would accept it."

And yet, coming out is nothing new in women's athletics, the most recent example being basketball star Sheryl Swoopes. During the past 18 months, Swoopes won her third gold medal for the U.S. Olympic team and her third most valuable player award from the Women's National Basketball Association.

In October, Swoopes announced that she was gay, saying life in the closet was "miserable."

Bean called Swoopes' announcement "heroic," in part because it was something he could never do during an eight-year career in Major League baseball.

"I was exhausted from lying about my life every single day," said Bean, who played for Detroit, Los Angeles and San Diego and is now a real estate agent in the Miami area. "I've learned that even if I had trusted just one person, it could have made the whole difference, but I just felt like I was on an island. I was a baseball player, but I knew I had this thing looming in the background, and it just seemed impossible to put the two together and make it work."

After some early struggles, tennis star Martina Navratilova has managed to do so after coming out almost 25 years ago. Professional golfer Rosie Jones has had an even easier time after announcing she was gay in March 2004. As a basketball player, Swoopes may be closer to the athletic sensibilities of the heartland, but even the buzz from her revelation seemed to pass quickly.

"That's because a WNBA player is still sort of on the periphery, compared to an NBA player," Bean said. "If it would have been Tracy McGrady (of the Houston Rockets), now we're talking."

FORCED TO KEEP A SECRET

Statistics suggest that as many as 400 professional male team athletes in the U.S. may be gay. But only three ex-athletes have come out.

According to the Urban Institute, anywhere from 2 percent to 10 percent of the United States population is gay. Applying that percentage to the four major men's professional sports, that means there could be as many as 400 gay athletes.

Yet through all the years of major pro sports, only three athletes—Bean, baseball player Glenn Burke and Esera Tuaolo, a National Football League defensive lineman for nine years in the 1990s—have acknowledged being gay, and each only after the conclusion of their playing careers.

As much as he would like an active male athlete to come out, Bean admits that such a move "would be a little daring."

"There are obviously closeted athletes who have learned to keep that secret in tow because they don't want it to affect their ability to play and make a wonderful living," Bean said. "It takes a long time to get to the top of the sports world, whether it's football or basketball or baseball. By the time someone wades their way through the minor leagues, the colleges, competing against other players, whatever that process of elimination is, you get so hardened by watching friends get peeled away, cut or released, injuries that ruin careers—by the time you get there, you're so damn grateful, however much you might want to come out, it's just another obstacle that makes your day a lot more complicated than it probably needs to be.

"People just make a conscious choice that until they see proof that it's not going to affect their job or the way people look at them or the fans' opinion of them, they're just going to hold on to that secret. It's unfortunate that that's where we are still, but I just think it's going to take more time."

A TABOO SUBJECT

Active athletes don't like discussing the possibility that some teammates may be gay. One player has said he wouldn't stand for a gay teammate.

If you want to see grown men, some of the most accomplished performers in athletics, squirm, just raise the topic of an active male athlete coming out.

"Hold up—do you know something I don't?" Anderson asks.

"No comment," Denver Nuggets center Marcus Camby said. "It's hard to think about. I just don't see it happening too soon."

"The last time I talked about this, I got into trouble," Broncos safety Nick Ferguson said.

"Man, I can't even go there," said PGA Tour golfer and ABC television analyst Paul Azinger. "This is like the taboo subject. It's like talking about race or something. If you talk about it, you're just going to get slaughtered."

Trying to find an example to point out the sensitivity level of some of his peers, Azinger recalls when LPGA star Nancy Lopez married Ray Knight. Although Knight had been an accomplished baseball player and manager, even winning a World Series, when he left his sport and spent the bulk of his time in the golf world traveling with his wife and managing his family, "everybody was just calling him 'Mr. Lopez,'" Azinger said.

As a member of the New York Jets a few years ago, Ferguson was sucked in by the media vortex after Jeremy Shockey of the New York Giants said he "wouldn't stand for" playing with a homosexual.

Ferguson takes a dissenting view.

"I have nothing against someone who wants to live their life in that particular way," Ferguson said. "I don't see why a gay athlete couldn't come out, as long as he handled his business on the field. (But) I don't know what it would be like for him outside of the game. You can have camaraderie inside the locker room, but outside of it, you probably wouldn't see too many people around him because they'd be afraid of getting labeled."

Nuggets general manager Kiki Vandeweghe argues that there's only one label that should matter.

"It's not like 30 years ago, it just isn't," he said. "It just wouldn't factor into what the guy does on the court. If he can play basketball, he can play basketball; that's the end of the story."

Though Bean finds Vandeweghe's sentiment encouraging, he doesn't believe it holds up, even in today's relatively more enlightened age.

"There's a perfect world, and then there's the real world," Bean said. "He's saying the right thing, but he's not the guy who's going to have to go out there in Madison Square Garden and stand at the free throw line with the game on the line and see someone hold up a big sign calling him a faggot."

DIFFERENCES BETWEEN SEXES

A golfer says she eventually made the adjustment after coming out. But it could be harder for men to do so because of sports' macho world.

Swoopes may be in that situation next summer. She is playing overseas for now, and her agent did not return repeated requests to contact her for this story. Swoopes recently signed an endorsement deal with Olivia, a travel company with a predominantly gay and lesbian clientele. Jones is another of the company's spokeswomen, her deal part of the reason she came out last year.

Today, Jones says her sexuality has become "a sidelight" to her play—"People say, 'Oh, yeah, she's gay.'" Though she says there have been no repercussions since coming out, with both gays and heterosexuals expressing thanks and admiration for her choice, Jones admits there was an element of discomfort initially.

"You're coming out to millions of people—it's not like it's just in your workplace, where there may be 30 or 100 people—it's to everybody," she said. "I felt like I was walking around naked for a couple of weeks; I don't know who wouldn't feel uncomfortable walking around naked playing golf in front of thousands of people.

"It was like I had stripped and shed layers off of me, and I felt vulnerable, but I wasn't a wreck emotionally. I played great golf, I was happy, and as time went by, I started playing better, I've had a lot more confidence. I'm just so glad I did it and I don't have to hide that part of my life anymore."

However, Jones feels the cultural chasm between men and women announcing their sexual orientations is miles and miles apart, a gulf that begins at a very early age.

"(Male) friends say to each other all the time, 'Oh, you're so gay,' or 'You're such a wuss' when they're playing sports," Jones said. "When that happens, you're not going to be accepted in that sport. You probably wouldn't survive."

Jean Hodges of Boulder is a regional director for Parents, Families and Friends of Lesbians and Gays. One of her current projects is a study of homophobia in sports, with early indications showing that schoolyard games of touch football or basketball play a strong role in how males begin to perceive their sexuality and the role that plays in interacting with others.

"Boys become afraid. There's such strong motivation for 'men to be men,'" Hodges said. "There's a deep-seated need not to be thought of as effeminate, with the fear factor of being regarded as such pretty great. And as you get older, it gets that much harder because there's so much peer pressure. It would take a huge amount of confidence for a young man to come out."

Bean couldn't do so. But he's hopeful that someone will step forward in time.

"I believe we can make this thing coexist," he said. "If an athlete is strong enough to handle all the scrutiny of being the first one, it's going to dissolve and dissipate as more people do it. But that first one, it's going to be news, and any athlete will tell you it's hard to concentrate and eliminate those variables and distractions when you have people asking you questions 24 hours a day about things that are going on off the field.

"Whoever does come forward will have to think long and hard about that, but they're going to be a hero for some people. But I hope when that happens, their play doesn't drop off. I hope it gets better, because that's what people are going to be looking for."

37

He Shoots, She Scores
The Story of a Transsexual Sportswriter

John Ireland

For all of its trappings of money, fame, and corruption, professional sports has a lot to do with character. Avid sports fans seem to respect those who face up to overwhelming challenge and overcome adversity. So it should not come as a surprise that readers rose in solidarity when a 23-year veteran sports writer announced in the *Los Angeles Times* that he would return from a short hiatus ... as a woman.

On April 26, Mike Penner wrote what he thought would be the toughest article of his career. "I am a transsexual sportswriter. It has taken more than 4o years, a million tears and hundreds of hours of soul-wrenching therapy for me to work up the courage to type those words." The piece ran in the Sports section, next to his regular column.

According to the *Los Angeles Times,* Penner's story was "by mid-evening, one of the most heavily viewed stories on latimes.com in the last year, with about half a million page views." Nancy Sullivan, executive director of communications for the newspaper, says "There was a massive response to this story, not only on our website, but across the media spectrum." The online message board accompanying the article was closed to comments in less than 8 hours, with 800 comments logged in. Hundreds more messages were sent via e-mail. Responses to the revelation came in three distinct flavors: kudos from sports fans, effusive thanks from other transsexuals and rants from bible-thumpers. Readers' initial shock, however, subsided almost immediately.

Source: John Ireland, "He Shoots, She Scores," *In These Times* 31 (July 2007): 24–27.

Michael Daniel Penner returned to work on May 23 as Christine Michelle Daniels. So far, it appears to be smooth sailing. But Daniels' very public transition has put a spotlight on a culture that is slow to acknowledge, let alone attempt to rehabilitate its ingrained intolerance and bigotry.

TRANSLATING HER WORLD

"The concept of one day having to come out publicly, as an *LA Times* sports columnist, was a paralyzing fear that, looking back, kept me from transitioning at least 5 years sooner," Daniels tells *In These Times*. She says she was "bracing for the worst."

Many of Daniels' colleagues have gone out of their way to champion her cause. "Some sportswriters," she says, "have written column items of support, some who know me pretty well have spoken to others on my behalf, without my knowledge, delivering the message that, 'This is just another writer, a normal person, facing a difficult challenge.'"

Sports blogs almost uniformly expressed admiration for her courage and wished her well. Overall, readers seem to be mildly bemused, but focused on her return to work. One commenter summed up the majority consensus: "Yea yea yea and all that girlie stuff, no problema.... But how 'bout them Angels this weekend? Gonna get back to bizz? Need you back Christine."

Some response has been negative. It's difficult to assess where it originates—within the sports community or those drawn by the spectacle. TheAngryT.com, an obscure sports blog, rants, "I am a straight male ... Do you care what I look like or whether I wear high cut panties out of the Sears women's wear catalogue? *LA Times* readers should no longer look for Mike Penner's column when they want hard-hitting sports journalism."

Sportswriters frequently express passion and enthusiasm for their subject, exposing more personality than reporters covering different beats. They often develop loyal followings and become a trusted voice that keeps readers up-to-date. In a world of high ticket prices, the sportswriter functions as the reader's passport to the field, court or stadium. For Daniels, this connection to her fans, and the known quality of her writing, may have smoothed her transition.

"I just always liked the spark in his writing, his wit and his use of language," says fellow Southern California journalist Joel Beers. "Penner's done a lot: covered the Olympics, wrote about media, NFL lead writer. But, after 23 years, it'd seem he'd be a dean of the *Times* sports section as opposed to just another very good writer in a section that has a lot of them. I always wondered why he seemed to bounce from beat to beat but never got what would seem to me the choicest of assignment: columnist."

It would seem that Daniels' bravery has yielded that opportunity twofold. She has two columns: *Day in L.A.*, which the paper describes as "a daily column on the sports events, personalities and themes that matter most to Southern Californians," and *Woman in Progress*, a blog on latimes.com in which she chronicles her transformation, comments on the angst that accompanied her public "coming out," and describes reconnecting with friends and colleagues she had kept at a distance since beginning hormone replacement therapy (HRT) in December.

Her first few weeks of posts indicate that each blog retains its distinct focus. Based on the heavy traffic to both blogs, much of her original audience has stayed on, in order to catch a glimpse of her personal journey. Daniels is making sports history by creating a space where questions of intolerance and bigotry can be posed and, through online comments, discussed.

Daniels knows that the average sports-page reader experiences cognitive dissonance when imagining a man donning a wig, a dress, pumps and lipstick to head out for a day at the mall. In a recent post, she related why many male-to-female "transwomen" are focused on the exterior. "We never had a girlhood. We missed out on all the fun (dolls, sleepovers, mother-daughter outings) and the rites of passage natural-born females take for granted ... [It's] just a normal part of growing up female."

Her employer's approach to the situation helped normalize Daniel's gender switch. When she revealed to her supervisor, Sports Editor Randy Harvey, that she would be transitioning, he insisted that she write the piece in order to stay in control of the story. Some critics thought that personal narrative belonged in the Op Ed section and not in the Sports section. Others believed she should be fired. One post to a blog sponsored by CBS SportsLine.com put it this way: "When a reporter makes himself the story, which he is clearly doing, he is definitely not serving the interests of his reading public and quite honestly should be fired for these ego-driven actions."

In the majority of states, being fired would be a distinct possibility. In February, the city of Largo, Fla., fired its city manager of 14 years after he revealed his plans to undergo sex reassignment surgery, also known as SRS. California, however, is one of the eight states (along with Illinois, Maine, Minnesota, New Jersey, New Mexico, Rhode Island and Hawaii, as well as Washington D.C.) that have passed laws that prohibit discrimination based on gender identity. Oregon will join the list on January 1, 2008, and the legislatures of Vermont, Iowa and Colorado have passed bills that await their governors' signatures.

AN UNEXAMINED CULTURE

Traditionally, the sports world is quick to minimize and ignore issues of bigotry when they arise and instead "focus on the game." In so doing, it misses a chance to discuss the issues and identify the underlying symptoms. Some would sweep Daniels' revelation under the rug in order to maintain the status quo and avoid what might be unsettling self-examination.

U.S. sports history is rife with examples of a pervasive culture of racism, sexism and homophobia. Football commentator Jimmy "The Greek" Snyder was fired by the CBS network in 1988 after describing on the air how African Americans were naturally superior athletes because they had been bred to produce stronger offspring during slavery. The words that got him fired were, "During the slave period, the slave owner would breed his big black with his big woman so that he would have a big black kid—that's where it all started."

Although primarily criticized as racist, Don Imus' April 4 reference to the Rutgers University women's basketball team as "nappy headed hos" revealed an insidious sexism that has been at the core of the sports world's resistance to professional female athletes. Just months before, retired NBA player Tim Hardaway was suspended from participating in NBA publicity events after saying on a local radio show: "Well, you know I hate gay people, so I let it be known. I don't like gay people and I don't like to be around gay people. I am homophobic. I don't like it." Homophobia has persisted like a healed-over injury that acts up when gender roles are challenged.

"That culture is very real," says Daniels. But she sees her proactive "coming out" and the *Woman in Progress* blog as an opportunity for fans to examine their discomfort with transsexuals in sports. Her blog holds up a magnifying glass for those who are willing to peer through it.

Daniels is in the process of getting new press credentials from local teams. "I have not ventured into a press box or locker room as Christine yet. But soon," she said with anticipation. "Most of the publicity directors from the local pro sports teams have contacted me to say, 'Welcome back, Christine, we look forward to working with you.'"

TRANSSEXUALS IN SPORTS

Daniels is not the first transsexual to emerge from the sports world. In 2003, Chris Kahrl, sportswriter and founding columnist of the annual *Baseball Prospectus,* the gold standard for baseball analysis, became Christina. At the time, Kahrl wrote, "nobody has batted an eye" calling sports "the ultimate American social bridge" transcending "race, gender, class, and culture." The history of transsexuals as sports players, however, hasn't always borne out such triumphant optimism.

In 1972, Richard Raskind reached the final of the men's national 35-and-over tennis championships. Three years later, he underwent sex-reassignment surgery, becoming Renée Richards. In 1976, the U.S. Tennis Association denied her entrance into the U.S. Open. In 1977, the New York Supreme Court ruled in her favor, allowing her to reach the doubles final at that year's competition. She went on to coach Martina Navratilova to win two of her 20 Wimbledon championship titles.

For nearly 20 years, women's golf, which has a significant number of lesbian players and fans, has excluded transsexuals from competition. Two years after transsexual Charlotte Wood placed third in the U.S. Senior Women's Amateur in 1987, the U.S. Golf Association (USGA) added a "female at birth" clause in its entry forms and many other golf organizations around the world followed suit.

In 2004, however, the Australian Ladies Professional Golf Association (ALPGA) reversed its 1991 "female at birth" decision and allowed Mianne Bagger to join. Bagger, who was born male and had SRS in 1995, was ranked sixth on the national amateur circuit before turning professional in 2004. She currently plays on the ALPGA and

Ladies European Tours. Bagger's success has had an international impact, as well. In 2005, the USGA changed its policy, allowing transgender athletes to compete in the U.S Women's Open. The same year, the Ladies Golf Union did the same, which allowed Bagger to play in the Women's British Open.

And in May 2004, the International Olympic Committee published its "Stockholm Consensus,"outlining eligibility for participation in gender-classified competitions. It states that eligibility of transgender athletes to compete should begin no sooner than "two years after gonadectomy," that "verifiable" hormone therapy has been administered, and that "legal recognition of their assigned sex has been conferred by the appropriate authorities."

CHANGING MEDICAL CONSENSUS

The confusion manifested in the sports world over transsexuality is understandable when one considers the lack of settled opinion in the medical world. Much has changed in the past 50 years and definitive classification is still in flux.

The term "transsexual" entered popular parlance in the '50s to describe a person who identified and often presented as a member of the opposite gender. In 1980, the American Psychological Association added "Transsexualism" to its Diagnostic and Statistics Manual (DSM-III). In 1994, the group replaced the diagnosis with "Gender Identity Disorder" (DSM-IV). The term "transgender" emerged around the same time to describe those with unusual gender identities without psychopathologizing them as "disordered." This is considered an umbrella term covering all types of "gender dysphoria," which literally means being uncomfortable with one's gender.

Medical professionals have different opinions as to the appropriateness of hormones, surgeries, transition counseling and even conversion therapy, which would seek to reverse the gender dysphoria and reconcile the individual to his or her biological gender. Treatments can cost between $15,000 and $50,000 and are not covered by most U.S. health insurance policies. Many countries that have comprehensive nationalized health care, including Canada and most European countries, do cover the cost of treatment, to varying degrees.

SURGERY AND LEGAL RECOGNITION

Legal recognition of gender change varies around the world. In the United States, only Idaho, Ohio and Tennessee prohibit the change of sex on a birth certificate. Every province in Canada permits this, as do most western European countries. The latter, however, require proof of a diagnosis and HRT, in addition to SRS. Spain requires proof of HRT for two years, but not surgery. Germany will grant the official change of gender only if the person is unmarried, permanently infertile, and has had surgery changing the "outer sexual characteristics." The United Kingdom requires only that the person prove s/he suffers from gender dysphoria. Japan will grant the legal change, but only if the person is unmarried and childless. Australia is one of the few countries that will issue a new birth certificate, as opposed to amending an existing one.

Thailand has become a haven for inexpensive SRS procedures for transsexuals from around the globe, making it a hotspot for this type of "medical tourism." Ironically, Thailand does not grant changes in gender in official records for its own citizens.

The small town of Trinidad, Colo., is known as the gender reassignment capital of the United States, due to the work of former Army surgeon Stanley Biber, who specialized in the surgeries in the late '60s. Before his death in 2006, he estimated that he had performed 5,800 such procedures and trained hundreds of other surgeons. The International Foundation for Gender Education estimates that more than 30,000 Americans have undergone SRS.

Unlike the rest of the Muslim world, Iran sanctions SRS, as it has been valid under Islamic Shariah since Ayatollah Ruhollah Khomeini issued a fatwa in 1983. Since homosexuality is punishable by death, however, it appears that surgery is the only option for many who might otherwise be hanged for being gay. As a result, an unregulated and marginally underground surgical industry has developed, leaving in its wake many postoperative patients who are not technically transsexual.

LIFE GOES ON

Discussing her public transition with *In These Times,* Daniels acknowledges that hard work lies ahead. "The overwhelming warm, positive and supportive response I have received has done much to buoy my spirits and get me emotionally prepared for the next career hurdle: covering sporting events and interviewing athletes and coaches as Christine," she says. "You know, for more than 20 years now, I have been a woman sportswriter going into locker rooms all the time. Only then, nobody, myself included, realized it."

Daniels will likely remain an expert in two realms. On her *Woman in Progress* blog, she will continue to share her own journey and transition from male to female, educating and provoking thousands of casual onlookers, while providing support and comfort to those on a similar journey. In her "Day in L.A." column, she will remain the first stop on many a fan's morning read-through of the Sports section, continuing to digest and contextualize the world of sports with her characteristic wit.

In a recent blog entry, Daniels addressed, if indirectly, the many questions people have asked about the extent and timetable of her transition. She wrote, "Gender identity is not about genitals. It is about what's in your head and in your heart. I am not taking a vacation to have SRS. I am taking a vacation to have a vacation."

Regardless of what comes her way, Daniels will do what she does best: churn out 2,000-plus words a day that speak to her readers. For reporter and reader alike, there's not much better than that.

✳ FOR FURTHER STUDY ✳

Amaechi, John. 2007. *Man in the Middle.* New York: Hyperion.

Broad, K. L. 2001. "The Gendered Unapologetic: Queer Resistance in Women's Sport." *Sociology of Sport Journal* 18 (2): 181–204.

Coakley, Jay. 2007. *Sports in Society: Issues and Controversies.* 9th ed. New York: McGraw-Hill.

Eitzen, D. Stanley, and George H. Sage. 2009. *Sociology of North American Sport.* 8th ed. Boulder, CO: Paradigm.

Fusco, Caroline. 2000. "Lesbians and Locker Rooms." Pp. 91–94 in Peter Donnelly, ed., *Taking Sport Seriously: Social Issues in Canadian Sport,* Toronto: Thompson Education.

Jacobson, Jennifer. 2002. "The Loneliest Athletes." *Chronicle of Higher Education* (November 1): A36–A38.

Lipsyte, Robert. 2000. "An Icon Recast: Support for Gay Athlete," April 30. Available at http://nytimes.com/library/sports/other/043000oth-lipsyte.html.

Lynch, Eamon. 2003. "Having a Gay Old Time." *Sports Illustrated* (June 16): G8–G12.

Nixon, Howard L. II. 2008. *Sport in a Changing World.* Boulder, CO: Paradigm.

Price, Michael, and Andrew Parker. 2003. "Sport, Sexuality, and the Gender Order: Amateur Rugby Union, Gay Men, and Social Exclusion." *Sociology of Sport Journal* 20 (2): 108–126.

Tomlinson, Dylan B. 1998. "Fear and Loathing." *Denver Post,* April 28, 10D.

PART THIRTEEN

Expanding the Horizons: Sport and Globalization

Globalization, according to Joseph Maguire, refers to transnational economics and technological exchange, communication networks, and migratory patterns resulting in interconnected world patterns.[1] Globalization, then, involves, among other things, markets, production, finance, the movement of people, and cultural homogenization. There has been a global economy for 500 years. In the sport realm the cultural imperialism employed by the British colonists of the nineteenth and twentieth centuries brought their sport (soccer, rugby, cricket) to their colonies (e.g., India). The Olympic movement spread around the globe during the twentieth century, and this, too, has been interpreted by some observers as a reflection of the colonial dominance of the West,[2] but in the last twenty-five years or so, it has accelerated rapidly.

While globalization is not new, the pace has quickened rapidly with the transportation and communications revolutions of the late twentieth century. Maguire states: "These globalization processes ... appear to be leading to a form of time-space compression. That is, people are experiencing spatial and temporal dimensions differently. There is a speeding up of time and a "shrinking" of space. Modern technologies enable people, images, ideas and money to criss-cross the globe with great rapidity."[3]

The three selections in this section provide information on the global dimensions of sport in today's world. The first, by anthropologist Alan M. Klein, describes the extent of globalization in Major League Baseball. His question: Will Major League Baseball see players and fans abroad as a twentieth-century-colonialist or as a twenty-first-century-decentered global enterprise?

The second chapter, by sociologist Jay Coakley, provides an overview of the global dimensions of sport in today's world. The final chapter, by sociologist/physical educator George H. Sage, focuses not only on the global reach of the Nike Corporation, the major worldwide producer and marketer of sports materials, but also the sordid history of the exploitation of workers in low-wage economies. Most significantly, Sage chronicles the success of various social movements to change policies of the Nike Corporation.

NOTES

1. Joseph Maguire, "Sport and Globalization," in *Handbook of Sports Studies,* Jay Coakley and Eric Dunning (eds.), (London: Sage, 2000), p. 356. For more on the defining characteristics of globalization, see Jeremy Breecher, Tim Costello, and Brendan Smith, *Globalization from Below: The Power of Solidarity* (Cambridge, MA: South End Press, 2000), pp. 1–4; and Robert K. Schaeffer, *Understanding Globalization: The Social Consequences of Political, Economic, and Environmental Change,* 2nd ed. (Lanham, MD: Rowman and Littlefield, 2003), pp. 1–18.

2. H. Eichberg, "Olympic Sport: Neocolonialism and Alternatives," *International Review for the Sociology of Sport* 19: 97–105.

3. Maguire, op. cit., p. 356.

38

Growing the Game

The Globalization of Major League Baseball

Alan M. Klein

Major League Baseball's efforts at globalization are not only provident for the future of the sport but also critical to its current prosperity. The ability of the game to rely upon its domestic base for fans and players has receded to the point where globalizing is imperative. This may be hard to square with the figures on attendance, which reached an all-time high in 2005, and with vigorous television ratings, but from a structural and long-term perspective the current boom is misleading. Major League Baseball must seek players and fans abroad, and indeed it is already doing so. The question is whether it will do so as a twentieth-century colonialist or as a twenty-first-century decentered global enterprise. The former strategy represents familiar ground but is doomed to slow growth and persistent resentment; the latter will at first feel uncomfortable but will aid the worldwide health of the sport.

In an effort to study this question systematically, I selected three of the game's organizations: two teams, the Los Angeles Dodgers and the Kansas City Royals, as well as the Commissioner's Office. All three are structurally representative of key dimensions of the industry, yet each is unique, and each approaches globalization in fundamentally different ways from the others. My attempt to chronicle their efforts spanned seven years (1999–2005) and covered eight countries. The core of this study looks at the political, economic, and structural arrangements of contemporary baseball on a global scale.

THE SPHERE OF BASEBALL

The Commissioner's Office is much like any other multinational corporation: large, complex, guarded, and autocratic. Fortunately, one division within the office deals with international dimensions of the sport: Major League Baseball International (MLBI). At the time of my research, it was presided over by Paul Archey, with Jim Small as the vice president for international marketing and the head of the Japan office.

MLBI is responsible for generating foreign revenue for the major league franchise owners. To that end MLBI sells broadcast rights, secures corporate sponsorships, licenses products, and stages events abroad. Expanding the business opportunities of the game is critical, but within the larger framework of the industry, it is equally important to develop the game itself abroad. Major League Baseball has to deepen its roots where it already exists and engender interest where it is absent or exists only weakly: it must, in the business-inflected jargon of the organization, "grow the game." Hence MLBI is concerned with generating profits as well as with increasing the institutional popularity of the sport internationally. This requires a coherent view of the baseball world outside of the United States.

Jim Small provided me with that social mapping in my first interview. According to him, all countries are divided into three strata according to their baseball sophistication and the potential economic rewards they offer. Tier one countries are those in which "baseball is mature, it's well known. Also, there is some sort of economic activity and the ability for us to market against that love of baseball."[1] In places like the Dominican Republic, Japan, or Mexico, baseball is deeply entrenched, and the number of players signed to professional contracts is significant and consistent.

Tier two includes countries where the game is somewhat less developed. There may be leagues, but they are amateur or semiprofessional, and much less competitive than in the first tier. Nor do these countries produce numbers of major league players comparable to those coming from the first tier. Italy, Australia, and the Netherlands are examples. With a certain kind of inducement (and no one really knows just what that might be), any of these countries might move up. Currently Australia is experiencing something of a baseball renaissance. After almost a decade of decline, the sport seems poised to make significant headway. A new league is planned, and players are being signed in impressive numbers. The 2005 Minnesota Twins, for instance, had sixteen Australians under contract at various levels in their organization.

Tier three comprises those countries in which the sport has a tentative footing, where the game either has only recently been introduced or has not yet taken root in the local sporting tradition. South Africa, England, and Germany are all long-term baseball projects. Players signing contracts with major league organizations are relatively rare in tier three, and the sport itself has yet to establish itself outside of scattered pockets. Because it is a long-term prospect, tier three is not on the radar screen of many major league organizations, but MLBI has worked diligently to grow the game there. Thus far the results have been mixed, but for baseball to become a real global sport, it will have to find a way to become entrenched in Europe and Africa. Jim Small cautions, however, that "tiers are more art than science. We look at a combination of good economies, where we can sell products, and baseball acumen. It's not like we sat down and actually assigned numbers to these."[2] These are all judgment calls, but the classifications can be useful.

In countries where the game is firmly established, the primary interest of Major League Baseball International is economic: "Ultimately, we're charged with returning money to the owners."[3] The largest share of MLBI revenues is derived from the sale of broadcast rights in foreign markets. Japan is the wealthiest such market ever, at $275 million, but deals have been signed in the past few years in Venezuela, the Dominican Republic, Australia, and the United Kingdom. Foreign corporate sponsors have also begun to seek out Major League Baseball with greater frequency. The tier one areas of Asia and Latin America lead the way, as might be expected, because the game is so entrenched there. Corporate sponsorships include everything from promotions to All-Star Game balloting to product lines. Licensing sales have also grown in direct proportion to the numbers of foreign players in major league organizations. The fourth leg of MLBI's revenue program comprises the events that it stages each year. They include preseason exhibition games, such as the weekend series in Valencia, Venezuela, in 2001 between the Houston Astros and the Cleveland Indians; regular-season games such as the 2004 opener between the New York Yankees and the Tampa Bay Devil Rays in Tokyo; and the biennial postseason visit of a major league all-star team to cities throughout Japan to play against stars of the Nippon Professional Baseball league.

In tier two and three countries the emphasis for MLBI is upon deepening the local involvement with the sport via a range of grassroots programs. The most fundamental program in the organization's arsenal is Pitch, Hit, and Run, a curriculum-based program administered through schools for children ages eight to twelve. Started in Australia in 1994, the program grew slowly. By 2002 more than three million children around the world had been introduced to it. Subsequent programs seek to build the base of young players until they are old enough to try out for their respective national teams.

Since these grassroots efforts are designed to change young people's minds as much as to develop the game, MLBI augments its hands-on programs with a range of televised programming. Getting youngsters to watch major league games is a major goal, along with promoting the creation of new sports heroes. Baseball Max, a weekly program filled with clips from games and interviews with stars, is produced by MLBI and disseminated around the world. By exposing young people in a lower-tier country to the game and to its colorful stars, MLBI hopes to make fans and players where few could be found before.

But while Major League Baseball International concentrates on being the game's ambassador to the world, ultimately it is the teams themselves that must be responsible for finding and grooming foreign talent. The Los Angeles Dodgers are an obvious choice for studying globalization in baseball because they pioneered it, and, while no longer alone, they continue to be among the most active in that arena. All major league teams are involved in the international hunt for talent, but big market teams like the Dodgers, the Atlanta Braves, and the New York Mets are exponentially the most involved. The cost of doing business overseas has risen considerably over the past decade. Consider that when Dominican superstars like pitcher Pedro Martinez signed with the Dodgers in 1988, almost no Latin American players signed for more than $10,000. Now a highly coveted prospect will easily get between $500,000 and $1,500,000; the record is Joel Guzmán's signing with the Dodgers for $2.25 million in 2001. It is precisely the wealth of big-market teams, combined with the rapid improvement of foreign talent, that has fueled these changes.

In certain foreign leagues owners who are concerned about losing their best players to the major leagues themselves further drive up the cost of signing their stars. A major league team seeking to sign a Japanese player, for example, must wait for ten years after his initial signing. When the player is finally posted as available to outsiders, interested teams must submit secret bids, the highest of which earns the team the right to negotiate with the player. Ichiro Suzuki cost the Seattle Mariners $13.125 million for the sealed bid, then $14 million for his contract.

The Dodgers may be representative of big-market teams, but they are also distinct in one key way: they are the pioneers in international baseball. While baseball entered the global arena in an institutional and business sense later than the National Basketball Association and the National Football League, in certain respects baseball has had a very long incubation period. The roots of its present-day efforts can be seen in the actions of Brooklyn Dodgers General Manager Branch Rickey more than sixty years ago. It was Rickey who, in 1945, flouted the barrier that had kept African Americans out of "organized baseball"—the major leagues as well as the recognized minor leagues—since late in the nineteenth century. In that monumental act, the first step toward globalization may be seen. On a social level, the Dodgers are to be credited with thinking outside of the box, showing a willingness to find players wherever they may be. This predisposed them to hurdle over national boundaries as quickly as they did racial ones.

Jackie Robinson entered a Dodger organization that was being configured to enable his ascent, and the handprint of Rickey was everywhere evident. Robinson possessed the right combination of personality traits, background, and baseball skill to make Rickey look like a genius, but Rickey planned Robinson's trajectory through three countries (Canada, Cuba, and the United States) to facilitate a smooth transition. Racial integration was a local response that had global repercussions unknown to Rickey and Robinson, but not to Dodger owner Walter O'Malley. Under O'Malley's stewardship (beginning in 1951), a foundation for a global perspective was laid. He built ties with Japan and the Caribbean and created an awareness of global possibilities when no one remotely considered such things. Schooled in proto-globalization, O'Malley's son Peter furthered these efforts when he took over at the helm. His progressive agenda included two signings with international impact: those of Fernando Valenzuela, from Mexico, and Hideo Nomo, from Japan.

While the Dodgers organization is a clear-cut choice for a study of big-market baseball's globalization, at first glance the Kansas City Royals seem anything but an obvious choice for the small-market representative. The Royals came to my attention after I read an article on their general manager, Allard Baird, who had made a grueling fact-finding trip to South Africa. He had hoped that South African baseball would be developed enough that a player might be signed with a good chance of making the majors. When Baird and his associate, Luis Silverio, began traveling about the country and holding tryouts, however, they quickly abandoned any notion of signing a prospect and launched into teaching baseball fundamentals instead. How many general managers would hold clinics for young people whom they know won't "matter" to their standings in the short term? I had to meet Baird, and promptly decided that he and the Royals were embracing a small-market mindset that had them globetrotting in advance of the big boys. Even in baseball-rich countries like the Dominican Republic, Kansas City has to adopt a different posture to sign players: they "shop without a credit card," as Baird puts it. The result is somewhat riskier, but affordable, signings. As a case study the Royals were perfect ... plus, they always returned my phone calls.

How large- and small-market teams operate in global baseball is one of the core features of this study. I liken the small-market teams to the Portuguese sailors of the sixteenth and seventeenth centuries, who sailed fearlessly to corners of the world and wound up establishing a toehold in the business of colonialism. They did this not because they were intrepid explorers but rather because they couldn't compete directly against the big-market traders like Italy and France. Large-market teams have the option of going where talent is more costly, and when they err in judgment—which can cost millions of dollars—they have the luxury of trying again. Not so for the Milwaukees, the Tampa Bays, or the Kansas Cities of the baseball world. This is why small-market teams shop in Europe, while the behemoths head for Japan.

BASEBALL GLOBALIZATION?

When people think of globalization and baseball, they typically conjure up cosmopolitan team rosters. The pitching staff of the 2005 New York Mets had players from Japan, the Dominican Republic, South Korea, Puerto Rico, and Venezuela, as well as from the United States. More than 29 percent of all major leaguers on opening day rosters in 2005 were foreign born. While most fans know that the Dominican Republic produces a lot of major leaguers (ninety-one of them as the season started), they may not realize that players are increasingly coming from Taiwan, Curacao, South Korea, Australia, and Panama. The face of baseball today looks more like the United Colors of Benetton—Ichiro, Pedro, and the Rocket (Ichiro Suzuki, Pedro Martínez, and Roger Clemens)—than at any time in its past.

But baseball's globalization has many faces that we don't typically see. The face of Ho-Seong Koh, a South Korean manufacturer of sports caps, for example, Koh specializes in producing caps for U.S. teams. Just minutes after a team has won a championship, Koh may receive an order. He has succeeded because he can overnight a shipment anywhere in the United States. His factories in Vietnam, Cambodia, and Bangladesh make two sets of hats ahead of time, awaiting only that last-minute phone order. The phenomenon of Koreans producing for American markets, in factories throughout Asia, and doing so at high speed, is typical of globalization.[4]

Dominicans have become synonymous with baseball excellence. Consider that Dominicans, either native or first generation, have won the American League's Most Valuable Player award each year between 2002 and 2005 (Miguel Tejada, Alex Rodríguez twice, and Vladimir Guerrero), as well as the National League's MVP in 2004 (Albert Pujols). Dominicans' rise to dominance has been nothing short of spectacular, and while their heroics make the front page of most sports sections in newspapers around the United States, in their home country Guerrero's selection was treated as a national story. Guerrero collected his trophy in a ceremony at the Presidential Palace. "It's a celebration all over the country and in the streets," declared Jason Payano, the Dominican sports minister.[5] Dominican accomplishment in baseball has its flip side as well. Young Dominicans—many impoverished—desperately seek to gain a toehold in the sport, giving rise to a host of problems that require action from MLB and the Dominican government. MLB's Commissioner's Office has made serious efforts, for instance, to regulate the way in which young players are signed and groomed to come to the United States—a less conspicuous, but equally important, component of globalizing the sport.

Globalization is found as well in the sudden appearance of an entire Japanese team in a newly formed professional league in California and Arizona. The Golden Baseball League has welcomed this Japanese cohort, the Samurai Bears, not shying away from any of the cultural or logistical issues posed by having such a foreign presence in their midst. When the Japanese players walk into the wrong bathroom or have to navigate an American menu or play their entire schedule on the road because they have no "home" field, the potential awkwardness is handled by all parties with aplomb and the requisite sense of humor.[6] Back in Japan, the megalithic corporation Dentsu signed a $275 million contract with MLB for the broadcast rights to games in Japan. The pact confirms the growing economic partnership between Japanese and North American baseball, as well as the parity of play that is increasingly coming within reach. One sees globalization also in the labyrinthine planning for a baseball World Cup, as the demands and concerns of the nations involved reflect their insistence on a level playing field. The politics of conceiving and producing such an event has been a major learning experience for MLB. In fact, Major League Baseball has had to learn the lessons of globalization on its feet, and to its credit, has come a long way in a short time.

Baseball is globalized even in countries that don't play the game. Máribel Alezondo is Costa Rican. As a citizen of a soccer-playing country, she might be expected to be ignorant of the game of baseball, but in one respect she knows quite a bit. She is one of the workers in the Rawlings sporting goods factory in Turrialba, where eleven hours a day she hand-stitches baseballs used by Major League Baseball. She earns about thirty cents per ball (MLB game balls cost $22.50 each, and regular Rawlings balls retail for $15.00 at stores). Well, she used to anyway; Máribel quit on her doctor's advice, because the work was deforming her fingers and arms. She misses the work nevertheless, and while she may be resentful about the conditions she endured, she grows incredulous upon finding out what happens to the baseballs she labored over: "It's an injustice that we kill ourselves to make these balls perfect, and with one home run they're gone."[7]

Globalization is also about building the game where it barely exists. In South Africa, where until recently hardly anyone knew what the sport was, hundreds of thousands of schoolchildren have been exposed to the game through Major League Baseball International's grassroots programs. Both MLBI and the Royals donated equipment to more than fifteen hundred schools in Black, White, and Colored (the country's three official racial categories) communities. In an unanticipated development, the government has acknowledged the race-free associations of baseball in postapartheid South Africa, proclaiming baseball as part of the "new South Africa." In a country where everything was identified by race, the government is eager to identify cultural elements that reflect new nonracial policies. Suddenly South African baseball is a part of the hoped-for future of the country. The Royals, unprompted, decided to help the game grow as well, teaching young players and holding coaching clinics. The effort has begun to pay off. Since 1999, seven South Africans have signed contracts with major league clubs, and three are still playing (fittingly, two in the Royals organization).

NOTES

1. Jim Small, interview by the author, January 12, 2000.

2. Ibid.

3. Ibid.

4. Ken Belson, "Getting Champions' Caps to the Game Before the Final Whistle," *New York Times,* May 28, 2003.

5. Bob Hohler, "Guerrero Wins by Country Mile," *Boston Globe,* November 17, 2004.

6. Charlie Nobles, "Baseball Players from Over There Get a Shot Over Here," *New York Times,* May 18, 2005.

7. Tim Weiner, "Baseballs Being Made in a Sweatshop," www.sportsbusinessnews.com (The Daily Dose), January 26, 2004 (originally published as "Low-Wage Costa Ricans Make Baseballs for Millionaires," *New York Times,* January 25, 2004).

39

Globalization and Sports
Issues and Controversies

Jay J. Coakley

NEW POLITICAL REALITIES IN AN ERA OF TRANSNATIONAL CORPORATIONS

Today, international sports are less likely to be scenes for nationalistic displays than scenes for commercial displays by large and powerful transnational corporations. This was clearly evident in Atlanta (1996), Nagano (1998), Sydney (2000), and Salt Lake City (2002), and it will be evident in future locations.

Global politics have changed dramatically over the past decade. Nation-states have been joined by powerful transnational organizations in global power relations. In fact, about half of the largest economies in the world are corporations, *not* nation-states. As nation-states have lifted trade restrictions, decreased tariffs, and loosened their internal regulations to promote their own capitalist expansion, transnational corporations have become increasingly powerful players in global politics. Many of them are now more powerful in economic terms than the nations in which their products are manufactured. This, of course, gives them political power as well.

Therefore, instead of focusing just on international relations when we study sports and political processes, we must broaden our focus to consider *transnational*

Source: Jay J. Coakley, *Sport in Society: Issues and Controversies,* 8th ed. (New York: McGraw-Hill, 2004), 460–469.

relations. This enables us to acknowledge that nation-states are now joined by major corporations and other powerful transnational organizations as global political players.

Nationalism still exists in connection with international sports, especially those played in regions where political and economic issues call attention to national differences and interests. However, in the case of many sport events, the differences between national interests and identities and corporate interests and identities are becoming increasingly blurred. This was highlighted by Phil Knight, the CEO of the U.S.-based Nike corporation, as he explained the basis for his team loyalty during the 1994 World Cup: "We see a natural evolution ... dividing the world into their athletes and ours. And we glory ours. When the U.S. played Brazil in the World Cup, I rooted for Brazil because it was a Nike team. America was Adidas." Knight's point was that he identified teams and athletes in terms of corporate logos, not nationalities. He knew that Nike's markets were not limited to the United States. They were and continue to be worldwide, and this was why Nike gave Brazil's national sport teams $200 million for the right to use the Brazilian soccer team to market Nike products around the world through the year 2005. Knight sees logo loyalty as more important than national loyalty when it comes to international sports; he sees consumerism replacing patriotism when it comes to identifying athletes and teams; he sees international sports events as sites for Nike and other corporate sponsors to deliver advertising messages promoting their companies' interests, and promoting general global capitalist expansion. Furthermore, he and fellow executives from other powerful corporations see this as good for the people of the world. Their conclusion would be similar to conclusions made by those using functionalist theory: Sport contributes to economic expansion, and this is good for everyone in the world.

To the extent that corporate sponsors influence sport events and media coverage, international sports televised around the world are used as vehicles for presenting to massive audiences a range of messages promoting the interests of corporate capitalism (Donnelly, 1996). These messages are directed to spectator-consumers, not spectator-citizens. Instead of focusing on patriotism or nationalism, the messages that come with international sports now focus on status consciousness and individual consumption. Sports that don't enable corporations to deliver their messages to consumers with purchasing power are not sponsored. If spectators and media audiences are not potential consumers, corporations see little reason to sponsor events, so, unless the media are publicly owned, they are not likely to cover events viewed by those who have little purchasing power.

Of course, the power of corporations is not unlimited or uncontested, as conflict theorists would have us conclude. Figurational research has identified cases in which local populations use their own cultural perspectives to interpret and apply the images and discourses that come with global sports and global advertising. However, those who use critical theories note that global media sports and the commercial messages that accompany them often cleverly fuse the global and the local through thoughtfully and carefully edited images of local traditions, sport action, and consumer products (Jackson and Hokowhitu, 2002; Jackson and Scherer, 2002). They argue that these fused images tend to "detraditionalize" local cultures by presenting local symbols and lifestyles in connection with consumer products.

Nike has been especially clever in this regard. As cultural theorist David Andrews points out, Nike commercials that aired in connection with global sport events during the late 1990s masterfully presented images from numerous localities around the world. These local images were "reassembled" and situated in connection with Nike products, such as soccer apparel worn by players from many nations as they kicked a soccer ball in numerous locations around the globe. Andrews argues that Nike captures local traditions and wraps its branded jerseys around them until there is little else to be seen or discussed. This has now become a common advertising strategy.

The conclusions made by critical theories have not been explored sufficiently in research, but it is clear that, as corporations join or replace nation-states as sponsors of athletes and teams around the world, sports do become framed in new political terms. According to John Horan, the publisher of *Sporting Goods Intelligence*, "It's not the Free World versus Communism anymore. Now you take sides with sneaker companies. Now everybody looks at the Olympics as Nike versus Reebok" (in Reid, 1996, p. 4BB). Horan's conclusion is probably distorted by his hope that global sports are perceived in this way. However, despite some distortion and exaggeration, Horan expresses the intent of transnational corporations as they spend billions of dollars to sponsor sports around the world.

The late Roone Arledge, former president of ABC News and director of ABC Sports, noted that this intent was becoming a reality in connection with sport events. He observed that the Olympic Games are "basically a commercial enterprise that tries every four years to make as much money as it possibly can," and that the games don't have "much to do with the heroic words that we use to describe them" (in Reid, 1996, p. 4BB). Reaffirming Arledge's conclusion, Dick Ebersol, president of NBC Sports, explained that NBC paid over $3.5 billion for the U.S. rights to televise all Olympic Games from 2000 to 2008, because the Olympics "has this amazing ability to put the whole family in front of the television together, which is what advertisers are grabbing at" (in Steinbreder, 1996, p. 38).

These statements, made only thirteen years after Peter Ueberroth, president of the Los Angeles Olympic Organizing Committee, described the Olympics as an athletic-*political* event, illustrate the power of corporate capitalism. In just over a decade, the characterization of the largest sport event in the world changed from athletic-*political* to athletic-*economic*.

Representatives from many major corporations around the world have come to see the potential of sports to establish new commercial markets and to promote the ideology of consumerism, which drives those markets. Although the sponsorship money coming from these corporations is welcomed by those who benefit from it, the primary goal of those who own and control the corporations is to make profits.

Coca-Cola may sponsor the Olympics because it wants to bring people together, but it is primarily interested in selling as many Cokes as possible to 6.3 billion people around the world. This is also why the Mars candy company pays millions to be the official snack food of the Olympics and why McDonald's uses the Olympics and nearly fat-free athletes' bodies to market hamburgers and fries around the world.

According to Sut Jhally, a noted communications profession from the University of Massachusetts, transnational corporations pay billions of dollars to sponsor global sports in an effort to become "global cultural commissars." Jhally says that if you listen closely and critically to the advertisements of these sponsors, you'll discover that, in addition to their products, they are selling a way of life based on consumption. They use sports to present images and messages emphasizing individual success through competition, production, and consumption. They know that elite competitive sports are ideal vehicles for presenting these images and messages, because such sports have become primary sources of entertainment around the world. When people are being entertained while watching these sports in person or on television, they are emotionally primed to hear what the sponsors have to say.

Of course, many people ignore the images and messages emphasized by sponsors, or they redefine them to fit local and personal circumstances. But this does not prevent large corporations from spending billions to deliver them. Advertisers understand that sooner or later the images and messages associated with sources of pleasure and entertainment in people's lives will in some form enter the imaginations and conversations of a proportion of those who see and hear them. Commercial images and messages do not dictate what people think, but they certainly influence what people think about, and, in this way, they become a part of the overall discourse that occurs in cultures around the globe.

We should not interpret this description of the new politics of sports to mean that sports around the world somehow have fallen victim to a global conspiracy hatched by transnational corporations. It means only that transnational organizations have joined nation-states in the global political context in which sports are defined, organized, planned, promoted, played, and presented, and given meaning around the world (Jackson and Scherer, 2002).

OTHER GLOBAL POLITICAL ISSUES

As sports have become increasingly commercialized, and as national boundaries have become less relevant in sports, an increasing number of athletes have become global migrant workers. They go where their sports are played, where they can be supported or earn money while they play, or where they can have the cultural experiences they seek. This global migration of athletes has raised new political issues in connection with sports.

Another global political issue is related to the production of sporting goods. As the demand for sports equipment and clothing has increased in wealthy nations, transnational corporations have cut costs for those products by manufacturing them in labor-intensive poor countries, where wage costs are extremely low. The result has been a clear split between the world's haves and have-nots when it comes to sports: Those born into privilege in wealthy nations consume the products made by those born into disadvantaged circumstances in poor nations. This is not a new issue, but it ties sports to global politics in yet another way.

Athletes as Global Migrant Workers

Human history of full of examples of labor migration, both forced and voluntary. Industrial societies, in particular, have depended on mobile labor forces responsive to the needs of production. Now that economies have become more global, the pervasiveness and diversity of labor migration patterns have increased. This is true in sports as well as other occupational categories (Maguire et al., 2002). Athletes frequently move from their hometowns when they are recruited to play elite sports, and then they may move many times after that, as they are traded from team to team or seek continuing opportunities to play their sports.

As geographer John Bale and sociologist Joe Maguire have noted in a book on athletic talent migration (1994), athletes move from state to state and region to region within nations, as well as from nation to nation within and between continents. They have noted also that each of these moves raises issues related to the following: (1) the personal adjustment of migrating athletes, (2) the rights of athletes as workers in various nations, (3) the impact of talent migration on the nations from and to which athletes migrate, and (4) the impact of athlete migration on patterns of personal, cultural, and national identity formation.

Some migration patterns are seasonal, involving temporary moves as athletes travel from one climate area to another to play their sports. Patterns may follow annual tour schedules, as athletes travel from tournament to tournament around a region or the world, as they may involve long-term or permanent moves from one region or nation to another.

The range of personal experiences among migrating athletes is great. They vary from major forms of culture shock and chronic loneliness to minor homesickness and lifestyle adjustments. Some athletes are exploited by teams of clubs, whereas others make great amounts of money and receive a hero's welcome when they return home in the off-season. Some encounter prejudice against foreigners or various forms of racial and ethnic bigotry, whereas others are socially accepted and make good friends. Some cling to their national identities and socialize with fellow athletes from their homelands, whereas others develop more global identities unrelated to one national or cultural background. In some cases, teams and clubs expect foreign athletes to adjust on their own, whereas others provide support for those who need to learn a new language or become familiar with new cultural settings (Klein, 1991).

Athletic talent migration also has an impact on the nations involved. For example, many Latin American nations have their best baseball players recruited by Major League teams in the United States. This not only depletes the talent the Latin American nations need to maintain professional baseball in their local economies but also forces them to depend on U.S.-based satellite television companies even to watch the players from their nations. As Major League Baseball teams in North America recruit stars from professional teams in Japan, some Japanese people worry that this trend could destroy professional baseball in their country. At the same time, they are proud that Japanese players excel on Major League teams. As they watch Major League games on satellite television, attendance and television ratings for Japanese baseball decline.

Furthermore, as people in other countries and continents watch sports based in the United States and Canada, they often are exposed to images and messages consistent with the advertising interests of corporations headquartered in the United States. Similar patterns exist in connection with European soccer teams that recruit players from around the world. In fact, soccer has higher rates of talent migration than other sports, although hockey, track and field, and basketball have high rates as well. The impact of this migration on national talent pools and on the ability of local clubs and teams to maintain economically viable sport programs is complex. Talent migration usually benefits the nation to which athletes move more than it benefits the nation from which athletes come, but this is not always the case.

The impact of global migration by athletes on how people think about and identify themselves in connection with nation-states is something we know little about. Many people appreciate athletic talent regardless of the athlete's nationality. At the same time, many people have special affections for athletes and teams representing their nations of citizenship or their nations of origin. Leagues such as the NHL are open to athletes from all nations. In fact, even though most of the teams are located in U.S. cities, less than 20 percent of the players are U.S.-born; about 60 percent are from Canada, and nearly 30 percent are from European nations. In Major League Baseball, over one-fourth of the players on Major League teams and over 40 percent of the players at all levels of professional baseball in North America were not born in the United States. Among the 416 players on 29 NBA teams at the start of the 2002–2003 season, 67, or 16 percent, were born outside the United States.

These trends have been worrisome to some people. This is why some leagues have quotas that limit the number of foreign-born or foreign-nationality players that teams may sign to contracts. For example, in the early 1990s, Japan banned U.S. women basketball players from its professional league. At the same time, professional leagues in Italy, Spain, and France allowed their teams to have up to two foreign players, many of whom were from the United States. In 1996, England lifted all quotas for both men's and women's pro basketball teams; during the same year, the new MLS (Major League Soccer) in the United States limited the number of non–U.S. players to four per team. Currently, some people in the United States are calling for limits on the number of foreign athletes who can play on intercollegiate teams. At the same time, many athletic departments are recruiting more athletes from outside the United States.

As commercial sport organizations expand their franchise locations across national borders, and as they recruit athletes regardless of nationality, talent migration will increase in the future. The social implications of this trend will be important to study and understand.

Global Politics and the Production of Sports Equipment and Apparel

Free trade agreements (for example, GATT and NAFTA), signed by many new nations in the mid-1990s, have created a new global economic environment. In this environment, it is cost-effective for large corporations selling vast amounts of goods to people in wealthy nations to locate production facilities in labor-intensive poor nations. These corporations are taxed at much lower rates when they move products from nation to nation, so they can make products in nations where labor is cheap and regulations are scarce and then sell them in wealthy nations, where people can afford to buy them.

These political-economic changes mean that, through the 1990s, most athletic shoes costing well over $100 a pair in the United States were cut and sewn by workers making less than 25 cents per hour in China and Indonesia, less than 75 cents per hour in Thailand, and less than $2.25 per hour in South Korea (Enloe, 1995; Kidd and Donnelly, 2000).

Similar patterns existed in connection with the production of clothes bearing patriotic-looking red, white, and blue NFL and NBA logos sold in the United States. Soccer balls sanctioned by FIFA, the international soccer federation, often were hand-sewn by child laborers making far less than poverty-level wages in poor nations, where people were desperate for any kind of work. And, while Nike athletes were making millions of dollars on their shoe endorsements, Nike shoes were being made mostly by young women in Southeast Asia working ten to thirteen hours a day, six days a week under oppressive conditions for 13–20 cents per hour (U.S. dollars)—far below a living wage in China, Vietnam, and Indonesia.

This exploitation attracted worldwide attention among religious, human rights, and labor organizations, as well as other activist groups. Sport sociologist George Sage has described the international Nike transnational advocacy network, which emerged during the mid-1990s. This network of dozens of organizations from many countries gradually mobilized consciousness and various forms of political action, which influenced various government policies on labor and human rights issues and Nike's relationship with production contractors in Southeast Asia. The network was so effective that the Nike logo became associated with sweatshops and unfair labor practices in the minds of many consumers. Nike's earnings declined, and its executives began to take responsibility for making changes in its production facilities; they even downsized the swoosh logo and converted the print logo to *nike* with a small *n* because they wanted to understate their presence and avoid negative attention among potential consumers.

Sage's case study of the Nike transnational advocacy network is heartening, because it documents the power of people to make change. The Internet and other global communications technologies make it possible for people around the world to mobilize in response to human rights violations and other important social issues. Of course, many factors influence the formation of a transnational advocacy network, but, when issues resonate across many groups of people, a network of organizations and individuals can organize, take action, and have an impact on global political processes. If this were not possible, what would stop transnational corporations, which are accountable to nothing but a generally underregulated global marketplace, from pursuing their interests in whatever ways they wish?

In November 2001, the University of North Carolina signed a contract with Nike, contingent on the sporting goods company following an anti-sweatshop code for all equipment and apparel provided to university teams. For the university, a primary goal of this $28 million contract was to force Nike to end its exploitive child labor practices. Representatives of the campus saw this as one step in dealing with the general exploitation of labor in poor nations where there are few or no laws protecting workers or regulating the conditions under which they work.

Other universities have considered taking or have taken similar steps. In the case of Nike, this type of action can be effective because it has contracts with 200 college and university athletic departments. But exploitation continues to exist as corporations seek the cheapest labor they can find to manufacture their products. This exploitation will end only when consumers in wealthy nations take collective social actions that demand changes in public and corporate policies around the world. Human rights and social justice groups have fought these battles for many years, but they need help.

MAKING SENSE OF TODAY'S POLITICAL REALITIES

It's not easy to explain all the changes discussed in this chapter. Are sports simply a part of general globalization processes through which various sport forms come together in many combinations? Are we witnessing the modernization of sports? Are sports being Americanized? Europeanized? Asianized?

Are we seeing sports simply being diffused throughout the world, with people in some countries emulating the sports played in other countries, or are sports being used in connection with new forms of cultural imperialism and colonization?

Are sports tools for making poorer nations dependent on wealthier ones, or are they tools for establishing cultural independence and autonomy in emerging nations?

Is it accurate to say that sports are becoming commercialized, or should we say that corporations are appropriating sports for the purpose of global capitalist expansion?

Are traditional and folk sports around the world being destroyed by heavily publicized sports based in wealthy nations, or do people take sport forms from other cultures and creatively adapt them to their own circumstances?

Are sports becoming more democratic, or have new forms of sponsorship actually restricted people's choices about when and how they will play sports?

Those who study sports as social phenomena now are devoting more of their attention to these questions. The best work on these issues involves data collected at global *and* local levels (Donnelly, 1996). This work calls attention to the fact that powerful people do not simply impose certain sport forms on less powerful people around the world. Even when sports from powerful nations are played in other parts of the world, the meanings associated with them are often grounded in the local cultures in which they are played. It is important to understand global trends, but it is also important to understand the local expressions of and responses to those trends. Power is a process, not a thing; it is always exercised through social relations, so the study of power must focus on how people agree and disagree with one another as they attempt to live their lives in meaningful terms. This is true in connection with sports, as it is in other dimensions of social life.

REFERENCES

Donnelly, P. 1996. "Prolympism: Sport Monoculture as Crisis and Opportunity." *Quest* 48, 1: 25–42.

Enloe, C. 1995. "The Globetrotting Sneaker." *Ms.* 5, no. 5: 10–15.

Jackson, S. J., and B. Hokowhitu. 2002. "Sport, Tribes, and Technology: The New Zealand All Blacks *Haka* and the Politics of Identity." *Journal of Sport and Social Issues* 2: 125–39.

Jackson, S. J., and J. Scherer. 2002. "Screening the Nation's Past: Adidas, Advertising, and Corporate Nationalism in New Zealand." Paper presented at the annual conference of the North American Society for the Sociology of Sport, November, Indianapolis.

Kidd, B., and P. Donnelly. 2000. "Human Rights in Sports." *International Review for the Sociology of Sport* 35, no. 2: 131–48.

Klein, A. 1991. *Sugarball: The American Game, the Dominican Dream.* New Haven, CT: Yale University Press.

Maguire, J., G. Jarvie, L. Mansfield, and J. Bradley. 2002. *Sports Worlds: A Sociological Perspective.* Champaign, IL: Human Kinetics.

Reid, S. M. 1996. "The Selling of the Games." *Denver Post,* July 21, 4BB.

Steinbreder, J. 1996. "Big spender." *Sky* (July): 37–42.

40

Corporate Globalization and Sporting Goods Manufacturing
The Case of Nike

George H. Sage

The sporting goods industry, like other major business industries, can be divided into relatively similar segments for the purpose of analyzing target markets, formulating marketing and positioning strategies, and identifying consumer groups. According to Brenda Pitts and her sport-management colleagues, the sport industry is composed of three major components: sport performance, sport promotion, and sport production. Sport performance consists of involvement in sport as a participant (athlete) or as a spectator; sport promotion encompasses various modes that promote sports—promotional merchandising, the media, sponsorships, endorsements, and so forth. The sport production segment of the sport industry comprises those products necessary or desired for the production of or to influence the quality of sport performance. Sporting goods—especially equipment, apparel, and footwear—are major products within this segment.[1]

The Sporting Goods Manufacturers Association (SGMA) defines this industry as "a composition of manufacturers of athletic footwear, sports apparel, and sporting goods equipment, as well as manufacturers of accessory items to the sports and recreation market." An essential segment of the sport industry, sporting goods constitute a $150 billion global industry; in the United States alone, sporting goods industry sales (at wholesale) were nearly $50 billion in 2003. Thus the production of sporting goods is a key component in the sport industry.

This chapter has been prepared for publication in D. Stanley Eitzen (ed.) *Sport in Contemporary Society: An Anthology* (8th edition). Any other use of this chapter is prohibited without the permission of George H. Sage.

Although there are three components in the sport industry, there are only two ingredients that are indispensable. Regardless of where sporting activities take place, one is the participants, the other is the apparel and footwear that are worn and the equipment—the sporting goods—that is used: uniforms, T-shirts, sneakers, balls, bats, gloves, protective equipment, and so forth that are necessary for playing sports. In many cases, these are required and regulated by the rules.

But sporting goods and equipment are not gifts of nature; all sporting apparel, footwear, and equipment are made by people, who, except for a random chance of nature that has put them where they are and us where we are, are just like us—they are human beings. It is their labor that allows all of us to play, watch, coach, and administer sports. Their labor, in effect, is the very foundation of our sporting experience.

What about those who toil in factories all over the world to make sporting experiences satisfying and pleasant for athletes, fans, coaches, and sport administrators? They are rarely the subject of the sports pages of newspapers and magazines, nor are they part of the daily network radio and television sports reports. Athletes, coaches, teams, leagues, and so forth are the focus of media sports. Sports sections in newspapers and radio and TV sports news daily report the minute details of individual athlete's performances, teams' performances, league standings, and they also provide "lead-up" stories of coming sports events. Entire television and radio networks are devoted to reporting the same information, in addition to broadcasting sports events. But there is virtually nothing—a huge silence, as it were—about those who labor in factories all over the world to manufacture the apparel and equipment necessary for the sporting events that drive the sport industry.

THE GLOBAL ECONOMY AND SPORTING GOODS MANUFACTURING

Foreign commerce, even direct investment between countries, has been a part of the national economies of industrialized countries for over a century. It has only been in the past 40 years that the production, distribution, and consumption of products and services of most corporations has taken place between countries. That expansion of what is now called the global economy can be seen by the increase in cross-border trade, which grew from $629 billion in 1960 to $7.43 *trillion* in 2002. Transnational corporations (TNCs) increased in number from 7,000 in the 1960s to 65,000 today, and they control over 850,000 foreign affiliates worldwide.[2] TNCs are huge, powerful economic enterprises. Economically, they exceed the size of most governments; indeed, of the world's 100 largest economies, 66 are transnational corporations and only 34 are nations. In his State of the Union address in January 2000, President Bill Clinton declared that "globalization is the central reality of our time."

Product manufacturing is the major driving force of globalization, as advanced capitalist and developing countries seek to increase their shares of the wealth of nations, and a key aspect of the global economy is a capital system and division of labor known as the "export-processing system." In this system, product research, design, development, and marketing take place in industrially developed countries while the labor-intensive, assembly-line phases of product manufacture are relegated to developing (aka Third World) nations. The finished product is then exported for distribution in developed countries of the world. Because manufactured goods from developing countries have increased sharply in the past 25 years, over one-third of the earnings of the 200 largest U.S. TNCs are now from their export-processing operations.

The prevailing organizational pattern used by TNCs in export-processing manufacturing is to either establish factories, or contract with foreign manufacturing firms, in countries with authoritarian governments, where production costs are cheaper, labor protections are not enforced, workers are most repressed, there is a non-union workforce, and weak or nonexistent safety and environmental laws prevail. This process is widely known throughout the world as the "race to the bottom," which refers to shifting production to the lowest-wage countries. The most dramatic shift of this kind in the past decade has been to China, where average wages are just 2.1 percent of U.S. average wages.[3]

One of the consequences of the export-processing system for workers in developed countries is that manufacturing employment in the United States has plummeted. TNCs have closed factories in industrialized countries and moved the jobs to people in developing countries throughout the world. As Figure 40-1 illustrates, manufacturing now accounts for only 11 percent of employment in the United States compared with roughly 28 percent 40 years ago. Just between 2000 and 2003—three years—American manufacturing lost 2.7 million jobs.[4] Thus, corporate layoffs in the United States are at a pace of about half a million jobs per year. For workers and their communities in developed countries, the consequences of export-processing industrialization have been grim: closed plants, replacement jobs paying minimal wages, and a variety of physical and mental worker afflictions, as well as community disintegration linked to the global economy.

Consequently, in the United States the number of imported manufactured goods has risen sharply in the past 25 years. Between 1970 and 1980 the percentages of imported and exported manufactured goods were about the same. But by 2000 imports had skyrocketed to 80 percent and exports had sunk to 20 percent. With China alone, the United States had a trade deficit of over $100 billion trade deficit in 2002.[5]

The consequences of export-processing industrialization in developing countries has been dreadful. Although this system has provided employment for many workers, there have been adverse consequence as well: wages so low that workers cannot provide for their basic needs, unjust and inhuman working conditions, prohibition of union organization, and environmental devastation. Add widespread child labor to these conditions. According to International Labor Organization estimates released in 2002, some 352 million children aged 5 to 17 are engaged in some form of economic activity in the world, with the Asian-Pacific region having the largest number of child workers.[6]

In spite of claims by TNCs, numerous economists, and governments that globalization tends to equalize economic equality between developed and developing

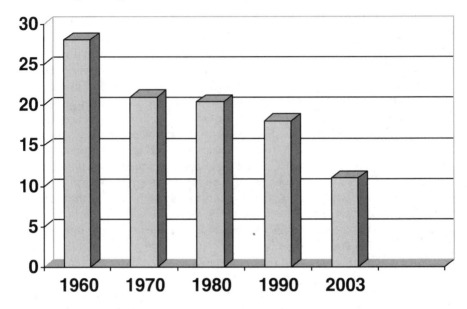

Figure 40-1 Percentage of U.S. Workers Employed in Manufacturing
Source: U.S. Bureau of Labor Statistics

countries, there has actually been increasing *inequality* between those countries. According to the United Nations Development Programme, the income gap between the 20 percent of the world's people living in the richest countries and the 20 percent in the poorest countries was 74 to 1 in 1997, up from 60 to 1 in 1990 and 30 to 1 in 1960. In other words, the economic gap between rich and poor countries *widened* dramatically. More recently this trend has been confirmed in the *United Nations Human Development Report 2003.* Fifty-four countries grew poorer, and 21 saw a decline in their human development indicators. Furthermore, gaps are widening both between and within countries.[7]

SPORTING GOODS MANUFACTURING IN THE GLOBAL ECONOMY: THE CASE OF NIKE

Sporting goods manufacturing is one of the most flourishing export-processing industries. Indeed, sporting goods manufacturers that produce all of their products domestically are now a minority because many of them have "run away" to various low-wage export-processing countries across the world. Over 90 percent of the sneakers and other sporting goods sold in the United States are imports made in foreign countries. China alone, arguably the country with the most abhorrent working conditions in the world, accounts for approximately 65 percent of global sporting goods production.[8]

The focus of this chapter is on a single sporting goods manufacturing firm— Nike—but it is important for readers to understand that there are 6,500 other sporting goods product manufacturers many of whose products are made in developing countries. Nike was chosen to illustrate how sporting goods firms have transferred their productive operations from the country in which they are incorporated to foreign export-processing operations in developing countries because it is the exemplar, the "poster boy" of this practice. In fact, the editors of the *Far Eastern Economic Review* even called the global economy "The New Nike Economy." Two writers for the *Washington Post* agreed, stating, "No company symbolizes the mobilization of American companies overseas more than Nike. Its 30-year history in Asia is as close as any one company's story can be to the history of globalization, to the spread of dollars ... into the poor corners of the earth.... [I]t is a story of restless and ruthless capital, continually moving from country to country in search of new markets and untapped low-wage labor."[9]

The corporation that is now Nike was founded in 1964 by its current CEO, Philip Knight, and Bill Bowerman, then the University of Oregon track and field coach. The original name of the company was Blue Ribbon Sports. Nike was adopted as the name for a new style of running shoes in 1971; the corporate name was changed to Nike later. Its corporate headquarters is located in Beaverton, Oregon.

At first, the sneakers sold by Blue Ribbon Sports were made in Japan, at that time a low-wage country. But by the time the corporate name Nike, Inc., was adopted, Japanese labor wages had become more expensive, so over the next few years Nike management opened footwear manufacturing plants in New Hampshire and Maine. But Philip Knight's thinking was well ahead of the curve with respect to understanding the profitability potential of manufacturing in developing countries, and in 1977 the first factory in South Korea was opened. By the early 1980s nearly 90 percent of Nike's sports footwear was produced by South Korean and Taiwanese shoe manufacturers. By then Knight was considering closing Nike footwear manufacturing in New Hampshire and Maine and shifting production to South Korea and Taiwan, because both were low-wage countries with cooperative governments for export-processing plants.

Nike's American shoe factories were closed in the mid-1980s. Productive operations in Asia were carried out through subcontracting with local manufacturers, thus eliminating the need for Nike to build plants, hire workers, and carry out the day-to-day tasks of production. Product research, design, promotion, and distribution became the main functions of the Nike corporation itself. As Phil Knight said, "We grew this company by investing our money in design, development, marketing and sales, and asking other companies to manufacture our products."[10]

In the late 1980s, democratic reforms came to South Korea and Taiwan; wages increased dramatically, and labor movements won the right to form independent unions and to strike. Responding to these developments, Nike began persuading its contractors to shift much of their Nike footwear operations out of these two countries into politically autocratic, military-dominated countries like Indonesia and Thailand and later to China and Vietnam, in a relentless drive for a favorable political climate and the lowest-cost labor to make its shoes and apparel.

In an interview with *Harvard Business Review*, Phil Knight explained the strategy underlying the series of moves from one Asian country to another: "We were ... good at keeping our manufacturing costs down. ... Puma and Adidas were still manufacturing in high-wage European countries. But we knew that wages were lower in Asia, and we knew how to get around in that environment."[11] Knight also knew that political leaders in these countries were attracting foreign corporations with promises of weak or poorly enforced labor and environmental standards, and unions were outlawed or state controlled.

By 1998 about 40 percent of all Nike shoes were produced in Indonesia, with China and Vietnam the other major Asian Nike footwear manufacturing nations. Currently, Nike has around 450,000 workers making Nike products in Southeast Asia; over 50 Nike footwear and apparel factories in China employ more than 120,000 workers. None of Nike's footwear is manufactured within the United States. Nike does not own its factories; it contracts with foreign manufacturers, mostly located in cheap labor countries in Asia, to supply it with shoes.

Nike's Asian Factories: Not a Pretty Sight

In the late 1980s, when Nike shifted footwear production from Taiwan and South Korea, the primary country of relocation was Indonesia, a nation led by a brutal dictator who was aggressively courting TNC investments in order to build up exports for Indonesia. From the beginning, Nike contractors in Indonesia engaged in what one writer called "management by terror." The minimum wage in the shoe factories was 83 cents per day, which was only 56 percent of the wage the government considered as meeting the "minimum physical needs" level—a wage governments use as a subsistence level for a single adult worker in a given country.[12]

Horrendous working conditions, extremely long working days, mandatory overtime, and abusive behavior by supervisors quickly led to strikes and protests in the Indonesian sport shoe factories, and later in Nike factories in Vietnam and China. These actions resulted in increased scrutiny of Nike's factories, at first by the Indonesian press. Then the foreign media and nongovernmental organizations (NGOs) began to focus on wages and conditions in Nike factories. Throughout the 1990s labor problems arose in every Asian country where Nike contractors were located.

During the decade of the 1990s sixteen major investigations were made of factories producing Nike footwear in Indonesia, China, and Vietnam. Investigations were carried out by a variety of organizations—academic, religious, labor, human rights, and development—from various countries. The length of time collecting data, expertise of the investigators, and methodology of data collection varied considerably, but the investigations revealed similar patterns and conditions in Nike's Asian shoe factories.

The reports can be summarized as follows: Appalling labor conditions were essentially the same in all of Nike's factories. Seventy-five to 80 percent of Nike workers were women—mostly under the age of 24—who regularly put in 10 to 13 hour days, worked six days a week, and were forced to work overtime two to three times per week. The typical worker was paid 13 to 20 cents (in U.S. dollars) an hour—which was $1.60 to $2.20 per day. This wage was below the "minimum physical needs" figure. Worker abuse was widespread in the Nike factories.

Local industrial safety laws were nearly useless in practice in all of the Nike Asian factories because Nike contractors simply ignored the rules and regulations set out in the laws. Not surprisingly, the investigations found that the results of cutting costs on safety and the health of the mostly women workers were alarming.

Several of the reports found that Nike's record on workers' rights in these countries was deplorable. Independent unions were not permitted in the factories. Where Nike workers attempted organizing to fight for their rights, Nike's contractors called in the police or military, and workers were arrested and subjected to torture and beatings.

Such conditions existed in these countries because the political leaders were blatantly corrupt; they could be paid off and they, in turn, made sure police and military units maintained vigilance for signs of labor activism. A Stanford University professor who studied Nike's Indonesian factories said: "Nike's got business in Indonesia because the workers are docile by virtue of government repression and they can't protest. The world that Nike and Philip Knight represent is the opposite of human rights and civilized values."[13]

At the same time as the investigations of Nike factories were being reported, and the abysmal workers' wages and working conditions were revealed, the Nike corporation was expanding rapidly and recording record-breaking revenue almost annually. Moreover, Nike was spending lavishly on promoting its products, paying out 1.13 *billion* on advertising alone in 1998.

As the reports from these investigations were published, and each largely corroborated the results of the others, mass media throughout the world began to report the findings of these investigations. Between 1992 and 1996, as global understanding and consciousness grew, it struck a collective chord of horror and outrage, spurring collective actions by workers in Nike's Asian factories, and launching what ultimately became the Nike social movement. This movement was composed of a coalition of organizations, each with its own maze of affiliates, members, friends, and allies. As it grew, it became so dense and diverse, with so many interlocking links, that the organizational matrix became difficult to identify clearly. Figure 40-2 illustrates the types of organizations that became part of the Nike social movement.

It was actually Nike workers in Indonesia who initiated the struggle against the low wages, unsafe and unhealthy working conditions, and abusive treatment in the factories. Worker complaints escalated to work stoppages and then to strikes against Nike contractors. For example, in 1992, 6,500 workers at the Sung Hwa Dunia factory in Indonesia began a one-day strike, demanding better wages and working conditions. These actions incited many NGOs throughout the world to take up the workers' cause, thus forming the broad structure for a Nike social movement, which then organized a variety of campaigns against Nike. Those campaigns, which took the form of demonstrations, protests, op-ed columns, TV spots, sit-ins, and marches, were devoted to making the public aware of Nike's labor practices.

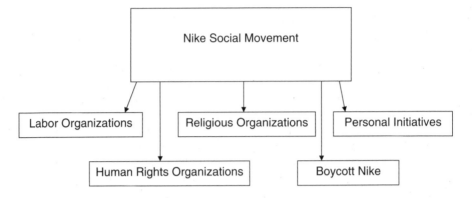

Figure 40-2 Types of Organizations Composing the Nike Social Movement
Source: Adapted from George H. Sage, "Justice Do It! The Nike Transactional Advocacy Network: Organization, Collective Actions, and Outcomes," *Sociology of Sport Journal* 16, no. 3 (1999).

The Nike social movement was the first global social movement to widely employ Internet communication. Literally dozens of Web sites connected the various organizations and served to inform the general public about Nike campaigns—announcing times, places, and purpose of future ones, and reporting the outcomes of previous ones. Cultivating the media by packaging information about workers in Nike factories in a timely and dramatic way, the social movement organizations were quite successful in attracting both electronic and print mass media coverage. For example, two hour-long programs about Nike factories were shown on the CBS program *48 Hours,* one in 1993 and the other in 1996. ESPN's *Outside the Lines* carried an hour-long documentary titled *Made in Vietnam: The Sneaker Controversy* that revealed unsafe and abusive working condition inside Nike factories.

The Nike social movement and its campaigns quickly agreed upon the most important objectives they were organized to accomplish. Those were:

- A subsistence wage for Nike workers
- Safe working conditions for Nike workers
- Freedom to organize for Nike workers
- Respect for the human rights of Nike workers

Their ultimate goal was to create enough public outrage against Nike that governments, business organizations, unions, religious organizations, and human rights groups would bring pressure on Nike to change its labor practices and move forcefully to improve conditions in the factories.

Through a loose system of networking, the Nike social movement was about to mobilize a multitude of mostly civil initiatives to respond to the various reports of Nike's factories documenting Nike's below subsistence wages, abysmal working conditions, employment of very young girls, abuse of workers, and antiunion practices. All of these campaigns portrayed Nike as a repressive, abusive, unjust, and inhuman corporation. Between 1993 and 1998 the Nike social movement reached its peak of actions and influence.

Nike's Responses to Factory Reports and the Social Movement

From its beginnings, Nike management carefully crafted the image of a company with an "attitude"—one journalist referred to it as a swagger—thus appealing to the "cool," "hip," and savvy side of the teenage and young adult populations, the major consumer groups for sports footwear. Its famous slogan, "Just Do It!" wordlessly asserts a "no excuses" viewpoint. Nike's advertising images have consistently communicated an irreverence and rebellious posture, which are also reflected in some of its endorsers, such as Dennis Rodman, John McEnroe, and Charles Barkley. Nike CEO Philip Knight himself admitted: "What we are all about is being against the establishment."[14]

At the same time, Nike had scrupulously honed a rhetoric of social responsibility, suggesting a socially conscious global corporate citizen with a sensitivity to racial, gender, and disability discrimination, as well as a concern for the environment. This was accompanied by its engaging in a variety of promotional ventures designed to illustrate Nike's support for empowering minority and disadvantaged groups.[15]

With such a corporate perspective, it is perhaps not surprising that Nike's initial response to the reports about its Asian factories was overwhelmingly denial, resentment, and anger. At first, Nike management denied responsibility for conditions in the Asian factories, arguing that Nike merely contracted with suppliers, who actually manufactured the shoes, and therefore Nike could not control what went on in the factories. Nike's vice president for production argued: "We don't set policy within the factories; it is their business to run."[16] This is, of course, absurd; Nike always had overall control of its productive operations through the power it had over its contractors. In all its contracts with suppliers Nike specified very precisely all of the quality standards that had to be met in the manufacture of their products. There is no reason at all that Nike management could not also specify labor standards with regard to the workers in the factories.

In response to some of its workers' unrest and mounting critical reports of its Asian footwear factories, Nike developed a Code of Conduct and Memorandum of Understanding in 1992 for its suppliers. Every factory employee was to receive a copy of the Code of Conduct, or the Code was to be placed where every worker could read it. However, several of the investigations of Nike factories found that many Nike workers had no knowledge of the existence of the Code and that the Code was flagrantly violated by Nike's contractors. Interviews with Nike's workers about the Code suggested that it was chiefly an instrument of damage control rather than a mechanism for worker protection in Nike factories.

Another form of response Nike made to the reports about conditions in its factories was to employ its own factory investigators. Nike hired the accounting firm

Ernst & Young in 1994 to conduct audits of labor and environmental conditions inside its contractors' factories to determine whether the factories were in compliance with Nike's corporate code of conduct. In 1997 Nike commissioned former American United Nations Ambassador Andrew Young and his GoodWorks International company to go to Asia and investigate its factory operations in Indonesia, China, and Vietnam. Later in the same year Nike released a summary of an investigation of its Asian factories it had funded, which had been done as a class project by a group of MBA students at the Amos Tuck School of Business at Dartmouth.

All three reports were prepared and paid for by Nike; none were independent inspections of Nike factories. Nevertheless, Ernst & Young reported numerous violations of labor laws on maximum working hours, inadequate safety equipment and training, and a series of hazardous and abusive working conditions inside the plants, including widespread worker exposure to hazardous chemicals. Andrew Young's review of Nike factories was silent on the issue of health and safety; did not address the use of hazardous chemicals, and made no mention of corporal punishment, except to acknowledge "there have been problems." Young totally avoided the most obvious and controversial issue—whether Nike paid its workers fair wages—saying that it was beyond the "technical capacity" of his investigation. For all intents and purposes, the Dartmouth Tuck Business School study was worthless. Analysts found the methodology of the study to be totally inadequate and questioned the validity of results obtained by students untrained for this type of research and paid for by Nike. Thus, all three reports came under scathing criticism from international human rights, labor, and religious organizations, as well as a number of journalists.

Meanwhile, in the mid-1990s Nike initiated a public relations blitz—including press conferences, letters to the editor, and so forth—to defend its corporate reputation and mute the mounting criticism of its labor practices. Ironically, the outcome was more negative public relations. For example, in 1998 Marc Kasky, a California consumer activist, sued Nike under the state's false advertising laws, claiming Nike was making false and misleading public statements. Nike countered that it was engaging in protected free speech. The California Supreme Court ruled 4 to 3 in favor of Kasky, holding that Nike's statements were commercial speech and thus could be regulated as advertising. Nike appealed to the U.S. Supreme Court; in 2003 that Court returned the case to California. In September 2003 Nike announced that it would pay Kasky $1.5 million to settle the case, thus staving off what could have been an unflattering court fight.

Perhaps the most consistent and persistent response Nike management made during the 1990s to the reports about its Asian factories was: "Why is Nike being singled out when the Asia factories of other sports footwear and apparel manufacturers are very similar to Nike's?" One of Nike's public relations spokespersons posed the question this way: "Why ... are we the sole target of all this interest" in foreign sport footwear production operations?

Several types of replies were made by the Nike social movement organizations: They argued that because Nike had been the industry pioneer in moving its productive operations overseas, complaints about its labor practices were the first to surface in the Asian sports footwear industry. It was also pointed out that a basic principle of labor collective actions is to go after the market leader, and that Nike was far and away the market leader in the sports footwear industry, with a 40 percent share of the market; moreover, by Nike's own research, its corporate icon—the swoosh brand—is recognized by 97 percent of Americans. As the "corporation marquée" in the sports footwear and apparel industry, other corporations in the industry looked to Nike for leadership. Even Nike CEO Philip Knight acknowledged: "Our competitors just follow our lead." Therefore, there was reason to believe that when Nike agreed to the demands of the Nike social movement, other companies in that industry would follow. As the founder of a Nike campaign called "Justice. Do It Nike" put it: "Nike is … the largest company [in the sport shoe industry] and has set the precedent for … [the] race to the bottom. If Nike reforms, they will trumpet the change and other manufacturers will have to follow."

Unspoken, but clearly one reason that Nike was being targeted, was an arrogance and hypocrisy in Nike's management and corporate culture that many Nike social movement organizers and supportive media journalists perceived. For Nike critics, CEO Phil Knight was viewed as contemptuous, insensitive, and iconoclastic in his public actions. As one leader of the Nike movement noted: "The company and its founder have always had a reputation for being aggressive and unconventional, the 'bad boys' of the shoe industry, built on an irreverence for the sporting establishment and for any authority which might cramp the individual's style." Nike's advertising seemed to take pride in communicating an in-your-face hipness and a win-at-all-cost image.[17]

Nike Social Movement Outcomes

The Nike brand name and reputation were severely damaged for millions of people throughout the world by the reports about conditions in Asian Nike factories and the campaigns of the Nike social movement. For many, the Nike swoosh became associated with sweatshops and the oppression of workers. Indeed, in a speech Philip Knight gave in May 1998 he admitted this, saying, "The Nike product has become synonymous with slave wages, forced overtime and arbitrary abuse." He also said, "I truly believe that … [consumers do] not want to buy products made in abusive conditions."

The Nike campaigns won sympathy and support for their objectives. They helped to change governmental policies in several foreign countries, such as the establishment of or increases in minimum wages, reforms in working-condition standards, and limitations on hours worked per day and week. Several governments adopted new public policies to permit independent union organization.

Nike campaigns also brought their message about Nike's Asian factories to American university campuses. Many students were moved to organize and campaign in a variety of ways to show their support for the movement. This led to the founding of the United Students against Sweatshops (USAS) in the summer of 1998.

Nike had a 49 percent decline in its 1998 fiscal net income compared to 1997. The company lost $68 million the last quarter (May–August 1998), the first time in

13 years the company had a quarterly loss. In the first quarter of 1999 (June–August 1998) revenue fell 9 percent; net income dropped 35 percent. These trends in earnings suggest that the Nike campaigns were likely adversely affecting Nike's revenues. However, the collapse of several Asian economies was affecting revenues of many TNCs between 1997 and 1998, and this may have also been a factor in Nike's revenue declines.

Nike Changes Course

Speaking before the National Press Club luncheon in Washington, D.C., on May 12, 1998, Nike CEO, Philip Knight, announced plans for a substantially new course for the company. This course—what he called "New Labor Initiatives"—was Nike's plan for significant reforms in the company's labor practices. The most notable of the new initiatives were:

- Nike was increasing the minimum age of footwear factory workers to 18, and the minimum age for all other light-manufacturing workers (apparel, accessories, equipment) to 16.
- Nike was adopting U.S. Occupational Safety and Health Administration (OSHA) indoor air quality standards for all footwear factories.
- Nike was expanding education programs, for workers in all Nike footwear factories.
- Nike was expanding its current monitoring program.

Organizations of the Nike social movement viewed these initiatives as an admission by Nike that there were serious problems in its Asian factories, and they also believed that these reforms came about as a direct result of the years of Nike campaigns that brought Nike labor practices to the awareness of world consumers. The feeling throughout these Nike social movement organizations was that Nike would not have taken these steps had it not been for the various Nike campaigns. In his book about international social activism, Randy Shaw said this about the Nike movement: "The growth of the anti-Nike campaign ... demonstrates not only the power of activists acting nationally to rewrite the rules of the global economy, but the triumph of the activists' vision of what is possible over prevailing, mainstream assumptions that have too often deterred social change efforts in all fields."[18] The Nike social movement showed that popular struggles can improve the plight of workers who labor under oppressive and unjust conditions in the global economy.

The Debate over Monitoring Sporting Goods Manufacturing Factories

Following Knight's announcement of the "New Initiatives" reforms, a vice president for corporate responsibility was employed, and shareholders at the 1998 Nike annual meeting were informed that by the end of the year the company would have an independent monitoring system underway. That same year, under the threat of a National Livable Wage Campaign, Nike announced it was raising wages of its

Indonesian workers by 25 percent (where wages were raised, they did not keep up with the rapid inflation in Indonesia). Finally, as predicted by the Nike social movement organizers, after Nike's "New Initiatives" announcement, other sporting goods manufacturers promised to reform their foreign-manufacturing operations, conform to codes of conduct, and agree to independent monitoring of their factories.

With Nike and other sporting goods companies promising labor reforms, attention turned to issues of independent monitoring of factories to assure that the corporations' promises could actually be verified through inspections by independent monitors. Over the following five years, vigorous and prolonged debate took place about the issue of independent factory monitoring. Sporting goods manufacturers supported the use of monitoring organizations that were "business friendly" and had weak labor and human rights representation. On the other side, labor and human rights, as well as the United Students Against Sweatshops, lobbied for monitoring organizations that would more likely be sensitive to the interests of workers.

Before discussing the problems associated with monitoring, it is necessary to comment on the role that university campus organizations played in the factory monitoring issue. In the mid-1990s the Nike social movement was reaching its peak of influence and reports about Nike's Asian factories became a popular topic on many American university campuses. Students began to raise questions about their own university's affiliations with Nike. As they did this, they demanded that their university take responsibility for the labor conditions under which its licensed and university-logo products were made by adopting Codes of Conduct to regulate the labor practices of the manufacturers of those licensed products. The idea behind the students' campaign was this: They opposed their colleges and universities supporting the appalling sweatshop system, and they did not want their institution profiting from the exploitation of the children, men, and women around the world who make the products that carry the university logo.

In July of 1998, student activists from over 30 different colleges and universities active in the anti-sweatshop movement formed USAS, the purpose of which was to be a cohesive coalition of students on campuses working on antisweatshop and Code of Conduct campaigns. One of the main goals of the USAS was to coordinate student participation and action around the development of manufacturers' Codes of Conduct and monitoring systems.

In less than one year, USAS spread to over 100 campuses across the United States and Canada (in 2003 USAS had chapters at over 200 university campuses), raising an awareness about the sweatshop issue to unprecedented levels. Students at Duke University took the lead in winning a commitment from the Duke administration to require full public disclosure of its licensees and in securing the university's approval of a Code of Conduct for all licensees who make products carrying the Duke name or logos and used by the university's sports teams.

Students at dozens of universities followed the Duke students' lead, winning commitments to full public disclosure by corporations, revealing the location of contractor's plants manufacturing the university's merchandise and athletic equipment, and securing approval of Codes of Conduct for all their licensees and assurances that those plants meet the code of conduct.[19] But on campuses across the country a major debate centered around the question of how these codes would be enforced. The answer, of course, was through a system of independent monitoring of factories where the university's products were made. So a central issue arose over which monitoring organization was the most appropriate.

Between 1998 and 2003 several organizations vied for recognition as the most credible and reputable independent factory monitoring firm. By 2003 two organizations had become the leaders: the Fair Labor Association (FLA) and the Worker Rights Consortium (WRC). The FLA initially gained the upper hand, primarily because it had been created out of the Apparel Industry Partnership that was formed from a diverse group of industry, labor, and human rights leaders that President Clinton brought to the White House in 1996 to discuss industry conditions. The FLA professed to be an independent monitoring organization that protects the rights of workers and holds manufacturers, as well as contractors and suppliers, publicly accountable for their labor practices. According to the FLA's information brochures, it certifies that corporations are in compliance with their Codes of Conduct and serves as a source of information for the public.[20]

The WRC was founded by the USAS in consultation with labor and human rights experts. The WRC Mission Statement on its Web site, asserts that it "is committed to building constructive working relationships with licensees.... [W]e recognize the licensees will play a central role in any progress that occurs toward better conditions in production facilities around the world. The WRC's goal is not to embarrass licensees but to promote real improvements in factory conditions."[21]

Despite the FLA's claim to be "independent" it is considered by many NGOs and labor unions to be "business-friendly," and, indeed, it is the preferred monitoring organization for manufacturing corporations as well as many university administrators. In 2003 some 170 colleges and universities were affiliated with the FLA. Major support for the WRC comes largely from labor, religious, and human rights organizations, and thus is considered unacceptable by most manufacturing corporations. According to the WRC, there were over 100 college and university affiliates in 2003.[22]

In 2004 the issue over the "best" monitoring organization for providing independent inspections and objective reporting of findings was still a hotly contested issue. The FLA has the edge in size and resources because it represents a multi-stakeholder coalition of companies, universities, and NGOs, whose foreign manufacturers supply their products. Nike is one of the FLA companies. The WRC was created by college and university administrations, students, and labor rights experts. Its purpose is only to assist in the enforcement of manufacturing Codes of Conduct adopted by colleges and universities. Thus, it has a more limited role in the factory monitoring industry.

Nike's New Initiatives: A Commitment to Reform or a Public Relations Ploy?

When Phil Knight made his "New Initiatives" speech, and then followed up with a number of actions appearing to show that those initiatives were under way, many of the individuals and organizations in the Nike social movement felt they had accomplished most of their objectives and turned to other issues. However, at the time of Knight's announcement he said nothing about the company being committed to paying a living wage for a normal workweek. Because this had been a fundamental demand of the Nike social movement from its beginning, a number of the movement organizations pledged to remain active until Nike committed to this issue. They also vowed to scrutinize Nike's future labor practices to make sure Nike delivered on the promises made in its initiatives. It turns out that their concerns about Nike were well founded. Over the next few years Nike invested substantial resources in public relations promoting its improved labor practices and invoked a corporate responsibility rhetoric for treating workers well, but reports from various labor and human rights organizations consistently told a different story, a story of unfulfilled promises.

A year after the "New Initiatives" announcement, the Urban Community Mission (Jakarta) conducted a survey of Nike's Indonesian workers. That report summarized the findings: "Contradicting claims by Nike to have reformed [its Asian factories], this survey indicated that excessive and compulsory overtime, abusive management practices and inadequate wages are still features of Nike contracted factories in Indonesia."[23] In Indonesian factories of another sport footwear company surveyed by the Urban Community Mission, the management practices were less cruel and the workers were under much less pressure than Nike workers. But low wages were a significant issue in those factories as well.

In the spring of 2000 a group of international labor rights organizations reported on a series of investigations made at various Nike factories in Thailand, Indonesia, Vietnam, and Cambodia during 1999 and 2000. The investigations found consistent evidence of abusive and exploitative working conditions including the following: wages below the level required for meeting basic needs, oppressively long working hours, excessive overtime, violent punishment of workers, and aggressive antiunion activity on the part of factory management. The report concluded: "This leads us to believe that labour abuses are the norm in ... suppliers' factories and not isolated incidents as Nike has frequently suggested to the media."[24]

In December 1999 and March 2000, the Hong Kong Christian Industrial Committee interviewed workers at Nike's factories in China. The reports disclosed that Nike's workers endured abusive and often illegal conditions. Some of those were: extreme hours of work—up to 12.5-hour days, 7-day workweeks, wages of 11 to 58 cents per hour where a living wage was over 87 cents per hour, cheating workers of their earned wages, and dangerous working conditions.[25]

In February 2001, the Global Alliance for Workers and Communities, formed by a consortium of companies and groups—including Nike—to study workplace experiences and life opportunities for workers in developing countries, released a 106-page report on the labor conditions at nine Nike factories in Indonesia. Nike had commissioned the project and spent $7.8 million to fund it. The report was titled *Workers' Voices: An Interim Report on Workers' Needs and Aspirations in Nine Nike Contract Factories in Indonesia;* many of the findings from interviews and focus groups involving more that 4,200 workers, confirmed what investigations of Nike Asian factories had been reporting for over 10 years. Even Nike management found the report findings "disturbing," and in a press release admitted that "no worker should be subject to some of the working conditions reported in this assessment."

The Global Alliance assessment process did not examine workplace conditions in depth, but a series of questions were included on workplace conditions. In the report, over half the workers said that basic monthly wages were not adequate to meet workers' subsistence living expenses. Forty-five percent were not satisfied with health facilities at the factories, workers at all nine factories reported experiencing or seeing various forms of harassment and abuse, and workers were forced to work overtime.[26]

In response to the Global Alliance report, Nike drew up a "remediation plan" that addressed compensation, terms of work, harassment, conditions of work, and reporting a worker's death, the most significant problems that were identified in the report. For each problem area, a plan of action was described.[27] Three months after the Global Alliance report, Global Exchange, an international human rights organization, published a 115-page report titled *Still Waiting for Nike to Do It.* The report revealed that three years after Phil Knight's speech to the National Press Club Nike workers were still forced to work excessive hours, were not earning a livable wage, and were subject to harassment and dismissal if they attempt to form unions. The report concluded: "Nike has misled consumers and let down the workers who make its products and who continue to suffer extreme injustice while Nike touts itself as an 'industry leader' in corporate responsibility." The Global Exchange corporate accountability organizer said, "Over the last three years, Nike has treated this issue as a public relations inconvenience rather than a serious human rights issue."[28]

In the same month that the Global Exchange report was published, a National Labor Committee (NLC) delegation left for Bangladesh. They went to study labor conditions in Bangladesh because it is the third largest export-processing country for apparel exported to the United States. In a booklet published in 2002 titled *Bangladesh: Ending the Race to the Bottom,* the NLC delegation reported on labor conditions in seven factories that produce logoed apparel for American universities, three of which produced Nike products, while the other four produced products for other sporting goods firms, such as Reebok, Pro Sports, and Wilson Sporting Goods.

In the Nike factories studied, the average hours of work per week at the three plants were 66, 78, and 80 hours; below-subsistence wages were paid at all the factories; health and sanitary conditions in the plants were appalling; workers were abused in a variety of ways; and attempts to organize a union were met with firing. (The right to organize and bargain collectively are guaranteed legal rights by Bangladesh labor law. However, the law does not apply in the country's Export Processing Zones, where all these factories are located.) In one Nike factory, no worker had ever heard of the Nike Code of Conduct. Conditions in the four factories not producing Nike products were very similar to those in Nike factories, confirming the point that I made earlier in this chapter.[29]

Also in 2002 a report titled *We Are Not Machines* was published by a coalition of labor rights organizations based on interviews with about 35 Indonesian workers from four sport shoe factories producing Nike and Adidas. This report was actually a follow-up of a report released in 2000 titled, *Like Cutting Bamboo, Nike and*

Indonesian Workers' Right to Freedom of Association, which detailed abuse of workers' human rights—verbal abuse, humiliation in front of other workers, excessively long work week, below-subsistence wages, and lack of respect for freedom of association and collective bargaining rights. When that report was published, Nike promised it would investigate, but it never published anything about the investigation.

The *We Are Not Machines* report was an attempt to assess whether any progress had been made in improving conditions in the factories since the first report was released. According to the new report, despite some small steps forward, poverty and fear still dominated the lives of Nike and Adidas workers in Indonesia, so any measures that Nike took fell well short of ensuring that workers were able to live with dignity. Fundamental wage inadequacies, working conditions, and lack of freedom of association were still present.[30]

These reports add to what has become a long list of factories that make products for Nike where serious labor violations have been found. The findings of the various studies of Nike's Asian factories in the five years after Knight's "New Initiatives" announcement convincingly show that many of Nike's factories continue to have many of the same conditions that have been reported for over 10 years. As one Nike social movement organizer remarked, "Persuading Nike to reform its factories is like pulling a reluctant tomcat across a carpet."

Three important points need to be made about Nike at this point: First it is important to note that Nike has over 450 factories in Asia, and not all of them have been part of the factories' reports. So it is possible that workers at some of Nike's factories do not suffer the conditions of those that have been studied. That seems unlikely, however. Second, most of the recent reports acknowledge that some of the conditions in Nike's factories have improved. For example, in the Global Alliance study, the majority of workers said they were satisfied with the health facilities at their respective factory as well as their work relationships with their direct supervisors and factory management. Nike has also prepared reports outlining how it proposes to address the findings of various reports. As mentioned above, it developed a "remediation plan" as a response to the Global Alliance release. In the fall of 2001, Nike published a detailed 56-page "Corporate Responsibility Report" that described its efforts toward understanding and managing global labor compliance and its commitment to diversity, and pledged its support for environmental sustainability. Still, Nike did not commit to a living wage for its workers in any of its documents.[31] Third, Nike has contributed substantial amounts of money to educational programs, community youth programs (e.g., Participate in the Lives of America's Youth [PLAY]), and promoted race and gender empowerment in various ways.

In spite of these actions, the contradiction between what Nike has claimed about its factories and what study after study has reported about those factories has continued because Nike persistently projected a corporate image of concern for the working conditions in its factories and a commitment to reform them, but the company's basic strategy relied on damage control and public relations.

Extraordinary resources have been expended by Nike deflecting blame and disparaging the findings in the reports about the company's factories. Simultaneously

Nike has integrated high-profile public relations initiatives while touting a wide-ranging social consciousness and a commitment to corporate responsibility, such as the educational, youth, and racial and gender projects mentioned above, all of which were designed to portray the company in a positive light. This strategy has preserved Nike's core company policies that have allowed it to profit from sweat-shop labor.

In some ways this strategy has served Nike well, especially with its stockholders and those loyal to its brand name. But in other ways it has not served well. While the company has been able to ameliorate some of the damage to its reputation with this strategy, it has opened itself to credibility problems. According to two Canadian sociologists, it "has created an image problem ... by setting the company's self-identity at odds with a growing public reputation for sweatshop practices. Activist criticism has been able to question Nike's credibility by exposing the gap between the company's social responsibility claims and its ... labor practices." They also note that "The motivation of the anti-sweatshop movement is a belief that Nike is hypocritical in the way it lays claim to social responsibility as an instrument of commercial promotionalism yet continues to exploit young, migrant, female workers in the developing world."[32]

Nike has been successful at creating wealth for its owners and shareholders, but while doing this it has also been a corporate leader in the race to the bottom, in seeking the lowest wage countries for its productive operations. But low wages have only been part of the story. The other part has been the miserable working conditions that its workers have had to endure. Reports over the past 10 years have consistently shown that Nike is a leader in exploitation of workers, not in the protection of workers. The evidence has shown that labor abuses have been central to the way Nike runs its business.

To be sure, Nike is not the only company that has followed this global economy model. Nike has received extensive public criticism not because it is the worst, but because it has had the largest share of the sports footwear market and the accompanying profits, and can therefore most easily afford to lead a change in corporate direction. Some researchers who have studied Nike's promotional strategies believe that "Nike faces the dual problem of making substantive improvements to working conditions, wages, and workers' rights and restoring its public credibility as a company whose claims to social responsibility are seen as sincere."[33]

Globalization is inevitable, and transnational corporate power and privilege will surely continue, but TNCs like Nike can play a very positive role in developing countries. Private sector investment can be an important driver for global economic growth and poverty reduction. TNCs can provide stable, long-term, decently paying jobs. They can ensure that workers' basic rights are respected in the workplace. Unfortunately, up to this point, many have not. But organizations and networks of the new civil globalism, like the Nike social movement, are determined to challenge the oppressive and exploitative power and practices of the transnational corporate global economy. The hopes for a better future throughout the world rest on a cooperative relationship and mutual respect between corporations and their workforce.

NOTES

1. Brenda G. Pitts, Larence F. Fielding, and Lori K. Miller, "Industry Segmentation Theory and the Sport Industry: Developing a Sport Industry Segment Model," *Sport Marketing Quarterly* 3, no. 1 (1994): 15–24.

2. United Nations Conference on Trade and Development, *World Investment Report 2002* (New York: United Nations, 2002); see also Tony Schirato and Jen Webb, *Understanding Globalization* (Thousand Oaks: Sage, 2003); Michael Veseth (ed.) *The Rise of the Global Economy* (Chicago: Fitzroy Dearborn, 2002).

3. Michael D. Yates, *Naming the System: Inequality and Work in the Global Economy* (New York: Monthly Review Press, 2003); see also David Zweig, *Internationalizing China: Domestic Interests and Global Linkages* (Ithaca: Cornell University Press, 2002); Tony Schirato and Jen Webb, *Understanding Globalization* (Thousand Oaks: Sage, 2003).

4. Alan Levenson, "As U.S. Economy Adapts to Change, Manufacturing Takes a Back Seat," *T. Rowe Price Report* (Fall 2003), pp. 13–14; see also Barbara Hagenbaugh, "U.S. Manufacturing Jobs Fading Away Fast," *USA Today,* 13 December 2002, pp. 1B-2B; Robert J. S. Ross, "The 'Race to the Bottom' in Imported Clothes," *Dollars and Sense* (January/February 2002), pp. 46–47.

5. Sue Kirchhoff, "U.S. Manufacturers vs. China," *USA Today,* 1 July 2003, p. 4B.

6. International Labour Office, *Every Child Counts: New Global Estimates on Child Labour* (Geneva, ILO, 2002).

7. United Nations Development Programme, "Overview," *Human Development Report 1999* (New York: Oxford University Press, 1999), p. 3; United Nations Development Programme, *Human Development Report 2003* (New York: Oxford University Press, 2003); see also J. Cox, "Poor Nations Just Getting Poorer," *USA Today,* 13 September 2000, p. 5B; Yates, *Naming the System.*

8. National Labor Committee, *No More Sweatshops!* (New York: NLC, 2002), p. 2; Maria Stefan, "Greetings from China," *SportsEdge* (October 2001), p. 30; for a brief history of the history of the sporting goods industry, see George H. Sage, "The Sporting Goods Industry: From Struggling Entrepreneurs to National Business to Transnational Corporations," in *The Commercialization of Sport,* ed. Trevor Slack (London: Frank Cass, in press).

9. Anne Swardson and Sandra Bugawara, "Asian Workers Become Customers," *The Washington Post,* 30 December 1996, pp. A1, A16.

10. Nike, Inc., "CEO Philip H. Knight's letter: Nike and Corporate Responsibility," *Corporate Responsibility Report* (October 2001), p. inside cover; for accounts of Nike's early history, see J. B. Strasser and Laurie Becklund, *Swoosh, the Unauthorized Story of Nike and the Men Who Played There* (New York: Harper Business, 1993); Donald Katz, *Just Do It: The Nike Spirit in the Corporate World* (New York: Random House, 1994).

11. Geraldine E. Willigan, "High Performance Marketing: An Interview with Nike's Phil Knight," *Harvard Business Review* 70 (July 1992), p. 92.

12. Jeff Ballinger and Claes Olsson, (eds.) *Behind the Swoosh: The Struggle of Indonesians Making Nike Shoes* (Global Publications Foundation, 1997).

13. Quoted in M. Mohtashemi, "Knight Defends Firm's Asian Wages," *Global Exchange Campaigns* (1997). http://www.globalexchange.org/watch/campaigns/gophilgo5.8.htm; see also George H. Sage, "Justice Do It! The Nike Transactional Advocacy Network: Organization, Collective Actions, and Outcomes," *Sociology of Sport Journal* 16, no. 3 (1999): 206–235.

14. Timothy Egan, "The Swoon of Swoosh," *New York Times Magazine,* 13 September 1998, p. 69.

15. Graham Knight and Josh Greenberg, "Promotionalism and Subpolitics: Nike and Its Critics," *Management Communication Quarterly* 15 (May 2002): 541–570; see also Carol A. Stabile, "Nike, Social Responsibility, and the Hidden Abode of Production," *Critical Studies in Media Communication* 17 (June 2000): 186–204.

16. Quoted in Donald Katz, *Just Do It: The Nike Spirit in the Corporate World* (New York: Random House, 1994), p. 191.

17. Robert Goldman and Stephen Papson, *Nike Culture: The Sign of the Swoosh* (Thousand Oaks: Sage, 1998); see also Walter LaFeber, *Michael Jordan and the New Global Capitalism* (New York: W. W. Norton, 1999).

18. Randy Shaw, *Reclaiming America: Nike, Clean Air, and the New National Activism* (Berkeley: University of California Press, 1999), p. 16.

19. See M. B. Marklein, "Colleges Apply Conduct Codes to Logo Sweatshops," *USA Today,* 1 June 1998, p. 1D; Thad Williamson, "Who Wants to Be a Cheerleader for a Sweatshop?" *Dollars and Sense* (July/August, 2002): 24–26; see also Chapter 7,"The Student Anti-Sweatshop Movement," in Jay R. Mandle, *Globalization and the Poor* (Cambridge: Cambridge University Press, 2003).

20. Fair Labor Association, Homepage, http://www.fairlabor.org. (2003).

21. Worker Rights Consortium, Homepage. http://workersrights.org. (2003).

22. David Moberg, "Too Cruel for School: Students Stand Up for Workers Rights," *In These Times* (27 May 2002): 21–22; see also Dara O'Rourke, "Sweatshop 101," *Dollars and Sense,* (September/October 2001): 14–17, 46.

23. Urban Community Mission Survey Report. "Cruel Treatment Working for Nike in Indonesia," (December 1999). http://summersault.com/~agj/clr/alerts/crueltreatmentworkingfornikeinindonesia.html.

24. Quoted in "UNITE! Report, 'Sweatshops Behind the Swoosh,'" p. 3 (2000). http://www.uniteunion.org/pressbox/nikereport3.html, p. 1.

25. "UNITE! Report, 'Sweatshops Behind the Swoosh,'" p. 2 (2000). http://www.uniteunion.org/pressbox/nike-report2.html, pp. 2–4.

26. See "Workers' Needs Assessment in Nike Contract Factories: A Summary of Findings," *Global Alliance for Workers and Communities: Progress Report* 2 (February 2001).

27. "Nike Releases Remediation Plan for Indonesian Factories," Nike Press Release, 22 February 2001.

28. Global Exchange, *Still Waiting for Nike to Do It* (2001). http://store.globalexchange.org/nike.html; Josh Richman, "Is Nike Still Doing It?" MotherJones.com (16 May 2001), p. 1, retrieve: MotherJones.com; click on "Search" and then type in "Is Nike Still Doing It?"

29. National Labor Committee, *Bangladesh: Ending the Race to the Bottom* (New York: National Labor Committee, 2002).

30. Timothy Conner, *Like Cutting Bamboo: Nike and Indonesian Workers' Rights to Freedom of Association* (2000), http://www.caa.org.au/campaigns/nike/association/report.html; Timothy Connor, We Are Not Machines (2002) http://www.caa.org.au/campaigns/nike/reports/machines/index.html.

31. "Corporate Responsibility Report fy01," Nike, Inc. (2001). http://www.nike.com/nikebiz.jhtml;bsessionid=5WUP5FEFZM3VQCQCGIMCF4YKAIZCQIZ.

32. Knight and Greenberg, "Promotionalism and Subpolitics," pp. 565, 554; see also Stabile, "Nike, Social Responsibility, and the Hidden Abode of Production."

33. Ibid., p. 544.

✳ FOR FURTHER STUDY ✳

Bairner, A. 2001. *Sport, Nationalism, and Globalization: European and North American Perspectives*. Albany: State University of New York Press.

Barney, Robert K., Stephen R. Wenn, and Scott G. Martyn. 2002. *Selling the Five Rings: The International Olympic Committee and the Rise of Olympic Commercialism*. Salt Lake City: University of Utah Press.

Coakley, Jay. 2007. *Sports in Society: Issues and Controversies*. 9th ed. New York: McGraw-Hill.

Cole, C. L. 2002. "The Place of Golf in U.S. Imperialism." *Journal of Sport and Social Issues* 26 (November): 331–336.

Eitzen, D. Stanley. 2009. *Fair and Foul: Beyond the Myths and Paradoxes of Sport*. Lanham, MD: Rowman and Littlefield.

Eitzen, D. Stanley, and George H. Sage. 2009. *Sociology of North American Sport*. 8th ed. Boulder, CO: Paradigm.

Foer, Franklin. 2004. *How Soccer Explains the World: An Unlikely Theory of Globalization*. New York: Harper Perennial.

Harvey, Jean, Alan Law, and Michael Cantelon. 2001. "North American Professional Team Sport Franchises Ownership Patterns and Global Entertainment Conglomerates." *Sociology of Sport Journal* 18 (4): 435–457.

Harvey, Jean, and Maurice Saint-Germain. 2001. "Sporting Goods Trade, International Division of Labor, and the Unequal Hierarchy of Nations." *Sociology of Sport Journal* 18 (2): 231–246.

Klein, Alan M. 2006. *Growing the Game: The Globalization of Major League Baseball*. New Haven, CT: Yale University Press.

Lafeber, W. 2000. *Michael Jordan and the New Global Capitalism*. New York: W. W. Norton.

Magee, Jonathan, and John Sugden. 2002. "'The World at Their Feet': Professional Football and International Labor Migration." *Journal of Sport and Social Issues* 26 (November): 421–437.

Magnusson, Gudmundur K. 2001. "The Internationalization of Sports: The Case of Iceland." *International Review for the Sociology of Sport* 36 (March): 59–70.

Maguire, Joseph. 1999. *Global Sport: Identities, Societies, Civilizations*. Cambridge, UK: Polity.

Maguire, Joseph. 2000. "Sport and Globalization." Pp. 356–367 in Jay Coakley and Eric Dunning, eds., *Handbook of Sports Studies*. London: Sage.

Nixon, Howard L. II. 2008. *Sport in a Changing World*. Boulder, CO: Paradigm.

Scherer, Jay. 2001. "Globalization and the Construction of Local Particularities: A Case Study of the Winnipeg Jets." *Sociology of Sport Journal* 18 (2): 205–230.

Wong, Lloyd L., and Ricardo Trumper. 2002. "Global Celebrity Athletes and Nationalism." *Journal of Sport and Social Issues* 26 (May): 168–194.

Zirin, Dave. 2005. *What's My Name, Fool? Sports and Resistance in the United States*. Chicago: Haymarket.

About the Editor

D. Stanley Eitzen is professor emeritus of sociology at Colorado State University, where he taught for twenty-one years, the last as John N. Stern Distinguished Professor. Prior to that he taught at the University of Kansas, where he earned his Ph.D. He was editor of *The Social Science Journal* from 1978 to 1984. He began his career as a high school teacher and athletic coach. Although he is well known for his scholarship on homelessness, poverty, social inequality, power, family, and criminology, he is best known for his contributions to the sociology of sport. He has taught a course on sport and society since 1972. He is the author or coauthor of twenty-four books (including three on sport), as well as numerous scholarly articles and chapters in scholarly books. He is a former president of the North American Society for the Sociology of Sport and the recipient of that organization's Distinguished Service Award. Among his other awards, he was selected to be a Sports Ethics Fellow by the Institute for International Sport. His most recent book, with George H. Sage, is *Sociology of North American Sport,* 8th edition (Paradigm Publishers 2009).